THE STORY OF
POETRY

By the same author

Criticism

Fifty Modern British Poets: an introduction
Fifty English Poets 1300–1900: an introduction
Reading Modern Poetry
Lives of the Poets
The Story of Poetry: Volume One
The Story of Poetry: Volume Two
The First Poets: Lives of the Ancient Greek Poets

Anthologies

Eleven British Poets
New Poetries I, II, III
Poets on Poets (with Nick Rennison)
The Harvill Book of Twentieth-Century Poetry in English
The Great Poets

Poetry

Choosing a Guest
The Love of Strangers
Selected Poems
The Resurrection of the Body

Fiction

The Colonist
The Dresden Gate

Translations

Flower & Song: Aztec Poetry (with Edward Kissam)
On Poets & Others, Octavio Paz

THE STORY OF
POETRY

VOLUME THREE

English Poets and Poetry
from Pope to Burns

Michael Schmidt

Weidenfeld & Nicolson

LONDON

First published in Great Britain in 2007
by Weidenfeld & Nicolson

1 3 5 7 9 10 8 6 4 2

A CIP catalogue record for this book
is available from the British Library.

ISBN 978 0 297 84870 7

Typeset by Input Data Services Ltd, Frome

Printed in Great Britain by
Clays Ltd, St Ives plc

The Orion Publishing Group's policy is to use papers that
are natural, renewable and recyclable products and made
from wood grown in sustainable forests. The logging and
manufacturing processes are expected to conform to the
environmental regulations of the country of origin.

Weidenfeld & Nicolson

The Orion Publishing Group Ltd
Orion House
5 Upper Saint Martin's Lane
London, WC2H 9EA

www.orionbooks.co.uk

For Kate and Bob Gavron
with love

CONTENTS

An Informal History

Anthology

An Informal History

THE LITTLE VIRTUES

... negligence and irregularity, long continued, will make knowledge useless, wit ridiculous, and genius contemptible.

Samuel Johnson, *The Life of Savage*

In London, during the spring of 1960, the Italian novelist Natalia Ginsburg wrote her most famous essay, 'The Little Virtues'. Her premise was simple. Having observed the British way of life, she had arrived at a contrary disposition. 'So far as the education of children is concerned I think they should be taught not the little virtues but the great ones. Not thrift but generosity and an indifference to money; not caution but courage and a contempt for danger; not shrewdness but frankness and a love of truth; not tact but love for one's neighbour and self-denial; not desire for success but a desire to be and to know.'

The British eighteenth century is largely about the little virtues. After the abundance and excess of the Jacobeans came the purity and self-denial of the Cavaliers, the vehemence of the Commonwealth and the Frenchified hedonism, hectic posturing and spiritual void of the Restoration; and after the heartless repression of Monmouth's rebellion of 1685, critics and writers alike were keen that John Bull should acquire recognisably good manners (in the European mode), and that London should be as powdered and polite as Paris. Wren's St Paul's was consecrated in 1697. John Vanbrugh had already begun perpetrating his comedies and would soon begin to execute those ponderously sumptuous buildings which are characteristically his: most notably his first, Castle Howard in Yorkshire, on which he collaborated with Nicholas Hawksmoor; and Blenheim Palace in Woodstock, Queen Anne's reward to her captain-general the Duke of Marlborough who won her wars for her.

George Farquhar and William Congreve were writing comedies which reveal a social order riven between the manipulative, the affected and the uncomprehending or provincial classes and mind-sets. A rural English wholesomeness survives, but only just. The wider world is one of cultural importations and studied politeness on the one hand, and aggressive xenophobia on the other. A year after Indian printed calicoes were banned because they were too popular, the novelist-to-be Daniel Defoe wrote his one famous poem, *The True-Born Englishman* (1701), making fun of national prejudices which threatened to impoverish English political and cultural life for years to come. The *political* point of his poem was rather more ingratiating, for the King of England was not English-born and the King was himself a catalyst of xenophobia.

> The Romans first with Julius Caesar came,
> Including all the Nations of that Name,
> Gauls, Greeks, and Lombards; and by Computation,
> Auxiliaries or Slaves of ev'ry Nation.
> With Hengist, Saxons; Danes with Sueno came,
> In search of Plunder, not in search of Fame.
> Scots, Picts, and fish from th' Hibernian Shore
> And Conqu'ring William brought the Normans o'er.
>   All these their Barb'rous Offspring left behind,
> The Dregs of Armies, they of all mankind;
> Blended with Britons who before were here,
> Of whom the Welsh ha' blest the Character.
>   From this Amphibious Ill-born Mob began
> *The vain ill-natur'd thing, an Englishman.*
> The Customs, Surnames, Languages, and Manners,
> Of all those Nations are their own Explainers:
> Whose Relics are so lasting and so strong,
> They ha' left a Shibboleth upon our Tongue;
> By which with easy search you may distinguish
> Your Roman-Saxon-Danish-Norman English.

It was a point worth labouring then, as it is now. The next year Defoe, a Dissenter, was put in the pillory and imprisoned for six months because of a savagely satirical prose pamphlet, *The Shortest Way with Dissenters.* The day of the explosive prose pamphlet was far from over: Swift's ruthless masterpieces, starting with *A Tale of a Tub,* on the theological conflicts of the day, appeared from 1704.

Against satirical and the oblique truth-tellers, the tyranny of fashion had begun to form. Snuff-taking from pretty little pewter, enamelled and silver boxes, with an elaborate series of rituals and gestures, became *de rigueur* for the man of fashion. Beau Nash started his half a century's reign at Bath, establishing himself as a model of dress and deportment. The 'polite world' of unquestioning obedience to often arbitrary laws and of cruel exclusions was emerging. People upgraded their names. Early in the century even Daniel Foe, son of James Foe the butcher, enhanced his with a 'De', a true-born Saxon-Norman Englishman.

The word 'polite' has nothing to do with *polis* or politics. It derives from the Latin verb *polire*, to smooth down, to polish. In the sixteenth century it had meant correct and scholarly. By the middle of the eighteenth it meant refined, cultivated, well bred; it was a measurable virtue, subserving fixed conventions and decorums of conduct in every sphere. In the handsome old subscription libraries, the Portico in Manchester for example, even today a whole quarter of the shelving is apparently devoted to what a large gilded inscription announces as Polite Literature. There is no space for the Impolite.

The time had come, now that the court was no longer a plausible arbiter of social or cultural propriety and the King could not be depended upon to speak, much less to read, English, for another kind of authority, another instrument of legitimacy, to emerge, for rules, schedules and regulations to be promulgated. They would be decreed not from the palace but from the coffee house. Before Joseph Addison gave us the *Tatler* and the *Spectator*, Doctor Samuel Johnson remarks, 'We had many books to teach us our important duties, and to settle opinions in philosophy and politics; but an *Arbiter elegantiarum*, a judge of propriety, was yet wanting, who should survey the track of daily conversation, and free it from thorns and prickles, which tease the passer, though they do not wound him.'

Some poets who entered the eighteenth century with substantial ballast from the century before made play with the new conventions. Matthew Prior (1664–1721) could be as serious as the next man, as great a flatterer, but a sense of realism and of the absurd irrupts in some of his poems, either in their diction, incident or tonality (**1–6**). A writer of *vers d'société*, on specific occasions and themes, his poems come alive because of their wit and irony, suddenly shifting from high diction to low. He goes so far as to make fun of his own voice and tone as a poet, standing outside his poems, cocking a snook at the artifice, if not the art, of verse itself, deliberately violating a chosen form to achieve specific effects. He caused Dryden tears when he parodied *The Hind and the Panther*. An enemy of hypocrisy, he is a kind of pre-emptive corrective to some of the excesses that were to come; he allies himself with Falstaff, the truth-telling liar.

As the eighteenth century let itself loose on the literature of the English past, it tidied it up considerably. Dryden had begun pruning and repairing what he took to be the broken arbours and derelictions of Chaucer and Shakespeare. Such restorations continued; scholarship became a function equally of erudition and propriety, culminating in 1818 with Thomas Bowdler's famous *Family Shakespeare*, from which every innuendo and impropriety had been, with greater or lesser subtlety, excised. Bowdlerised.

In terms of making literature, it was not a question of scaling down: literary works produced in the eighteenth century are as ambitious and innovative as any that had come before. It was rather a matter of reproportioning, of adjustment of parts to the whole. Just as the handsome old Jacobean mansion was given a neoclassical façade and new buildings strove for an elegant, neutral harmony, so in poetry integration, semantic depth, prosodic correctness, give rise to an elaborated, correct diction and all that follows from such an enrichment and codification of certain *kinds* of meaning at the cost of other poetic resources.

'Correct diction', 'poetic diction', the terms are used so loosely that they retain as much, and as little, meaning as the term 'post-modern'. One twentieth-century critic insisted that the only way we could begin to understand the poetry of the eighteenth century was to understand poetic diction in a very specific way. In his first major critical work, *Purity of Diction in English Verse* (1952) Donald Davie distinguished between 'the language of poetry' and 'the diction of verse'. A diction is a selection, made according to certain rules of propriety, class, etymology, precedent, from the language as a whole. There are poets, he says, who give him the feeling 'that a selection has been made and is continually being made, that words are thrusting at the poem and being fended off from it, that however many poems these poets wrote certain words would never be allowed into the poems, except as a disastrous oversight'. A writer with a pure diction of this kind writes, Davie insists, *verse*. The verse may also be *poetry*, but it is different in texture, intent and provenance from the kind of poetry which seems as though it might, given a context, admit any word in the language.

Davie makes it clear that while Milton has a *style*, he does not have a *diction*. We can imagine any word at some stage finding lodging in one of his poems. However, poets who follow Milton closely, like James Thomson and others in the eighteenth and nineteenth centuries, use a Miltonic diction. They use those words whose use Milton licensed, those words that his style seems to sanction. Thomson's 'selection of language' is a subset of the selection made by John Milton. Early on, William Wordsworth too used a Miltonic diction. Early on, Milton used a Spenserian diction.

If we can reserve the word 'diction' to mean 'a selection from the whole language', it begins to play a more useful part in our discussion of the eighteenth century and of the revolutions against its rules as the century progressed. A poetry which depends on rules of diction will also evolve rules of decorum and propriety: what range of diction is appropriate to the ballad, the hymn, the lyric, the epic and the satire? Johnson found King Lear's 'Undo this button' a dreadful error of tact: the word 'button' had no place in tragedy.

The choice of appropriate diction imparts information and a range of expectations to readers, who know what poetic area they are in from the first line. Furthermore, poems can be judged against, as it were, very nearly objective (though in origin arbitrary) criteria. So long as all those participating in a literary culture, as readers, critics and writers, accept the appropriateness of the criteria, a succinct and expressive poetry can develop. Its expressiveness and succinctness are accessible, of course, only to those familiar with the criteria. Such consensus might imply a rather narrow literary class: metropolitan for the most part, polite in a special sense, and taking pleasure in the intensity of word-play going on in a few lines which sound to the uninitiated as merely rhetorical. Davie reminds us of what Oliver Goldsmith made of three lines of Thomson:

> O vale of bliss! O softly swelling hills!
> On which the power of cultivation lies,
> And joys to see the wonders of his toil.

'We cannot conceive a more beautiful image than that of the Genius of Agriculture, distinguished by the implements of his art, imbrowned with labour, glowing with health, crowned with a garland of foliage, flowers, and fruit, lying stretched at his ease on the brow of a gently swelling hill, and contemplating with pleasure the happy effects of his own industry.' Goldsmith visualises conventionally, to be sure, in neoclassical generalities. Such detail as he adduces is characteristic rather than specific. His reading of the three lines is not unjust. The 'vale of bliss' imports into the eighteenth-century reader's mind the foliage of Spenser, the accents of Comus, even perhaps Milton's Paradise; the personifications are all there in precedents as well. The world of allegory is not far off. There are common meanings to be surmised here, characteristic meanings. Poetry is a social art from which every reader will receive the same meaning, though in different degrees; it cannot be misconstrued. Achieved poetic diction is a most precise shorthand, if we have the skill and will to interpret it.

Not for Keats, however. Writing a century later in *Sleep and Poetry*, he was categorical, setting up Queen Anne as a Georgian Aunt Sally with haughty eloquence:

> Ah, dismal-soul'd!
> The winds of heaven blew, the ocean roll'd
> Its gathering waves – ye felt it not, the blue
> Bared its eternal bosom, and the dew
> Of summer night collected still to make
> The morning precious: Beauty was awake!
> Why were ye not awake? But ye were dead
> To things ye knew not of – were closely wed
> To musty laws lined out with wretched rule
> And compass vile; so that ye taught a school
> Of dolts to smooth, inlay, and clip, and fit,
> Till, like the certain wands of Jacob's wit,

Their verses tallied. Easy was the task:
A thousand handicraftsmen wore the mask
Of Poesy. Ill-fated, impious race!

The chief culprit, in Keats's view, was French fashion, and in particular Nicolas Boileau, the maker of polite rules, for whom, Gustav Flaubert said, bad taste was an intense personal affront. Like most of those who vehemently criticise the eighteenth century, Keats is categorical, reductive – and young. Yet his personifications, his 'eternal bosom' (less material even than Thomson's 'softly swelling hills'), the abstractions 'Beauty' and 'Poesy', the way many of the nouns are carried under the arm of a convenient adjective – concrete and abstract or abstract and concrete – show how far from emancipation Keats himself was. The main difference between his rancour and Alexander Pope's, in this passage compared with something from *The Dunciad*, is not in the couplets but in the skill of their deployment (Keats can reverse into a rhyme, and the couplets run on, without epithetic closure); not in the uneven symmetries of syntax, but in the tone. Keats is angry and puffed up; Pope in such circumstances is wily, wry and deadly. Pope addresses us as intelligent individuals, Keats (in this passage) as a literary rabble; he tries to persuade us with eloquence, not convince us in our own intelligences.

At the end of the eighteenth century another young man, William Wordsworth, set his cap against the kinds of writing generated by prescriptive 'diction', divorced from the 'real language of men'. In his 'Preface' to *Lyrical Ballads* he touched upon the theme, but with insufficient clarity, so that he returned to it in an 1802 'Appendix'. 'The earliest poets of all nations,' he asserts, 'generally wrote from passion excited by real events.' The premise is certainly dubious; but he proceeds with his Rousseauvian history to describe this happy 'original' poetic occasion: passion, real events, and a language without a history of poetic usage, result in 'daring and figurative' language. That language, once set down, becomes a pre-existing language *of poetry* for the successors of those 'earliest poets', who, 'desirous of producing the same effect without having the same animating passion, set themselves to a mechanical adoption of those figures of speech'. As time passed, the language of poetry, without it being the poet's conscious intention that it should do so, came to differ 'materially from the real language of men in *any situation*' (Wordsworth's italics). It became archaic, formulaic, conventional. The question for Wordsworth was: how to re-root the language of poetry in 'real language'?

Yet just as for the conventional poet of the eighteenth century there were norms of diction, which made men write not 'in character' or with 'a distinctive voice' but rather in a common code, the diction itself effacing individual idiosyncrasy, so too Wordsworth proposes a norm. He proposes it over and over again without ever quite tying it down: 'real language'. Could he mean dialect? The language of a specific class? The language of an age? He means one or all these things, depending on his context. In other words, he is speaking of dictions too, only his dictions are those of best speech which he hopes will restore to poetry 'daring and figurative' language, the compelling particularity which, in the interests of 'moral value' of a conventional kind, the poets of the eighteenth-century 'main stream' had purged from their verse.

The eighteenth century is, like any other, irreducible. Wordsworth's take on it simplifies a diverse reality in the interests of his own timely polemic. But it is Wordsworth's rhetorically simplified account of the century which persists. Eighteenth-century British poetry is not widely appreciated outside, or even inside, the academy. Only the insane and the profoundly depressive exceptions – Christopher Smart, for example, and Edward Young: 'Fate! drop the curtain; I can lose no more' – are read with general gusto: the exceptions, whose response was a way of dealing with intolerable cultural and political prescription. General readerly aversion to the characteristic manner of the eighteenth-century begins with Dryden who died on the century's threshold, in 1700, and persists until William Cowper and Charlotte Smith begin to break the 'chains of conventionality' from within, the French Revolution gets seriously under way, and first William Blake and then Wordsworth rise above the horizon. Romanticism is at hand.

If we miss out or over-simplify the eighteenth century, we misread the nineteenth and twentieth and, more to the point, we ignore some extraordinary poetry.

THREE FRIENDS

Jonathan Swift, John Gay, Alexander Pope, Mary Leapor

> Books and the man I sing, the first who brings
> The Smithfield muses to the ear of kings.
>
> Alexander Pope, The Dunciad, in Three Books

If writers are friends in the eighteenth century, it is best that they plough different furrows or live in different cities. A prose-writer and a poet might be friends, but men active on the same patch might fall out over a patron, a reward, an error of taste or emphasis. Yet some of the great writers of the early eighteenth century knew and applauded one another. *Gulliver's Travels*, *The Vicar of Wakefield*, *The Beggar's Opera* and *The Dunciad* are cousin works by men who had one another's interests – to some extent – at heart.

Jonathan Swift's mother was a Leicestershire Herrick, of Robert Herrick's family – so it happens that the savage satirist and the gentle Cavalier poet grow on a single family tree. They also share, in different centuries, a religious vocation and a politics. Yet their poetic imaginations belong on opposite sides of the divide that was the Commonwealth and Restoration. Swift is a brilliant savage who understands – though he cannot control – the political and literary jungle in which he lives.

> If on Parnassus' top you sit,
> You rarely bite, are always bit:
> Each poet of inferior size
> On you shall rail and criticise ...

His reputation as a poet rose higher last century than it had done before. Several poets identified original virtues in the verse which had been regarded as peripheral to his major prose work. Robert Graves called the verses 'trifles', 'But these trifles, though darkened by a morbid horror of man's physical circumstances, demonstrate the proper use of English: they are clear, simple, inventive, pungent, unaffected, original, generous, utterly outspoken.'

Born in Dublin in 1667, Swift insisted on his Englishness. He was of Yorkshire stock. His father died before Swift was born. His education was paid for by an uncle, first in Kilkenny and later at Trinity College, Dublin, where he did not distinguish himself. He travelled to England and became secretary to Sir William Temple at Moor Park in Surrey. There, among other studies, he laboured at verse, subjected his work to endless revisions, and fell under the influence not of Milton, whose religion and politics were anathema to him, but Abraham Cowley, whose Pindaric odes appealed (disastrously) to many young poets. Swift's odes are negligible. His first significant poem, 'Mrs Harris's Petition', was not composed until he was thirty-two (1699), by which time he had put Cowley aside and opened his ears to the spoken language of the day, the new eighteenth century. The 'Petition' is thoroughly colloquial, in irregular long-lined couplets that assume the tone of a woman speaking at great speed. Undecorated, it displays what Thomas De Quincey called his 'vernacularity'. When Wordsworth called for a poetry rooted in 'real language', he did not have in mind a language quite as real as this.

When Swift composed the 'Petition' he had left Temple, abandoning after real promise his secular career, and taken holy orders (1694). He was to rub shoulders with men of power and in his prose writings to make a mark on English affairs, but he was not destined to be a man at Court. His first living, in Kilroot, Ireland, displeased him. He returned briefly to England but in 1699 was back in Ireland as chaplain to the Earl of Berkeley, a post from which he was ousted by private intrigue. He became vicar of Laracor. Deeply embroiled in religious and political affairs, he eventually became Dean of St Patrick's, Dublin. With the death of Queen Anne the Whigs, his enemies, came to power. There was to be no further preferment for him.

In his later years he became a political enigma, 'with the Whigs of the State and the Tories of the Church', Johnson said. His treatment by patrons and parties provoked a healthy distrust of men in power and intensified his sense of personal grievance. He considered life in Ireland to be exile. Yet he did much for the Irish, earning their respect if not their love. Through correspondence he maintained his friendship with Alexander Pope and John Gay, with Dr John Arbuthnot, Henry St John Viscount Bolingbroke and others in England, but his mind ran on Irish affairs. He was aware of conditions at every social level; his Toryism was of that rare particularist kind which will not overlook exploitative corruption from any quarter.

His vexed relations with women, especially 'Stella' and 'Vanessa', and his disgust with physical functions, have given much latitude to Freudian interpreters. Although disgust informs much of the prose and verse, so also does a real interest in common people, their language, actions and concerns.

The verse opens on this area of his genius, and on his darker musings. It possesses the satiric virtues of the prose with an additional element: the 'I' speaks, speaks *as itself,* with an uncompromised acerbity which few poets have mastered. When he died in 1745, Ireland and England were in his debt. The topicality that limits the appeal of some of his prose is itself the appeal of the verse: it catches inflections and remembers small actions now lost – the voices of gardeners, street vendors, labourers, which we hear a little over-refined in Gay; the tone of a cryptic man of conscience speaking of his world, his bitter life, his wary loves. He is commemorated by a great epitaph: he lies '*ubi saeva indignatio ulterius cor lacerare nequit. Abi, viator, et imitare, si poteris, strenuum pio virili libertatis vindicatorem.*' W. B. Yeats translated it thus:

> Swift has sailed into his rest;
> Savage indignation there
> Cannot lacerate his breast
> Imitate him if you dare,
> World-besotted traveller; he
> Served human liberty.

Boswell found Johnson's 'Life of Swift' too harsh. In thirty pages, the poems receive three succinct paragraphs. In the poems 'there is not much upon which the critic can exercise his powers. They are often humorous, almost always light, and have the qualities which recommend such compositions, easiness and gaiety.' Their diction, prosody and rhyme are correct, conforming to Swift's own notion of good style: 'proper words in proper places'. Johnson's highest praise follows: 'perhaps no writer can be found who borrowed so little, or that in all his excellences and all his defects has so well maintained his claim to be considered as original'. He is original in part because – in his mature poems – he is so spare. As Johnson says, his thoughts were 'never subtilised by nice disquisitions, decorated by sparkling conceits, elevated by ambitious sentences, or variegated by far-sought learning'. In this his verse resembles Defoe's prose: it never shirks a difficult subject or elaborates for elaboration's sake.

Trifles and bagatelles, Johnson tells us, were necessary to Swift. Many of the poems are occasioned by little more than a fascination with language as it is differently spoken, and with the people who speak it. The activity of humble folk provides substance: to represent can be a sufficient end. There are the 'Descriptions' of 'Morning' (7), 'A City Shower' in particular, which realises a peopled scene with slight satirical colouring:

> Brisk Susan whips her linen from the rope
> While the first drizzling show'r is borne aslope,

> Such is that sprinkling which some careless quean
> Flirts on you from her mop, but not so clean.

Bustling verbs animate scene and metaphor. Human actions rather than natural phenomena arrest attention. Ford Madox Ford comments on his 'most unusual power of conveying scenes vividly ... scenes rather of the sensibility than of material objects and landscapes'. Sometimes, in *despite* of the sensibility, because the material objects are 'real'. Coleridge calls Swift – with the prose more than the verse in mind – 'the soul of Rabelais dwelling in a dry place'.

In the more ambitious pieces Swift challenges his reader. F.R. Leavis indicates the paradoxical nature of his approach: 'Lacking the Augustan politeness, he seems with his dry force of presentment, both to make the Augustan positives ... look like negatives, and to give the characteristic Augustan lacks and disabilities a positive presence.' Without 'Augustan urbanity', 'spiritual poverty' and 'hollowness' are underscored. There is a unique irony at work, not normative, like Dryden's, but radical: thematic rather than stylistic. This is why his poems, even the most topical, retain force today. 'I take it to be part of the honesty of poets,' Swift wrote, 'that they cannot write well except they think the subject deserves it.' The subjects he chose he approached as if for the first time, as if we stepped from the chill, clear world of reason into a world of *actual* men. Bolingbroke was not quite fair when he suggested, 'If you despised the world as much as you pretend, and perhaps believe, you would not be so angry with it.' Swift is a vigorous hater, but with a hatred rooted in disappointed expectation. He is merciless not to those below him on the social ladder but to those above, the empowered, and to the vain who persist in self-deception. The grossest sin is flattery, chastised in the satirical 'On Poetry: A Rhapsody', a poem which had terrible consequences for its printer, Motte, who spent a year in prison for it, and Swift's friend Mary Barber, who brought it over from Dublin. It was not kind about the King or his Court.

> O, what indignity and shame
> To prostitute the Muse's name,
> By flatt'ring kings whom heaven designed
> The plagues and scourges of mankind,
> Bred up in ignorance and sloth,
> And every vice that nurses both.

In the twentieth century Edgell Rickword and later C.H. Sisson took Swift's verse to heart. In a crucial essay, 'The Re-Creation of Poetry' (1925), Rickword describes a 'poetry of negative emotions, of those arising from disgust with the object'. For him, 'Swift is a great master of this kind of poetry. His verse has no pleasure-value beyond that of its symmetry and concision, but it is the most intricate labyrinth of personality that any poet has built around himself, not excepting Donne.' Rickword loves Donne, which makes his point compelling. Donne creates a beguiling labyrinth; Swift undecorates as he goes. The narrow, narrowing power of the verse is great. 'The Progress of Beauty' and 'The Furniture of a Woman's Mind' exemplify the voice of 'negative emotion'. So does 'The Progress of Marriage' or 'Verses on the Death of Dr Swift' (11), where he directs satire at himself. His imitation of Horace II.6, with wry self-knowledge and a canny understanding of the world, evokes the man and those who use him. Conventional love is remote from this verse.

Swift is hard to recommend as a poet because he is hard to quote from. There are few purple passages, detachable maxims; the sense is drawn evenly through the poem in ways that out-of-context quotation violates. The epitaphs, the spoofs, the eclogues, the anecdotes spoken by various voices, the ironic love poems, the first person poems, will not be broken up into tags like the rich couplet bric-à-brac of Pope. Swift might have preferred to be called a versifier rather than a poet. There is a difference in kind between his work and that of his predecessors; and he is not 'polite' enough to have charmed his contemporaries into imitation. He stands alone, he doesn't sing, he never ingratiates himself. He speaks, and he understands how the world wags.

The most brilliant poet of the eighteenth century would have been a composite figure made up of the three poet-friends, Swift, Pope, and John Gay. Swift's savagery rooted in a concern for common people, Pope's verve and imaginative profligacy, and Gay's gentle good cheer might, taken together, have given us a writer of Shakespearean – or at least Chaucerian – proportions. Genius was parcelled out, not combined, in the eighteenth century, and Gay was fortunate to have been given what seem like gentle, beguiling elements. 'Tell me, ye jovial sailors, tell me true, / If my sweet William sails among the crew.' (12) His epitaph reads, 'Life is a jest; and all things show it, / I thought so once; but now I know it.' It is true, though perhaps not quite as Swift's epitaph is to him. Recent biographers have sensed beneath the apparently guileless voice of John Gay a man who could scheme, and perhaps a man with a secret which dared not speak its name. On this matter the jury will be for ever out.

For Pope and his circle Gay was more a 'play-fellow' than a 'partner'. Pope reports that he was treated 'with more fondness than respect ... he was a natural man, without design, who spoke what he thought and just as he thought it.' This isn't quite just. Gay, when he sets pen to paper, is a great parodist. His method is different from Pope's. Ironist rather than satirist, he lacks the sure-seeming moral voice of Pope and the firm orientation of Swift: he will not be tied to an opinion. Amused and alarmed by human fallibility, vanity and self-deceit, he does not rise to that rage which makes and mars the satires of his friends. Evil is unclear to him, he avoids moral absolutes. He is also skilful in securing patrons and, when necessary, as effective a flatterer as any.

He was born in Barnstaple, Devon, in 1685. His father, who died when Gay was ten, was a Nonconformist man of affairs from established Devonshire stock. The boy was educated at the local grammar school, then apprenticed to a silk mercer in London. He disliked the job, secured his release, and returned to Devon, where he began writing verse. In 1707 he went back to London to become a writer, and the next year published *Wine*. It celebrates wine in Miltonic parody: 'Of happiness terrestrial, and the source / Whence human pleasures flow, sing heavenly Muse.' Of a muse that failed another poet, he writes as of the fallen angel Lucifer:

> Now in Ariconian bogs
> She lies inglorious floundering, like her theme
> Languid and faint.

He parodies the debate of the fallen angels. Closing time is like the departure of Adam and Eve from the garden. He wryly sends up not only Milton's language and style, but his plot and structure, with a trivial subject handled in the grand manner. The moral: water drinkers cannot be successful writers. It is clever and sustained but, Johnson dourly reflects, inconsequential: an exercise that any decent versifier might perform. It lacks the purpose of his later parodic satires. Yet it shows how deeply embedded Milton is in the eighteenth century, how the choice of Milton over Cowley was almost complete. In Gay there are no vestiges of Swift's earliest master.

In 1711 he met Pope and found himself in the best possible literary milieu, with a friend and critic who, though younger than he, could help and advise, a warrior eager to exploit his talents in his own literary vendettas. If Pope did not fully appreciate Gay's benign genius, he valued his friendship and helped him in times of need. Gay's nicest tribute to Pope, 'Mr Pope's Welcome from Greece' (25), celebrates the translator of Homer as himself an Homeric hero upon concluding his famous translation.

Gay's talent for eccentric, accurate observation, and his sense that the established literary modes were vulnerable to real experience and needed to open out towards an actual world, inform all his verse. He could deflate epic, georgic, eclogue and dramatic modes by literalising rather than ridiculing them. He laughed them back to a more inclusive life. In his 'low style' he did things Swift must have appreciated, wrote ballads and burlesques. In two of his several attempts he was a considerable dramatist. He had an instinctive, if not an infallible, sense of his public. Like Swift, he ought to have escaped Wordsworth's strictures. In many ways Swift and Gay were more wedded to 'real language' than Wordsworth is.

During his two years of service as secretary to the Duchess of Monmouth (1712-14) Gay wrote his first notable poems and began contributing to Steele's *Guardian*. It was his friend Pope and not a noble patron who was honoured with the dedication of his first major poem, *Rural Sports* (1713), based on *Windsor Forest*. The overall form leaves much to be desired, but the detail lives. Johnson called it 'realistic pastoral'. It prepared the ground for *The Shepherd's Week* (1714), Gay's best 'pastoral'. *Rural Sports* exploits the pathetic fallacy to effect. Fish and worms behave in such a way as to suggest the animal fable, a genre he later practised. An uninsistent religious strain sounds through the poem. Country streams are 'Sweet composers of the pensive soul'.

The Shepherd's Week, a sort of truncated *Shepheards Calendar*, was part of Pope's campaign against Ambrose Philips, whose pastorals had been praised in preference to Pope's own. Gay imports into the polite, idealised world of swains and shepherdesses some of the rollicking Devonshire peasants of his youth. Spenser and Virgil, as well as Philips, are among his targets. Convention is invaded by flesh and blood. In 'Monday' he footnotes his own lines 83-88 and refers to their source in Virgil:

Populus Alcidae gratissima, vitis Iaccho,
Fermosae Myrtus Veneri, sua Laurea Phoebo.
Phillis amat Corylos. Illis dum Phillis amabit,
Nec Myrtus vincet Corylos nec Laurea Phoebi.

Johnson says the pastoral can only be brought to life through burlesque. Gay adapts these lines as:

Leek to the Welsh, to Dutchmen butter's dear,
Of Irish swains potato is the cheer;
Oats for their feasts the Scottish shepherds grind,
Sweet turnips are the food of Blouzelind.
While she loves turnips, butter I'll despise,
Nor leeks nor oatmeal nor potato prize.

This form of traduction into common diction and experience marks Gay's parodies, especially his dramatic masterpiece *The Beggar's Opera* (1728), a 'Newgate pastoral' composed at Swift's suggestion. It sets out to discredit the Italian opera that had held the stage in London for ten years. This 'ballad opera', as Johnson called it, was an unparalleled success and jeopardised Gay's friendship with one of his chief patrons who was also a promoter of Italian opera. The sequel, *Polly*, banned by Walpole, sold well when it was published in 1729. Swift commented on the predominance of humour over wit in these works: rules are parodied and satirised – those of marriage and honour for example – but finally upheld. Despite having parodied opera, Gay became Handel's librettist for *Acis and Galatea* (1732) and – staged after his death – *Achilles* (1733).

He had left the service of the batty Duchess of Monmouth in 1714 and served under the Duke of Clarendon at Hanover. Queen Anne's death brought this brief appointment to an end and he enjoyed no courtly preferment thereafter. Like Swift, he experienced disappointment: his sense of the social world clouded, his poetry matured. In 1713 he had published *The Fan;* but in 1716 he published *Trivia*. The change is remarkable. *The Fan* follows too closely on the heels of Pope's *The Rape of the Lock.* It is weak because it is unsystematic and unsubtly overstated. It does not grasp the real firmly enough to mythologise it. It is literary, in the spirit of *Wine.* But *Trivia: or the Art of Walking the Streets of London* (**26**) is the great evocation of London in verse. It originates in the Roman poet Juvenal's uncompromising third satire, as Johnson's 'London' does, but Gay is gentler than his original and than Johnson and, though less powerful, more complex. The target of his parody is Virgil's *Georgics* and the again fashionable Georgic tradition. An ironic contrast between the rural order which the form imposes, and the disorder of city life which is the subject, generates the humour. In an even, Georgic tone he describes bizarre and terrible incidents. The Great Frost, described in the second section, includes an account of the death of an apple vendor:

> 'Twas here the matron found a doleful fate:
> Let elegiac lay the woe relate.
> Soft as the breath of distant flutes, at hours
> When silent evening closes up the flowers;
> Lulling as falling water's hollow noise;
> Indulging grief, like Philomela's voice ...

Doll, the fruit vendor, is decapitated as she falls through the ice, her voice dying in the 'pip-pip-pip' of her pippin cry. The incongruity between manner and matter is a measure of Gay's ironic power. The reader can never be quite certain of the poet's tone.

'Nothing about *Trivia* is straightforward,' says Gay's editor Marcus Walsh, 'not even the title, which means primarily crossroads, but is also a Roman name for the goddess Hecate', that night-time goddess conjured for magic. Not only the title: single words, parodic passages and scenes are equally complex. A bootblack is begotten by immaculate conception; Vulcan visits Patty and makes her patterns. As in a good Georgic, we receive advice, but here it is about our dress for walking the London streets: suitable shoes, coat, walking stick, hat; about the weather and the sights to see. We hear creaking shop signs, street cries, wagons and carriages rumble by. There is mud, a street fight, pick-pockets, whores, chairmen, vendors, watchmen, rakes. The values that inform georgic poetry are parodied and rejuvenated.

In 1720 Gay successfully published his *Poems on Several Occasions*. He lost the money he made, however, in the speculative fiasco known as the South Sea Bubble which destroyed many fortunes, large and small. Gay was so disappointed that, had Pope and his circle not rallied round, he would have died. He became Commissioner for the Public Lottery in 1722, and spent his later years at various houses, especially with the Duke and Duchess of Queensberry who took his chaotic affairs in hand. In 1725 he published 'To a Lady on her Passion for Old China', a sustained polite moral satire: 'What rival's near? a China jar.' Two years later *The Fables* appeared, written for Prince William, later Duke of Cumberland. In 1738 sixteen posthumous *Fables* were published, more overtly moral and satiric than the earlier pieces, and in epistolary form after the manner of Pope. Gay died in 1732 and was buried in Westminster Abbey.

The *Fables* proved popular, running through fifty editions before 1800, a poetry bonanza for his publisher, along with Thomson's *The Seasons* and Pope's work. The *Fables* were illustrated by Thomas Bewick and later by Blake. Gay uses his animals to illuminate human nature, either by contrast or caricature, varying the tone and approach. Some are serious, others simply comic. The moral, as Johnson says, cannot always be drawn. When he adopted fable form, he found literary parody difficult, since fable itself is a species of parody. Gay is compelled to neglect one of his best skills and modern readers feel its absence 'The Elephant and the Bookseller' (**27**), 'The Butterfly and the Snail', 'The Two Monkeys', and the fox fables stand out from the rest. But they are less entertaining than *Trivia*. No one has written a poem to vie with *Trivia* as living verse documentary and brilliant parody. Pope wrote Gay a fuller epitaph than the one he provided for himself, and it touches on the paradox of his innocent integrity:

> Of manners gentle, of affections mild;
> In wit, a man; simplicity, a child;
> With native humour temp'ring virtuous rage,
> Form'd to delight at once and lash the age;
> Above temptation, of a low estate,
> The uncorrupted, ev'n among the great;
> A safe companion, and an easy friend,
> Unblam'd thro' life, lamented in thy end ...

'A safe companion': Alexander Pope had few of those. Ford's account of him, though perfunctory and unkind, is not inaccurate. 'It has well been said of Pope that his work divides itself into three periods which correspond to the three reigns under which he wrote. Under Queen Anne he was a personal pastoral English poet; Under George I he was a translator and "made much money by satisfying the French-classical taste of his day with versions of the *Iliad* and the *Odyssey* and with bitter-sweet poems of the bag-wig and sword-knot type" . . . The heavy materialism and gross agnostic alcoholism settled on the country that had driven out the Stuarts and forgotten the piety and music of Herbert and Donne; so Pope turned his mind to the problems of his age. And in a series of poems that were "serious" and censorious enough he made his muse sing his day.'

Pope is among the first British verse businessmen, setting out to make a living free of any patron but public esteem; he was among the first to flatter for a living not a monarch or a peer (though he does both) but a party. He writes with assurance and authority which set at nothing the animosity his character arouses. Even his letters he composed for publication; in his privacies (there are few intimacies) he felt himself to be on show, accountable, as it were, to his idea of himself.

Developing the measure that Dryden used with such finality, the heroic couplet, Pope restores poetic complexities which Dryden had refined away. He does not decorate a line of thought: he thinks in metaphor, shape and form. And ideas, the sequence of rational thought, matter less in his work than in Dryden's. There are few of the spiritual crises which matured Dryden's ideas and gave them abiding weight. For Pope, crises were not religious or political but social and literary. If as a man he was crudely ambitious, in some respects dishonest, in love with his role as a poet and with material profit as a writer above all else, he did command deep friendship from discriminating men – Swift and Gay, but also Bolingbroke, Arbuthnot and others. That is so much to his credit that bad report is partly answered. At the heart of his work an unresolved philosophical contradiction provokes much of the best verse. Of twentieth-century poets W. H. Auden most resembles him in his omnicompetence, ambivalence and social character.

Pope was born in Lombard Street, London, in 1688. His Roman Catholic father was a merchant, and both his parents were advanced in years when the little misshapen poet came into the world. From a protective home he acquired not religious certainties, but the instincts of a successful and settled entrepreneur. In the year of Dryden's death, when Pope was twelve, the family joined a Catholic Community in Windsor Forest. Soon the young Pope was writing imitations of Waller, Cowley, Rochester, Chaucer, Spenser, and translating from Thomas à Kempis, Ovid, Statius and Homer.

At the age of twelve he contracted the first of a series of illnesses which, with his physical disability (a hunched back), left him *nearly* an invalid for the rest of his life. He read eclectically and was encouraged to write. In the year when illness beset him, he wrote a poem imitating Cowley and indebted to Horace, 'On Solitude':

Happy the man, whose wish and care
A few paternal acres bound,
Content to breathe his native air,
    In his own native ground.

Whose herds with milk, whose fields with bread,
Whose flocks supply him with attire,
Whose trees in summer yield him shade,
    In winter fire.

Blest! who can unconcern'dly find
Hours, days, and years slide soft away,
In health of body, peace of mind,
    Quiet by day,

Sound sleep by night; study and ease
Together mixed; sweet recreation,
And innocence, which most does please,
    With meditation.

Thus let me live, unseen, unknown;
Thus unlamented let me die;
Steal from the world, and not a stone
    Tell where I lie.

Like the voice of an inmate of Thomas Gray's country churchyard, its resignation (a literary attitude) is credible because the form is so accomplished, phrases building precisely, now gathering evidence, now deploying it, so that the conclusion is not only just but inevitable. The second stanza anticipates the future poet: fields yield bread and sheep provide clothing, natural images translated into manufacture and a marketable commodity. It matters less what they are than what they produce.

When he was nineteen, his *Pastorals* appeared in the sixth volume of Tonson's *Miscellany*. Pope insists more than once that he wrote the poems when he was sixteen, along with 'A Discourse on Pastoral Poetry' in which he sets out, in a short space, to summarise the critics' conflicting accounts of the mode: 'You will also find some points reconciled, about which they seem to differ, and a few remarks which I think have escaped their observation.' Such adolescent hubris is beguiling, if a little intimidating: Dryden is a guide, Spenser a model, but in both he finds faults which he sets out to remedy as much in his prose discourse as in the poems themselves. The poems are of little interest today, stiff with eager correctness. But the poet's accomplishment was auspiciously welcomed. In 1711 perhaps his best non-satirical composition, *An Essay on Criticism* (**30**), appeared and the *Spectator* and the *Guardian* took up the young prodigy. He was 23.

Pope attributed the virtues of his *Pastorals* not to observation of nature but 'to some old authors, whose work as I had leisure to study, so I hope I have not wanted care to imitate'. Here is literary – wholly literary – eclogue. In the first lines, along with classical echoes, we hear Spenser, Milton and Waller. The syntax is classicising and at times silly. 'Two swains, whom Love kept wakeful, and the Muse, / Poured o'er the whitening vale their fleecy care.' The muse appears to be both wakeful and a shepherdess – until we realise that she is a second cause for insomnia after love. Lapses of syntactical clarity are common in Pope. Thomas De Quincey sees the problem as 'almost peculiar to himself. It lay in an inability, nursed doubtless by indolence, to carry out and perfect the expression of the thought he wishes to communicate. The language does not realise the idea: it simply suggests or hints it.' Pope *indolent?* Surely not, surely not at the age of sixteen. Injudicious, inexperienced perhaps, but never indolent. De Quincey is talking about the mature work. Pope is a treacherous 'model of correctness'.

Yet couplets from the *Pastorals* reveal the virtues of his writing, too: 'their fleecy care' is a round-about way of saying 'sheep', but it has the effect of stressing the shepherds' responsibility (an abstract meaning) and of physically evoking sheep (and their use). It combines pictorial and moral elements. The technique is deployed in 'Eloisa to Abelard' (1716), a romantic 'heroic epistle' unique in his work (**34**).

> In these deep solitudes and awful cells,
> Where heav'nly-pensive, contemplation dwells,
> And ever-musing melancholy reigns;
> What means this tumult in a Vestal's veins?

'Deep' and 'cells' are apprehensible to the senses; 'solitudes' and 'awful' are abstract. Parallel construction mingles the terms: hermitage and state of mind. Within solitude a hierarchy is proposed: melancholy reigns, contemplation dwells: a pensive, ever-musing kingdom, shaken by earthly desire. 'Vestal's veins' is oxymoronic in effect. Pope attaches shapes and scenes, most vividly in the passage in which tears distort the visible world for Eloisa, the speaker:

> Can'st thou forget what tears that moment fell,
> When, warm in youth, I bade the world farewell?

As with cold lips I kissed the sacred veil,
The shrines all trembled, and the lamps grew pale ...

This passage suggests the kind of poet Pope might have become with different priorities, other admirers. 'Eloisa to Abelard', undramatic yet gripping because of its close-textured, consistent evocation – developing imagery of lips, eyes, tears, pallor, coldness and burning – can lay claim to being the last achieved English epyllion, just as his *Pastorals* provide the last, almost asphyxiated gasp of Spenserian eclogue. The subjects are human nature and passion at their most paradoxical. Pope never tried the mode again, perhaps because it gave him only limited scope for what De Quincey described as his 'talent for caustic effect'. Besides, the subject was 'unwholesome'; it may have shaken him.

'Windsor Forest' (**31**) suggests another might-have-been. He observes nature less through 'old authors' than through his own eyes; we see (stylised) something like the Forest itself. The scene is full of brittle, natural detail presented in terms of artifice and carrying a moral or interpretative weight. Transitive verbs energise the verse, fusing concrete images and abstract qualities:

Oft, as in airy rings they skim the heath,
The clam'rous lapwings feel the leaden death;
Oft, as the mounting larks their notes prepare,
They fall, and leave their little lives in air.

'Leaden death' for 'shot' or 'bullet' suggests the physical weight of ammunition and checks the free movement of the previous line. The speeding larks are shot and fall, their music left suspended.

In 1712 Pope was getting to know Swift, Gay, the neglected poet Thomas Parnell and the genial physician and polemicist Dr Arbuthnot who as a pamphleteer opposed to the wars with France invented John Bull. These men became pillars of his social world and collaborators in works for stage and page, and they began inventing the Scriblerus Club, which included not only writers but men of affairs disaffected with the political current of the time. *The Rape of the Lock* (**33**) was published by Barnaby Bernard Lintot in his *Miscellany*. (In *The Dunciad* (**39**) Pope later compared Lintot to 'a ' dabchick', which was ungracious since Lintot had printed his work and was a not dishonourable publisher.)

Two years later an extended version of *The Rape* appeared. This chief of British mock-heroic poems, the verse masterpiece of Queen Anne's reign, grew out of an actual event but, in a satirical onslaught on polite ladies, pursued a social foible to absurd lengths, into 'the moving toyshop of their heart'. The protagonist's very boudoir is displayed, her ritual of social preparation disclosed. The drama of her stolen lock is delicious, trivial, the satire tart rather than corrective – and it charms. Pope is at home in the world he describes, half-seduced by its opulence, and if not willing to forgive, reluctant to chastise excesses which he pushes in his poem to further excess. Yet at the fringes of his poem a cruel social world peeps in:

> Meanwhile declining from the noon of day,
> The Sun obliquely shoots his burning ray;
> The hungry judges soon the sentence sign,
> And wretches hang that jury-men may dine;
> The merchant from th' Exchange returns in peace,
> And the long labours of the *toilette* cease –

We skitter merrily past the 'wretches', but they stay on hold, incongruous above a world of 'Puffs, powders, patches, Bibles, billet-doux'. A canny politician reading these lines might have foreseen what the little poet might do on a different scale.

In 1713 Pope issued proposals and started to raise subscriptions for his translation of Homer's *Iliad*. It appeared between 1715 and 1720 and profited him greatly, despite a spoiling effort by Thomas Tickell who published an *Iliad* I two days after Pope's *Iliad* I-IV appeared, and numerous critical attacks. All publicity proved to be good for the project. In 1725-6 the *Odyssey* less successfully followed, prepared with two assistants (by then, like a painter, he had an *atelier* to prepare the huge Homeric canvases: his minions primed them and he added a verbal stroke here and there and called them his, as indeed the contracts for them were). In his *Iliad* Pope fully mastered the couplet, with a finality at times glib, for the form forces parallelisms and imposes a rigid pattern on the matter. It is suited more to aphorism and satire than to narrative. Yet he made the couplets – intermittently – flow. Johnson's estimate of the translation is as high as Pope's estimate of Dryden's Virgil: 'the noblest version of poetry which the world has ever seen'. Less generous and less successful Grub Street residents dubbed him the 'poetical undertaker', profiting from dead writers. In 1725 his six-volume edition of Shakespeare was published: he was almost as much of a literary factory as Johnson.

His Shakespeare was not good and its numerous errors and inconsistencies were exhibited by Lewis Theobald in *Shakespeare Restored*, a timeless error on Theobald's part since he earned for himself the role of principal butt in the original *Dunciad*, and even his admirable 1734 edition of Shakespeare, a model for later editors, did not restore his name to posterity. Pope was not a man to cross. Fortunately Colly Cibber offended Pope even more severely than Theobald had done, for Cibber, whose life as an actor and writer was remote from Pope's experience, was made Poet

Laureate in 1730. In the 1743 four-book version of *The Dunciad* Cibber replaces Theobald.

What does it mean when we say that Pope profited from his writings? Patronage was at its height under Queen Anne, and there was a settled market price: five to ten guineas for the dedication of a play, less for the dedication of a poem. With the accession of George I this changed. Writers became too proud and independent to sue for patronage. From Lintot Pope got £16 2s 6d for the first book of Statius (1712); £7 for *The Rape of the Lock;* £32 5s for *Windsor Forest.* Pope's Homer was published by subscription; Lintot paid him £200 for each of six volumes. In the end Pope realised £5324 4s on this work. Johnson estimated that the cost of living, around the year 1730, was in the region of £30 per annum. Thus Pope's little epigram 'On Authors and Booksellers' is a little harsh:

> What authors lose, their booksellers have won,
> So pimps grow rich, while gallants are undone.

The best printer-booksellers dealt more or less honourably with their better selling authors, as dairy farmers deal with good cows. A sense of the economics of the trade emerges when full records exist, and of course for a businessman of letters like Pope, records survive.

On the proceeds of his writing, Pope was able to settle in Twickenham in 1718, acquiring his famous house with a grotto and making room for his recently widowed mother. There he lived until his death in 1744. He practised a frugality that rivalled Swift's, but without Swift's excuse. Success did not spoil him, but the pleasures of prosperity induced him to undertake projects he should have left alone, especially the Shakespeare.

The substitution of Cibber for Theobald in the *Dunciad* – poet for scholar – is arbitrary and tells against the virulent generality of the satire. That the substitution required so little adjustment to the text shows how removed from its targets, how merely scornful, and how unintegrated it is. Pope attended to the surface of the work, but the satire only occasionally deepens and tells. The four books progress towards the triumph of eternal Dullness ('born a Goddess, Dullness never dies') and he exploits different modes of humour from book to book. First Pope deploys literary satire and parody, advancing through coprological, sexual and even sadistic forms of humour. The fourth book remains most vital, scourging habits and institutions of education. But the verve of the language exceeds its occasions, a kind of overkill. In all but the fourth book the satire, unlike Dryden's, lacks a moral norm which, by contrast, it endorses. Where is Pope firing from? He did not dislike the society in which he found himself, though he did at times dislike himself. De Quincey calls the rage 'histrionic', for effect, and goes further: Pope was a hypocrite whose insincerity spilled over into his non-satiric work. There may be a prejudice, but there is no rule that a writer should *not* be a hypocrite.

Pope translated Horace's satires with his usual skill, but even there we may be tempted to agree with De Quincey. We should resist the temptation: Pope, morally uneven, eludes categorical condemnation or endorsement. He is often at his best with borrowed anger. In 1735 he wrote his 'Epistle to Dr Arbuthnot' (37) (later called 'The Prologue to the Satires'), combining satire with personal statements of intense candour. His skill in composing whole poems is intact, even after the *Essay on Man* (1733–4) which, despite memorable aphoristic passages, fails as didactic and philosophical verse. It was attacked and defended for its morality; now it is excerpted for its good passages but neglected as a whole (36). Johnson's verdict is just: 'Never was penury of knowledge and vulgarity of sentiment so happily disguised.' Technically a *tour de force*, it is hollow at the centre. De Quincey asks, which *should* have been Pope's greatest poem? The *Essay on Man*. And which was in fact his worst? The same. It 'sins chiefly by want of central principle, and by want thereof of all coherency amongst the separate thoughts'. Compared with the *Essay on Criticism*, written twenty-two years before, it looks still more invertebrate. Pope became professional in the worst sense.

His techniques can deal with almost any theme; but his sense of structure and his ability to present consecutive, consistent thought are limited. Johnson remarks on his 'poetical prudence': 'he wrote in such a manner as might expose him to few hazards. He used almost always the same fabric of verse; and, indeed, by those few essays which he made of any other, he did not enlarge his reputation. . . . By perpetual practice, language had, in his mind, a systematic arrangement; having always the same use for words, he had words so selected and combined as to be ready at his call.' A dangerous facility: 'his effusions were always voluntary'. For De Quincey his satiric rages were similarly factitious. In the *Essay on Man* he bit off not more than his style could chew, but more than his intellect could digest.

Pope's intellectual incompleteness can be attributed in part to the age, for much more than Dryden he was a man of his time. He has been called a 'cosmic Tory', a social optimist (though closer to Hobbes in his evaluation of the individual), believing 'whatever is, is right' and converting the *status quo* into a universal ethic. In such an approach there is a cool, impersonal arrogance which he shares with some of his journalist contemporaries – a new breed – who couldn't quite bring themselves to choose between deism and John Locke's psychology, but felt confident in rejecting traditional theology as outmoded. Pope remains intellectually 'between'. He distrusts empirical enquiry as strongly as Swift did, but without Swift's reasons. For such a mind the appeal of authority should be great; but Pope is wary of authority as well.

The imagination 'gilds all objects, but alters none'. Such an aesthetic is a world away from that of Sir Philip Sidney in the *Apology for Poetry*. Pope wants not to expand imagination and understanding but to formulate and give permanent expression to thought and experience; not to particularise but to establish general truths. That nature conceals, under its varied surface, a basic pattern or harmony, is a worked-up belief, as willed as the language itself. He was able in the *Essay on Man* to change the description of Nature as a 'mighty maze, and all without a plan' to a 'mighty maze but not without a plan' when it was suggested that his original formulation was too negative. So radical a change, casually made, suggests that at times the current of his thought ran shallow. Thus Theobald and Cibber, scholar and poet, were interchangeable in the *Dunciad*. His rancour was arbitrary. The closing lines reflect on the themes of the poem, but perhaps also on its wilful structure or *construction*.

Lo! thy dread empire, Chaos! is restor'd;
Light dies before thy uncreating word
Thy hand, great Anarch! lets the curtain fall;
And universal Darkness buries all.

The best of Pope is wonderful, but excellence is found *in extenso* only in the earlier poems, translations and satires. Later it emerges locally: the shiny surface of his philosophical disquisitions yields like thin ice when we venture out too far upon it. His best writing depends on the elusive way he makes solid an abstract or moralising passages by combining unexpected words, and by rhyme which seals the 'conjunction disjunctive' (Coleridge's phrase) of the couplets. Dryden's couplets tend to be self-contained; Pope's contain at their best a paradox, an irresolution, which compels us to read on. They create suspense. He makes whole poems when he avoids the temptation to try for a total statement.

In the distorting mirror of his devoted admirer, the servant-poet Mary Leapor (1722–1746), his legacy can be clearly read. Critics of this slight writer suggest that her best effects come when she is unable quite to achieve the precisions and closures of Pope. These 'best effects' are in fact defects of technique: her genuine accomplishment is in her approximations to the clarity of Pope, and in the occasional surprise in her imagery. Her work was composed in spare moments stolen from the busy demands of a life as chamber-maid and kitchen-maid.

She was born in Brackley, Northamptonshire, and hardly moved beyond that neighbourhood. Her first employer was herself a minor poet, and it is assumed that the girl admired and emulated her mistress, but with great modesty and self-effacement, to such an extent that she resisted publication and her book, *Poems upon Several Occasions*, appeared in 1748, after she had died of the measles at the age of 24. She had changed jobs, lost her second job, and retired to look after her father in Brackley, where she was befriended by Bridget Freemantle, the daughter of the rector: this was a close relationship, given their social difference, which sustained and developed her concerns. It was Freemantle who edited and published her poems after she died.

Leapor possessed sixteen or seventeen books of her own, including a volume of Pope and one of Dryden, and these she knew by heart. She was familiar with the polite literature of the day and she seems to have been intrigued by the new scientific learning, not least the development of the microscope and what it did to the imagination's sense of scale, of minutenesses.

The publication of her work was surrounded by a condescension informed both by her class and by her sex. A letter to the *Gentleman's Magazine* spoke of her cruelly, as a repulsive curiosity: she was 'extremely swarthy, and quite emaciated, with a long crane-neck, and a short body, much resembling, in shape, a bass-viol'. The language of her poems, which talk knowingly of 'the Town' and pretend to move in those circles where the pastoral was a pleasant affectation, are a kind of ventriloquism; a set of conventions and decorums informs the verse, ballasting it with values, prejudices, social inflections remote from those of the class, location and daily experience of the writer. Had Mary Leapor fallen for the work of John Gay, she might have found more space in verse for the vocation and for the lessons of her own brief life. But for her poetry was a mode of aspiration, a way of entering a larger world (not only social but intellectual) by means of the imagination, because, most certainly, she had no other mode of access to it.

> You see I'm learnèd, and I show't the more,
> That none may wonder when they find me poor.
> Yet Mira dreams, as slumb'ring poets may,
> And rolls in treasures till the breaking day:
> While books and pictures in bright order rise,
> And painted parlours swim before her eyes:
> Till the shrill clock impertinently rings,
> And the soft visions move their shining wings:
> Then Mira wakes, – her pictures are no more,
> And through her fingers slides the vanished ore. (**69**)

One might expect a woman in her position to write devotional verse; Mary Leapor was devoted to the social world, its colours, gestures and tonalities. Her vision of nature is coloured and cultivated by the good order of the well-managed estate.

THE HYMN

Isaac Watts, Charles Wesley

O Bible chopped and crucified
in hymns we hear but do not read,
none of the milder subtleties
of grace or art will sweeten these
stiff quatrains shovelled out four-square –
they sing of peace, and preach despair;
yet they gave darkness some control,
and left a loophole for the soul.

Robert Lowell, 'Waking Early Sunday Morning'

Religious poetry has a place in any anthology. But hymns? Are they poetry at all? Stiff, congregational, common, without 'the milder subtleties / of grace or art', what right have they to keep company with Pope, and Johnson, and Scott, and Burns? Unless we have removed all the barriers of judgement, how can we tolerate in this place Isaac Watts's lines,

Soft and easy is thy cradle;
   Coarse and hard thy Saviour lay,
When his birthplace was a stable
   And his softest bed was hay.

'That simple verse, bad rhyme and all, is poetry beyond Pope,' said A. E. Housman in 1933. He was not a believer, but he was a poet with an ear for authenticity and for serviceable English, especially plain English which had been set down in an age of marbling, gilding and artificial deportment.

Accommodating hymns should be no harder than accommodating the ballad, another popular quatrain-based tradition. But anthologist and critic distrust so insidious a form as the hymn: it subverts memory through music and choral repetition, it has designs not only on the imagination of the reader but on the reader's spiritual being. Ballads are often unstable texts because there are various versions, none with absolute authority; and hymns too are textually various, because use and fashion prune and alter them. It is seldom that we sing a hymn as it was originally composed. Still, we might argue that the effective hymn demonstrates the actual power language has to make things happen in the individual or the congregational mind, and how its efficacy is maintained by collaboration with succeeding generations.

The hymn tradition starts long before Caedmon's Hymn, the first surviving poem in English, before ancient Greece, somewhere in poetry's prehistory. Sacred hymns were attributed to the legendary Orpheus, but the most famous Greek hymns are laid (implausibly) at Homer's door. These poems provided models for Pindar, Callimachus and later Greek poets and for their Latin imitators. Charles Boer, who translated them in the 1960s,[1] suggests in a useful if fanciful afterword that the word *hymn* is of eastern derivation and the Greek word *hymnos* relates to the word for *woven* or *spun*. An ancient poet speaks of 'weaving a hymn'; Homer *(Iliad* III, 1. 212) 'speaks of Menelaus and Odysseus as having "spun" *(hyphainon)* "their words and their counsels"'. Boer declares, 'in its primal sense, a hymn was thought of as what results when you intertwine speech with rhythm and song. And it is in this sense precisely that the word "hymn" appears in its oldest recorded usage, in the *Odyssey* (VIII, 429) when Alcinoös invites Odysseus to "enjoy dinner and listen to the spinning of a yarn" *(aoides hymnon).*' Boer's 'yarn' is unfortunately an English rather than a Greek figure of speech.

The language of the surviving Orphic and Homeric hymns has something in common with Christian hymns. The density of allusion to scriptures can make them peculiarly rebarbative as poetry, especially to the unbeliever. Introducing his Orphic translations in the late eighteenth century, at a time of effective Christian hymn-making, Thomas Taylor writes: 'Thus most of the compound epithets of which the following Hymns chiefly consist, though very beautiful in the Greek language, yet, when literally translated into ours, lose all their propriety and force. In their native tongue, as in a prolific soil, they diffuse their sweets with full-blown elegance, but shrink like the sensitive plant at the touch of the verbal critic, or the close translator. He who would preserve their philosophical beauties, and exhibit them to others in a different language, must expand their elegance, by the supervening and enlivening rays of the philosophic fire; and, by the powerful breath of genius, scatter abroad their latent but copious sweets.'

So, too, with Christian hymns, when they are taken out of church or chapel, out of the hymnal, and planted in the alien soil of a poetry anthology. They feel exposed without the base-note of the organ, without the airy treble, placed mum and anonymous-feeling alongside 'real' poetry. Donne's, Herbert's and Vaughan's devotional verse is at home in secular or

[1] Charles Boer, *The Homeric Hymns* (Swallow, 1970)

literary anthologies because faith is a crucial constituent of the poet's imaginative world; it is individually experienced and tried; indeed the poetry is often a trial of faith. Belief is an aspect of the poetic medium itself, and it is struggled for and held in the poem, as Proteus is briefly, magically held in his cave, yielding up his truth. The doubts and certainties in Herbert are expressed with an aristocratic finesse and clarity; no complexity is sacrificed or smoothed over, and the dramas (for they are all dramas of a kind) resolve in a timeless moment. But the reader, like the poet, is then delivered back to time. The moment of the poem, the arrested sense it gives, is profoundly reassuring, but ephemeral; it may promise but it does not yield repose.

Thomas Taylor speaks of the 'philosophical mythology' of the Orphic hymns, as though the argument in early philosophy and religion could be conducted solely through narrative, symbol and metaphor. This is, indeed, how the Christian hymn conducts itself. It is designed to be sung, an experience different from reading, even from reading aloud. It is, along with the stained glass and the statuary, didactic, congregational. The verse of the hymn, like the voice of the confession, 'We have erred and strayed from thy ways like lost sheep,' is a shared voice, and the hymn writer delivers his words up to the 'we' and recedes into anonymity, as it were. In many old hymnals it is hard to discover who wrote the hymns we sing; indeed in my *Hymns Ancient and Modern,* printed in 1947, it is impossible. Milton's, Herbert's, Watts's, Wesley's, Cowper's and John Henry Newman's hymns belong to choir and congregation. What modern law identifies as an author's 'moral right' has been overruled.

It is hard to stand back from a hymn one has known by heart for decades and to appraise it as poetry. Many hymns and carols that we love, separated from their music, do not survive critical scrutiny. We can respond to Herbert's religious poems whether or not we are believers ourselves; but the hymn presumes belief. It addresses a shared experience which, if we have not had it, we may resist or find absurd, as we are inclined to find Taylor's Orphic versions more than a little bizarre. Here Hecate is invoked:

I call Einodian Hecate, lovely dame,
Of earthly, wat'ry, and celestial frame,
Sepulchral, in a saffron veil arrayed,
Pleased with dark ghosts that wander through the shade,
Persian, unconquerable huntress hail!
The world's key-bearer never doomed to fail;
On the rough rock to wander thee delights,
Leader and nurse be present to our rites;
Propitious grant our just desires success,
Accept our homage, and the incense bless.

Here the syntax works as syntax, but it is almost unspeakable as verse. Taylor comments usefully: 'the reader will please to observe through the whole of these Hymns, that the Orphic method of instruction consists in signifying divine concerns by symbols alone'. The same might be said of 'Crown him with many crowns,/The Lamb upon the Throne ...' In terms of imagery, this is surreal confusion, but as Christian metaphor and symbol it is succinct, a way of true speaking and a way of affirming true vision. Taylor expresses a view bordering on that of the mystics of faiths from the Sufi to the Christian: 'Now the authors of fables, having perceived this proceeding of nature, that it expresses itself by inventing resemblances and images of divine concerns in their verses, imitated the exalted power of exemplars by contrary and most remote adumbrations: that is, by shadowing forth the excellency of the nature of the Gods by preternatural concerns: a power more divine than all reason, by such as are irrational: a beauty superior to all that is corporeal by things apparently base, and by this means placed before our eyes the excellence of divinity, which far exceeds all that can possibly be invented or said.' This language of the late eighteenth century touches a profound truth of pre-Hellenic poetry, and also of Christian hymnology. Taylor is a little too tolerant of the occult, but many writers tended to err thus at the exhausted end of the eighteenth century; his credulousness lets him see further than a logician or satirist could do.

The eighteenth century was for the English hymn what the sixteenth was for the English lyric. Why should this have been? Perhaps because in the hymn deep feeling could be expressed without a sense of impropriety and embarrassment: the use of expressive italics, the volume control of small and large caps, were often fully exercised, and hearts could hang wet and throbbing from otherwise polite sleeves. Perhaps, too, because it was the next great age of religious emancipation after the Reformation, the period in which the authority of the Bible became (for the radical soul) the authority of the individual Christian, and witness became personal once again. The growth of evangelicism, accompanying political and economic developments, entailed the development of evangelical instruments, the hymn being one of them, the sermon another. But primarily, perhaps, the hymn came of age because two great and several good hymn-writers happened to emerge, building on what was already a firm foundation, to which Sidney, Donne, Quarles, Herbert, Milton and Bunyan had contributed.

The two great hymn-writers were Isaac Watts (**12–20**) and Charles Wesley (**44–49**). Watts (1674–1748) is not in fact 'father of the English hymn', a title which belongs by rights to Caedmon, though he has been described as such. Donald Davie risks evoking him as 'a poet of the tribal lay, a true analogue in Augustan England of David, the bard and warrior king of ancient Israel'. It may at first seem ironic to do so. Watts was notable for his looks: he stood no higher than five feet, he had a frail body and a huge head with a sharp, beaked nose. The portraits are merciful, involving him in gowns and topping him with a copious wig, but his contemporaries described him as grotesque-looking. Like Pope, he had social difficulties as a consequence of his physical self.

He suffered severe psychological illnesses, the most vehement expressed in theological doubt. He had a weedy voice but, when the spirit took him, he could bind a congregation in the spell of a sermon. He was, Davie says, 'demure and grave and domesticated in Hanoverian London'. Yet Davie insists: the hymns were written for 'the tribe', dissenting Christians who saw themselves as uniquely chosen; and Watts was of their party.

He was born in Southampton, the eldest of eight – or nine – children. His father was a Dissenter and suffered for his beliefs, enduring a year in prison, during which time Isaac was born. His mother is said to have nursed him on the steps of the gaol.

Little Isaac, if we are to believe the biographers, learned Latin by the age of four, Greek by the age of nine, French by eleven, Hebrew by thirteen. How deeply in Virgil and Livy the four-year-old had read is not reported. As with most stories of precocity, there are no exam results to confirm whether the boy knew more than the rudiments of Hebrew, or if he was settling down of an afternoon with the Torah at thirteen. French was useful, Southampton at the time being full of religious refugees from France.

From his earliest years he was a slave of metre and rhyme. He would rhyme his conversation, irritating his father who resorted to beating the boy. Once, during family prayers, Isaac started chuckling. His father demanded the cause. He had opened his eyes and spotted a mouse climbing up a rope over in a corner of the room, and these words occurred to him: 'A little mouse for want of stairs / Ran up a rope to say its prayers.' His father got out the strap to punish him, but he cried out, 'Father, father, mercy take, / And I will no more verses make.' It is to be hoped that the father showed him mercy. At seven he composed an acrostic poem on his name in which there is a remarkable dose of fundamental theology:

I am a vile polluted lump of earth
So I've continued ever since my birth;
Although Jehovah grace does give me,
As sure this monster Satan will deceive me.
Come therefore, Lord, from Satan's claws relieve me.

He was offered the opportunity to go to Cambridge or Oxford if he renounced his religious views, but he refused, attending instead a dissenting academy in Stoke Newington, London, where he composed much verse, principally in Latin, and where he completed his studies in 1694. In later life, as a working clergyman, he wrote a logic text which was a set book at Oxford and other universities for many years; a book on astronomy; a volume of edifying children's verses (the first collection of its kind, it went through almost a hundred editions in as many years, and Lewis Carroll parodied them in *Alice in Wonderland*[2]); he published catechisms for children of different ages; and he wrote hymns.

Watts as a boy grew bored with the metrical settings of the psalms. They certainly had their place, but Calvin and his immediate followers were too restrictive when, despite Lutheran and Moravian traditions of hymn-singing and, even richer, the Anglican practice, they insisted that *only* metrical psalms were appropriate for singing in church. Watts 'did' the Psalms (his 1719 volume proved his best-selling book of verse), but he wanted to do much more, to play variations, to attempt more original approaches not only to sanctioned Old Testament passages but to New as well. He confided his impatience to his father who challenged him to write something for the congregation to sing. He composed 'Behold the Glories of the Lamb', based on a text from Revelations V: 6-12.

> Behold the glories of the Lamb
>   Amidst his Father's throne;
> Prepare new honours for his name,
>   And songs before unknown ...

He wrote almost seven hundred 'songs before unknown' in the years that followed.

The use of his hymns in worship was a matter of contention and split many congregations, not least the one whose leader, a generation or two before, had been John Bunyan. His approach to the Psalms themselves was distinctive. His David was required to sing in 'the language of a Christian'. He gave an account of his method: where the Psalmist stressed the fear of God, he appended faith and love to it; where David spoke of God's mercy, he added the merits of a Saviour. It was translation not only of the words but of symbols: the sacrificial lamb becomes inseparable from the Lamb of God. 'Where he promises abundance of wealth, honour, and long life, I have changed some of these typical blessings for grace, glory, and life eternal'. His authority is the Gospel. 'And I am fully satisfied, that more honour is done to our blessed Saviour by speaking his name, his graces, his actions, in his own language, according to the brighter discoveries he hath now made, than by going back again to the Jewish forms of worship, and the language of types and figures.'

[2] 'How doth the little busy bee improve each shining hour' becomes 'How doth the little crocodile improve his shining tail'.

When it came to choosing an appropriate language for a hymn, Watts is deliberate and clear, and his justification, on religious grounds, sounds not entirely unlike Wordsworth's advocacy of a language actually spoken by men as proper for poetry. Watts declares, 'In many of these composures, I have permitted my verse to rise above a flat and indolent style; yet I hope it is every where supported above the just contempt of the critics; though I am sensible that I have often subdued it below their esteem; because I would neither indulge any bold metaphors, nor admit of hard words, nor tempt the ignorant worshipper to sing without his understanding.'

When he had completed his formal education, Watts became a tutor for five years, using the time to continue his other studies and to prepare for publication the first version of his *Hymns and Spiritual Songs* (1707). Even here, the poetic perspective of Watts's poems is astronomical: his sense of man's smallness is part and parcel of his sense of the universe's unfathomable magnitude, which thus emphasises the precision and defined intentionality of God's individual grace. He isolates and defines, against a cosmic darkness as it were, the Incarnation, the Crucifixion and Resurrection, pinpoints in time and space which in their significance and resonance transcend time and space. The cosmic scale within which his imagination works is vaster and colder than Milton's great architecture; and the almost imponderable fact of God's grace to man within that scale of things is duly magnified.

His cupboard was swept clean of the formal consolations of allegory and the psychological consolations of superstition and mere custom. His hymns were modern in a specific way, a way which has remained modern: he was a spiritual logician, troubled when a proof seemed wilfully withheld. Yet he rejected from the hymns the brittle 'high' language of Addison and the decorous writers. Unlike them, he never merely entertained but rather *lived* his belief. It hurt him, it stretched him and changed him. His greatest battle, which he never resolved in mind or spirit, was with the enigma of the Trinity. Indeed his frustration with the doctrine and the ways in which it was expressed was at the root of his supposed later 'madness'.

He became, in his own lifetime, a writer loved by Anglican and dissenting interests alike; his words were relished and used by John Wesley, a third of whose first Hymn Book consisted of Watts's hymns. But Watts's life was not an easy one. After his work as a tutor, he became an assistant minister at Mark Lane Independent (Congregational) Chapel in London, and full pastor in 1702. He was attacked by a chronic fever and was unable to follow what he had hoped to be a lifelong vocation. Sir Thomas Abney, a wealthy dissenter from Herefordshire, took the ailing poet-pastor under his protection, initially for a week. The Abney family looked after him for the remaining thirty-six years of his life. He died in 1748 and was buried at Bunhill Fields, where Defoe, Bunyan and Blake lie also in dissenting dignity.

A monument in his honour was raised in Westminster Abbey.

More than forty of his hymns remain in use, sung indifferently by Anglicans, Baptists, Methodists, Lutherans, Presbyterians and even by Roman Catholics. This ecumenical legacy is remarkable in another sense: the variety of inflection and form, the strict freedom of approach, became instructive to later hymn-writers Watts's rich success freed dissenting congregations from thralldom to the metrical psalm. Watts also nourished common culture in an unparalleled way.

Without his experiments and achievements, the work of Charles Wesley, 'sweet singer of Methodism', would have been rendered much more difficult, and Cowper in turn would have been a lesser hymn writer. As it is, Watts cleared a way for Wesley, a substantial successor who wrote several great hymns, and whose writings have a different identity and definition from Watts's.

Samuel and Suzanna Wesley had had eighteen children before, in 1707, Charles was born, their third surviving son. John Wesley, the great religious thinker, reformer and activist, was four years his senior. Shortly after his first birthday, the family rectory at Epworth, Lincolnshire, was burned to the ground by parishioners protesting at Samuel's high church ways. Both boys were narrowly rescued from the conflagration by a servant girl, and John, who clearly remembered the event, spoke of himself ever after as 'a brand plucked from the burning'.

Their father made no plans for his innumerable daughters but expected his three sons to be proper scholars and to follow him into the church. Charles went to Westminster, where he was a good student and an opponent, often at risk to himself, of the school bullies. He was admitted to Christ Church, Oxford. John by then had taken orders and been elected a Fellow, lecturing on Greek, of Lincoln College in the same city, where he kept a wary eye on his brother. Charles resisted discipline, declaring in the spirit of St Augustine, 'Would you have me to become a saint all at once?' The time for saintliness would come.

Charles was impetuous and emotional but not egotistical. He was self-effacing, unambitious in worldly terms, naturally humble. After university, he became spiritually troubled. Surely faith was not something one merely professed: it was something one *did*. He shared a new, questing religious seriousness with some of his contemporaries and in 1729 they established a 'Holy Club'. The members acquired nicknames: 'Bible Moths', 'Sacramentalists' and (the one that took) 'Methodists', due to their strict rules governing fasting, praying and taking communion. John later led the little group, but Charles founded it and came to be known as 'the first Methodist'. George Whitefield of Pembroke College joined the group in 1732. He and Charles, now a College tutor, drew close, and John was near at hand: the Methodist triumvirate took shape, changing the course of English-language protestantism. When we think of early Methodism the figure of John Wesley most readily comes to mind, the indefatigable evangelist, the great sermoniser, the unaffected and vigorous writer, who delivered over 40,000 sermons and travelled a quarter of a million miles on horseback delivering a living God to the British people. Yet Charles gave his elder brother direction and purpose, and Charles's are the words we remember, even if he remains in the shadow of his brother.

Charles was a prolific poet as well as a hymn-writer. His poems are no longer read, but his best hymns are as well-loved and widely-sung as Watts's, and share many of their formal virtues. Charles's love for George Herbert, however, and his adaptation of a number of poems from *The Temple* into hymns, provides a clue to his temperament, different in tenor from Watts's radical but deeply Anglican approach. Herbert writes poems, not hymns, and yet it is the quality of poetry, its very specific gravity, that Wesley wants in his hymns, an element which, while not forfeiting the congregational purpose and manner of the hymn, allows for the 'I'. In liturgical terms, he wanted to combine the voice of the general confession with the voice of the individual Creed: '*We* have erred and strayed', but also '*I* believe in one God'. The congregation is not a collective: it is a confluence or merging of individual witness.

The story of Samuel Wesley *père*'s death feels rather staged, but even so it tells an indicative truth. In the spring of 1735, approaching death, he said to John, 'The inward witness, son, the inward witness, this is the proof, the strongest proof of Christianity.' Then he lifted his feeble hand and laid it on his youngest son's head: 'Be steady. The Christian faith will surely revive in this kingdom. You shall see it; though I shall not.' It would have been more appropriate had he reversed the order of his statements and spoken to Charles of witness, because that is what the hymns are about: bringing to light in memorable, singable language the unarguable, powerful 'inward witness', the very 'proof' Watts was never quite able to find, or if he found, never quite able to credit.

Shortly after their father's death, Charles went with John to America, on a mission to Georgia, then a new colony, where he worked for a time as secretary to General James Oglethorpe, the governor, and was moved by the fervent sincerity and clarity of belief of the Moravian settlers. The mission was, however, a trying failure for both brothers, unprepared (at that stage) temperamentally and physically for the rigours of the new world. Their outspoken sermons against slavery and their high church approach did not endear them to the new colonists. The failure gave John greater energy, but it robbed Charles of confidence and damaged his practical spirit. He returned to England a year before John.

He met in London the leader of the Moravians and was delegated by the University of Oxford to appear before the King. His was a life of unsettled activity. John's return in 1738 helped stabilise him, but ill health kept him from ever returning to America, as he intended, to try again as a missionary. The Moravian influence became more pronounced and in 1738 the brothers learned from a young man, Peter Bohler, crucial truths about evangelical faith. In effect, both brothers had to re-make their belief. Bohler wrote to his leader, 'The elder, John, is a good-natured man; he knew he did not properly believe in our Saviour, and was willing to be taught. His brother is at present very much distressed in his mind, but does not know how he shall begin to be acquainted with the Saviour.' But surely Charles had already been well-acquainted with his Saviour? Apparently not: there was profound spiritual work to be done.

Hymns are, at their best, parts of a process of affirmation, and affirmation is itself a coming to terms not only with the Saviour but with the self the Saviour seeks. In May 1738 the light of grace gleamed into Charles's eyes out of the Bible. He was amongst the Moravians. He opened the book at Isaiah xl.1: 'Comfort ye, comfort ye my people, saith your God.' The strife was over, 'I now found myself at peace with God, and rejoiced in hope of loving Christ' and 'I saw that by faith I stood, by the continual support of faith'. The support of faith entailed congregation, forms of prayer and common worship. This was his 'conversion', and John's followed soon after. But both, after their genuine enthusiasm for the Moravians, found themselves retreating from what were, in their view, heresies in Moravian teaching.

In the end Anglican evangelicism, which issued ultimately in the schism John and Charles strenuously resisted, between the national communion and the Methodists, was far from radical in its political consequences. Much has been made in recent years of the parallels between the hymns of Charles Wesley and the songs of William Blake, a juxtaposition which illuminates both men's work. Blake is deeply implicated in the hymn trad-ition; he revered Watts and Wesley. But deep differences divide them as well, none quite so profound as this: 'Wesley believes in paradox, Blake believes in dialectic.' Donald Davie suggests that acceptance of dialectic leads to radical analysis and action; acceptance of paradox leads to con-templation. 'Wesley's verse takes on rhetorical splendour and intensity when paradox is concentrated into its appropriate rhetorical figure, oxy-moron.'

The impact of conversion on any individual is great; the need for its renewal or repetition is great also, for if it recedes the believer is left empty and subject to despair. This happened notably to Cowper; it happened, to a lesser degree, to Charles Wesley. After an impassioned sermon his emptiness was painful to bear. It is a constant trial for the evangelical Anglican and the Methodist, to retain the clarity of conversion, the moment when everything comes into true focus, and to speak aloud, extempore, in witness. 'His preaching at his best was thunder and lightning,' an early enthusiast declared; he held large congregations spellbound. He made no bones about his feelings. If the text of his sermon was Christ's words, 'It is finished', he would utter the text and burst into tears at its implications. And the congregation, too, would weep and wail.

The severity, formality and reserve of the traditional Anglican service dissolved. The sermons were delivered, often, out of doors. The holy spirit had escaped its gilded cage. And it was the hymns that entered people's hearts. The first collection was published in 1739. Joseph William reported of Wesley's congregations: 'Their singing was not only the most harmonious and delightful I ever heard, but they sang "lustily and with a good courage"'. The hymns would often go before the preacher: they had the popular energy of ballads: memorable tunes carrying in their current memorable words.

What secured Charles's peace of mind was his marriage to Sarah Gwynne in 1749. Until she started bearing children (their two sons became gifted musicians), she went with Charles on his preaching tours. They settled in Bristol, and then moved to London where Charles oversaw the work of the Methodists. He continued writing hymns, producing in the end between five and six thousand. Shortly before his death in 1788 he dictated to his wife these last lines:

> In age and feebleness extreme,
> Who shall a helpless worm redeem?
> Jesus! my only hope Thou art,
> Strength of my failing flesh and heart,
> Oh, could I catch a smile from Thee
> And drop into eternity!

The longing is like George Herbert's, for an affirmation so positive as to remove the strain of faith.

In the light of the hymns of Watts and Wesley, we can dispute John Betjeman's dogmatic contention that 'hymns are not good poems'. One need not over-extend the definitions of poetry or the requirements of prosody to affirm that some hymns are great poems: the hymn is a genre in its own right, and deserves a place, even without its music, alongside the ballad and other 'tribal' poetry without the tabor, and alongside the lyric poem without the lyre.

DEAD PASTORAL

James Thomson, William Collins

The success of the great hymn-writers was measured by the survival of their poems in popular memory. Such vulgar recognition hardly mattered in the Bourse of poetic reputation. One of the most conventionally successful British poets of all time – in Pope's terms of unit sales and vast editions – is James Thomson, the man who momentarily reinvented Pastoral and is now read primarily by scholars who prefer dust to living dirt and by students puzzled by the reputed tedium of the eighteenth century. In British poetry nothing today is more enigmatic than his huge and long success. Contemporary neglect of Spenser and Milton does not diminish them; the neglect of Thomson is eloquent.

Once he was the poetic equivalent of the Gideon Bible: his poems were to be found in every inn and cottage in the land. The verse was reassuring and instructive but seldom taxing.

What, what is virtue but repose of mind?
A pure ethereal calm that knows no storm,
Above the reach of wild ambition's wind,
Above those passions that this world deform,
And torture man, a proud malignant worm!

His one immortal poem is 'Rule Britannia' (**42**), though few remember to attribute it to him. He inspired respect from men as different as Doctor Johnson and William Wordsworth. His poetic antecedents – Milton above all – and his adoption of the fashionable scientific and philosophical thought of his time – confine him to his age. Self-conscious modernity dates. Miltonic blank verse does not liberate but muffles his peculiar genius. His novelty is his subject matter: literal seasons, actual countryside, seen through wholly eighteenth century spectacles. His contemporaries did not sense this disparity between style and matter. Donald Davie demonstrated how it was natural for readers to tease out – to *unpack* – meaning, translating out of metaphoric code. Modern readers hardly recognise a happy peasant at all: they have mislaid the key.

Thomson was born at Ednam, in the Borders, in 1700, the year of Dryden's death, and reared in Southdean, a neighbouring parish to which his father, a minister, was transferred. Educated at Jedburgh and at Edinburgh University, he studied Divinity. He published poems in Edinburgh journals, and when his prose was deemed 'too ornate' for the pulpit by his instructors, he left the Scottish for the English capital to become a writer. He was tutor to the son of the Earl of Haddington and was introduced into Pope's circle. In 1726 he published a poem partly completed before he reached London. It was *Winter,* first of *The Seasons,* which were published together in 1730 and in various updated and revised forms between then and his death in 1748. The book was part of a programme he enunciated in 1726: poetry should free itself of social satire. He abandoned heroic couplets, accepted what he took to be Milton's disciplines, and looked for subject-matter beyond the city gates.

Before 1730 he published shorter poems, and *Sophonisba,* an ill-fated tragedy. He travelled to the Continent and received a sinecure on his return. In 1735 he published the poem *Liberty,* and thereafter composed plays and collected a further sinecure and a pension from the Prince of Wales. A bachelor, he settled comfortably in Richmond. In 1745 he wrote his most successful play, *Tancred and Sigismunda.* Three years later he composed *The Castle of Indolence.* He died of a fever and was memorialised in William Collins's superb Ode, the best thing Thomson ever occasioned:

> In yonder grove a Druid lies,
>> Where slowly winds the stealing wave!
> The year's best sweets shall duteous rise
>> To deck its poet's sylvan grave! (**68**)

Johnson describes Thomson as of 'gross, unanimated, uninviting appearance'. He admired the work, however, and gave Thomson high marks for his original 'mode of thinking, and of expressing his thoughts'. 'His blank verse is no more the blank verse of Milton, or of any other poet. ... His numbers, his pauses, his diction, are of his own growth, without transcription, without imitation, He thinks in a peculiar train, and he thinks always as a man of genius.' What is more, he possesses 'a mind that at once comprehends the vast and attends to the minute'.

Proximity to the subject, together with an enthusiasm for the novelty of Thomson's subject-matter in an age poor in novelty, lead Johnson to this – what must seem to us – misvaluation. Thomson's language in *The Seasons* owes debts to Milton on almost every line. *The Castle of Indolence* is indebted to Milton and Spenser for language and manner. His originality of form consists of reviving the Georgic – which had been done by several of his immediate predecessors. He includes new science and new attitudes not original to him. His poetry reflects fashionable thought and springs from the discursive experimental activity of his time. He is skilful in handling blank verse, there are notable passages, but even Johnson had to admit, 'The great defect of *The Seasons* is want of method.' Formal failure is masked by verbal exuberance. It is hard at times to see through the adjectival undergrowth to a subject. Thomson continually revised his verse, both to perfect it and to keep it abreast of new scientific findings. To the original 4000 lines he added roughly 1400 in successive revisions.

The Seasons – like John Gower's *Confessio Amantis* – is encyclopaedic, a compendium of the wisdom, knowledge and *bien pensant* prejudice of the age, including zoological, botanical, meteorological and geological information, political and moral reflection, sentimental tales. ... It reflects a dissatisfaction with decorous and stylised poetry but reacts without the radical passion of Smart, Blake or Wordsworth. Thomson plays acceptable music in a different key, with different themes, not new music. Milton was responsible for the change of key. Thomson did not adopt the dynamics of Milton's language: he borrowed from the surface. He vulgarised Milton as he vulgarised new science. It suited his ends to blend the discoveries of Newton with the optimistic deism of the sickly third earl of Shaftesbury, whose benign and anti-Hobbesian views stressed innate human 'affections', and a continuity between private and social or political 'affections'.

Coleridge disliked Thomson's style but saluted the poet and his optimism. 'The love of nature seems to have led Thomson to a cheerful religion; and a gloomy religion to have led Cowper to a love of nature. The one would carry his fellow-men along with him into nature: the other flies to nature from his fellow-men. In chastity of diction, however, and the harmony of blank verse, Cowper leaves Thomson immeasurably below him; yet still I feel the latter to have been a born poet.' Born in the wrong age, perhaps. Thomson presented a version of nature itself as subject, and this *was* original. Wordsworth owes him a verbal and thematic debt because he *can* be convincing in presenting detail. In *Winter* the movement of birds foretells a storm:

> Retiring from the downs, where all day long
> They picked their scanty fare, a blackening train
> Of clam'rous rooks thick-urge their weary flight,
> And seek the closing shelter of a grove.
> Assiduous in his bower, the wailing owl
> Plies his sad song. The cormorant on high

Wheels from the deep, and screams along the land.
Loud shrieks the soaring hern; and with wild wing
The circling sea-fowl cleave the flaky clouds.

There is also a delicious luxury in some of his Summer effusions:

Bear me, Pomona! to thy citron groves;
To where the lemon and the piercing lime,
With the deep orange glowing through the green,
Their lighter glories blend. Lay me reclined
Beneath the spreading tamarind, that shakes
Fanned by the breeze, its fever-cooling fruit.

But, by ascending from sensual observation to generalisation, he forfeits our attention. His optimism is aloof and reductive. Unlike Swift, he is not eager to rouse others – the humble, for example – to a sense of their potential. In *Summer* he reflects:

While thus laborious crowds
Ply the rough oar, Philosophy directs
The ruling helm.

Hobbes left no mark here. Thomson celebrates commerce, enterprise, ambition, in ways that would have been impossible half a century later. His is the Whig epic. He prefigures Walter Bagehot.

Thomson's verse lives in its descriptions and in odd lines. A poet of fragments, he seems to fragment Nature, celebrating a first cause through it, not – as Wordsworth does – a force latent within it. He lacks Wordsworth's engagement. His is an enthusiasm of the various senses: the whole man is withheld. Wordsworth's imagination is continuous with the experienced world, Thomson's tangential to it.

He finds bizarre poetic epithets for scientific terms, and obsolete science disrupts certain passages. Even his most particular definitions answer no necessary poetic purpose. He screws his language up by heightened diction and elaborates syntax to produce the *effect* of poetry, but the poetic occasion remains at best nebulous. Gilbert White's prose portrays a clearer nature than Thomson's verse does. White addresses a subject, Thomson an audience. His most useful contribution – to Cowper, George Crabbe and Wordsworth among others – was to show how landscape might be used for emotional projection, to reveal an observer's mind as much as the thing observed.

In *The Castle of Indolence* he adopted Spenserian form and diction and wrote what some regard as his finest poem. Formally it is more coherent than *The Seasons*. The old wizard Indolence speaks persuasively. The poem is a smoothly satirical record of temptation overcome, with knights and witty transformations. Each sense is tempted in turn. Thomson pillories various human types and espouses various causes. There are memorable figures – for example, 'A little, round, fat, oily man of God' with 'a roguish twinkle in his eye', who is a bit of a lecher and might be at home in a poem by Crabbe. We come across members of Thomson's circle which, in his later years, was distinguished chiefly by the occasionally incomparable William Collins (1721–1759), the son of a Sussex hatter who became one of the most severely self-critical and brilliant lyricists and ode-writers of this time and who lost his mind or, Johnson suggests, his energy, ending his days looked after by a sister in Chichester. His prosodic subtlety surpasses even Gray's. In his celebrated 'Ode to Evening' (**66**) he dispenses with rhyme and writes an extended 'sentence' so closely integrated, so deeply infused with Spenserian lightness and Miltonic concentration, that no Ode until Keats's attains a similar wholeness. 'Mr. Collins was a man of extensive literature,' says Johnson, 'and of vigorous faculties' – at least before his ailment. 'He was acquainted not only with the learned tongues, but with the Italian, French, and Spanish languages. He had employed his mind chiefly upon works of fiction and subjects of fancy' – his *Persian Eclogues* (1742) among his earliest and most ambitious – 'and by indulging some peculiar habits of thought was eminently delighted with those flights of imagination which pass the bounds of nature, and to which the mind is reconciled only by a passive acquiescence in popular traditions. He loved fairies, genii, giants, and monsters; he delighted to rove through the meanders of inchantment, to gaze on the magnificence of golden palaces, to repose by the water-falls of Elysian gardens.' And he knew a Druid when he met one, even if it was sporting a periwig.

The Castle of Indolence's Spenserian form imposes on Thomson tautologies, ill-considered similes and solecisms which Collins would have avoided, but they do not destroy altogether the effect. In the allegory, Art and Industry in knightly form destroy the castle and its wizard lord. As in *The Seasons,* here is the verse of whiggery which, set beside Goldsmith's or Johnson's, remains rooted in period, class and place. No wonder it sold. It is the sort of verse which was modern in its time.

DOCTOR JOHNSON

Samuel Johnson is a natural poet born into the age of prose, condemned to develop skills which were unnatural to him and to write, at great length, in the wrong medium. Edmund Wilson, the most Johnsonian of American writers, is harsh: 'For all of Johnson's vigorous intellect and his elaborate brilliance, he is a figure of secondary interest: it is not altogether that he is prejudiced and provincial but rather that his prejudices do not have behind them quite enough of the force of the creative mind.' Hazlitt's view: 'He has neither ease nor simplicity, and his efforts at playfulness, in part, remind one of the lines in Milton: – "– The elephant / To make them sport wreath'd his proboscis lithe." ... This want of relaxation and variety of manner has, I think, after the first effects of novelty and surprise were over, been prejudicial to the matter. It takes from the general power, not only to please, but to instruct.' He adds a wonderful observation which is true more of Johnson's early than his later prose: 'The structure of his sentences, which was his own invention, and which has been generally imitated since his time, is a species of rhyming in prose, where one clause answers to another in measure and quantity, like the tagging of syllables at the end of a verse; the close of the period follows as mechanically as the oscillation of a pendulum, the sense is balanced with the sound; each sentence, revolving round its centre of gravity, is contained with itself like a couplet, and each paragraph forms itself into a stanza.'

His age tended to distort natural impulse, driving it to madness in the case of Christopher Smart or to 'specialism' in the cases of Swift, Gay and Pope. Such distortions were givens. Ford Madox Ford declares, 'The language used by the eighteenth century – and Samuel Johnson – was a translation.' He itemises stock phrases. 'The eighteenth century retired from life that was coarse into a remoter region where individuals always became types and language more and more rarefied itself.' Writers came obsessively to use the definite article: 'the poet', not 'a poet'; 'the hill', not 'a hill' – until, 'We arrive, then, at Johnson, the most tragic of all our major literary figures, a great writer whose still living writings are always ignored, a great honest man who will remain forever a figure of half fun because of the leechlike adoration of the greatest and most ridiculous of all biographers.' This was the strange, respectful, attentive microscopist James Boswell, whose biographical subject was 'a man who loved truth and the expression of truth with a passion that when he spoke resembled epilepsy and when he meditated was an agony. It does not need a Boswell to tell us that; the fact shines in every word he wrote, coming up through his Latinisms as swans emerge, slightly draped with weeds, from beneath the surface of a duck pond. His very intolerances are merely rougher truths; they render him the more human – and the more humane.' If he was released from bondage to a prescribed language and the values that determined it, it was through becoming a conversationalist and learning to deploy a rhetoric which was not constructed upon the page, a rhetoric for the ear. The development in his style from the Latinising of his amazing little novel *Rasselas* to the terse directness of *Lives of the Poets* is decisive. He brought his prose back towards the language of *his* considered speech.

Doctor Samuel Johnson: novelist, lexicographer, biographer, critic, editor, pamphleteer, conversationalist, moral and critical centre of his age, point of reference and illumination for later ages: he represents with broad wisdom and authority of style the radically English intelligence, its power of generality and of discrimination. The poems, often neglected, are a fragment of his huge work. In them, as T. S. Eliot says, he has contrived 'to be original with the *minimum* of alteration', a feat 'sometimes more distinguished than to be original with the *maximum* of alteration'.

Born in Lichfield in 1709, the son of a bookseller in the modern sense,[3] he took an interest in his father's wares. Educated at Lichfield Grammar School and later at Stourbridge Grammar School, he went up to Pembroke College, Oxford, at the age of nineteen. There he felt acutely out of place because of his poverty and social class origins. Friends clubbed together to buy him shoes. He left the university in 1731 without taking a degree. He did not enjoy his year as a schoolmaster or 'usher', being unable to keep order or to convey his learning or his dogged enthusiasms. He was a phlegmatic man who, if moved by need or passion, was capable of heroic labours and surprised even himself with his powers. He undertook as his first literary job a hack translation of Father Lobo's *Voyage to Abyssinia*

---

[3] The word 'bookseller' often meant 'publisher' in earlier times, and even in the eighteenth century.

(published 1735), useful to him when he composed *Rasselas* twenty-four years later, in the evenings of one week, to defray his mother's funeral expenses and to pay her debts. His memory was orderly and encyclopaedic, even if he tended to surround himself with clutter.

He married in 1735 and the next year opened a private school in Edial, Staffordshire, where he looked after six to eight pupils. They are said to have found their master intriguing and a little strange; they spied on him and Mrs Johnson, considerably his senior, on whom he doted. Among his pupils was David Garrick, his theatrical protégé. With Garrick he went to London in 1737 and took root there. It was not – at the beginning – an easy transition, for success came slowly. In 'London' (**51**), an imitation of Juvenal's third satire, written the year after he arrived, he evoked an unregenerate, hostile environment:

> This mournful truth is ev'ry where confessed,
> Slow rises worth, by poverty depressed:
> But here more slow, where all are slaves to gold,
> Where looks are merchandise, and smiles are sold ...

The poem is spoken by a man preparing to leave the city. Johnson may have been tempted to go, but London remained his sometimes bitter destination. 'Why, Sir, you find no man at all intellectual who is willing to leave London: No, Sir, when a man is tired of London, he is tired of life; for there is in London all that life can afford.'

He made progress with his tragedy *Irene* and began writing, and later reporting parliamentary debates, for the *Gentleman's Magazine*. His friendship with Richard Savage at this time led to the celebrated *Life of Savage,* the most deeply *felt* of his indispensable *The Lives of the Poets* (1779–81). In 1745 he published his plan for an edition of Shakespeare, and two years later his preliminary plan for the great *Dictionary*. His poetic activity, always fitful, culminated in 1749 with 'The Vanity of Human Wishes' (**50**), an imitation of Juvenal's tenth satire, and his first signed work. In the same year *Irene* was produced and published, without notable success.

Independent periodical work on the *Rambler,* of whose 208 issues he wrote over 200, occupied him from 1750 to 1752, when his wife died. 'He deposited the remains of Mrs Johnson in the church of Bromley, in Kent,' says his peremptory biographer. 'The funeral sermon which he composed for her, which was never preached ... is a performance of uncommon excellence, and full of rational and pious comfort to such as are depressed by that severe affliction which Johnson felt when he wrote it. When it is considered that it was written in such an agitation of mind, and in the short interval between her death and burial, it cannot be read without wonder.' Despite this loss and his natural indolence, the projects he had initiated carried him along with their momentum and came to fruition, the *Dictionary* in 1755, the Shakespeare ten years later. He also contributed to the *Idler*. In 1762 he was awarded a Royal Pension.

The next year James Boswell descended like a benign Scottish parasite on his life, or his Life; thus began the biography – a monologue with commentary and digression – and much of the legend of Doctor Johnson. Boswell interposes himself between readers, the Doctor and his world. It was quite a broad world: Johnson presided over the Literary Club from 1764, and in his circle were Sir Joshua Reynolds (who left a striking portrait of him), Edmund Burke, Oliver Goldsmith, and several others. In the same year he met Mrs Thrale, who tended him devotedly in his extended difficulties.

After his Shakespeare was published, literary activities diminished. In the nineteen years before his death in 1784 he published political pamphlets, A *Journey to the Western Islands of Scotland* (1775) where Boswell had conducted him two years earlier, and *Lives of the Poets,* begun in 1777, which he struggled to complete for publication in 1779-81. He was awarded the degree of Doctor in Civil Law at Oxford in 1781, exactly half a century after he had left the place with no degree at all. He also received the flyting dedication of Robert Fergusson's poem 'To Dr Samuel Johnson: Food for a new Edition of his Dictionary', an early gauntlet thrown down by the Scots against their assimilation into the metropolitan current of English literature and language (**99**). Fergusson's short life (1750-1774) was a brilliant Catherine wheel. He died desperate and destitute in the Edinburgh mental asylum.

An account of Johnson's evolving literary manner does not reflect the turbulence of mind which his prayers, letters and actions suggest. Literary work was not a place to explore subjective impulse and distress; it was where fact, critical discrimination, imaginative and moral insight were called for, a place of self-effacement and thus of relief. Pessimism and acerbity colour much that he wrote and intensify the imaginative work. The comments on poets and on Shakespeare are those of a man matured by untold – but not all unrecorded – torments, who understood weakness and failure because he recognised the human paradoxes in himself. It is hard to understand his hostility to Swift the man, for of his near contemporaries only Swift was his equal in imagination, integrity and inner turmoil.

Johnson's severe Augustan perspective, when he came to appraise works, must have appeared a bit old fashioned in its standards and expectations even in his own day, and not wholly congruent with his lived tastes. 'Sir, there is nothing which has yet been contrived by man, by which so much happiness is produced as by a good tavern.' He added grandly, 'A tavern chair is the throne of human felicity'. Donald Davie insists that 'it is the mind which knows the power of its own potentially disruptive propensities that needs and demands to be disciplined'. This is true of Swift and Cowper, and in the twentieth century of A. E. Housman and Yvor Winters; but especially so of Johnson with his heavier burdens and larger projects. His choice of poetic forms is governed by such considerations. His couplets, for 'gravity, sheer weight', are unprecedented; if not 'personal' in a modern sense, they are fraught with personal consequence.

He condemns 'the cant of those who judge by principle rather than perception'. Yet 'principle' seems to turn him off Milton, and he misreads 'Lycidas' for this reason, but perception, especially in his reading of *Paradise Lost,* overrides principle. Reason is strong; strong reason knows limits beyond which it cannot be trusted. Beyond those limits one must make do with feeling or faith. Johnson on Shakespeare confirms the power of perception, even in passages where Shakespeare most violates Johnson's cherished principles.

Particularism is at the heart of Johnson's conservatism. His Tory stance was a matter of orientation, not party affiliation: indeed he criticised parties with severity. He hated whiggery, however, from his earliest years in London. In 'London', Thales cries out as he leaves the city:

> Here let those reign, whom pensions can incite
> To vote a patriot black, a courtier white;
> Explain their country's dear-bought rights away,
> And plead for pirates in the face of day,
> With slavish tenets taint our poisoned youth,
> And lend a lie the confidence of truth.

Political scepticism guarantees that his declarations are disinterested

His comprehensive knowledge of past literature gave him means with which to measure the work of his day. His versions of Juvenal and Horace take for their ground the efforts of earlier translators and writers, but he follows Horace's advice and, in rendering an 'original', gives it to his own age. He updates references where he can, evoking London rather than Rome. At the age of fifteen he had translated Horace's 'Eheu fugaces', a suitable preliminary to 'London' and 'The Vanity of Human Wishes':

> Your shady groves, your pleasing wife,
> And fruitful fields, my dearest friend,
> You'll leave together with your life,
> Alone the cypress shall attend.

It is not literal translation, even here. In his 'Life of Shenstone' he describes the nature and pleasure of 'imitation' as a creative mode: 'The adoption of a particular style, in light and short compositions, contributes much to the increase of pleasure: we are entertained at once with two imitations, of nature in the sentiments, of the original author in the style, and between them the mind is kept in perpetual employment.' The reader who knows no Juvenal, Horace or Latin, will experience half, or less than half, the poem, but will still find something of weight. This product of Johnson's teenage pen does not compare in accomplishment with Pope's 'On Solitude'.

When he was seventeen he wrote 'Upon the Feast of St Simon and St Jude', interesting chiefly for its skilful, rather than spirited, use of the stanza form Christopher Smart was to adopt in 'A Song to David'. Despite early prosodic precocity, Johnson came to rely upon the heroic couplet for serious poems. Some of the ephemeral pieces do live. Although 'An Ode on Friendship', expresses conventional sentiment in conventional quatrains, it has the authority of conviction. The 'Epitaph on Sir Thomas Hamner' is civic verse of a high order. His 'Prologue', composed for Garrick, is a verse essay on the English stage with notable observations on Shakespeare, Jonson, the Restoration poets ('Intrigue was plot, obscenity was wit'), and the effect of excessive rule and refinement: 'From bard to bard, the frigid caution crept, / Till declamation roar'd, while passion slept.' (52) He con-jures the 'vicissitudes of taste' from which he, arriving in London a mature man of twenty-eight, stood aloof. His sense of merit is one with his sense of cultural history: there can be no compromise with tradition. Modern excellence must measure itself against proven excellences of the past.

As a reader and critic, he appreciates *sensually* both overall form and realised subject-matter. No critic before him so often uses the word 'image'. Donald Davie commented on the power of *verbs* in the best Augustan writing. Johnson's verbs are strong. For him wit (the 'constant presence of critical intelligence') fuses idea and image to convey truth. He condemns Pope for reducing strength of thought to felicity of language. Wit is seeing what is not obvious but what is acknowledged as just in all its parts when first produced. He distinguishes between intrinsic and extrinsic forms. It is intrinsic form we perceive in the best works. In his 'Life of Cowley' he writes, 'words being arbitrary must owe their power to association, and have the influence, and that only, which custom has given them. Language is the dress of thought'. The dress must fit not only the thought but the dignity of the speaker or occasion. Decorum proves crucial in dis-crimination. The complex association of words with thought, image, speaker and prosody we call form, intrinsic form; it may include con-ventional given form like the sonnet, which we recognise, but we respond only if the intrinsic form is correct.

Johnson looks for certain qualities in verse. First: generality of reference. Natural detail should suit thought, not distort or displace it. Like most of his contemporaries, he overuses the definite article. 'The Vanity of Human

Wishes' tries for universality but instead tends towards abstraction. He also seeks to instruct. A poem should detect order and suggest moral direction, even if it reminds the reader of a known truth rather than discovering a new one. He seeks to make a work pleasing, sensuous gratification deriving from sound, imagery and organisation and the moral and intellectual pleasure of its rightness. Poetry is the 'art of uniting pleasure with truth'. Genius is 'a mind of large, general powers'.

T. S. Eliot regards 'The Vanity of Human Wishes' as the most accomplished satire in the language. Some readers see it as a work – like *Samson Agonistes* – in which the extremity of the moral is intolerable and reduces the artistic achievement. And the epigrammatic completeness of many of the heroic couplets militates against its overall integration. Continuity of argument and imagery, however, impart a kind of unity. The imagery in particular is worth attention. It can remain implicit in allusive verbs or adjectives. Theatre, pageant (with fireworks) and performance recur. In line 64 he mentions 'scene', followed by 'solemn toys' and 'empty shows', 'robes and veils', until we come to the word 'farce' which draws the allusions into coherence, connecting 'stage' images in an emblem of vanity. In line 74 he uses the word 'burning', then 'call', but not until line 76 do we surmise fireworks. The suggested image remains unstated. The evaporation of the 'call' connects with earlier images of mist, phantoms, the unreal masquerading as the solid. Johnson qualifies concrete nouns with abstract adjectives. Such techniques coordinate and connect the couplets. Pope strives for a similar verbal alchemy, though often for rhetorical effect; Johnson uses it to integrate the elements of the poem.

Johnson owes Pope a big, not uncritical debt. The moral and intellectual concentration of his couplets exceeds Pope's. Johnson is the more serious; 'his warrant for public utterance,' Leavis says, 'is a deep moral seriousness, a weight – a human centrality – of theme. It is a generalising weight.' His abstractions concentrate meaning, do not gesture at it. In his generalising imagery, half remains static and located, the other half is in motion or acts: 'the *steady* Roman *shook* the world'. Connection between mutable and immutable (sometimes ironically reversed) or between the physically stable and the evanescent, releases the general truth. Few poets in English share Johnson's specific gravity. This is what recommends him to some and condemns him for others. Blake was not the first, though he was the most scathing, to despise what Johnson was and represented:

'Lo the Bat with Leathern wing
Winking & blinking
Winking & blinking
Winking & blinking
Like Doctor Johnson'

says Suction in Chapter 9 of *An Island in the Moon.* The tenor of subsequent literary periods can be judged by the nature of their general response to Doctor Johnson.

METHODS AND MADNESSES

Thomas Gray, Christopher Smart, Oliver Goldsmith, Edward Young

Around the Springs of Gray my wild root weaves.
Traveller repose & Dream among my leaves.

William Blake, a couplet

It is not surprising that Thomas Gray's 'Ode to Adversity' (58) appealed to Doctor Johnson. The poem is about endurance, and the Doctor admired the efficiency of the writing and Gray's 'sentence' or meaning. It is not a poem characteristic of Gray who, though he can be solemn, never smells of dust and dirty linen. Gray appealed to Blake as well. Johnson and Blake read very different poets in him.

As boys at Eton, Orozmades (Gray), Celadon (Horace Walpole), Favonius or Zephyrus (Richard West) and Almanzor (Thomas Ashton) established the Quadruple Alliance, coming together in mutual hatred of the sporting fraternity and a shared love for classical poetry. Gray, often ill-at-ease in general company, found fortitude and self-assurance in subgroups. Shrill-voiced, witty and playfully inventive among friends, to the world at large he presented an austere façade. At seventeen, soon after he went up to Peterhouse, Cambridge, he sent 'Celadon' a poem he says he got off the ghost of John Dennis after a visit to the Devil Tavern. Poet, dramatist and critic, Dennis had been sent up by Pope in *The Dunciad.* He had died earlier in the year and his memory was warm enough to kindle mild satire. Gray's conceit is that Walpole conjured the ghost, who gives an echo-account of his worldly existence.

That little, naked, melancholy thing,
My soul, when first she tried her flight to wing,
Began with speed new regions to explore,
And blundered through a narrow postern door.
First most devoutly having said its prayers,
It tumbled down a thousand pairs of stairs ...

The casual nature of the composition is clear: the soul is 'she' then 'it', ungendered in a careless transition. The stairs are in 'pairs', signifying perhaps the couplet form. At last the poem arrives in a weird metropolitan Elysium: 'Here spirit-beaux flutter along the Mall'. Dennis tires, abandoning description, but adding a lewdly adolescent *postscriptum:*

> Lucrece for half a crown will show you fun,
> But Mrs Oldfield is become a nun.
> Nobles and cits, Prince Pluto and his spouse
> Flock to the ghost of Covent-Garden House:
> Plays, which were hissed above, below revive,
> When dead applauded that were damned alive . . .

There is no solemnity in sight. Though the later poems achieve at their best an impeccably decorous manner, the figure who shaped them, not a happy man, was capable of deep friendship and light-hearted good cheer.

Not a happy man: such a verdict supposes that modern readers can glean from the recorded facts of a life something of its subjective quality. If that quality is not patent in the poems, have we a right to presume? Surmises about poets of the eighteenth century are especially hard because their hearts, when worn on their sleeves, were usually frilled with lace, and as often as not decorously disguised. Direct expression is what many of them, and Gray in particular, longed to risk: some way of naming objects in the world and passions in the heart. Hence his attraction to all the experiments and forgeries that claimed to emanate from a world of feeling and language beyond the confines of Augustan diction and received form.

> In climes beyond the solar road,
> Where shaggy forms o'er ice-built mountains roam,
> The Muse has broke the twilight-gloom
> To cheer the shivering native's dull abode.

The *ignis fatuus* he pursued was the pseudo-primitive; in it he found space, however spurious, in which to breathe a different air. For Coleridge he seldom breathed real air at all; most of his lyrics are 'frigid and artificial'. Coleridge has a point and should be answered, 'Yes, but . . . '

Doctor Johnson's best poetry is imitation of Juvenal and Horace. It is improper for the poet to pretend to originality. He prefers transposition, restatement in a new context of proven, especially classical work. Other Augustan poets took 'imitation' differently, in the spirit that led T. S. Eliot to weave his verse out of new thread mingled with strands from other works. Eliot, often in ironic spirit, borrows to define his themes. Gray, without programmatic irony, 'imitated' in this spirit. His critics and the poet himself annotated the 'sources' of many lines. Roger Lonsdale, a great editor of our time, writes, 'one seems at times to be confronting a kind of literary kleptomania, such is his dependence on the phrasing and thoughts of other poets'. He is most original in the extent of his derivativeness, his tactful borrowing, from Greek, Latin, English and other writers. William Collins runs him a close second.

Gray turns in his early verse less to Pope and Dryden and more to Spenser, Shakespeare and Milton for metaphor and organisation. This underlines a dissatisfaction with the prescriptions of Augustan verse.

> But not to one in this benighted age
>> Is that diviner inspiration given,
> That burns in Shakespeare's or in Milton's page,
>> The pomp and prodigality of heaven.

His enthusiasm for Thomson's *The Seasons* (in which he sensed, as we no longer can, an actual nature alive), for James Macpherson's Ossianic forgeries, for the 'primitive' Celtic poets, and his longing to infuse primal energy into the effete literary tyrannies of his day, his interest even in the absurd Pindaric mode, all reflect dissatisfaction, a casting about for a way through and *out*. Some of his poems, including 'The Fatal Sisters' (**63**), 'The Descent of Odin' and 'The Bard', imitate Welsh and Norse poetry. He could not make the break: he strove to regenerate poetry only from poetry. He never wrote, he said, 'without reading Spenser for a considerable time previously'. His best poems are not those laboured 'original' compositions, but the thoroughly Augustan pieces, above all the odes and elegies.

A *poeta doctus,* or learned poet, he translated passages of Statius, Tasso and Propertius. Most of his waking hours were spent in study. He attempted a blank verse tragedy in *Agrippina*. In all, he produced relatively little poetry, some of it in Latin and Greek. His debt to Dante, whom he imitated in the opening of the 'Elegy Written in a Country Churchyard' (**61**), is great: he understood the Florentine better than any other Augustan and went so far in his early twenties as to translate the cruel, moving Ugolino passage in which a father devours his own children (**54**). He deploys not Dante's *terza rima* but a blank verse that recalls now Milton, now Spenser. The story itself touched a deep nerve in him, the sole survivor in a family of twelve children: the drama and grim pathos are communicated in something like a speaking voice.

He was born in 1716 in Cornhill. His father was a scrivener – in an earlier age he might have been a scribe – and his mother and aunt kept a milliner's shop. They prospered and gave him the best education their money could buy. In 1735 he was admitted to the Inner Temple. His intention was to pursue a legal career. In 1739 he embarked on a tour of France and Italy with Walpole. A falling-out with his friend hastened his return to England

in 1741. They remained estranged for four years but then became faster
friends than ever. Walpole commissioned a portrait of Gray at 31. He holds
the manuscript of 'Ode on a Distant Prospect of Eton College' (57). It is a
fair likeness, the lips drawn into a tight line, gentle almost-smiling eyes, a
handsome straight nose; collar open, casually disarranged – a boyish Gray,
the person Walpole held dear from school days.

Several bereavements marked him deeply, and his father's death in 1741
left him financially insecure. The law lost its attraction. He settled back at
Cambridge, first at Peterhouse, later at Pembroke College, and apart from
a few absences – in London for research, Stoke Poges for relaxation with
his family, York and the Lakes for rambles – he remained in Cambridge
until his death in 1771. In 1768, after a long campaign, he was appointed
Regius Professor of Modern History. He engaged in university politics and
stooped to partisan satire in 'The Candidate', a poem that distressed his
admirers by its vulgarity. He rhymed the word 'bitches' with 'stitches' (a
term for lying with a woman).

Shortly before his return to Cambridge his poetic energies were released,
possibly by the force of bereavement. In 1742 he completed the 'Ode on the
Spring' (56), his first important composition, a confident mastery of pure
convention. The verse, as Lonsdale says, is entirely self-conscious, moral-
ising the subject *and* moralising the moralising convention as well, as if to
undercut itself. The Eton ode is a finer poem, his first to appear in print,
full of the anxiety that personal losses (including the death of West)
induced. The intricate ten-line stanza form in tetrameters and trimeters is
taut and understated. It is a 'topographical poem', relating to an actual
prospect – from his uncle's summer-house in Stoke Poges he could look
across the Thames to Windsor and Eton; but the poetic prospect is across
time, into the past. The view provokes elegy, not without bitterness. This
is the most transparently subjective of his poems. The pessimism of a
worldly-wise man surveying innocent youth leads to a final stanza whose
terrible force Keats and Wilde were to echo.

> To each his sufferings: all are men,
>   Condemned alike to groan;
> The tender for another's pain,
>   The unfeeling for his own.
> Yet ah! why should they know their fate?
> Since sorrow never comes too late,
> And happiness too swiftly flies.
> Thought would destroy their paradise.
> No more; where ignorance is bliss,
>   'Tis folly to be wise.

So negative a view receives correction in the 'Ode to Adversity' (**58**).

> Thy form benign, oh Goddess, wear,
> Thy milder influence impart,
> Thy philosophic train be there
> To soften, not to wound my heart.
> The generous spark extinct revive,
> Teach me to love and to forgive,
> Exact my own defects to scan,
> What others are to feel, and know myself a man.

Solemn, certainly. He struck other notes from his classic lyre. Walpole's cat drowned in a goldfish bowl, an accident which produced one of the best animal fables, or elegies, in English, 'Ode on the Death of a Favourite Cat' (**59**), satirising the character of woman. Walpole superintended Gray's publications from his Strawberry Hill Press, whose chief activity was to publish Walpole's own works, *The Castle of Otranto,* a gothic novella, and his writing on painting and history. The Strawberry Hill books are the product of a kind of vanity, Walpole's desire to control not only language but its dissemination. He did not distribute them widely. He was a make-believe publisher, some of whose dreams survive.

Walpole was available for consultation on the 'Elegy Written in a Country Churchyard' which Gray completed in 1750 at his uncle's house in Stoke Poges (**61**). The success of this great poem became irksome to him. He was after another sort of originality, yet his later work was criticised in the light of the definitive Augustan achievement. He married in this poem two incongruous but mutually attractive styles: the sedate, tidy elegiac and a Miltonic rhetoric.

We may at first balk at the welter of present participles – more than ten in the first twenty-one lines – or at Gray's tendency to define by negatives, but present participles suggest continuation in time and evoke a natural process; definition by negatives implies what they specifically exclude, so the poem evokes what is *not,* even as it portrays what is. The quatrains function rather like extended couplets: most of them have the finality of epigram.

The 'Elegy' animates the conventional with actual observation, a literal and a formal world come together and agree. If his success is, in Leavis's words, 'of taste, of literary sense' rather than 'of creative talent', then what good sense, what good taste! The distinction is hardly relevant to the poem we have. It is invidious to suggest that taste and sense at such a level of achievement are not a form of 'creative talent'. Johnson's judgement, that the poem 'abounds with images which find a mirror in every mind, and with sentiments to which every bosom returns an echo', is borne out by the popularity of the work and the number of passages and lines which have entered common speech. Robert Wells calls it 'many poems in one'. He admires 'the way that it unfolds and surprises itself. The strong wayward current of its rhetoric is exploratory. Just over half-way through (with the stanza "Yet ev'n these bones ...") Gray veers away from the conclusion he had originally planned, and re-enters his subject, to discover the unwritten poem standing at the edge of the one he has been writing, a preoccupation at variance with his conscious theme.' The concerns that hover at the edge of the 'Elegy' are personal: Gray is a man of homosexual temperament inhabiting a world rich in all things, not least denials. His feeling for what Wells calls 'suppressed potential' has personal resonance, a 'preoccupation which steals up on the first theme, changing the course of the "Elegy", is the need for answered affection and the presence of a "kindred spirit", for the knowledge that a real meeting has taken place this side of the grave'. It is the theme of the Eton poem more subtly and fully developed, more consolingly acknowledged.

Gray, Johnson says, 'thought his language more poetical as it was more remote from common use'. The odes are vitiated by 'a kind of cumbrous splendour which we wish away ... glittering accumulations of ungraceful ornaments ... they strike, rather than please; the images are magnified by affectation; the language is laboured into harshness. The mind of the writer seems to work with unnatural violence.' This is the case with Gray's experimental works and can be explained by his desire to suggest energy where he felt none, to drum up a passion but without motive force. Donald Davie identifies the fault: 'Gray seems to have been distinguished by low vitality.' He does not pour forth his verse, even in his vatic poems. He labours line by line.

Low vitality meant that he abandoned major schemes. The projected *History of English Poetry* was one, for which he composed 'The Progress of Poesy' (62), a species of *translatio regni* of poetry from classical cultures to England, with due praise for English liberty – though not in the complacent tones of Thomson. To Thomas Warton he handed on his plan and notes for the *History*, and Warton incorporated much of Gray, though he went his own way and achieved his own incomplete book. Later Gray wrote 'The Bard', a poem whose lack of inner dynamic produces effects similar to those in Blake's most zany visions, where an *excessive* dynamic fragments the work and leads to ill-judged absurdities. Inevitably Gray returned to translation, to recharge his batteries.

He was indebted to earlier poets, but he is a creditor to many successors. Wordsworth owes him some debts in phrasing, image and theme, especially in 'Hymn to Ignorance', and a negative debt, for Gray was a poet against whom he could react in formulating his own practice and theory of poetic diction. Goldsmith owes Gray specific debts. 'The Alliance of Education and Government' is not generically remote from Goldsmith's much better poems, 'The Traveller' and 'The Deserted Village' (**76**). Goldsmith's verse is less preconceived than Gray's, less careful, more impassioned. Gray's poem is unfinished.

T. S. Eliot says that the second-rate among eighteenth-century poets were those who, disaffected with conventional modes, 'were incompetent to find a style of writing for themselves'. Gray tried, but he lacked the energy. His formidable conventional skills do not suggest that he could have been other than he was. What he is – as a letter-writer as well as a poet – attests to the positive, learned virtues of an age, but also to its limitations. There is no acceptable space for such a man to live a full life. The 'Elegy' remains for anyone who cares for poetry to enjoy. Read in the light of his life, it reveals as much about him as *The Waste Land* does about Eliot. The most 'impersonal' poets, those who borrow voices, wear elusive masks, when regarded attentively are often terrifyingly candid.

Christopher Smart, Robert Graves tells us, 'wrote "A Song to David" (**71**) in a lunatic asylum, and when his collected poems were published in 1791, it was omitted as "not acceptable to the reader". This poem is formally addressed to King David. Smart knew that he was no madder than King David had been, and a tradition survives that he scrabbled the verses with a key on the wall of his cell ... ' However they were written, they remain a wonder and a mystery, begotten of the Bible, of broad and deep learning, and of some catalyst which made a confusion that the poet resolved, against chaos as it were, to put in some sort of order. In his *Jubilate Agno* (**72**) the pressure of chaos has come closer.

> For the word of God is a sword on my side – no matter what other weapon a stick or a straw.
> For I have adventured myself in the name of the Lord, and he hath marked me for his own.
> For I bless God the Postmaster general & all conveyancers of letters under his care especially Allen & Shelvock.
> For my grounds in New Canaan shall infinitely compensate for the flats & maynes of Staindrop Moor.
> For the praise of God can give to a mute fish the notes of a nightingale.

Is it nonsense? Yes. Is it nonsense? No. 'It is not impossible that when Smart is judged over the whole range of his various productions – conventional in form as well as unconventional, light and even ribald as well as devotional, urbane or tender as well as sublime – he will be thought of as the greatest English poet between Pope and Wordsworth.' Is his apparent madness a reaction to the severities of the Augustan Muse? Can a mad poet be, as that strictest of modern critics Donald Davie suggests, 'the greatest English poet between Pope and Wordsworth'? There are such poets in other languages, notably Friedrich Hölderlin in German, though his poetry and his madness are of another order.

Smart's originality is the product not of a candid, puzzled, anxious personality like William Cowper's, nor the lucid, nostalgic and humane sensibility of a Goldsmith. It is the product of a distinctly *poetic* imagination, using that term in a classical sense. Smart seldom composes verse: he is a poet rare in any age, most rare in the eighteenth century, a spiritual enthusiast and a consummate verbal artist. He might resemble Blake, except that he has greater formal tact, a better ear, a better (that is, a less didactic) nature. His poems exist to celebrate God, not to cajole, instruct and persuade us. They are not instruments but instances of faith.

The more we know about Cowper's life, the more we appreciate his verse. With Smart the case is different. Biography obscures his achievement because it seems to apologise for it. He is regarded for his madness (so much more colourful than Cowper's or Collins's) at the expense of the poems. Wilfred Owen famously said of his verse, 'The poetry is in the pity'; the apologist for Smart says, 'The poetry is in the madness.' It is and it is not. Some critics readily assume that he wrote in madness, that what he wrote, in forms and themes, partakes of his derangement. Others divide the work into 'sane' and 'insane' and judge the parts by distinct criteria. But his madness can be seen less as a disorder, more as an *alternative* order, his religious vision not as eccentric but as direct, comprehensive. To say an artist is 'mad' is to say very little. What matters is what he makes of language. Smart makes passionate poetry. Doctor Johnson gives a memorable account of Smart's illness: 'I did not think he ought to be shut up. His infirmities were not noxious to society. He insisted on people praying with him; and I'd as lief pray with Kit Smart as anyone else. Another charge was that he did not love clean linen; and I have no passion for it.'

'A Song to David' was not, as far as we now know, composed in madness. It was certainly not composed in confinement. Structurally rigid, it comes alive in its astounding prosody, not in its theological content. *Jubilate Agno (Rejoice in the Lamb)*, though produced in confinement, deserves to be read as celebration, too. Recent critics and editors who follow Smart's own order for it claim that it is based on a clear scheme, the 'antiphonal structure of Hebrew poetry', as Davie says, the prosodic principles described by Robert Lowth: lines beginning with 'Let' run parallel (ideally on a facing page) to lines beginning with 'For': responses. The poem gives a sense of having been extemporised, written at speed. It was in fact composed at the rate of between one and three lines a day, almost as though it was a devotional journal. Erudite and allusive, the psalmodic lines are deployed with rhythmic versatility. Because Smart did not prepare the *Jubilate* for press, much of its obscurity and difficulty may result from how editors have presented it, not quite understanding his intention and without his manuscript before them. There will never now be a 'definitive version'. It is doubtful that Smart himself could have overseen one.

No known cause in his upbringing can be adduced as the cause of what he called the 'peculiarity' of his imagination. He was writing verse at the age of four. He fell in love with a girl three times his age who used to cosset and caress him. A man pretended he would wed her; when the child told him he was too old, the man threatened to send his son in his place. Terrified at the prospect, Kit wrote eight lines to pre-empt his imaginary rival:

> Madam, if you please
> To hear such things as these.
> Madam, I have a rival sad
> And if you don't take my part it will make me mad.
> He says he will send his son;
> But if he does I will get me a gun.
> Madam if you please to pity,
> O poor Kitty, O poor Kitty!

Pretty, irregular, pathetic: already in infancy insecure in love, already subject to the teasing and treachery of the adult world.

Smart was born in Shipbourne, Kent, in 1722. Peter, his father, was steward of the Vane family establishment of Fairlawn. After his father's death when he was eleven, Kit spent his youth in Durham under the supervision of the Barnard branch of the Vanes. He may have experienced another frustrated passion there. He spent his holidays at the Vanes' Raby Castle in Staindrop. They helped him to Cambridge, where at Pembroke College he became a sizar (receiving a living allowance from the college). He distinguished himself as a scholar and poet. In 1745 he was elected a fellow of Pembroke. While at Cambridge he translated Pope's 'Ode for Music' ('Ode on St Cecilia's Day') into Latin, won Pope's approbation, and composed comical Tripos verses for the Commencement ceremonies. He also wrote secular poems, amorous and otherwise. He became a friend of the organist and composer Charles Burney, from whom he learned about music; through him he got to know Johnson's circle.

Despite his academic success, he was not an ideal student or college fellow. Over-fond of drink and something of a spendthrift, in 1747 he was arrested for debts to his tailor. In 1749 he went to London to try his hand in Grub Street. He wrote ballads and fables for London periodicals. He became a competent editor. In 1752, the year of his marriage to Anna Maria Carnan, step-daughter of his own publisher, *Poems on Several Occasions* was published. It included a georgic, 'The Hop Garden', a tribute to hops and to his native Kent. Between 1750 and 1755 he won the Cambridge Seatonian Prize five times for religious verse, Miltonic in manner. 'On the Goodness of the Supreme Being' (1755) is the best of these, invoking 'Israel's sweet Psalmist' David, one of Smart's peculiar muses: 'thy tuneful touch / Drove trembling Satan from the heart of Saul, / And quelled the evil Angel'. Music remained a solace to him, as to Saul. He translated Horace into prose and later turned the versions into verse. Horace was his other muse. David and Horace, Judaic and Classical: an odd but, as it proved, a fruitful combination.

Between 1756 and 1763 he was confined for insanity, brought on in part by religious fervour, in part by financial improvidence (by now he had a wife and two daughters and had not learned good husbandry). Doctor Johnson and others did what they could to alleviate his difficulties. He saw the inside of St Luke's Hospital for the Insane and of Mr Potter's madhouse in Bethnal Green (in 1758 his wife retired to Dublin and his marriage was at an end). He worked hard after his release, but six years later was again imprisoned, for debt. He died, aged 49, in 1771 in the King's Bench Prison. Most of his best religious poetry dates from 1759–63. 'A Song to David' was completed and published in 1763, the year of his release from asylum. The *Psalms, Hymns* and *Spiritual Songs,* published in 1765, date from this period. *Hymns for the Amusement of Children* appeared in 1770.

'Pope's "Messiah" is not musical, but Smart's "A Song to David", with its pounding thematic words and the fortissimo explosion of its coda, is a musical *tour de force,*' says Northrop Frye. From the first stanza there is a relentless but never monotonous regularity, syntax urging the reader on across stanza endings, creating expectation and suspense; and a taut sound organisation, with strong alliteration and assonance, cunning deployment of monosyllables and polysyllables almost as though they came from different language registers, and concentrated climaxes in three word sequences, usually expressing progression, as in the final stanza, which picks up the word 'glorious' from the stanza before:

> Glorious – more glorious is the crown
> Of Him that brought salvation down
>   By meekness, called thy Son;
> Thou at stupendous truth believed,
> And now the matchless deed's achieved,
>   DETERMINED, DARED, and DONE.

'Thou *at* stupendous truth believed'! A stupendous risk to take with a preposition, and a wholly successful one, giving 'truth' a location in spiritual space, if not in time.

Smart returned to this form as suitably ecstatic for some of his Psalm translations. Two lines of tetrameter tauten into trimeter, and the rhyme scheme is made rigorous by Smart's preference for assonance and approximation between the rhymes. Over a span of eighty-six stanzas, he proved his versatility in this strict form, from the opening invocation of David and Christ to that concluding stanza. The first three stanzas – the treble construction is especially significant for him – initiate the music and establish the themes:

> O thou, that sit'st upon a throne,
> With harp of high majestic tone,
>   To praise the King of kings;
> And voice of heav'n-ascending swell,
> Which, while its deeper notes excell,
>   Clear, as a clarion, rings:
>
> To bless each valley, grove and coast,
> And charm the cherubs to the post
>   Of gratitude in throngs;
> To *keep* the days on Zion's mount,
> And send the year to his account,
>   With dances and with songs:
>
> O Servant of God's holiest charge,
> The minister of praise at large,
>   Which thou may'st now receive;
> From thy blest mansion hail and hear,
> From topmost eminence appear
>   To this the wreath I weave.

Such verbal weaving combines with a schematically rigid structure. R. D. Havens pointed out in 1938 (when the slow process of dusting down the poet began in earnest) how the stanzas are bunched in 'threes, or sevens or their multiples – the mystic numbers'. Donald Davie summarises the structure: 'after three stanzas of invocation come two groups of seven describing David, then three sets of three describing David's singing, and a further set of three describing the effects of his singing' and so on. The alternation between longer and shorter stanza runs and the syntactical and rhythmic parallelism and repetition within the 'bunches' creates an aurally beguiling progression.

The power of rhythm combined with the inventive accuracy of his diction set Smart in a class of his own. Had Gray taken the poem to heart he might have found a way out of his poetic congestion. Here, learning and artifice do what Gray wanted pseudo-primitivism to do for him. Early in his career Smart achieved uncluttered and unabstract poetic *impressions,* if not images; in his mature work even obscure and recondite allusions have a direct impact, not visual so much as sensual. David was master of Smart's rhythms, both taut and expansive; Horace taught him 'the curiosity of choice diction'. Marcus Walsh quotes Smart's preface to Horace: 'The beauty, force and vehemence of *Impression* ... by which a Genius is empowered to throw an emphasis upon a word or sentence in such a wise, that it cannot escape any reader of sheer good sense, and true critical sagacity.'

Behind the language and structure of *Jubilate Agno* stand the examples of the Old Testament in the King James version, the Prayer Book and, more remotely and distortedly, Milton. Smart allegorises detail but not overall design. Each line has a various significance revealed in punning and in contrived parallelisms which Addison described as 'false wit', a wit aurally rather than analytically recognised to be right. 'Let Jotham praise with the Urchin, who took up his parable and provided himself for the adversary to kick against the pricks.' It is the old adversary, the Devil, whose spell is deflected by continually, musically praising creation and Creator. The rightness strikes us over long passages, cumulative, as in the evocation of Jeoffrey, the cat, which Benjamin Britten set to music:

> For he keeps the Lord's watch in the night against the adversary.
> For he counteracts the powers of darkness by his electrical skin and
> glaring eyes.
> For he counteracts the Devil, who is death, by brisking about the life
> For in his morning orisons he loves the sun and the sun loves him.
> For he is of the tribe of Tiger.
> For the Cherub Cat is a term of the Angel Tiger.

The Devil in the heart of Saul, the madness in the mind of Smart, provoke the Psalms of David and the *Jubilate,* exorcisms, charms against chaos, celebrations of a divine force. Works of nature and art ('For flowers are peculiarly the poetry of Christ', 'For the TRUMPET of God is a blessed intelligence and so are all the instruments of HEAVEN') are aids against the adversary.

Smart goes where Gray could not: enthusiasm and vaticism overflow from a full if troubled spirit. He is not an imitator even in his translations, which hold the original in a form and language that make no concessions. He feels and conveys the force of the poetry he admires. His intuition is attuned to a broad tradition, not caught in the rut of convention. Marcus Walsh calls Smart's mature style 'mannered, religiose and self-conscious' – and each becomes a positive critical term, for together they produce a 'homogeneous' style which 'unifies' – the crucial word – 'a number of divergent influences'. It is the paradoxical combination of influences,

Biblical and Classical, and the disruptions his imagination registers, that make him outstanding and eccentric. Learning and accidents of biography deliver him from the bondage of Augustan convention into the sometimes anarchic, vertiginous freedom of *Jubilate Agno* and the originality of the 'A Song to David'. He has few heirs; in the context of his century his work is a symptom more than a resource. How could it be a resource when the definitive editions belong to the twentieth, not the eighteenth, century?

Beside his world, that of Oliver Goldsmith looks comfortable and consoling. 'All the motion of Goldsmith's nature,' writes Thomas De Quincey, 'moved in the direction of the true, the natural, the sweet, the gentle.' He had an 'unpretending mind': a fair judgement. Versatile he certainly was: his literary activity was almost as varied – though not so copious – as Johnson's: poet, novelist, dramatist, journalist, nature writer, essayist, correspondent. Like Johnson's, his reputation as a poet rests on a few fine poems.

He was a remarkable Anglo Irishman, like his friend Edmund Burke, the statesman, whose roots remained deep in Ireland, yet who flourished in England. His 'Irishness' is different from Burke's, as their milieux and destinies were to prove. But their concerns and values are similar.

> Yes! let the rich deride, the proud disdain,
> These simple blessings of the lowly train;
> To me more dear, congenial to my heart,
> One native charm, than all the gloss of art . . .

Probably in 1730, Oliver, fifth child and second son of the Reverend Charles Goldsmith, was born in County Westmeath. His father became curate of Kilkenny and moved to Lissoy where the boy spent his childhood. He went to Trinity College, Dublin, at the age of fifteen as a sizar. Two years later his father died. The young Oliver, who did not distinguish himself academically, was publicly reprimanded for participating in a student riot. In 1750 he managed to take a degree. When he failed to get ordained, he became a tutor, perhaps toyed with the possibility of emigration to America, and at last in 1752 settled into medical studies, supported by his family, first at Edinburgh and later at Leyden. He travelled widely in Europe, where he conceived and developed 'The Traveller, or a Prospect of Society' (1764), the germ of 'The Deserted Village' (1770).

In 1756 he was in London, pursuing medicine as an apothecary and as a physician in Southwark. He may have served as a proof-reader in the novelist Samuel Richardson's printing-house and as an usher or under-schoolmaster. So many jobs suggest that he prospered in none. His literary aspirations grew, journalism and translation work began to find him. He nearly sailed to India as a physician with the East India Company at

Coromandel, but it was not to be. Writing began to feed him. In 1759 *An Enquiry into the Present State of Learning in Europe* was published. He became known as Dr Goldsmith and numbered among friends and associates the novelist Tobias Smollett, the poet Edward Young, Edmund Burke and Doctor Johnson.

His essays, 'letters' – satirical epistolary essays by imagined foreign travellers – and other writings found a market and a price. But like Smart he was impecunious. He made the acquaintance of bailiffs. A new waistcoat swallowed up the money another man might have saved for accommodation or food. Goldsmith was sociable beyond his means.

His *Essays* (1765) and the novel *The Vicar of Wakefield* (1766) set him in the first rank among his contemporaries. But his immediate circle failed to take him seriously – much as Gay was undervalued by his friends. There is condescension in their banter, and in their criticism of his political analysis in 'The Deserted Village'. Johnson said bluntly, 'Goldsmith had no settled notions upon any subject; so he talked always at random. It seemed to be his intention to blurt out whatever was in his mind, to see what would become of it.' Goldsmith's incomplete 'Retaliation' (1774) is said to have been composed in response to Garrick's extempore 'Epitaph': 'Here lies Nolly Goldsmith, for shortness call'd Noll, / Who wrote like an angel, but talk'd like poor Poll.' The 'Retaliation' savours a little of resentment. There is, however, nothing resentful in the tone of his plays and lighter poems, notably 'The Haunch of Venison' (1770), or in the sheer unpedantic readability of his prose, which has not the gravity of Johnson's nor the orotundity of Burke's, but is full of the virtues of character which De Quincey admired. No wonder he commanded an audience and had a market for his prose and plays.

Of the plays, *She Stoops to Conquer* (1773) proved perennial. His themes in all his works were serious even though the tone was often light: regret for a vanishing rural order (which he idealised); impatience with the whiggery which was replacing ideals of patrimony with the practice of investment and profit, with appalling social consequences. Goldsmith is the poet of Burke's prose, catching the essence if not the logic of Toryism. By the time he died in 1774, he had witnessed poignantly to the end of a social order almost as decisive as the earlier end that came with the execution of Charles I.

Like Gray and Collins, Goldsmith as poet was a confirmed borrower and imitator; unlike them, his chief resource was his own prose works. There is an almost linear continuity between prose and verse, rather as in the work of Thomas Hardy, Rudyard Kipling and Edward Thomas. His poems – like most in the eighteenth century – were pre-planned and pursue a discursive rather than 'imaginative' development. But as Donald Davie writes of 'The Deserted Village' – and it goes for 'The Traveller' as well – though it is 'an example of poems consciously planned like essays', it appeals 'through a hidden imaginative continuity'. The poetic process functions not in the argument but in the natural imagery, presented as frail and subject to change, exploitation and destruction. 'The natural,' Davie says, 'which we think of as robust, is thus associated with what is vulnerable and fugitive.'

Most of Goldsmith's surviving verse is work of his maturity. The earliest pieces include translation and epigram, proofs of wit and formal skill, and exercises in social and literary irony. La Monnoye's 'Ménagiana' provided a model for his satirical elegies, where a fourth line in each quatrain undermines conventional sentiment with 'the truth'. Typical is a stanza from 'An Elegy on that Glory of her Sex, Mrs Mary Blaize':

> She strove the neighbourhood to please,
>   With manners wondrous winning,
> And never followed wicked ways,
>   *Unless when she was sinning.*

'On the Death of the Right Honourable —' follows the same pattern. Satire is only accidentally social: its object is to ridicule a sentimental literary mode, most wittily in 'Elegy on the Death of a Mad Dog'(**74**). Goldsmith could serve up poetry of the very sort he parodied, a sentimental mixture favoured at the time, as in his touching romance 'Edwin and Angelina'. T. S. Eliot's judgement is fair: Goldsmith had 'the old and the new in such just proportion that there is no conflict; he is Augustan and also sentimental and rural without discordance'.

'The Double Transformation: A Tale', the first largely original poem he wrote, owes a debt to Swift, though he is more temperate than the Dean:

> Jack sucked his pipe and often broke
> A sigh in suffocating smoke;
> While all their hours were passed between
> Insulting repartee or spleen.

The moral of this tale is general, contrasting beauty and vanity, exploring what a wife owes a husband. By contrast, 'The Description of an Author's Bedchamber' (**73**) smacks of autobiography: poverty was a condition the poet knew. Scroggen lies in his room safe from the bailiffs under a rug:

> A window patched with paper lent a ray,
> That dimly showed the state in which he lay;
> The sanded floor that grits beneath the tread;
> The humid wall with paltry pictures spread . . .

Goldsmith's portrait of his cold, hungry and thirsty alter ego is rueful rather than angry. Scroggen's condition is an unhappy given of his vocation. One is put in mind of Hogarth's engraving of 'The Distrest Poet', and the verb 'grits' runs our own shoe soles across the unswept floor.

'The Traveller' owes something to Goldsmith's own prose and something to Samuel Johnson, who contributed a number of lines and urged the lethargic poet to complete the work. He drew on Montesquieu's *L'Esprit des Loix* in formulating the ideas: the poem was patiently conceived and exhaustively revised. He drafted it first with wide gaps between the lines, filling them with deliberations and deletions. He exploited the popular topographical genre: the physical suggests a moral panorama; natural detail acquires moral weight as in Gray's Eton poem, but on a grand scale. It proceeds from Italy through Switzerland, France and Holland, to Britain. 'The Traveller' started in a letter Goldsmith wrote to his brother; perhaps for this reason there is a frank directness of address in its couplets which have little of the stiff formality of Johnson's or the decorousness of Pope's. The argument often stretches across couplets: they are not emphatically end-stopped and can hardly be called 'heroic'. Intellectual expansiveness loosens the form and reflects an imagination concerned more with the process of thought than with ripe, polished conclusions.

He judges the virtues and faults of each nation he surveys. It is striking how he evokes a nation, its culture and temperament, through landscape, insisting on a continuity between man and environment. Lord Macaulay thought this work the noblest and most simply planned philosophical poem in the language. There is novelty in the way he introduces, as Roger Lonsdale shows, his own 'predicament and sensibility as matters of interest and importance' at the beginning and end. Here (and more so in 'The Deserted Village') Goldsmith repeats words, not as Pope does locally for special emphasis, but throughout the poem – words which are pivots of thought and mood, whose reiteration adds to the meditative tone. We have arrived at the frontier of Romanticism.

But we are not ready to cross over. In the epistle dedicatory to his brother, Goldsmith attacks blank verse, Pindaric odes and metrical experiments. 'Every absurdity has now a champion to defend it, and he is generally much in the wrong, so he has always much to say; for error is ever talkative.' He promises wholesome formal conservatism. Worse than poetic is political partisanship: 'Party entirely distorts the judgement and destroys the taste. When the mind is once affected with this disease, it can only find pleasure in what contributes to increase the distemper.' For himself, 'Without espousing the cause of any party, I have attempted to moderate the rage of all.' Goldsmith as moderator, but not as a pragmatist. He has his own orientation. 'At gold's superior charm all freedom flies, / The needy sell it and the rich man buys.' His praise of liberty puts Thomson to shame. He rails against party:

> O then how blind to all that truth requires,
> Who think it freedom when a part aspires!
> Calm is my soul nor apt to rise in arms,
> Except when fast approaching danger warms:
> But when contending chiefs blockade the throne,
> Contracting regal power to stretch their own;
> When I behold a fractious band agree
> To call it freedom, when themselves are free;
> Each wanton judge new penal statutes draw,
> Laws grind the poor and rich men rule the law;
> The wealth of climes, where savage nations roam,
> Pillaged from slaves to purchase slaves at home;
> Fear, pity, justice, indignation start,
> Tear off reserve and bare my swelling heart;
> Till half a patriot, half a coward grown,
> I fly from petty tyrants to the throne.

He laments rural depopulation, enclosure of the common land, the decay of the countryside. Thus the Industrial Revolution was recorded in poetry, not in itself, but in its effect on the principles of permanence. Few poets experienced the industrial cities. They registered change almost entirely in terms of its impact on rural England. Cowper, Crabbe, even Thomas Hardy, observe the decay of the established order, but perceive the new order and its vicissitudes only from a distance.

'The Deserted Village' (**76**) focuses initially on one 'place', Auburn, which Goldsmith idealises and generalises: it comes to represent all such communities. The poem, drafted in prose, was then corseted into couplets which disciplined and condensed expression, but always with reference to an initial design. The idealisation of Auburn, possibly based on the Lissoy of his childhood, is not excessive. If it is sentimental, it is not falsely so; it serves as the ground against which he develops his meditation, without the prosaic argument of 'The Traveller'. Place and thought give way to elegiac feeling, a sense (not just an idea) of irrevocable loss: organic, traditional communities sacrificed to the inconstant will of commerce, enclosure, exploitation. For him this represents a loss of personal roots, yet his lament is comprehensive because his is by extension a general experience. The blisses of village life – 'charm' and 'sweet' recur too frequently in his evocation – are so pervasive as to be almost abstract. The general judgement is appealingly simple and just:

> Ill fares the land, to hastening ills a prey,
> Where wealth accumulates and men decay:
> Princes and lords may flourish or may fade;
> A breath can make them, as a breath has made;
> But a bold peasantry, their country's pride,
> When once destroyed, can never be supplied.

Times 'When every rood of ground maintained its man' are over. Trade is the undiscriminating instrument of change. In the past, the peasant crowned 'A youth of labour with an age of ease'. The lines about the man who 'Bends to the grave with unperceived decay, / While resignation gently slopes the way', are often cited for the appositeness of their verbs, the exact fit of language with image and moral content. Such usage gives the lie to those who say Goldsmith has an 'essentially prosaic' imagination. He is the author of *The Vicar of Wakefield*, admittedly – the Vicar himself is invoked in lines 133–92. But the imaginative procedures of poet and novelist are distinct, even if the poem took off from a prose draft. The verb 'slope' is a measure of this eminently civilising poet.

Satire is too weak a term for Goldsmith's passionate sorrow at the effects of the deeds of those who would replace modest happiness with egotistical splendour, displace the organic and vital with the formal, monumental and ornamental ('The country blooms – a garden and a grave'). They compel common men – their countrymen – to leave their native soil and emigrate to unknown lands. The humble have no redress against the power of wealth. Doctor Johnson contributed the poem's final quatrain. We are moved by the poem to sadness, not to action; to resignation, for the poet seems to know that what he elegises is gone beyond recall, that whiggery is the order of the day. As in the early poem about the poet's threadbare room, 'The Deserted Village' does not resist: it accepts what is. This is the source of its aesthetic wholeness (it is not 'instrumental', it does not incite) and its political inadequacy.

Goldsmith felt deeply, but it would be misleading to call him a 'Poet of Feeling'. Edward Young (1683–1765), a generation his senior, claims that ambiguous title, being a poet peculiar to his century, a man who escaped the trammelling of fashion and decorum by privileging his sensibility, by refusing to efface himself in the interests of a 'common language', and by, as it were, finding a kind of philosophical adequacy in the aesthetics of feeling. In an age of restraint and control, he is a poet of letting go, not with religious enthusiasm but with the delicious excesses of a kind of abstract emotion.

His father, the Dean of Salisbury, addressed the boy's tutor at Corpus Christi College, Oxford, in these terms: 'I know my son had a fastidious, whimsical fancy which was like to lead him to the love of such studies only as were apt to gratify and nurse up his infirmity.' The boy in turn became a tutor to a wonderfully irregular and volatile young nobleman, and then a Law Fellow of All Souls, but failing to find secular preferment entered the Church. There too he failed to advance, remaining rector of Welwyn, Hertfordshire, from 1730 until his death. It was the infirmity his father had identified which in turn 'nursed up' his writing: the tragedies *Busiris* and *The Revenge,* both produced not unsuccessfully at Drury Lane; his satires which were popular until Pope's superior satires displaced them (though Young survived Pope and his mature mode displaced Pope's in due course); and, from his rectory, his best-remembered work, *Night Thoughts on Life, Death and Immortality* (1742–5) (**22**).

The poem is spoken by a deliberately created voice, a *persona,* the skill for generating such a feelingful voice having been developed in his dramatic writing. Doctor Johnson applauded, uncharacteristically, Young's use of blank verse, commenting that rhyme would have destroyed the intention. He also commented on the way in which the *sense* was spread out evenly through the writing, not condensed into single lines or runs. Fanny Burney, herself a voice of Feeling, was ecstatic in the presence of his work: 'I forgot, while I listened,' she confided to her diary, 'all my own little troubles and disturbances.' She was not alone in experiencing the strange lenitive powers of the verse, 'every line an anodyne of pain', as one admirer put it. He was loved by Burns and by several of the Romantics.

It was left to George Eliot, impatient as much with the poet's self-indulgence as with the praise he had garnered, to deal him a fatal blow, identifying 'his *radical insincerity as a poetic artist'.* Later advocates have found it hard to hoist the bust back on to its pedestal, and Young has remained one of those 'precursors of Romanticism', a poet read in his own right largely by academic enthusiasts.

It is hard not to concur with George Eliot's objections, in particular her sense that Feeling and Sentiment of the type he expresses naturally attach to particulars, and yet he is sufficiently a child of the eighteenth century to be at home only with categories, 'the tree' rather than 'this specific tree'. His satires are at once more particular and more precise.

> Critics on verse, as squibs on triumphs, wait,
> Proclaim the glory, and augment the state.
> Hot, envious, noisy, proud, the scribbling fry
> Burn, hiss, and bounce, waste paper, sting, and die.
> Rail on, my friends! What more my verse can crown
> Than Compton's smile, and your obliging frown?

The removal of rhyme and of the compulsion to give shape to thought and feeling in a series of controlled closures gave Young a freedom to fly in all directions. He could warm up the language with the fitful embers of a grief now deeply felt (the death of his wife), now blown upon and almost ash. Mix Feeling with the great Abstractions such as Death, Folly, Youth and Passion, and see how high they rise into an empty and indeed starless *Night Thoughts* sky. When Ezra Pound said, 'Go In Fear Of Abstractions', he offered good counsel to some of the abstracting heirs of Young. At his best, in the Poetry of Feeling, Young resembles the Pope of 'Eloise and Abelard' without the benefit of plot; at his worst he foreshadows William Blake in his zanier visionary moments. No wonder Blake took him to heart and gave wonderful pictorial form to some of his flimsiest abstractions.

> Thus, Darkness aiding intellectual light,
> And sacred Silence whispering truths Divine,
> And truths Divine, converting pain to peace,
> My song the midnight raven has outwing'd,
> And shot, ambitious of unbounded scenes,
> Beyond the flaming limits of the world
> Her gloomy flight. But what avails the flight
> Of Fancy, when our hearts remain below?

'A STRICKEN DEER'

William Cowper, Charlotte Smith

I had considered it as a defect in the admirable poem of *The Task* that the subject which gives the title to the work was not, and indeed could not be, carried on beyond the first three or four pages . . .

Samuel Taylor Coleridge, *Biographia Literaria*

William Cowper wrote some of the best-known hymns and poems in English – so well-known that they travel incognito, having acquired the authority of anonymity, much as the ballads, 'Rule Britannia', 'Drink to me only' and 'The Passionate Shepherd' have done. Such a fate never overtook a Romantic poem. Cowper is not quite a Romantic, though his hand is on the latch. He is the *other* poet with a claim to being the 'greatest' between Pope and Wordsworth. As mad as Smart, though with a different kind of madness, he broke through to God in his hymns, and then agonisingly lost contact; and in 'social' and 'normative' verse he discovered the social language, if not the society, of his time.

His poetry proved of value to Coleridge and Wordsworth. Coleridge's original lectures on English poetry define three periods, the third running from Cowper to 'the present day'. For him something important begins with Cowper, a poet who read the poems of George Herbert with delight when Herbert was almost forgotten, who knew Milton's work as few before him had done, and developed a personal discursive blank verse style that in directness and variety of tone foreshadows Wordsworth's. He loved Robert Burns and regretted only the dialect, not because it was inexpressive but because English readers gave up on it too easily ('His candle is bright, but shut up in a dark lantern'). De Quincey joins Cowper's name with Edward Young's and Wordsworth's as meditative poets of a kind, always allowing to Wordsworth the greenest laurel. But Cowper decisively displaces Young, though it is probably more useful to approach his work from the eighteenth than from the nineteenth century. To see him always as a pre-Romantic makes him into a harbinger and we misvalue him as a poet in his own right.

Cowper's spiritual and secular unhappiness were of a piece with those of other poets of his century. But he dwells insistently on his own guilt, with the hubristic humility of a Protestant who knows himself to be the *most* abject of all sinners: such exaggeration guarantees him the attention, even if derisive, of God.

> Your sea of troubles you have past,
>   And found the peaceful shore;
> I, tempest-tossed, and wrecked at last,
>   Come home to port no more.

Critics are reluctant to make the claims for Cowper that he deserves. There is something about him: the unironic self-obsession of Thomas Hoccleve, the variable copiousness of Thomson, the excellence of the hymns which are, like the ballad, a genre not *quite* polite ... Jn one anthology the head-note for Cowper begins, 'Of all the poets in this selection, Cowper is perhaps the smallest in poetical stature. He would probably have counted himself lucky to figure in such grand company.'

In important ways Cowper is original, and the emotional and intellectual range of his poems is wide. A 'milder muse' dominates, but there are reasons for this: Cowper had to court that Muse more intensely than any poet in the language, because for him poetry was a means of talking himself back from the edge, not – in the fashion of the 1960s and 1970s – of coaxing himself over it. Acquaintance with his darker verse makes the 'milder muse' a formidable and healing figure. Cowper's work gains in definition when we understand his motives in writing. His Augustanism is illuminated when we accept, as Donald Davie puts it, that the poems 'were written under the shadow of psychosis'.

Cowper was born in 1731 at Great Berkhamstead, where his father, a grand-nephew of the first Earl Cowper and one-time royal chaplain, was rector. On his mother's side he could claim remote kinship with John Donne. His first trauma was his mother's death when he was six, a loss consolingly weighed in the remarkable poem, 'On the Receipt of my Mother's Picture Out of Norfolk', written after his earliest experience of madness. 'Oh that those lips had language! Life has pass'd / With me but roughly since I heard thee last ... ' Intense pathos, untouched by sentimentality. At his first school he was bullied. He went on to Westminster School where he was happier and able to excel. Among his classmates was the satirist Charles Churchill. He read Homer, Milton and Cowley deeply. He started translating Homer, which became a major vocation, and rendered the Latin poems of Milton into English.

At the age of eighteen he entered the Middle Temple and in 1754 he was called to the bar. He fell in love with his cousin Theodora whose father, sensing Cowper's instability and poor prospects, opposed the match. It was another blow to him. His 'Delia' poems, addressed to Theodora, though not his best work, attest to his devotion. He came to expect failure – even, at times, to court it. He began to withdraw from the world, and his father's death, leaving him only a modest inheritance, precipitated his decline. He was a Commissioner of Bankrupts (1759–65). His family exerted itself to secure him a better post, but when it was offered he was unable to accept it. He attempted suicide and was confined to an asylum. He was not surprised by his breakdown: it was part of the pattern he expected.

Recovery coincided with an evangelical conversion. Later he could write, 'The path of sorrow, and that path alone, /Leads to the land where sorrow is unknown.' He was lifted up by reading a Biblical text in Romans. Tenuously 'cured', he went to live in Huntingdon with the Reverend and Mrs ('My Mary') Unwin (1765–7). The Unwins, Anglican evangelicals, supported him, and after her husband's death Mrs Unwin tended Cowper in his illnesses. His love for her was the subject of several poems more mature and memorable than those to 'Delia':

> Thy indistinct expressions seem
> Like language uttered in a dream,
> Yet me they charm, whate'er the theme,
>   My Mary! (**81**)

This was written in the twentieth year of their friendship; she is fading, and he believes himself (as usual) responsible for her decline. They had almost married, but desisted at a recurrence of Cowper's malady. She fell ill in 1791 and he helped look after her until her death in 1796. He died, miserable and ill, in 1800, having composed his harrowing poem 'The Castaway' (**79**) two years earlier:

> No voice divine the storm allayed,
>   No light propitious shone,
> When, snatched from all effectual aid,
>   We perished, each alone:
> But I beneath a rougher sea,
> And whelmed in deeper gulfs than he.

The 'he' was mercifully drowned; the 'I' survives to suffer. Images of storm, shipwreck, drowning and isolation are *leitmotifs* through the poetry, even in unexpected humorous contexts. Shipwreck and drowning epitomise human vulnerability. Theological and psychological elements coexist in the images: they come at points when Cowper is peculiarly, darkly himself. 'Alexander Selkirk' (**78**), ostensibly about the human prototype for Daniel Defoe's Robinson Crusoe, is a personal vision: Cowper is castaway. 'The

Loss of the Royal George' (80), a superb dirge, comes fraught with personal cargo. The ship sank in calm water, unexpectedly.

> Toll for the Brave!
> The brave! that are no more!
> All sunk beneath the wave
> Fast by their native shore!

Happy or at least contented times precede his miserable end. With Mrs Unwin he moved to Olney. There they encountered a rather dreadful Calvinist, the Reverend John Newton. Whatever else he may have done, he elicited from the poet the *Olney Hymns* (84) at a time when Cowper was again suffering mental and spiritual torment. His faith revived, but he still doubted his own election for salvation. He dreamed that God had damned him and the hymns are heavy with a hopeless hope. Davie suggests that Cowper's depressive madness was connected with the extreme Calvinism of the evangelicals. He recovered from the dream of damnation, resigned worldly ambitions, accepted his fall from grace. In nature he found external solace. Tending leverets and birds gave purpose to his retirement. The nature he describes in his verse with minute and loving particularity appealed to those caught up in the vogue for the Picturesque. Unlike them, he came to nature directly, not through art.

His earliest attempts at extended verse were the eight *Moral Satires*, suggested to him by Mary. He worked best when someone requested poems from him. Newton catalysed the hymns; Lady Austen provoked *The Task* (85), the roistering ballad 'John Gilpin' and other occasions for poems were offered by those solicitous for his health and keen to prevent him from reflecting on his spiritual condition. The verse is much more than the therapy they intended it to be. It has the mild urgency of a man intent to look abroad, away from himself, to attach himself to the created, contingent world. At least Nature won't condemn or rebuff him. What he writes is strenuously normative, judiciously moralised: self-doubt in quest of certitude. The tenuous structure of the long poems reveals the uncertainty of his control, but it is hard to fault the surface. Coleridge praises above all the 'clarity of diction' and 'harmony' of the blank verse.

Cowper translated ambitiously, 'fishing in other men's waters', to use C. H. Sisson's phrase, when his own streams ran dry. His blank verse Homer is not a masterpiece: set beside Pope's couplet version it shows how much even late Augustans abandon (as Young did in *Night Thoughts*) when they omit to rhyme. But his Horace, Virgil and Ovid are variously excellent. He translated from French and from the Greek Anthology, displaying technical competence in epigrams, hymns, anthems, elegies, lyrics, pastorals, discursive poems and epistles (in verse and prose: he is among the best letter-writers in the language).

Norman Nicholson concentrates on the paradoxical nature of the poet, 'a recluse who became the spokesman of a great popular religious and democratic movement; and an oddity, an eccentric, a refugee from society, who, perhaps more than any other English poet, expressed the aspirations of the average man of his time'. The poems have 'the merit of good conversation', an intimacy with their readers. Normative verse is powerful when it is hard won, when the troubled poet strenuously achieves normality.

Conversational verse was uncommon in an age still overshadowed by Pope, whom Cowper admired with reservations, and still under the spell of Milton. Cowper's Milton is not mediated through Thomson: it is Milton himself, whose Latin he translated, whom he set out to edit in 1791. He avoids Milton's grandiloquence because he is aware of having particular readers, concerned with specific issues and images. He has a defined *personality*, and he selects in *The Task* a loose associative form over a narrative structure. His debt to Milton is not, like Gray's and Collins's, to the shorter poems, but to *Paradise Lost* and *Paradise Regained*. His other master is Homer; he doubts only the morality of devoting so much time to a pagan poet. The absence of Shakespeare is evidence of how essentially literary a poet Cowper was in his earlier work.

D. J. Enright compares Cowper with Herbert. Cowper asks that we assent to his presentation of faith, while Herbert's representations are of faith as experience. Cowper teases out his morals, Herbert as often as not leaves the moral implicit. Cowper is didactic where Herbert is devotional, with the immediacy of prayer and not the remove of sermonising. Coleridge admires in *The Task* the 'vein of satire which runs through that excellent poem, together with the sombre hue of its religious opinions'. 'Opinions' is the right word, opinions argued and affirmed, only seldom conveyed to the pulse. Yet the opinions must have been widely held, for between its publication in 1782 and 1800 eleven editions of *The Task* appeared.

In 'Table Talk', the first of the *Moral Satires*, Cowper modestly presents his claims as a poet. 'I play with syllables, and sport in song.' The understatement goes too far. This poem begins with philosophy and politics and, like good table talk, takes much else in its stride, most memorably the halcyon poetic Genius, whose literary firmament includes Homer, Virgil and Milton.

In 1783, the year of Crabbe's *The Village* and Blake's *Poetical Sketches*, Cowper began *The Task*. Lady Austen requested an epic about a sofa. 'I sing the Sofa. I, who lately sang / Truth, Hope, and Charity.' Soon enough he gets back to Truth, Hope and Charity. After a history of seats, a comment on the suitability of sofas for sufferers from the gout, he expresses a desire that he may never experience that illness. Why?

For I have loved the rural walk through lanes
Of grassy swarth, close cropped by nibbling sheep,
And skirted close with intertexture firm
Of thorny boughs ...

The sofa establishes a tone: drawing room, comfort, conversation. It inaug-
urates, too, what is virtually a theme: the rich texture of things in the world,
physical sensations; and the theme of illness and enforced repose. The
poem connects not by argument or narrative but through tone. It develops
by association, an interchange between particular observation and moral
generalisation. Cowper's blank verse suggests the tone and subject-matter
of Wordsworth:

Nor rural sights alone, but rural sounds
Exhilarate the spirit, and restore
The tone of languid nature ...

'Languid' may not be Wordsworthian, but more than a common debt to
Milton associates the poets in our minds. They partly share a vision of
nature. Of the cacophonous birds, Cowper writes that they

have charms for me,
Sounds inharmonious in themselves and harsh,
Yet heard in scenes where peace for ever reigns,
And only there, please highly for their sake.

Cowper is less elemental, more consoling than Wordsworth.

Abstracted from the poetry, the thought of *The Task* is not distinguished,
but in context it is realised and vivid. Only the positive moral exhortations,
against slavery and blood sports, for example, or in favour of certain
religious views, weary the reader. In promoting reform Cowper prefers
exhortation to satire. Yet in verse, satire is generally the more effective, at
least for the modern reader.

One of the triumphs of Cowper's art and vision comes in the third, most
quoted book, 'I was a stricken deer', evoking the function of Christ and the
true nature of redemption. For an exalted moment Cowper is almost on a
par with Herbert.

I was a stricken deer, that left the herd
Long since, with many an arrow deep infixt
My panting side was charg'd, when I withdrew
To seek a tranquil death in distant shades.
There was I found by one who had himself

Been hurt by th' archers. In his side he bore,
And in his hands and feet, the cruel scars.
With gentle force soliciting the darts,
He drew them forth, and heal'd, and bade me live.
Since then, with few associates, in remote
And silent woods I wander, far from those
My former partners of the peopled scene;
With few associates, and not wishing more.

This is oblique autobiography. Other vivid descriptive passages, about cucumbers, greenhouses, animals, the winter landscape and the hearth, add a documentary interest to the poem, but always animated by a spiritual and a psychological interest. One need only compare *The Task* with Thomson's *The Seasons* to see how the Augustan imperatives were being eroded by a first person singular coming to terms with its singularity.

In 'John Gilpin', 'Epitaph on a Hare' (**82**) with its accuracy and gentle humour, 'The Poplar-Tree' which meant a great deal to both Coleridge and Gerald Manley Hopkins, and the unfinished 'Yardley Oak' (**86**) – the majestic unfinished moral poem – readers find readiest access to Cowper. They first hear him (without proper introduction) in church when they sing his *Olney Hymns,* 'Oh! for a closer walk with God' and 'God moves in a mysterious way'. In the poems it is the same voice, and a music not of organs but of intimate speech.

Eighteen years after Cowper's birth, in 1749, an unaccountably neglected poet, Charlotte Smith (half-remembered as a novelist) was born. If Cowper had his hand on the latch of Romanticism, her foot was firmly in the door. Wordsworth read her: Dorothy recalls him turning the pages of her *Elegiac Sonnets* – the fifth edition, for she was popular in her time; and he visited her in Brighton. She treated him politely, introducing him to other women writers in the town. In London at the end of the century she dined with the young Coleridge. A recurrent footnote, doggedly represented in anthologies by a sonnet which is wonderful ('Pressed by the moon, mute arbitress of tides' [**97**]) and to which few attend closely, she is a key poet of the transition to Romanticism, but it is best to approach her from the eighteenth century, too, so as to appreciate her origins and her originality.

Among women writers she is, after Mary Sidney, the first substantial poet. The famous sonnets resemble Cowper's verse in tone, but without his specific anxieties. Meditative, judicious, she also has a clear, unconventional vision. Her language seeks out representative detail, too many exclamations and vocatives irrupt into the verse, yet scene and sensibility are sharply delineated:

... The wild blast, rising from the western cave,
  Drives the huge billows from their heaving bed;
  Tears from their grassy tombs the village dead,
And breaks the silent sabbath of the grave!
With shells and seaweed mingled, on the shore
  Lo! their bones whiten in the frequent wave;
  But vain to them the winds and waters rave;
They hear the warring elements no more:
  While I am doomed – by life's long storm oppresst,
  To gaze with envy on their gloomy rest. (**97**)

Gothic, yes: but beneath or despite the gothic, astonishing in visual, prosodic and *tonal* precision. Her coy self-description – 'an early worshipper at Nature's shrine' – sells the poetry short. True: she observes nature, walking out on the hills and along the shore. But her 'worship' is more 'witness', her nature is not transcendent despite her rhetoric. What distinguishes her as a writer is her formal assurance. In the much-anthologised 'Thirty-Eight' (**96**) she masters with wit and wisdom a difficult form and develops a crucial theme, that of a woman growing older, with tact, feeling and wit.

She was born Charlotte Turner at Bignor Park in Sussex and enjoyed a privileged childhood, though her mother died when she was three. Terrified at the prospect of her father's remarriage, she herself disastrously married Benjamin Smith, profligate son of a West India merchant, when she was sixteen. He spent them into debt and then debtors' prison. She bore Mr Smith ten children, eight of whom survived; she left him, and began – having already started in 1784 with the *Elegiac Sonnets* – to make her way as a writer. She wrote on average a book each year for two decades. Mr Smith remains, in various fictional guises, the villain of her life and occasions some of the gloomy skies in her poems. But she had read Rousseau and was inspired by the French Revolution. Her poetic imagination emerges generally at night; in the dark shapes loom larger, lights burn brighter, the landscape takes on an alternative, accepting definition. In her major poem 'Beachy Head', she does not appropriate, colonise, or look through nature to an absolute. She witnesses and celebrates with gratitude to nature rather than, through nature, to God.

What makes her neglect unaccountable is that she achieved, *avant la lettre,* so much that is celebrated in the work of Wordsworth in particular, as well as the Coleridge of 'This Lime-Tree Bower My Prison' and the blank verse narratives. 'Beachy Head' (**91**) evinces, beyond its assured tone, a mastery of blank verse meditation and a compelling, complex syntax which mimes the movement of thought. Clearly she is rooted in the eighteenth century, but emancipation has taken place, she has created first a distance from the stylistic vices and reflexes of the age, and then a space for her own sensibility to identify a physical world and a physical and spiritual self.

> The high meridian of the day is past,
> And ocean now, reflecting the calm heaven,
> Is of cerulean hue; and murmurs low
> The tide of ebb, upon the level sands.
> The sloop, her angular canvas shifting still,
> Catches the light and variable airs
> That but a little crisp the summer sea;
> Dimpling its tranquil surface.

Pure description, and from its purity something more comes, as though we are returning to a literal uncomplicated world after the packed diction and decorum of the 'social century'. Charlotte Smith is not, like Smart and Cowper, an exception, someone set apart as a consequence of illness or the estrangements of genius. She is propelled forward by Milton, Thomson and Pope. There are the epithets, the rhetorical bric-à-brac, the large abstractions, yet in the foreground a literal eye is trained upon an actual world. She has a landscape quite as specific as Wordsworth's, the Sussex of her unimpeded childhood. Her personal hardship is there in her tone, but seldom in the frame; celebration and reflection are given in judicious measure:

> Ah! hills so early loved! in fancy still
> I breathe your pure keen air; and still behold
> Those widely spreading views, mocking alike
> The poet and the painter's utmost art.
> And still, observing objects more minute,
> Wondering remark the strange and foreign forms
> Of sea-shells; with the pale calcareous soil
> Mingled, and seeming of resembling substance.
> Though surely the blue ocean (from the heights
> Where the Downs westward trend, but dimly seen)
> Here never rolled its surge. Does Nature then
> Mimic, in wanton mood, fantastic shapes
> Of bivalves, and inwreathed volutes, that cling
> To the dark sea-rock of the wat'ry world?
> Or did this range of chalky mountains, once
> Form a vast basin, where the Ocean waves
> Swelled fathomless? . . .

Such blank verse, with variable enjambements that create the kinds of syntactical suspense that urge us on, so that description is vibrant, unpredictable and alive in the verse reflection, is unusual in any century. The diction is assured and 'modern' in the manner of Thomson, using a precise, scientific register, yet naturally, as an informed person would. If the verse were anonymous, would we be inclined to surmise that it was written by a woman? I think we would, especially if we knew the date of its composition. 'Beachy Head' was published in 1807, the year after Charlotte Smith died. It is the work of an unsung maturity: at times humorous, full of a love of specific nature, marked too by longing, less for youth and romance than for that lost world when imagination was unconstrained, the world before Benjamin Smith and children and the labour of sustaining a family as a single parent. The world before she was, like some of her intimate friends and some of the Romantics she prefigures, an opium addict. Yet these circumstances are not adduced in the poems. They inform only the tone.

Charlotte Smith's poetry may have been delivered from the trammels of the eighteenth century by means of her fiction writing: the verse is wonderfully efficient, in its disclosure of scene and theme, evenly measured, rising to grandeur, scaling down to microscopic observation. Her fault in the longer poems is formal: extension rather than structure. Yet if we read her as we tend to read Cowper, Pope or Thompson, in extract, she is not out of place. Her work was once popular, but it was not absorbed into the critical culture of the day; its claims were not made. We can say that she was appreciated by Wordsworth, but his appreciation was not eloquent. We can say that her example empowered Elizabeth Barrett Browning. But Charlotte Smith is much more than a footnote to Romanticism. She should adjust our take on the eighteenth century. She is a reckonable poet who deserves to be read today.

YOUTH AND AGE

Thomas Chatterton, Phillis Wheatley, George Crabbe

Then proudly smiléd that old man
  To see the eager lad
Rush madly for his pen and ink
  And for his blotting-pad –
But, when he thought of *publishing*,
  His face grew stern and sad.

Lewis Carroll, 'Poeta Fit, Non Nascitur'

Thomas Warton wrote a judicious account of Thomas Chatterton in the decade of the 'marvellous boy's' death. It is a tribute to the success of Chatterton the forger that, though some critics believed they had rumbled him, others sat on the fence. In Thomas Rowley's poems, Warton declares, the fifteenth century will be vindicated: 'a want of genius will no longer be imputed to this period of our poetical history, if the poems lately discovered at Bristol, and said to have been written by Thomas Rowlie, a secular priest of that place, about the year one thousand four hundred and seventy, are genuine'. Warton's indecision is on poetic rather than scholarly grounds; the poems 'possess considerable merit', he declares; there were still grounds for regarding them as genuine. In the end Warton, on the evidence of parchments and handwriting, and on spelling conventions, comes down on the side of the disbelievers. Yet he is reluctant to do so. He is enchanted: 'This youth, who died at eighteen, was a prodigy of genius; and would have proved the first of English poets, had he reached a maturer age.'

Which was more marvellous: that a fifteenth century poet of real moment should be rediscovered, or that a teenager from the provinces should create so plausible and sustained a poetic work? In the end the spell Chatterton cast was broken. 'He was an adventurer, a professional hireling in the trade of literature, full of projects and inventions, artful, enterprising, unprincipled, indigent, and compelled to subsist by expedients.'

Begin, my Muse, the imitative lay,
Aonian doxies sound the thrumming string;

Attempt no number of the plaintive Gray,
Let me like midnight cats, or Collins sing.

Chatterton survives for what he meant to the Romantics more than for anything he wrote. Much of his (false) work is outstanding, all of it provides evidence of genius that did not give itself time to mature fully, though mature it certainly is. His writings fill three volumes; there are longueurs. He was not Arthur Rimbaud. To the Romantics he symbolised genius untutored, misunderstood, misprized by 'the ingrate world' (Keats). Keats used to intone the magnificent lines from the Minstrels' song in the play *Aella* (**105**):

Comme, wythe acorne-coppe and thorne,
Drayne mie hartys blodde awaie;
Lyfe and all yttes goode I scorne,
Daunce bie nete, or feaste by daie.
　Mie love ys dedde,
　Gon to hys death-bedde,
　Al under the wyllowe tree.

To Chatterton's memory he dedicated an indifferent sonnet, and then *Endymion*, the poem he described as 'a feverish attempt, rather than a deed accomplished'. Keats sets his hero 'among the stars / Of highest Heaven'. In a letter to Reynolds he confides, 'I always somehow associate Chatterton with autumn. He is the purest writer in the English Language. He has no French idioms, or particles like Chaucer – 'tis genuine English idiom in English words.' In a letter to his brother he adds, 'Chatterton's language is entirely northern. I prefer the native music of it to Milton's cut by feet.' Chatterton's 'pure' English proved useful in Keats's emancipation from Milton. He loved the 'Rowley poems' in 'Middle English', not the precocious but otherwise unexceptional English poems.

Wordsworth refers to Chatterton in 'Resolution and Independence' and carries the poet's name further in time and space than any other tribute does: 'I thought of Chatterton, the marvellous Boy, / The sleepless Soul that perished in his pride.' Coleridge was behindhand in his tribute. For over thirty years he tinkered with his 'Monody on the Death of Chatterton', spoken figuratively at the poet's grave (as a pauper suicide, his grave was unmarked). The life and death of the poet detain him. The poems which he praises in passing are the 'Rowley poems'. Coleridge's significant poetic debt to Chatterton is in the metrical organisation of his own 'Christabel'.

What, apart from the life, was the appeal of Chatterton? Why do some claim him as 'the first Romantic'? There are undeniably fine poems and stanzas among the forgeries. Best are certain passages of *Aella*, 'An Excelente

Balade of Charitie (As wroten bie the goode Prieste Thomas Rowley 1464)'
(**107**), and 'Eclogue the Third'. The authority of his 'language' is felt in the
amusing and, in tone at least, plausibly medieval quatrain:

> There was a Broder of Orderys Blacke
> > In mynster of Brystowe Cittie:
> He layd a Demoisell onne her Backe
> > So guess yee the Tale of mie Dittie.

Remarkable for its oddity, such verse also has a separable *quality*. The best
passages in *Aella* do not lose their imaginative force when translated back
into modern English (Chatterton drafted them in English, then medi-
evalised the language). It is disappointing, however, that when it is antho-
logised, most critics de-medievalise the language more or less completely,
and Chatterton loses the deliberate semantic varnishing that so deepens
the mystery of his fanciful work.

He remained popular until the middle of the nineteenth century as a
Romantic legend, a lesson in resisting to the death literary and social
convention. From his setting forth he was marginal. He was born in Bristol
in 1752. His father, a schoolmaster and sub-chanter at the Church of St
Mary Redcliffe, died before the boy was born. Chatterton's mother sup-
ported him, working as a seamstress and running a 'dame school'. It was
she who, one day disposing of some antique documents, aroused in the
hitherto listless child an enthusiasm, first for the illuminated letters, then
for the old words. She taught him to read. Later he busied himself studying
at home and at St Mary's (where he claimed to have gained access to a
mysterious box containing Rowley's manuscripts).

When he was seven he was sent to a grim Bristol school, Colston's
Hospital. He kept himself to himself, writing occasional satirical poems
about his schoolmate-tormentors to keep his spirits up – poems like one
to 'Sly Dick', 'in arts of cunning skilled'. At the age of ten he began to write
more earnest poems. 'On the First Epiphany', written when he was eleven,
was published. He composed more satirical as well as religious verse, reveal-
ing a precociously informed (or cleverly imitative) scepticism in matters of
public morality. In 1764 he presented a pupil-teacher with a forged medieval
poem. His first gull was duped.

In 1767 he was apprenticed to an attorney. He composed further forgeries.
Most of the 'Rowley poems' were completed in 1768–9. He persuaded
several Bristol burghers, some of his friends, and for a time he succeeded
with the great Horace Walpole. Ambition to be a writer took him to London.
Pride forbade him to return home a failure. In 1770, in his eighteenth
year – starving, possibly riddled with venereal disease, and in despair – he
poisoned himself with arsenic in a rented room in Holborn.

His ambition, talent and pride were frustrated at each endeavour, perhaps because he started off on the wrong, borrowed medieval foot: his own feet would have carried him far. He could find no peer in Bristol to converse with. There his forgeries were admired as antique manuscripts, not as poems. He could find no patron. Grub Street exploited his energy but not his genius. Yet he had achieved the 'Rowley' poems. Was he a 'native' or 'born' poet? Romantic writers needed to believe in such creatures. Coleridge pointed out in a note on 'Resolution and Independence' that Wordsworth could name only two 'natural poets': Chatterton and Burns.

Chatterton's invention of Sir Thomas Rowley, fifteenth-century 'Secular Priest of St John', was not perverse. His perverse forgeries consisted in providing 'authentic' pedigrees for drab notables or convenient documents for local historians. Rowley by contrast was a serious enterprise. He has character, a tone of his own quite distinct from Chatterton's in his modern English verse. He lives in an idealised medieval Bristol. Rowley's rank, religious vocation ('The Church of Rome [some Tricks of Priestcraft excepted] is certainly the true Church,' Chatterton wrote in his 'Articles of Belief'), his erudition, all extended Chatterton beyond the cramped, commercially evolving Bristol of the slave trade in which he existed without wealth, status or prospect, and in which he was compelled to observe a faith he found colourless and hypocritical. Rowley was necessary to him; his best poems partake of that necessity.

Forgery was a device for escaping the conventions that checked the genius of Gray and disoriented the work of Young, Smart and Cowper. Macpherson's Ossian, and Walpole's own *The Castle of Otranto* which pretended to be translated from an Italian original, were two of the best-known. A harking back to pre-Renaissance culture, a hankering after 'native' roots and styles kept writers such as Gray and Warton active. An interest in philology and earlier versions of the language was developing.

Chatterton's dramatic instinct allows him not only to describe but to enter the world of Rowley. He owes debts to Shakespeare, and *Aella,* his most sustained Rowley work, though unstageable, is dramatic. His language derives mostly from Chaucer, but his imagination is at home in the sixteenth century. The forgeries are not mosaics of philological plagiarism, any more than Gray's poems are mosaics of poetic plagiarism. They make a solid structure of old- and new-baked bricks. Behind Chatterton's English poems stand Pope, Gay and Swift. Without Rowley Chatterton would have remained a minor Augustan, unless Grub Street had provided him with more than crusts. With Rowley he became an original, using the past as a way of apprehending the world and rejecting the conventions of a narrowed culture.

Keats in the preface to *Endymion* speaks of himself and of adolescence in terms applicable to Chatterton. 'The imagination of a boy is healthy, and the mature imagination of a man is healthy; but there is a space of life between, in which the soul is in ferment, the character undecided, the way of life uncertain, the ambition thick-sighted.' It was in this space that Chatterton perished in a sordidness to which the Romantics imparted tragic glamour.

A story stranger even than Chatterton's, and in its ending sadder, is that of Phillis Wheatley (**109–111**), who – born around 1753 somewhere in Africa (perhaps Senegal) and under a name entirely lost – was transported into slavery in America. She was bought as a child on her arrival in Boston by a tailor, John Wheatley, and reared by him and his wife, whose servant she became. Phillis learned English quickly, then Latin. Her masters introduced her to the poetry of Pope and Gray, to the classics in translation (one gets a sense that she could read Latin, judging from certain allusions and constructions), and at the age of thirteen she was writing religious verse. Her first published poem was an elegy on the death of an evangelical minister, composed when she was seventeen. A prodigy of imitation rather than invention, she travelled to England in 1773 where her first book, *Poems on Various Subjects, Religious and Moral,* was published, with a preface signed by various American men of substance including John Hancock. The Countess of Huntingdon entertained and patronised her in London and was the dedicatee of her book. In America she met with George Washington, to whom she addressed a poem. Her celebrity ended here: returning to Boston, she watched her masters die, and then married a freed slave who succumbed to debtors' prison. She had three children, one of whom survived. She drudged to support the child and herself, then died in 1784; the surviving child followed soon after. Poetry abandoned her in her hardship or, it is truer to say, any poetry she may have written in her later, sketchily charted years has not survived. Those who supported and sponsored her in her early success lost sight of her or perhaps averted their eyes.

Her poems disappoint those seeking, in the first substantial black poet in English (she called herself 'the *Afric* muse'), and the first black woman writing in the language, evidence of her circumstances as a slave, as a woman, as a freed woman. They should not. Their competence is real, their achievement conventional because their occasions were: the deaths of clergymen, other bereavements, poems of gratitude and unbridled praise, mild devotional verse. The work (it *is* work) belongs to a tradition more British than American: there is less of her world in her verse than of Anne Bradstreet's in hers. She does refer to her origins, addressing a poem to another black artist, a painter; and a letter of thanks to the Earl of Dartmouth; an epigram on her origin affirming that 'Negroes, black as Cain / May be refined and join the angelic strain'; but her heroic couplets march along in terms of such generality as to be at most points indistinguishable from other conventional work of the day. Indeed her poem to General Washington, which concludes with the couplet, 'A crown, a mansion, and a throne that shine, / With gold unfading, WASHINGTON! be thine' shows how conventional language could betray an enthusiastic sensibility, how an ideology can inhere in imagery and form when they are not tested against the particulars of experience. Phillis Wheatley is a tragic individual, fascinating, but hardly a harbinger. She does not disappoint if we read her in her own period rather than insist upon the concerns of ours and project those concerns upon her. She is not an anachronism, but this ought not to be laid against her.

For abundant particulars we turn to another Romantic precursor, glamourless George Crabbe, who, unlike Chatterton and Wheatley, survived well into the nineteenth century and, having influenced Wordsworth, lived to learn from him in turn. Wordsworth imitated him in *The Excursion* and Crabbe attempted Wordsworthian blank verse and explored his childhood (*Infancy, A Fragment,* 1816), though by then his best work was done. He very nearly attained the age of eighty. His remorseless vision of human nature and society makes Thomas Hardy seem almost cheerful. His poems chronicle the human condition – or predicament – mercilessly, a sort of Suffolk Zola. His place in the genealogy of Romaticism is assured because of *how* he portrays that condition, and the landscapes through which his characters are led by their lives.

Hazlitt puzzled over his work. 'Mr Crabbe's style might be cited as an answer to Audrey's question – "Is poetry a true thing?" There are here no ornaments, no flights of fancy, no illusions of sentiment, no tinsel of words. His song is one sad reality, one unraised, unvaried note of unavailing woe. Literal fidelity serves him in the place of invention; he assumes importance by a number of petty details; he rivets attention by being tedious.' He continues, with a degree of wry appreciation: 'The world is one vast infirmary; the hill of Parnassus is a penitentiary, of which our author is the overseer: to read him is a penance, yet we read on! Mr Crabbe, it must be confessed, is a reclusive writer. He contrives to "turn diseases to commodities", and makes a virtue of necessity.' Then, again: 'Mr Crabbe gives us one part of nature, the mean, the little, the disgusting, the distressing ... he does this thoroughly and like a master, and we forgive him all the rest.' We *do* read on; once we develop a taste for his characters, his world and its sombre tonalities, we do forgive him.

Doctor Johnson was able to admire him, even against the grain of his natural prejudice against plain style. Crabbe kept more or less to the style he devised early *because* it was admired: approbation atrophied and to an extent impeded him. But he could describe nature (not Nature) at every stage of his work with a minuteness and inwardness that set him above Thomson: 'even Thomson describes not so much the naked object as what he sees in his mind's eye, surrounded and glowing with the mild, bland, genial vapours of his brain: – but the adept in Dutch interiors, hovels, and pig-styes must find in Mr Crabbe a man after his own heart.' And indeed Crabbe, given his Suffolk, given the Dutch trade, is the most Dutch of English poets in terms of *depiction*, with a rich palette of dark colours, intoxicating variegations on a small scale, the humble, the apparently trivial. His sourness and misanthropy we make allowance for. 'The situation of a country clergyman is not necessarily favourable to the cultivation of the Muse. He is set down, perhaps, as he thinks, in a small curacy for life, and he takes his revenge by imprisoning the reader's imagination in luckless verse.' So he says, 'Lo! the gay lights of Youth are past – are dead, / But what still deepening clouds of Care survive!' In the twilight of Augustanism Crabbe was doomed to tend a parish remote from the metropolitan heart. He commanded a large readership. Byron declared him 'Though nature's sternest painter yet the best'.

'A provincial Pope' or 'Pope in worsted stockings' are versions which rouse F. R. Leavis to an extravagant defence of a writer who combines novelistic with poetic virtues. He praises Crabbe's use of couplets in dialogue. They are not evidence of 'awkward elegance clothing an incongruous matter': the couplet 'represents, one might say, "reason's self"'. Leavis goes further: 'in the use of description, of nature, and the environment generally, for emotional purposes he surpasses any Romantic.' Here he goes too far. Crabbe *is* a master story-teller, and it is more useful to see him in the poetic narrative tradition of Chaucer than in the novel tradition of his century. In 'Peter Grimes' (114), 'Procrastination' (113), 'The Frank Courtship', 'The Lover's Journey' and elsewhere, the verse connects individual and communal experience, the weathers of the heart and of the world, mental and physical landscapes. There is humour if not wit in some of the portrayals. His originality is dramatic and psychological, accomplished not by formal or stylistic invention, but by conventional skills.

He was born in Aldeburgh, Suffolk, in 1754, son of a collector of salt-duties. His background was not affluent. For his early schooling he went to Bungay and Stowmarket, Suffolk. When he was thirteen he was apprenticed to an apothecary and farmer for three years, then for another three to a surgeon-apothecary. He started writing poems. When he was seventeen he became engaged to Sarah Elmy, but did not marry for eleven years. At the age of twenty one, after working briefly as a labourer, he set up as an apothecary and was appointed surgeon to the poor in Aldeburgh. *Inebriety*, a moral poem modelled on Pope, was his anonymous début. At twenty-two he went to London to advance his medical training, returning there again in 1780 with £5 in his pocket, to make his way as a writer. It was a struggle, and in the unsettled years there he witnessed the anti-Papist Gordon Riots, so terrifyingly evoked by Dickens in *Barnaby Rudge*. He secured Edmund Burke's patronage: Burke attempted to 'civilise' or 'Londonise' the poet but remodelled only the surface: Crabbe was not able to change his spots or willing to disguise his nature. *The Library,* another long poem in the manner of Pope, appeared. Burke introduced him to some of the great men of the day. He was ordained deacon and returned to Aldeburgh as curate in 1782. Shortly after, he was ordained priest and appointed chaplain to the Duke of Rutland at Belvoir Castle.

The Village (112), his first major work, appeared in 1783. Doctor Johnson read, corrected and praised it. It reveals a skilled poet with broadly social concerns and a documentary technique. It is no surprise that Henry Fielding was Crabbe's favourite novelist – a moralist teaching through laughter, his moral categories corresponding to psychological types. Crabbe is a literalist, a portrayer and interpreter rather than a visionary. He does not conceal rural ills 'in tinsel trappings of poetic pride'. His poetry is richer in social detail than Cowper's because his range of experience, of character and of human involvement was greater. A conservative when faced with needless change, he was radical in one respect: he showed what was, before suggesting what ought to be. What was being destroyed – by individuals and by political and commercial interests in the life of the community – was of greater value than what was replacing it. Social issues interested him less than social verities:

> ... cast by fortune on a frowning coast,
> Which neither groves nor happy valleys boast;
> Where other cares than those the Muse relates,
> And other shepherds dwell with other mates;
> By such example taught, I paint the cot
> As Truth will paint it, and as Bards will not ...

Of the poor he asks, 'Can poets soothe you, when you pine for bread, / By winding myrtles round your ruined shed?' In the first book of *The Village* he expresses firmly, if repetitiously, a poetic commitment to which he remained true, by and large, in his later work. His craft improved, his concerns became more profound as they became more particular, but his orientation was constant. He can be 'old fashioned' but seldom nostalgic.

In 1785 he became curate of Stathern, Leicestershire, was doctor to the poor of the parish, and studied botany and entomology, work useful in his later poetry and which he published separately (in 1795). In 1789 he moved to the living of Muston, Leicestershire, where he stayed for three years before moving back to Suffolk, and which he kept until 1814, returning in 1805 when laws against absentee clergy were passed. About 1790 he began taking opium on doctor's orders to control vertigo and continued the practice for the rest of his life, whose length and general health he attributed to the virtues of the 'medicine'. His wife's manic-depressive illness, the death of his third son and other troubles afflicted him. He went through a period of abortive activity, wrote and destroyed three novels, began work on *The Parish Register* (1807) and *The Borough* (1810). In *The Parish Register* he found the voice that distinguishes his best work. In *The Borough* he went further, writing twenty-four 'letter' poems about the life of a country town. The twenty-two year gap in poetic publication was not time wasted. After so many false starts he found his pace and manner: *Tales* (1812), including twenty-one stories in various tones on various subjects, is his masterpiece.

After the death of his wife (1813) and with the growing success of his books, his remaining years were active but not fruitful. He met other writers, including Wordsworth (to whom Francis Jeffrey had preferred him in the *Edinburgh Review*), Southey and Scott. He travelled, he wrote further poems and tales, but even the once popular *Tales of the Hall* (1819) is inferior to *Tales* (1812). In 1832 he died in Trowbridge. His son George was his excellent first biographer, his account now unaccountably neglected.

Crabbe's final years were passed in a world remote from the one that had shaped his imagination. Leavis declares he was 'hardly at the fine point of consciousness in his time'. C. H. Sisson responded, 'What an excellent thing not to have been! How many false hopes did this solid and pertinacious observer decline to share!' Thomson was the sort of poet who kept 'at the fine point of consciousness' doggedly, forgettably. Crabbe's provincial conservatism no longer requires apology. The ills he recognised have worked themselves into human consequences which writers 'at the fine point' fail to register. Crabbe was no prophet, but in Suffolk he could see before his eyes depopulation, enclosure, grinding poverty, corruption among the gentry and by the gentry of the poor, mental illness, breakdown in community, the triumph of Methodism (which ate into his own congregations). It was a world against which John Clare contended, at a different level. Crabbe was a witness, honest and uncompromised.

He was born in the same decade as Blake and Burns; his first writings appeared five years after the publication of Goldsmith's 'The Deserted Village'; his verses were adjusted and blotted by Johnson; he met, influenced, and was influenced by Wordsworth; he survived Keats by eleven years. The only other British poet who provides so impressive a time-bridge is Michael Drayton (1563–1631). But while Drayton remade his art with each change of fashion. Crabbe did not.

Novelists admire Crabbe, Jane Austen and E. M. Forster most fondly. But the connection between his and a novelist's art is tenuous. The general scope of the *Tales* is novelistic but the individual scope of each tale is not. Each is different in manner and intention; they share a landscape, but that landscape alters from tale to tale. In the mature tales, morality is explored through plot, and in several it is less morality than psychology that interests him. The consequences of action are social or personal, in any event moral, tending to particular rather than general resolutions. In his compressed style, his affinity with Chaucer and his distance from the novelists of his time clearly emerges. Lovers pass through a landscape which smiles, each detail illuminating an aspect of their happiness; when love founders, they return through the same landscape as through another world, altered, frowning. Crabbe's precise correspondences are the essence of his originality. In 'Procrastination' (113), the objects with which people surround themselves define their characters; moral abstraction acquires physical weight:

> Within that fair apartment, guests might see
> The comforts culled for wealth by vanity:
> Around the room an Indian paper blazed,
> With lively tint and figures boldly raised;
> Silky and soft upon the floor below,
> Th' elastic carpet rose with crimson glow ...

The objects blaze, rise, glow – animated, as in Keats' 'The Eve of St Agnes' – while the inhabitants, surrounded by the spoils of empire, are almost inanimate. Most vivid is the time-piece above the heiress's head:

> A stag's-head crest adorned the pictured case,
> Through the pure crystal shone th' enamelled face;
> And while on brilliants moved the hands of steel,
> It click'd from prayer to prayer, from meal to meal.

The device in the final line recalls Pope, but the effect is purely Crabbe's. Elsewhere a hostess of the new breed (though 'a pale old hag' – Crabbe does not mince words), 'carves the meat, as if the flesh could feel'. Such observation lays character bare. In one of the best poems in *The Borough*, 'Peter Grimes' (114), on which Benjamin Britten based his opera, changing seascapes figure changes in the protagonist's troubled mind, without ever ceasing to correspond to the actual world. In a tale such as this, motive is always clear: Peter Grimes's cruelty to the boys he kills is his vicarious attempt to punish the waywardness of his own youth. His actions are not abstract sadism: they have a psychological reality. A recent biographer, Neil Powell, suggests that the story is rooted in the poet's own childhood, the character of Grimes being an echo of his father. Crabbe's is, in any case, a poetry of consequences.

He did not achieve the best tales easily. He advanced from an early Pope-like rigidity of narrative and description to a more relaxed, comprehensive manner. His concerns, at first documentary, became social and then individual – a movement towards character, but always from a firm apprehension of a given, common world. The moraliser becomes a moralist as the tales learn to contain, in a single statement, morality and psychology. Sequence gives way to careful parallelisms, and within a single tale verbal, syntactical and rhythmic repetitions prepare the way for climaxes, reversals and conclusions, as in 'Peter Grimes': 'And hoped to find in some propitious hour / A feeling creature subject to his power', or, 'He'd now the power he ever loved to show, / A feeling creature subject to his blow.'

Crabbe's *Tales* are described by Howard Mills as a 'mixture of inertia and originality'. The language is at times off the peg. We do not look for purple passages or honed couplets. We look through, rather than at, the language, which is efficient, not flashy. We see a Suffolk world through its transparency, not heightened with Augustan decorum but very nearly literal in its drizzle, or dust, or simple twilight.

KILLING DOCTOR JOHNSON

William Blake

'Contest of Bards' (1977) is an idiosyncratic baroque erotic narrative, by-product of several weeks' uninterrupted reading of Blake's complete poetical works.

Allen Ginsberg, 'Apologia of Selection' (1996), *Selected Poems 1947–1995*

'I do not condemn Pope or Dryden because they did not understand imagination, but because they did not understand verse,' says a peremptory William Blake. Robert Graves shares his impatience with the decorous couplet tradition from which Blake vigorously wriggled free. He praises the early *An Island in the Moon* (1784, composed when the poet was twenty seven) as worth 'a thousand prophetic books'; he quotes with relish the cruel lines on Doctor Johnson and the whole Augustan crew. 'The prophetic robe with its woof of meekness and its warp of wrath was forced on [Blake] by loneliness and his modest station in life ...' Edward Thomas is more judicious: 'In his youth, [Blake] had a gift of simple and fair speech; but he lost it. Although he could always catch the heavenly harmony of thoughts' – and here Thomas chooses to ignore the rigours Blake believed he had transcended – 'he could seldom mount them on a fitting chariot of rhythm and rhyme. His fine passages were the direct gift of the Muse, and are followed by lines of other origin.'

Blake is not often *judiciously* read. He polarises readers, eliciting ecstatic enthusiasm from Allen Ginsberg (who, like Blake, 'lost it' in later years) and severe antipathy from poets repelled by the visionary and the Beats. Blake confuses poets – and readers. T. S. Eliot responds in a puzzling way. Speaking of Blake's honesty, a quality peculiar to great poets, he declares: 'It is an honesty against which the whole world conspires, because it is unpleasant.' Well, the *whole* world does not conspire against Blake. For more than half a century the world has seemed to take his side, parroted his aphorisms, adopted the simplifications with which he ridicules traditional discipline, scholarship and the fought-for (as against the asserted) truth. Blake's visionary poems have pumped up their muscles with steroids into a pulsing simulacrum of moral and spiritual health. If we accept their terms we can cast out whole centuries of art and literature and revel in the dubious freedoms of an unbridled century.

Blake's apprenticeship in a manual profession and his self-education, the fact that he was not lured into journalism or into the painting academy, secured his freedom. There was 'nothing to distract him from his interests or to corrupt those interests', says Eliot. Nothing except the limitation of those interests themselves, scorn for a culture that bred a different kind of intelligence, a different – was it a lesser? – order of imagination. Eliot makes a sentimental case against formal education. He distrusts 'the conformity which the accumulation of knowledge is apt to impose'. He portrays learning in this context as corrupting, Blake as an innocent. He humours the tendentious naïf. In the *Songs of Innocence* (**120**) and *Songs of Experience* (**121**), Eliot says, 'The emotions are presented in an extremely simplified, abstract form. This form is one illustration of the eternal struggle of art against education, of the literary artist against the continuous deterioration of language.' Equally curious is Eliot's unsustainable claim: 'He is very like Collins. He is very eighteenth century.'

Eliot praises the early work and the first mature work but can't overcome his distrust of the excesses, the 'automatic' writing of the later work. 'We have the same respect for Blake's philosophy ... that we have for an ingenious piece of home-made furniture: we admire the man who has put it together out of the odds and ends about the house.' This condescension to a poet whose claims he is trying to advance sets the critic on a superior plane. He patronises with the refinement of an education whose clutches he praises Blake for having eluded. There is more confusion to come. Blake is exalted as a free spirit but also as a poet condemned in his freedom. 'What his genius required, and what it sadly lacked, was a framework of accepted and traditional ideas which would have prevented him from indulging in a philosophy of his own, and concentrated his attention upon the problems of the poet.' Eliot is eloquently off beam, and this last point is the most telling. In the end Blake lacks concentration: without stable givens, each idea, each constituent intellectual and imaginative element has to be asserted, set down, before a poem can begin to move. When a musician abandons tonality, he finds his scope altered, but what seems a freedom *from* leads into drastically narrowed technical terrain. Eliot compares Blake implausibly with the luminous Friedrich Nietzsche of *Also Sprach Zarathustra*.

The visionary poet commences his career with electrifying clarity.

For mercy has a human heart,
Pity a human face:
And love, the human form divine,
And peace, the human dress.

This is the best of him, arch-poet of embodiment who strives to bring abstractions before our eyes as manifest, just as he allows us to glimpse, all too fleetingly, the streets and green places of a London undergoing dramatic change, the London where he spent all but three years of his life.

He was born there in 1757, and there seventy years later he died. His father was a haberdasher. What formal education he received was in art: he became an engraver's apprentice and studied at the Royal Academy of Art. His graphic work is integral to his literary activity, and his literary activity invariably has spiritual dimensions, or pretensions. Even as a child he had visions. 'Ezekiel sitting under a green bough' and – in Peckham – 'a tree full of angels'. These figures stayed with him. And he became a vision for later poets, most vocal among them Allen Ginsberg.

The young Blake pursued his own passions in reading; he followed no Augustan curriculum. When he was twenty-four he married the illiterate Catherine Boucher, daughter of a market gardener. He taught her to read and she became his assistant in etching and binding. His first book was *Poetical Sketches* (1788). He etched, watercoloured and bound most of his other books: *Songs of Innocence* and *The Book of Thel* (1789), *The Marriage of Heaven and Hell* and *The Gates of Paradise* (1793), *Visions of the Daughters of Albion, Europe, Songs of Experience* and *The Book of Ahania* (1795) and others. Later large ventures were *Milton* (1804–8) and *Jerusalem* (1804–20).

At the suggestion of his painter friend John Flaxman, William Hayley invited Blake and his wife to Felpham on the Sussex coast in 1800. Hayley, the autobiographer and poet-biographer of Milton and Cowper, gave him three years' work as an illustrator. The arrangement went badly wrong. Hayley chose an artist of greater imaginative integrity than he had bargained for. He tried to bring Blake to heel artistically in various ways – after all, he was paying the bills – but Blake could not oblige for long. Whatever the Blakes eventually came to feel about Hayley, a friend of Cowper and Southey, they enjoyed Felpham and the sea: it was their one extended stay outside the metropolis. In 1803 an infamous soldier turned up in the Felpham garden and sealed their fate. The gardener asked the soldier to cut the grass. Blake disliked soldiers and ordered him off, cursing (among others) the King, and speaking of Napoleon in terms insufficiently hostile. When he was tried on a charge of high treason at Chichester in 1804, he was acquitted thanks to Hayley's testimony. Thus ended the Blakes' not entirely unhappy seaside idyll.

As poet-illustrator Blake was too startlingly original to attract many admirers at the time. The neglect of his poetry became virtual oblivion after his death in 1827, and only Alexander Gilchrist's *Life,* completed by his wife Anne and published two years after his death (1863) revived interest. (Anne wrote essays on Whitman's poetry, too: her ears were open to the new cadences.) Since the *Life* Blake's reputation has burgeoned.

In his last twenty-odd years, when he had occasional acolytes but no settled readership, intellectual isolation may have determined the development of his writing. F. R. Leavis remarks, 'he had no public: he very early gave up publishing in any serious sense. One obvious consequence, or aspect, of this knowledge is the carelessness that is so apparent in the later prophetic books. Blake had ceased to be capable of taking enough trouble.' This isn't quite right. Judging by the manuscripts, Blake took considerable trouble; but trouble of an odd sort. Leavis rightly points to 'the absence . . . of adequate social collaboration'. He is also right to say that Blake's 'symbolic philosophy is one thing, his poetry another'. The more pronounced the philosophy, especially in the prophetic books, the more opaque and poetically inert the symbolism. Blake's best poems work despite his symbolic philosophy.

Yet his genius produced that philosophy which hates the word 'philosophy'; it generated what Leavis calls 'a completely and uncompromisingly individual idiom and technique', rendering the poet 'individual, original, and isolated enough to be without influence' – in his own age, in any case. This genius limited his large work. For all but the *aficionado*, Eliot's verdict on the prophetic books rings true: 'You cannot create a very large poem without introducing a more impersonal point of view, or splitting it up into various personalities. But the weakness of the long poems is certainly not that they are too visionary, too remote from the world. It is that Blake did not see enough, became too much occupied with ideas.' Eliot perceives in Blake a loss of cultural and philosophical bearings, an eccentricity that ends in solipsism. Crabbe, a lesser poet, is a better teacher, at least about the world we *actually* inhabit. His ghost would never have strayed into Allen Ginsberg's reverie or answered the call of Dexedrine: he would have been in the street outside, doggedly observing the lives of passers-by.

Blake's prophetic and biblical pretensions are clear from his titles: 'The Book of' this or that, and even 'Songs' suggest Old Testament prophets and King David. Biblical reference, allusion and cadence inform his work even when he tilts at conventional religion. Disillusion schooled him. Like Wordsworth, he regrets the direction the French Revolution took. Between *Songs of Innocence* (1789) and *Songs of Experience* (1794) his social optimism faltered. Innocence speaks with a voice all transcendence, Experience with a voice incapable of transcendence. Behind Blake's poems is an apprehended social reality, he is conscious of evils and injustices in the ways of man to man. When he approaches such themes directly, as in 'London' (**121h**), he is among the first and fiercest poets of the modern city. In his prophetic books he translates perceived reality away from direct presentation, into a symbolism which sets out grandly to effect a process of regeneration. But the regeneration is itself symbolic: the actual world above which it hovers is perplexed but untouched by it. Blake, when he is 'timeless', becomes oblique, a poet demanding exegesis. His earlier work possesses immediacy which the older Blake forfeits for a brocade of symbols.

From his first *Sketches,* he has his own tone and method. In rejecting 'imitation' of form and perception he established his originality. 'An Imitation of Spenser' is quite un-Spenserian. He experiments with an archaic mode, looking for a way out of the eighteenth century: 'That wisdom may descend in faery dreams.' The imitation fails because mythology and archaised language do not answer his needs. Eliot overstates the affinity between Blake and his eighteenth century. There are common epithets and strategies, but what is striking is Blake's original formal imagination and his freedom from conventional diction.

Imitation is the shadow of a shadow; art for Blake is *creation*. What the eye sees as real *is* real, whether simple raincloud or the weeping child within the cloud. Blake's best poetry is a seeing and seeing into, with unconventional eyes. He does not describe, he projects. Man's divine part is his ability to create, a faculty Blake exercised for over half a century. He sees what is and what is implicit. He rejects prescribed forms as part and parcel of his rejection of social institutions. In *The Book of Thel* (**119**) he declares that Wisdom cannot be contained or simplified in 'a silver rod' nor Love in 'a golden bowl', both ecclesiastical and sacramental allusions. The lines from *Thel* were originally included in *Tiriel,* a cry against the tyranny man imposes on man.

Remarkable among the early *Sketches* ('the production of untutored youth, commenced in his twelfth, and occasionally resumed by the author till his twentieth year') is 'To Autumn' (**115**). Here he proposes a collaborative relationship with Nature:

> O autumn, laden with fruit, and stained
> With the blood of the grape, pass not, but sit
> Beneath my shady roof; there thou may'st rest,
> And tune thy jolly voice to my fresh pipe;
> And all the daughters of the year shall dance!
> Sing now the lusty song of fruits and flowers.

The conventional pastoral of a city boy becomes original poetry in the wonderfully paced second line. Autumn becomes a figure, walking, stained with autumnal juice. Is it sacrificial or Dionysian? The fifth line suggests the latter. The poem continues:

> 'The narrow bud opens her beauties to
> The sun, and love runs in her thrilling veins;
> Blossoms hang round the brows of morning, and
> Flourish down the bright cheek of modest eve,

Till clust'ring summer breaks forth into singing,
And feathered clouds strew flowers round her head.

'The spirits of the air live on the smells
Of fruit; and joy, with pinions light, roves round
The gardens, or sits singing in the trees.'
Thus sang the jolly Autumn as he sat;
Then rose, girded himself, and o'er the bleak
Hills fled from our sight; but left his golden load.

Autumn sings through a young poet. Love, a substance flowing in the veins of flowers, is contained in imagery, not abstracted from it. Nature has an aspect: 'brow', 'cheek'. The clouds are 'feathered' and active, strewing not rain but (the effect of rain on plants displaces the rain itself) flowers, and the 'singing' of the line before turns clouds into birds. No simile is used: Blake evokes equivalences, connections, a natural wholeness. What in another poet would be abstraction in early Blake breathes the air, though it would be impossible to paraphrase, or to draw a diagram of the scene. The images are visionary and transparent.

If the poem is conceptually impressive, prosodically it could hardly be more interesting. The enjambements throughout, but especially in the first line of the second stanza, dramatically affect ear and eye, enhancing the surprise of the vision. Other *Sketches* suffer from an excess of adjectives. Here adjectives pull their weight. Syntactical and rhythmic parallelism from stanza to stanza produces the effect of rhyme, though the poem is unrhymed. There is 'through rhythm' but no metrical regularity despite the blank verse norm it plays away from.

Soon after completing the *Sketches,* Blake annotated Swedenborg's *Divine Love.* We love what contains us most, what is most human, a dog more than a wolf. The poet leads the reader to love, the end of the golden chain that leads to Eden. 'Think', Blake writes, 'of a white cloud as being holy, you cannot love it, but think of a holy man within the cloud, love springs up in your thoughts, for to think of holiness distinct from man is impossible to the affections. Thought alone can make monsters, but the affections cannot.' Around this time he put an infant in a cloud in the introduction to *Songs of Innocence,* a poem that recalls the procedure of 'To Autumn'. When the child in the cloud weeps, with pity rather than sorrow, we are a little disconcerted by such rain; and the cutting of the reed or pipe and the making of a pen are equally perplexing. The poet forfeits a measure of independence when he consents (it is consent, unlike the introduction to *Songs of Experience* with its imperative 'Hear the voice of the Bard!') to write. In *The Marriage of Heaven and Hell* Blake says, 'the Poet is Independent and Wicked, the Philosopher Dependent and Good'. The poet should be his own law, creating the world in which he walks. For him the world is an extension of the senses; he proceeds from sense to vision. The grandest poetry, Blake says, is immoral, as are the greatest heroes: Iago, Satan, Christ 'the wine bibber'. When he set Milton in the devil's camp he was praising the poet who outshone the theologian, his Satan over his God.

Annotating Wordsworth, Blake gives further evidence of the process of his imagination. Physical objects, he says, are at variance with the imagination: objects do not exist apart from perception. When we adapt this statement to Blake's imagery, we resolve a problem. Many of his images are deflected from particularity into abstraction. In the opening of *The Marriage of Heaven and Hell* (123), however, his imaginative process is vividly demonstrated:

> Once meek, and in a perilous path,
> The just man kept his course along
> The vale of death.
> Roses are planted where thorns grow,
> And on the barren heath
> Sing the honey bees.

The first three lines are figurative, moral language; the three that follow are images. Figurative and particular correspond rhythmically; rhyme connects 'vale of death' with 'barren heath'; and parallelism connects the rose and the meek man, the honey bees and the just man. The images body forth the figurative language. Here Blake does not deflect image into abstraction: he segregates two registers of language, bodiless and embodying. His language enacts the division between heaven (the word) and hell (the substance). In the stanzas that follow he mingles and then re-segregates registers in pursuit of the theme.

In his best work he avoids simile unless its point of reference is contained in the poem. For example, in 'The Echoing Green' he writes in line 26, 'like birds in their nests', recalling 'skylark and the thrush' earlier in the poem. He distrusts similes because they single out qualities – moral or otherwise – from a subject and the thing to which it is compared. Simile *disembodies* and is at variance with his vision. 'Ah! Sunflower' and 'The Sick Rose' are not referred back to human experience; they include it. Lamb and Tiger are not equated with Christ, though they include him.

Blake's allegiance to the plain language of the King James Bible, his innocence of rigorous eighteenth-century diction and convention, and his social vision made it possible for him to write balladic lyrics ('The Little Black Boy', both poems entitled 'The Chimney Sweeper', and others) in an idiom more direct than Wordsworth's in his more studied ballads. The effortlessness of *Songs of Innocence* and *Songs of Experience* proceeds from a sensibility untroubled by decorum, and from a rhythmic tact that takes his poems directly to the pulse. They work at the deep level from which 'Lycidas', 'A Song to David', 'Kubla Khan', and very few other poems reach us.

In both sequences the subject-matter is similar. Tone, emphasis and conclusions differ. Innocence does not understand beyond its Innocence (though what *is* beyond hovers near, as in 'A Blossom', 'The Echoing Green', 'The Chimney Sweeper'); Experience is melancholy because it remembers but no longer possesses Innocence. Yet in the Experience poems positive powers are at work in the gloom, as in 'Holy Thursday' and 'The Lily'.

Auguries of Innocence carries Blake's aphoristic wisdom to extremes in a couplet monotony unrelieved by effective enjambement. The couplets, separately, are striking paradoxes; taken together they detract from one another. The poem asks to be read as a polemical creed, with all that that implies of wilful devising. There is none of the transparency of the *Songs*. No couplets were ever less Augustan, despite metre and paradox. The paradoxes are (intentionally) discontinuous.

Among the prophetic books, *The Book of Thel* – an early composition – is the most poetically lucid. It too considers innocence and experience from an original perspective. The unborn soul foresees her life and looks back from her grave. She travels through various states of creative innocence, symbolised successively by lily, cloud, worm and clod. Each, with its limits, terrifies free unborn Thel. She rejects such life, unable to comprehend the 'curb upon the youthful burning boy' and the 'little curtain of flesh on the bed of our desire'. But *The Book of Thel* is not satisfactory. It demands exegesis in terms of Blake's symbolic philosophy. So does *Urizen,* which enacts a process of reduction, from unlimited potential to human and natural bonds. 'Like a human heart, struggling and beating, / The vast world of Urizen appeared' – but that world is by stages constrained, dwindling to the one-dimensional world of Ulro. Part of the concluding section is power-ful and succinct:

> They lived a period of years;
> Then left a noisome body
> To the jaws of devouring darkness.

The giants themselves diminish, their progeny are pygmies: in short, philo-sophers:

> And their children wept, and built
> Tombs in the desolate places,
> And found laws of prudence and called them
> The eternal laws of God.

They become the creatures of 'non-entity' frequently evoked, particularly in *Los*.

For Blake, liberty, a state of mind and spirit, entails the ability to create. His philosophy connects with this belief. There are four states of perception, the highest with four dimensions: in descending order, Eden, Beulah, Generation and Ulro. Four antitheses rule the development of the prophetic books: imagination and memory; innocence and experience in religion; liberty and tyranny in society; outline and imitation in art – each pair, as Northrop Frye notes, is a variation on the antithesis of life and death. Yet knowledge of Blake's scheme, or explication of figures, does not improve the poetry. If a poem lives on a primary level, knowledge and explication perfect understanding; without communication to the mind or senses, a poem becomes a game for exegetes.

Like the philosophies he rejects, his own philosophy obscures what was visible before and distorts the real. *Milton* (**123**) opens with four of his best and best-known quatrains, sung by the Women's Institute and by the nation: 'And did those feet in ancient times . . .' He urges 'mental fight'. Yet the prophetic chapters that follow are a poetic disappointment, quite apart from their philosophy. We feel the same disappointment in *Jerusalem*, despite electrifying lines, for example, 'Trembling she wept over the space and closed it with a tender moon.' The later prophetic books are scattered with such moments but undercut by a rhetorical and philosophical scheme that corresponds remotely to the world it would illuminate. Failure of clarity is a failure of thought. Did Blake despair of an audience and write to expand his own consciousness, or that of his friends the angels? These works have served the careers of many critics and scholars. 'In a Commercial Nation impostors are abroad in every profession.' They have answered to a number of modern causes because they will accommodate a variety of contradictory interpretations. 'Thought alone can make monsters.' Blake forgot that early wisdom.

HUMBLE TRUTH

James Macpherson, Robert Burns

'I was with Wilson, my printer, t'other day, and settled all our bygone matters
between us. After I had paid him all demands, I made him the offer of the
second edition [of *Poems, Chiefly in the Scottish Dialect* (1786)], on the hazard
of being paid out of the first and readiest, which he declines . . . By his account,
the paper of a thousand copies would cost about twenty-seven pounds, and
the printing about fifteen or sixteen: he offers to agree to this for the printing,
if I will advance for the paper, but this you know is out of my power; so
farewell hopes of a second edition till I grow richer! an epocha which, I think,
will arrive at the payment of the British national debt.'

Robert Burns, from a letter to Robert Aiken

The achievement of the fifteenth-century Scottish Makars was almost out
of memory when James Macpherson (1736–1796), inventor of the Gaelic
poet Ossian and the most successful forger in British poetry, burst on a
jaded eighteenth-century world. He did not meet with universal acclaim.
Oliver Goldsmith found the writing vacuous: 'Macpherson write[s]
bombast and call[s] it a style.' The apparent energies of his translations for
others seemed to mark a new beginning for a distinctly Scottish literature.
Twenty-three years after Macpherson was born, and without his social or
material advantages, a genuinely new force emerged, speaking and singing
not in pseudo-Gaelic but in English and in the dialect of his part of Scotland.
This poet lived hard and died poor at thirty-seven – the same year that
Macpherson's remains were ceremoniously deposited, at his request, in
Westminster Abbey.

Of the eighteenth-century poets, Robert Burns is most out of place. He
belongs among the Romantics, not because they romanticised him but
because he emancipated himself from Augustan language and decorum as
decisively as Blake did, not by means of madness or through the agency of
angels but by listening to the traditional songs and poems of common
people and daring to write in their language, which is to say, his own. 'By
our own spirits are we deified', to follow Wordsworth a line further. He and
his sister Dorothy visited Burns's last home and his grave in a spirit, to

judge from Dorothy's letter, of tutting melancholy. The poet, only six years dead and yet undeified, lacked a respectful headstone.

For Coleridge, Burns was 'Nature's own beloved bard', and '*always-natural* poet'. Edward Thomas quotes a poem of his and says: 'It is as near to the music as nonsense could be, and yet it is perfect sense.' His poetry is a relief because he uses language not according to rules but according to deeper laws. 'Spirit and body are one in it – so sweet and free is the body and so well satisfied is the spirit to inhabit it.' The poems 'seem almost always to be the immediate fruit of a definite and particular occasion'. They remain true to an occasion by remaining true to its speakers.

Burns was so successful (though he tasted few material fruits of his success) that for many he stands for the whole of Scottish poetry. With Burns Nights to celebrate his memory each year in Scotland, Moscow ('That Man to Man the warld o'er, / Shall brothers be for a' that') and Chicago, with a Burns industry which has (it is not his fault) cast a tartan haze over the whole literature of his country, it is no surprise that Scottish writers keen to revive their poetry in the twentieth century, after the inertia of the nineteenth, should lay so many literary and cultural ills at his door. His most vehement detractor is Hugh MacDiarmid. 'The highest flights of [Burns] – from any high European standard of poetry – may seem like the lamentable efforts of a hen at soaring; no great name in literature holds its place so completely from extra-literary causes as does that of Robert Burns.' It is true that Burns has been appropriated by the heritage industry. He is sanitised, bowdlerised, sentimentalised. If we turn away from this, and from MacDiarmid's corrective verdict, to the poems, we do not need to reserve judgement. This is not the work of a chicken Icarus:

> O wert thou in the cauld blast,
>   On yonder lea, on yonder lea,
> My plaidie to the angry airt
>   I'd shelter thee, I'd shelter thee.

Keats had a more complex view of Burns than Wordsworth did and was more generous than MacDiarmid. In 'On Visiting the Tomb of Burns' he writes:

> All is cold Beauty; pain is never done:
> For who has mind to relish, Minos-wise,
>   The Real of Beauty, free from that dead hue
>   Sickly imagination and sick pride
>   Cast wan upon it! Burns! With honour due
>   I oft have honour'd thee. Great shadow, hide
> Thy face; I sin against thy native skies.

Writing to Reynolds from Scotland Keats says, 'One song of Burns is of more worth to you than all I could think of for a whole year in his native country. His Misery is a dead weight on the nimbleness of one's quill . . . he talked with Bitches – he drank with blackguards, he was miserable. We can see horribly clear in the works of such a Man his whole life, as if we were God's spies.' Yet neither misery nor joy characterises the work. He is sufficiently of his century to find more interest in man, his foibles, his institutions, his ballads, than in mere personal revelation or natural description. Byron, less drawn than Keats to the accidents of his biography, valued the lucid pathos of the poet, and something more. 'What an antithetical mind! – tenderness, roughness – delicacy, coarseness – sentiment, sensuality – soaring and grovelling, dirt and deity – all mixed up in one compound of inspired clay!' Matthew Arnold in 1880 wrote a warm appreciation of his comic and satirical work, criticising the sentimental poems. His assessment was crucial in the re-appraisal of Burns's merits. The modernists – MacDiarmid excepted – generally ignored him.

There is a political version of Burns. Radicals English, Scottish and European have set up a bronze bust, emphasising the anticlerical satires, the tilting against hypocrisy and rank, the 'egalitarianism'. Burns's life attracts them: it does little credit to the Scottish bourgeoisie and gentry. His sympathy for the American and French revolutions adds to his *usefulness*. His appeal in the Soviet Union was partly explained by this. In 'Scots Wha Hae' he wrote:

> By Oppression's woes and pains,
> By your sons in servile chains,
> We will drain our dearest veins,
>   But they shall be free!

In more familiar manner he says, in 'For a' that' (**139**),

> Is there, for honest poverty
>   That hings° his head, an' a' that?   *hangs*
> The coward-slave, we pass him by –
>   We dare be poor for a' that!
> For a' that, an' a' that,
>   Our toils obscure, and a' that,
> The rank is but the guinea's stamp,
>   The man's the gowd° for a' that   *gold*

The version of Burns which irked MacDiarmid, who led the Scottish renaissance with the cry, 'Not Burns – Dunbar!', was the one which read the poet in narrow chauvinistic terms. Scottish expatriates and nostalgic

Scots at home championed him with what Arnold called 'national partiality'. And in MacDiarmid's view Burns's rural and ballad poetry in Scottish dialect set a disastrous example for a century of dialect poets who imitated what had become an outmoded idiom and subject-matter, perpetuating an anachronism and producing a linguistic and cultural caricature. Burns answers to each partial description and includes rather more than their sum. He wrote over six hundred poems; his formal, tonal and thematic range is greater than that of his Scottish predecessors and most of his English contemporaries.

He was born in Alloway, Ayrshire, in 1759, into the family of a tenant farmer, an event the poet later commemorated in 'There was a lad was born in Kyle'. The gossip in the poem predicts, 'He'll be a credit till us a''; that he'd have a lively future among the ladies (which he did). Burns's father and neighbours, though poor, had a respect for learning and hired a tutor to see to their children's schooling. Later, the father himself undertook to teach them. At the age of fifteen, working on his father's farm, he wrote his first verses. His Latin was indifferent, but he was well-read in the English poets and understood French enough to read Racine. The Scots poetry of Allan Ramsay suggested to him the possibilities of dialect. Robert Fergusson's Scots verse proved the eventual catalyst: after reading it, Burns began his 'demotic' career in earnest, but he was already that way inclined. At sixteen he wrote,

> O once I loved a bonnie lass,
>> An' aye I love her still,
> An whilst that virtue warms my breast
>> I'll love my handsome Nell.

Nell was Nelly Kirkpatrick, and he noted: 'For my own part I never had the least thought or inclination of turning poet till I got once heartily in Love, and then Rhyme and Song were, in a manner, the spontaneous language of my heart.' He had a native tradition and a native tongue. To Fergusson he addressed three poems, largely about that poet's (and perhaps his own) hardships and neglect: 'Curse on ungrateful man, that can be pleas'd, / And yet can starve the author of the pleasure.' Burns's English poems have merit, but pale beside the Scots writing. He knew this himself: 'These English songs gravel me to death,' he wrote. 'I have not the command of the language that I have of my native tongue. In fact, I think that my ideas are more barren in English than in Scotch.' His attempts to 'translate' his poems were fruitless.

The key year in Burns's poetic career was 1786, when the Kilmarnock edition of *Poems Chiefly in the Scottish Dialect* was published. In the years between the poet watched his father's death in 1784, a year after his bankruptcy. Burns was now provider and head of the family. His mother's servant Betty Paton gave him his first child out of wedlock in 1785, a daughter.

> Tho' now they ca' me, Fornicator,
> And tease my name in kintra clatter°,   *country gossip*
> The mair they talk, I'm kend the better;
>   E'en let them clash!
> An auld wife's tongue's a feckless° matter   *worthless*
> To gie ane fash°.   *trouble*

He also composed 'The Fornicator. A New Song'. 'The rantin dog the Daddie o't' is a song put in the mouth of Betty. Throughout his work we find songs of a sexual frankness and jollity as outspoken as some of the poems of the Restoration, and yet a good deal more down-to-earth than those. Eighteenth-century Scotland might at first seem an unlikely environment for them.

In 1785 Burns met Jean Armour, whom he married in 1788 after she had borne him two sets of twins. His brilliant satirical attacks on Calvinism begin at the time of her pregnancy. In the same month in which *Poems* was published the Calvinists took revenge and exacted from him a public penance for fornication with Jean. He was tempted to emigrate with another girl, composing poems about his planned departure. The gossips were right; he had a complicated and thorough love-life.

Poems proved a success; the next year a second, enlarged edition was published. Both versions omitted the church satires and included instead more general satirical pieces. Apart from the church satires, the *Poems* contain the core of his original work. Most of it was composed in 1785 and early 1786 – a remarkable production, including 'To a Mountain Daisy', 'Halloween', 'The Address to the Deil' (**136**), 'To a Mouse' (**137**), 'To a Louse' (**129**), 'The Cottar's Saturday Night', the best epistles, 'The Twa Dogs' and many others satires, pious pieces, dramatic monologues, mock-elegies, songs, lyrics and flytings. The poet was twenty-six. Four years later he wrote 'Tam O'Shanter' (**138**), completing his important original work. He wrote more poems but his chief labour thereafter was to collect and publish Scottish folk songs and ballads.

Literary Edinburgh took him up – no doubt as one who 'walked in glory and in joy / Behind his plough', a role he found it hard to sustain without big doses of alcohol and the camaraderie of low types. As a result, literary Edinburgh in general put him down again. Sir Walter Scott as a boy of fifteen saw the poet and recalled his 'manners rustic, not clownish', his 'massive' countenance, his shrewd look: 'The eye alone indicated the poetical character and temperament. It was large, and of a dark cast, and literally glowed when he spoke with feeling and interest.' Lord Glencairn and Mrs Dunlop became his patrons and friends. His admirers secured him a post in the Excise Division in Dumfries and rented a farm for him. He worked hard, investing his imaginative energy in collecting and revising material for *The Scots Musical Museum* (1787–1803) and the *Select Collection of Original Scottish Airs* (1793–1818). He travelled, gave up farming, was promoted in the Excise Division. His work took him out in all weathers. He caught rheumatic fever and died in 1796, leaving a wife and a large progeny. Jean was not his only current love. There was Betty; also Mary Campbell, Mrs McLehose ('Clarinda'), and others.

Perhaps he died bitter. Though he had friends and advocates, he was certainly ill-used. He had foibles, could be curmudgeonly and difficult, held firm and outspoken opinions, did not suffer fools. But he hardly deserved the hardships that befell him, or the hostility. Thomas Carlyle in his essay gets the proportions right: 'Granted the ship comes into harbour with shrouds and tackle damaged, the pilot is blameworthy ... but to know how blameworthy, tell us first whether his voyage has been round the globe or only to Ramsgate and the Isle of Dogs.'

Burns's place in Scottish culture is very different from his place in English. Debts to the Augustans are few: the polite tradition of Edinburgh, with some exceptions, was an echo of Dryden and Pope, a world of fixed rules of diction and form. We can see him in connection with English romanticism. But as Donald Davie reminds us, he was 'adopted posthumously'. In reading Wordsworth's and Keats's tributes, do we recognise any but a simulacrum of Burns? Only Byron – another Scot, 'mad, bad and dangerous to know' – heard him more or less clearly. F. R. Leavis goes too far when he suggests Burns 'counts for much in the emancipation represented by the *Lyrical Ballads*'. He counts for something: a comparison between Burns's and Wordsworth's ballads reveals how much and also how little. Arnold precedes Leavis when he writes, 'Wordsworth owed much to Burns, relying for effect solely on the weight and force of that which with entire fidelity he utters, Burns could show him.' Wordsworth's 'At the Grave of Burns' and other poems written on him and his neighbourhood borrow one of the Scottish poet's forms, but not his energy. Wordsworth records a debt:

> He has gone
> Whose light I hailed when first it shone,
>   And showed my youth
> How verse may build a princely throne
>   On humble truth.

A pious moral, more than a poetic lesson learned. Burns might have grimaced at such sanctimony.

Arnold stripped away some of the sentimental gloss. 'Let us coldly say that of much of this poetry, a poetry dealing perpetually with Scotch drink, Scotch religion, and Scotch manners, a Scotchman's estimate is bound to be personal.' Burns's is 'often a harsh, a sordid, a repulsive world' – part of its attraction and also its limitation. Much of the bacchanalian verse is 'poetically unsound', vitiated by a factitious bravado, written in reaction, to shock and amuse, but not to extend or interpret experience. He often lacks 'the high seriousness which comes from absolute sincerity' (which is just as well). One feels this in the poems about fornication and those about drink: defiance in verse is rare, especially difficult to achieve when the poet defies an audience without questioning his own position. Yet there is a great poet in Burns. Arnold compares him to Chaucer: 'Of life and the world, as they came before him, his view is large, free, shrewd, benignant – truly poetic, therefore; and his manner of rendering what he sees is to match.' Unlike Chaucer, he has 'a fiery, reckless energy' and 'an overwhelming sense of the pathos of things'. After all, his great poems were written when he was a young man.

Arnold directs attention to a poem central to Burns, but until then generally neglected, 'The Jolly Beggars'. It has 'hideousness', 'squalor', 'bestiality', 'yet the piece is a superb poetic success. It has a breadth, truth, and power which . . . are only matched by Shakespeare and Aristophanes.' Other good poems possess 'archness and wit' as well as 'shrewdness'. These include 'Duncan Grey', 'Tam Glen', 'Whistle, and I'll come to you my lad', 'Auld Lang Syne' (**135**) – and, no doubt, 'A Red, Red Rose' (**127**), 'Green Grow the Rushes', 'The Banks o' Doon' (**130**), and a score of others.

After reading a lot of Burns we may reluctantly agree with Gerard Manley Hopkins, who wrote in a letter to Robert Bridges of 'a great want' in his utterance. Hopkins defined this a little imprecisely: 'he had no eye for pure beauty', a lack he shares with another equally versatile poet: Dunbar. There is little repose in Burns. The closest he comes to it is in a few lyrics and the epistles, where he addresses one or two and speaks with the candour Arnold described in his essay. In 'Epistle to Davie, a Brother Poet' Burns confesses how sour he is about his own wants, and the unequal distribution of wealth. But he finds consolation in the open air:

What tho', like commoners of air,
We wander out, we know not where,
   But either house or hall?
Yet *Nature's* charms, the hills and woods,
The sweeping vales, the foaming floods,
   Are free alike to all.
In days when daisies deck the ground,
And blackbirds whistle clear,

With honest joy, our hearts will bound,
　To see the *coming* year:
　　On braes when we please then,
　　We'll sit and sowth a tune°;　　　　　　　　　*try a tune with a low whistle*
　Syne rhyme till 't, we'll time till 't,
　　And sing 't when we hae done.

Poetry heads for the open air, having spent half a century working out strategies to free itself from the periwigs and formal patterns, prescriptions and proprieties, arbitrary rules and decorums, that had taken it over. If nowadays we concentrate our reading of the second half of the eighteenth century more on its eccentrics than on those who performed correctly, it is because poetry, as a rule, is more exciting in the breach than in the observance. The periods when rules are being formulated, manacles are being forged, are fascinating, whether those periods are in the fourteenth, sixteenth or late seventeenth and early eighteenth centuries. Once forged, for a time there is a common language and, one is tempted to infer, a common audience. But in time poetry begins to stifle, poets finds themselves unable to say what they want to say, go where they want to go. The little virtues are so dominant that the potential of the larger ones is quite forgotten. Some poets, perhaps not the most educated, the most privileged or the best connected, hanker after the freedom that poetry is actually about: ways of concentrating meaning, feeling, perception, and finding new meanings, feelings and modes of perception through language, or recovering those that the tyranny of convention has dulled and discarded.

Anthology

PREFACE

'Are Dryden and Pope poetical classics? Is the historic estimate, which represents them as such, and which has been so long established that it cannot easily give way, the real estimate?'

Matthew Arnold, 'The Study of Poetry'

John Dryden died in 1700. His mastery of the heroic couplet, the singular efficiency of his satirical, ruminative and essayistic verse, of his translations, plays and the occasional poems and lyrics, stand as a measure to the century that follows, and as a menace to it. Much is gained in precision and economy of expression, in poetic *authority*, but whole registers of language and feeling seem to vanish. The language of poetry becomes an agreed territory, marked by strict decorums, by the refinements of diction, by a politeness of manner which could be savage but could not be direct or passionate. Departure from the norms would be taken to signal a failure of tact and taste. It is as though there is no more room for the rustic cottage, the Tudor and Jacobean mansion, the fluent Perpendicular: everything is made of squared, honey-coloured stone, porticoed, and the really important edifices are frosted with marble.

Dryden devoted part of his time to correcting the literature of the past, and this included refacing the mansions of Chaucer and Shakespeare. One can only correct if there is a measure of correctness, and this is what Dryden sought to provide, by example and in his magisterial essays, great formative documents in the arts of English criticism. Ben Jonson had been a strict master, but Dryden by example and precept becomes an unopposed legislator for poetry. And in his wake follows the even more efficient Alexander Pope; though Pope lacks Dryden's philosophical convictions, his deep religious and political *engagement*, he has an intriguing politics and a fascinating psychology.

In the first half of the eighteenth century, the most influential critics and poets, not to mention the great lexicographer Doctor Samuel Johnson, were building towards cultural stability in the wake of the religious, civil and cultural disruptions of the century before. Language, it seemed to them, could be defined and stabilised, the task of the lexicographer being not, as in modern times, descriptive, following in the wake of language, but prescriptive. The lexicographer affirmed what a word meant, drew a line around its sense, as it were, and gave it a pedigree. The assumption was that, whatever a word had meant in the past, for the present and future it would have a fixed meaning.

Such an approach in effect legislated against the natural development of language as an expressive tool. Not only are words added daily to the resources with which we communicate; the words we use daily evolve and change meaning. Against prescription some poets rebelled for national reasons (Fergusson, for example, as a Scot); others found such legislation offensive to the imagination. In general, those who used language precisely used it ironically as well; that ironic voice is the durable relic of the eighteenth century, a social or class tone which depersonalises or universalises a statement. It can be imitated and acquired and seeks to suggest that the speaker is at once superior and disengaged. In the hands of lesser practitioners it can become a vice. Resistance to this tone marks some of the most distinctive poetry of the period.

One nineteenth-century essay has done much to empty the eighteenth-century reading-room of poetry readers: Matthew Arnold's 'The Study of Poetry'. By winding the century around Dryden (its John the Baptist) and Pope, Arnold produces a brilliantly illuminating and reductive perspective. 'But after the Restoration,' he writes, 'the time had come when our nation felt the imperious need of a fit prose. So, too, the time had likewise come when our nation felt the imperious need of freeing itself from the absorbing preoccupation which religion in the Puritan age had exercised. It was impossible that this freedom should be brought about without some negative excess, without some neglect and impairment of the religious life of the soul; and the spiritual history of the eighteenth century shows us that the freedom was not achieved without them. Still, the freedom was achieved; the preoccupation, an undoubtedly baneful and retarding one if it had continued, was got rid of. And as with religion amongst us at that period, so it was also with letters.' Arnold concludes: 'A fit prose was a necessity; but it was impossible that a fit prose should establish itself amongst us without some touch of frost to the imaginative life of the soul.'

This 'touch of frost' is local, but Arnold has extended it to the whole century and made a kind of permafrost. If we break through it we find that, yes, Pope does evince in his verse what Arnold calls 'the needful qualities for a fit prose', namely, 'regularity, uniformity, precision, balance'. He adds that an 'almost exclusive attention to these qualities involves some repression and silencing of poetry'. In general, readers have nodded assent to this proposition. Those readers have not engaged with the Pope who wrote 'Eloisa to Abelard', 'An Epistle to Dr Arbuthnot', or the scatological, disturbed and disturbing virulence of *The Dunciad*. It is possible to exaggerate the 'regularity, uniformity, precision, balance' in Pope, to mistake the apparent shape and control of the vehicle for the sense itself. What looks like balance is often, in fact, a precariously unstable structure; what looks like regularity often overlies a most irregular human territory. There is precision, but what it is precise about may not be precisely what it appears to *be* about, and there is more deliberate variation in Pope's accomplished couplets than Arnold's account allows.

We should withhold assent from Arnold's resonant conclusion, which deploys the rhetoric of the great sermon-writers of the eighteenth century: 'We are to regard Dryden as the puissant and glorious founder, Pope as the splendid high priest, of our age of prose and reason, of our excellent and indispensable eighteenth century.' He admires their verse, but largely because it has the virtues of prose. We must learn again to admire their poetry because of its *poetic* resourcefulness as well. For Arnold, there are two genuinely poetic voices in the eighteenth century worth attending to: Gray's and Burns's. This limited admission shows how trammelled in decorum Arnold's own age still was. For Pope, Gray and Burns are one measure of the century, but Swift, Watts, Smart, Cowper, Charlotte Smith and Blake are another. And both are, *pace* Arnold, poetic measures. And in Watts, Cowper and Blake there is as much spiritual nutriment as in some of the great poets of the seventeenth century.

Yet we must concede to Arnold that in the eighteenth century there was an acceptable middle voice, the polite man speaking to polite men, and it became possible for lesser writers to compose yards and yards of verse with smooth efficiency, and to be celebrated in the coffee house or in the *Spectator*. Verse composition was a polite, acquirable skill. One had strict rules of diction and form to follow, and whoever observed them could claim the title of poet. There was a market, too, meagre but measurable, for such verse in the magazines and among publishers, a market that, though unstable, made it possible for poets to depend on something other than private patronage. After the wonderful volatilities of the preceding century, the endeavour of many poets was to be to stabilise the language and the market for verse, to bring it wholly within the parameters of the polite, the instructive and serviceable. Poetry turned towards its market, the print-buying public. It was a market in which some poets, Smart, Chatterton and Fergusson among them, spectacularly failed.

The political world, settled into hostile factions whose chosen weapons were the pamphlet, lampoon and satire, had need of verse writers. Verse was instrumental: didactic not only in the essay but in the savage language of satire. A poetry which is instrumental in this way, with butts and quarries in its own time and locality, becomes hard to understand when the memory of ephemeral events and of 'important' men and women subsides. Satire wedded to its age's contingencies becomes incomprehensible unless it is great verse and carries, in the very terms of the satire, a narrative that clarifies its themes. In this respect Swift, Pope and Johnson are transcendent practitioners, rooted as they are in the generic precedents of Roman satire. Romans, not in togas but in periwigs, occupied some of the choicest spots on Parnassus, but English poetry was not all columns and marble.

The purpose of this anthology is to present the poetry of the eighteenth century, to show how it relates to the preceding century, inheriting and re-investing many of its best qualities; and how diverse and rich it is as a period. Readmitting the hymn to the specifically poetic tradition is important, just as re-admitting those portions of the King James Bible which are poetry is important to the preceding century. The hymn belongs to an audience wider than the one addressed by Pope or Collins or Macpherson; it presents to the poet and to the reader an unusual challenge. But there are other unusual challenges which, had he confronted them, would have changed Arnold's sense of the age. The poetry of extreme experience, psychological and spiritual (Gray's, Smart's, Cowper's, Blake's), tests and extends common prejudices about the eighteenth century. The extraordinary qualities of Charlotte Smith's verse raise key questions about the formation of poetic canons and the gender bias that may have accompanied them.

It is a mistake to read backwards, from the nineteenth to the eighteenth century, and apply familiar templates to what is richly unfamiliar. Anthologies which seek the 'roots of romanticism' in Edward Young, Chatterton, Cowper or Blake tend to theorise retrospectively, to impose intentions and discover themes where they do not in fact exist, or do not exist in the forms adduced. Just as Arnold impoverishes the eighteenth century by coming to it with a vivid general preconception, so we diminish Blake, for example, by not holding him steady beside Doctor Johnson and seeing how they work together to define a present rather than to foreshadow a future.

In this anthology, as in the two preceding volumes, I have modernised texts. In the eighteenth century typographical conventions went through various transformations. At one time it was usual for virtually all nouns to be capitalised, whether or not they represented allegorical and symbolic figurations. The lavish use of italics, not necessarily to indicate emphasis, enhanced the appearance of a poem on the page. I have adopted, for the most part, modern conventions of presentation, punctuation and spelling, so as to make the texts consistent with one another (though there are exceptions, as with Smart's and Blake's work, where the idiosyncrasies are sometimes irreducible). In compiling and modernising texts, I have had recourse to various editions. In the case of ballads and hymns, I have endeavoured to work from original and early editions, because the accretion of variants is quite daunting: hymns in particular have an ongoing textual life of their own.

The anthology is intended to be used with the excerpts and whole poems in the Informal History that precedes it. I have represented several of the poets in rather substantial selections, in part because the long poem was often the rule rather than the exception for the Augustan poet, and in part because it helps readers to get their bearings when they have the space in which to do so.

Matthew Prior (1664–1721)

1. A Better Answer to Chloe Jealous

Dear Chloe, how blubbered is that pretty face;
    Thy cheek all on fire, and thy hair all uncurled!
Prithee quit this caprice, and (as old Falstaff says)
    Let us e'en talk a little like folks of this world

How can'st thou presume thou hast leave to destroy   5
    The beauties which Venus but lent to thy keeping?
Those looks were designed to inspire love and joy:
    More ord'nary eyes may serve people for weeping.

To be vexed at a trifle or two that I writ,
    Your judgment at once, and my passion, you wrong: 10
You take that for fact which will scarce be found wit –
    Od's life! must one swear to the truth of a song?

What I speak, my fair Chloe, and what I write, shows
    The diff'rence there is betwixt nature and art:
I court others in verse, but I love thee in prose;   15
    And they have my whimsies, but thou hast my heart.

The god of us verse-men (you know child) the sun,
    How after his journeys he sets up his rest;
If at morning o'er earth 'tis his fancy to run,
    At night he reclines on his Thetis's breast.   20

So when I am wearied with wand'ring all day,
    To thee, my delight, in the evening I come:
No matter what beauties I saw in my way,
    They were but my visits, but thou art my home.

Then finish, dear Chloe, this pastoral war,   25
    And let us like Horace and Lydia agree;
For thou art a girl as much brighter than her,
    As he was a poet sublimer than me.

2. An Ode

The merchant, to secure his treasure,
   Conveys it in a borrowed name:
Euphelia serves to grace my measure;
   But Chloe is my real flame.

My softest verse, my darling lyre   5
   Upon Euphelia's toilet lay:
When Chloe noted her desire,
   That I should sing, that I should play.

My lyre I tune, my voice I raise;
   But with my numbers mix my sighs: 10
And whilst I sing Euphelia's praise,
   I fix my soul on Chloe's eyes.

Fair Chloe blushed: Euphelia frowned:
   I sung and gazed: I played and trembled:
And Venus to the Loves around   15
   Remarked, how ill we all dissembled.

3. To a Lady

She refusing to continue a dispute with me, and leaving me in the argument

Spare, generous victor, spare the slave,
   Who did unequal war pursue,
That more than triumph he might have,
   In being overcome by you.

In the dispute whate'er I said,   5
   My heart was by my tongue belied;
And in my looks you might have read
   How much I argued on your side.

You, far from danger as from fear,
   Might have sustained an open fight: 10
For seldom your opinions err:
   Your eyes are always in the right.

Why, fair one, would you not rely
    On reason's force with beauty's joined?
Could I their prevalence deny,   15
    I must at once be deaf and blind.

Alas! not hoping to subdue,
    I only to the fight aspired:
To keep the beauteous foe in view
    Was all the glory I desired.   20

But she, howe'er of victory sure.
    Contemns the wreath too long delayed;
And, armed with more immediate power,
    Calls cruel silence to her aid.

Deeper to wound, she shuns the fight: 25
    She drops her arms, to gain the field:
Secures her conquest by her flight;
    And triumphs, when she seems to yield.

So when the Parthian turned his steed,
    And from the hostile camp withdrew,   30
With cruel skill the backward reed
    He sent; and as he fled, he slew.

4. A Simile

Dear Thomas, didst thou never pop
Thy head into a tin-man's shop?
There, Thomas, didst thou never see
('Tis but by way of simile)
A squirrel spend his little rage   5
In jumping round a rolling cage?
The cage, as either side turned up,
Striking a ring of bells a-top? –
    Moved in the orb, pleased with the chimes,
The foolish creature thinks he climbs: 10
But here or there, turn wood or wire,
He never gets two inches higher.

So fares it with those merry blades,
That frisk it under Pindus' shades.
In noble songs, and lofty odes,   15
They tread on stars, and talk with gods;
Still dancing in an airy round,
Still pleased with their own verses' sound;
Brought back, how fast soe'er they go,
Always aspiring, always low.   20

5. Two Beggars Disputing their Right to an Oyster they had Found

a Lawyer thus decides the Cause

Blind plaintiff, lame defendant, share
The friendly Law's impartial care.
A shell for him, a shell for thee,
The middle is the lawyer's fee.
So judge's word decrees the people's right,   5
And Magna Carta is a paper kite.

6. On a Fart, Let in the House of Commons

Reader I was born, and cried;
I cracked, I smelt, and so I died.
Like Julius Caesar's was my death,
Who in the senate lost his breath.
Much alike entombed does lie   5
The noble Romulus and I;
And when I died, like Flora fair,
I left the Commonwealth my heir

Jonathan Swift (1667–1745)

7. A Description of the Morning

Now hardly here and there a hackney-coach
Appearing, showed the ruddy morn's approach.
Now Betty from her master's bed had flown,
And softly stole to discompose her own.
The slip-shod 'prentice from his master's door   5
Had pared the dirt, and sprinkled round the floor.
Now Moll had whirled her mop with dext'rous airs,
Prepared to scrub the entry and the stairs.
　The youth with broomy stumps began to trace
The kennel-edge, where wheels had worn the place.   10
The small-coal man was heard with cadence deep;
Till drowned in shriller notes of 'chimney-sweep'.
Duns at his lordship's gate began to meet;
And brickdust Moll had screamed through half a street.
The turnkey now his flock returning sees,   15
Duly let out a-nights to steal for fees.
The watchful bailiffs take their silent stands,
And schoolboys lag with satchels in their hands.

8. Advice to the Grub Street Verse-Writers

Ye poets raggéd and forlorn,
　Down from your garrets haste;
Ye rhymers, dead as soon as born,
　Not yet consigned to paste;
I know a trick to make you thrive;   5
　O, 'tis a quaint device:
Your still-born poems shall revive,
　And scorn to wrap up spice.
Get all your verses printed fair,
　Then let them well be dried;   10

And Curll[1] must have a special care
   To leave the margin wide.
Lend these to paper-sparing Pope;
   And when he sets to write,
No letter with an envelope   15
   Could give him more delight.
When Pope has filled the margins round,
   Why then recall your loan;
Sell them to Curll for fifty pound,
   And swear they are your own.   20

9. On Stella's Birthday

March 13, 1719

Stella this day is thirty-four,
(We shan't dispute a year or more)
However, Stella, be not troubled,
Although thy size and years are doubled,
Since first I saw thee at sixteen,   5
The brightest virgin on the green;
So little is thy form declined,
Made up so largely in thy mind.
   Oh, would it please the gods to split
Thy beauty, size, and years, and wit;   10
No age could furnish out a pair
Of nymphs so graceful, wise, and fair;
With half the lustre of your eyes,
With half your wit, your years, and size.
And then, before it grew too late,   15
How should I beg of gentle Fate,
(That either nymph might have her swain)
To split my worship too in twain.

[1] Edmund Curll (1675–1747), a pamphleteer and bookseller, remembered through the satires of Pope and Swift as a literary fraudster. He was involved with Alexander Pope's own fraud: he got Curll to publish his early correspondence (which Pope had edited to 'adjust the history' and improve the record) and then pretended the book was issued against his wishes, leaving Curll holding the puppy.

10. The Lady's Dressing Room

Five hours, (and who can do it less in?)
By haughty Celia spent in dressing;
The goddess from her chamber issues,
Arrayed in lace, brocades, and tissues.
Strephon, who found the room was void   5
And Betty otherwise employed,
Stole in and took a strict survey
Of all the litter as it lay;
Whereof, to make the matter clear,
An inventory follows here.   10
   And first a dirty smock appeared,
Beneath the arm-pits well besmeared.
Strephon, the rogue, displayed it wide
And turnèd it round on every side.
On such a point few words are best,   15
And Strephon bids us guess the rest;
And swears how damnably the men lie
In calling Celia sweet and cleanly.
Now listen while he next produces
The various combs for various uses,   20
Filled up with dirt so closely fixt,
No brush could force a way betwixt.
A paste of composition rare,
Sweat, dandruff, powder, lead and hair;
A forehead cloth with oil upon't   25
To smooth the wrinkles on her front.
Here alum flower to stop the steams
Exhaled from sour unsavory streams;
There night-gloves made of Tripsy's hide,
Bequeathed by Tripsy when she died,   30
With puppy water, beauty's help,
Distilled from Tripsy's darling whelp;
Here gallypots and vials placed,
Some filled with washes, some with paste,
Some with pomatum, paints and slops,   35
And ointments good for scabby chops.
Hard by a filthy basin stands,
Fouled with the scouring of her hands;
The basin takes whatever comes,
The scrapings of her teeth and gums,   40
A nasty compound of all hues,

For here she spits, and here she spews.
But oh! it turned poor Strephon's bowels,
When he beheld and smelt the towels,
Begummed, besmattered, and beslimed   45
With dirt, and sweat, and ear-wax grimed.
No object Strephon's eye escapes:
Here petticoats in frowzy heaps;
Nor be the handkerchiefs forgot
All varnished o'er with snuff and snot.   50
The stockings, why should I expose,
Stained with the marks of stinking toes;
Or greasy coifs and pinners reeking,
Which Celia slept at least a week in?
A pair of tweezers next he found   55
To pluck her brows in arches round,
Or hairs that sink the forehead low,
Or on her chin like bristles grow.
The virtues we must not let pass,
Of Celia's magnifying glass.   60
When frighted Strephon cast his eye on't
It showed the visage of a giant.
A glass that can to sight disclose
The smallest worm in Celia's nose,
And faithfully direct her nail   65
To squeeze it out from head to tail;
(For catch it nicely by the head,
It must come out alive or dead).
Why Strephon will you tell the rest?
And must you needs describe the chest?   70
That careless wench! no creature warn her
To move it out from yonder corner;
But leave it standing full in sight
For you to exercise your spite.
In vain, the workman showed his wit   75
With rings and hinges counterfeit
To make it seem in this disguise
A cabinet to vulgar eyes;
For Strephon venturèd to look in,
Resolved to go through thick and thin;   80
He lifts the lid, there needs no more:
He smelt it all the time before.
As from within Pandora's box,
When Epimetheus oped the locks,

A sudden universal crew   85
Of humane evils upwards flew,
He still was comforted to find
That Hope at last remained behind;
So Strephon lifting up the lid
To view what in the chest was hid,   90
The vapours flew from out the vent.
But Strephon cautious never meant
The bottom of the pan to grope
And foul his hands in search of Hope.
O never may such vile machine   95
Be once in Celia's chamber seen!
O may she better learn to keep
'Those secrets of the hoary deep'![2]
As mutton cutlets, prime of meat,
Which, though with art you salt and beat   100
As laws of cookery require
And toast them at the clearest fire,
If from adown the hopeful chops
The fat upon the cinder drops,
To stinking smoke it turns the flame   105
Pois'ning the flesh from whence it came;
And up exhales a greasy stench
For which you curse the careless wench;
So things which must not be exprest,
When plumpt into the reeking chest,   110
Send up an excremental smell
To taint the parts from whence they fell,
The petticoats and gown perfume,
Which waft a stink round every room.
Thus finishing his grand survey,   115
Disgusted Strephon stole away
Repeating in his amorous fits,
Oh! Celia, Celia, Celia shits!
But vengeance, goddess never sleeping,
Soon punished Strephon for his peeping: 120
His foul imagination links
Each dame he sees with all her stinks;
And, if unsavoury odours fly,
Conceives a lady standing by.
All women his description fits,   125

---

[2] Milton, *Paradise Lost* II, line 892, describing Chaos.

And both ideas jump like wits
By vicious fancy coupled fast,
And still appearing in contrast.
I pity wretched Strephon blind
To all the charms of female kind.   130
Should I the Queen of Love refuse
Because she rose from stinking ooze?
To him that looks behind the scene
Satira's but some pocky queen.
When Celia in her glory shows,   135
If Strephon would but stop his nose
(Who now so impiously blasphemes
Her ointments, daubs, and paints and creams,
Her washes, slops, and every clout
With which he makes so foul a rout),   140
He soon would learn to think like me
And bless his ravished sight to see
Such order from confusion sprung,
Such gaudy tulips raised from dung.

11. Verses on the Death of Dr Swift, D.S.P.D.

*Dans l'adversité de nos meilleurs amis nous trouvons quelque chose,
qui ne nous déplaît pas.*[3]

As Rochefoucauld his maxims drew
From Nature, I believe 'em true:
They argue no corrupted mind
In him; the fault is in mankind.
     This maxim more than all the rest   5
Is thought too base for human breast:
'In all distresses of our friends,
We first consult our private ends;
While Nature, kindly bent to ease us,
Points out some circumstance to please us.'   10
     If this perhaps your patience move,
Let reason and experience prove.
     We all behold with envious eyes

---

[3] In our best friends' travails we find something that does not quite displease us.

Our equal raised above our size.
Who would not at a crowded show
Stand high himself, keep others low?   15
I love my friend as well as you
But would not have him stop my view.
Then let me have the higher post:
I ask but for an inch at most.   20
   If in a battle you should find
One, whom you love of all mankind,
Had some heroic action done,
A champion killed, or trophy won;
Rather than thus be overtopt,   25
Would you not wish his laurels cropt?
   Dear honest Ned is in the gout,
Lies racked with pain, and you without:
How patiently you hear him groan!
How glad the case is not your own!   30
   What poet would not grieve to see
His brethren write as well as he?
But rather than they should excel,
He'd wish his rivals all in hell.
   Her end when emulation misses,   35
She turns to envy, stings and hisses:
The strongest friendship yields to pride,
Unless the odds be on our side.
   Vain human kind! fantastic race!
Thy various follies who can trace?   40
Self-love, ambition, envy, pride,
Their empire in our hearts divide.
Give others riches, power, and station,
'Tis all on me a usurpation.
I have no title to aspire;   45
Yet, when you sink, I seem the higher.
In Pope I cannot read a line,
But with a sigh I wish it mine;
When he can in one couplet fix
More sense than I can do in six;   50
It gives me such a jealous fit,
I cry, 'Pox take him and his wit!'
   Why must I be outdone by Gay
In my own hum'rous biting way?
   Arbuthnot is no more my friend,   55
Who dares to irony pretend,

Which I was born to introduce,
Refined it first, and showed its use.
    St John,[4] as well as Pultney,[5] knows
That I had some repute for prose;   60
And, till they drove me out of date,
Could maul a minister of state.
If they have mortified my pride,
And made me throw my pen aside;
If with such talents Heav'n has blest 'em,   65
Have I not reason to detest 'em?
    To all my foes, dear Fortune, send
Thy gifts; but never to my friend:
I tamely can endure the first,
But this with envy makes me burst.   70
    Thus much may serve by way of proem:
Proceed we therefore to our poem.
    The time is not remote, when I
Must by the course of nature die;
When I foresee my special friends   75
Will try to find their private ends:
Though it is hardly understood
Which way my death can do them good,
Yet thus, methinks, I hear 'em speak:
'*See, how the Dean begins to break!*   80
Poor gentleman, he droops apace!
You plainly find it in his face.
That old vertigo in his head
Will never leave him till he's dead.
Besides, his memory decays: 85
He recollects not what he says;
He cannot call his friends to mind:
Forgets the place where last he dined;
Plies you with stories o'er and o'er,
He told them fifty times before.   90
How does he fancy we can sit
To hear his out-of-fashioned wit?
But he takes up with younger folks,
Who for his wine will bear his jokes.
Faith, he must make his stories shorter,   95

---

    [4] Henry St John, Viscount Bolingbroke, a major political figure, writer and key friend of Scriblerians.
    [5] William Pultney, fellow Scriblerian and man of affairs, a Whig turned Tory and a committed foe of his one-time friend Sir Robert Walpole.

Or change his comrades once a quarter:
In half the time he talks them round,
There must another set be found.
   '*For poetry he's past his prime:*   100
He takes an hour to find a rhyme;
His fire is out, his wit decayed,
His fancy sunk, his Muse a jade.
I'd have him throw away his pen; –
But there's no talking to some men!'   105
And then their tenderness appears,
By adding largely to my years:
'*He's older than he would be reckoned*
And well remembers Charles the Second.
He hardly drinks a pint of wine;   110
And that, I doubt, is no good sign.
His stomach too begins to fail:
Last year we thought him strong and hale;
But now he's quite another thing:
I wish he may hold out till spring.'   115
Then hug themselves, and reason thus:
'*It is not yet so bad with us.*'
In such a case, they talk in tropes,
And by their fears express their hopes:
Some great misfortune to portend,   120
No enemy can match a friend.
With all the kindness they profess,
The merit of a lucky guess
(When daily '*How d'ye's*' come of course,
And servants answer, '*Worse and worse!*')   125
Would please 'em better, than to tell,
That, '*God be praised, the Dean is well.*'
Then he who prophesied the best
Approves his foresight to the rest:
'*You know I always feared the worst,*   130
And often told you so at first.'
He'd rather choose that I should die,
Than his prediction prove a lie.
Not one foretells I shall recover;
But all agree to give me over.   135
Yet, should some neighbour feel a pain
Just in the parts where I complain,
How many a message would he send?
What hearty prayers that I should mend?

Inquire what regimen I kept,   140
What gave me ease, and how I slept?
And more lament when I was dead,
Than all the sniv'llers round my bed.
  My good companions, never fear;
For though you may mistake a year,   145
Though your prognostics run too fast,
They must be verified at last.
  Behold the fatal day arrive!
'*How is the Dean?*' – '*He's just alive.*'
Now the departing prayer is read;   150
'*He hardly breathes.*' – '*The Dean is dead.*'
Before the passing-bell begun,
The news through half the town has run.
'*O, may we all for death prepare!*
What has he left? and who's his heir?' –   155
'*I know no more than what the news is;*
Tis all bequeathed to public uses.' –
'*To public use! a perfect whim!*
What had the public done for him?
Mere envy, avarice, and pride: 160
He gave it all – but first he died.
And had the Dean, in all the nation,
No worthy friend, no poor relation?
So ready to do strangers good,
Forgetting his own flesh and blood?'   165
  Now Grub-Street wits are all employed;
With elegies the town is cloyed:
Some paragraph in ev'ry paper
To curse the Dean or bless the Drapier.[6]
The doctors, tender of their fame,   170
Wisely on me lay all the blame:
'*We must confess his case was nice;*
But he would never take advice.
Had he been ruled, for aught appears,
He might have lived these twenty years;   175
For, when we opened him, we found
That all his vital parts were sound.'
  From Dublin soon to London spread,

[6] *The Drapier's Letters* (1724) were among Swift's most effective political writings. The four *Letters*, written under the assumed identity of an Irish draper, altered government policy in relation to a major coinage scam.

Tis told at Court, the Dean is dead.
Kind Lady Suffolk in the spleen   180
Runs laughing up to tell the Queen.
The Queen, so gracious, mild, and good,
Cries, '*Is he gone! 'tis time he should.*
He's dead, you say; why, let him rot:
I'm glad the medals were forgot.   185
I promised them, I own; but when?
I only was the Princess then;
But now, as consort of a king,
You know, 'tis quite a different thing.'
Now Chartres,[7] at Sir Robert's[8] levee,   190
Tells with a sneer the tidings heavy:
'*Why, is he dead without his shoes?*'
Cries Bob, '*I'm sorry for the news:*
O, were the wretch but living still,
And in his place my good friend Will[9]!   195
Or had a mitre on his head,
Provided Bolingbroke were dead!'
Now Curll his shop from rubbish drains:
Three genuine tomes of *Swift's Remains*!
And then, to make them pass the glibber,   200
Revised by Tibbalds, Moore, and Cibber.[10]
He'll treat me as he does my betters,
Publish my will, my life, my letters:
Revive the libels born to die;
Which Pope must bear, as well as I.   205
     Here shift the scene, to represent
How those I love my death lament.
Poor Pope will grieve a month, and Gay
A week, and Arbuthnot a day.
St John himself will scarce forbear   210
To bite his pen, and drop a tear.
The rest will give a shrug, and cry,
'*I'm sorry – but we all must die!*'
Indifference, clad in Wisdom's guise,

---

[7] [Swift's note] 'Chartres is a most infamous, vile scoundrel, grown from a foot-boy, or worse, to a prodigious fortune both in England and Scotland: he had a way of insinuating himself into all ministers under every change, either as pimp, flatterer, or informer. He was tried at seventy for a rape, and came off by sacrificing a great part of his fortune (he is since dead, but this poem still preserves the scene and time it was writ in).'

[8] Sir Robert Walpole, Chief Minister of State

[9] William Pultney

[10] [Swift's note] 'Three stupid Verse Writers in London ...'

All fortitude of mind supplies: 215
For how can stony bowels melt
In those who never pity felt?
When *we* are lashed, *they* kiss the rod,
Resigning to the will of God.
The fools, my juniors by a year, 220
Are tortured with suspense and fear;
Who wisely thought my age a screen,
When death approached, to stand between:
The screen removed, their hearts are trembling;
They mourn for me without dissembling. 225
 My female friends, whose tender hearts
Have better learned to act their parts,
Receive the news in doleful dumps:
'*The Dean is dead: (and what is trumps?)*
Then, Lord have mercy on his soul! 230
(Ladies, I'll venture for the vole.[11]*)*
Six deans, they say, must bear the pall:
(I wish I knew what king to call.)
Madam, your husband will attend
The funeral of so good a friend.' 235
'No, madam, 'tis a shocking sight:
And he's engaged to-morrow night:
My Lady Club would take it ill,
If he should fail her at quadrille.
He loved the Dean – (I lead a heart) 240
But dearest friends, they say, must part.
His time was come: he ran his race;
We hope he's in a better place.'
 Why do we grieve that friends should die?
No loss more easy to supply. 245
One year is past; a different scene!
No further mention of the Dean;
Who now, alas! no more is missed,
Than if he never did exist.
Where's now this fav'rite of Apollo! 250
Departed: – and his works must follow;
Must undergo the common fate;
His kind of wit is out of date.
Some country squire to Lintot goes,
Inquires for 'Swift in Verse and Prose.' 255

---

[11] Winning of all the tricks in some card games.

Says Lintot, '*I have heard the name;*
He died a year ago.' – 'The same.'
He searcheth all his shop in vain.
'*Sir, you may find them in Duck-lane;*
I sent them with a load of books,   260
Last Monday to the pastry-cook's.
To fancy they could live a year!
I find you're but a stranger here.
The Dean was famous in his time,
And had a kind of knack at rhyme.   265
His way of writing now is past;
The town hath got a better taste;
I keep no antiquated stuff
But spick and span I have enough.
Pray do but give me leave to show 'em;   270
Here's Colley Cibber's birth-day poem.
This ode you never yet have seen,
By Stephen Duck[12], *upon the Queen.*
Then here's a letter finely penned
Against the Craftsman *and his friend:*   275
It clearly shows that all reflection
On ministers is disaffection.
Next, here's Sir Robert's vindication,
And Mr Henley's last oration.
The hawkers have not got 'em yet: 280
Your honour please to buy a set?
    '*Here's Woolston's tracts, the twelfth edition;*
'Tis read by every politician:
The country members, when in town,
To all their boroughs send them down;   285
You never met a thing so smart;
The courtiers have them all by heart:
Those maids of honour who can read
Are taught to use them for their creed.
The rev'rend author's good intention   290
Hath been rewarded with a pension.

---

[12] Stephen Duck, 'the Thresher Poet', (1705?–1756) was a sensation for a time: a working-man who wrote verse, a rustic prodigy. Unfortunately he had not the genius of Clare; but he was much mythologised by the Augustans. After an audience with Queen Caroline he became a beneficiary of allegorical and rather absurd royal favours, which lost him literary respect. In his best-remembered poem, 'The Thresher's Labour', he contributes to the myth of himself. His flattering royal poems do him less credit. After the Queen died he took holy orders, became Rector of Byfleet, Surrey, and ended up a suicide, drowning himself behind a Reading tavern.

He doth an honour to his gown,
By bravely running priestcraft down:
He shows, as sure as God's in Gloucester,
That Jesus was a grand imposter;   295
That all his miracles were cheats,
Performed as jugglers do their feats:
The church had never such a writer;
A shame he hath not got a mitre!'
Suppose me dead; and then suppose   300
A club assembled at the Rose;
Where, from discourse of this and that,
I grow the subject of their chat.
And while they toss my name about,
With favour some, and some without,   305
One, quite indiff'rent in the cause,
My character impartial draws:
    'The Dean, if we believe report,
Was never ill received at Court.
As for his works in verse and prose   310
I own myself no judge of those;
Nor can I tell what critics thought 'em:
But this I know, all people bought 'em.
As with a moral view designed
To cure the vices of mankind: 315
His vein, ironically grave,
Exposed the fool, and lashed the knave.
To steal a hint was never known,
But what he writ was all his own.
    'He never thought an honour done him,   320
Because a duke was proud to own him,
Would rather slip aside and choose
To talk with wits in dirty shoes;
Despised the fools with stars and garters,
So often seen caressing Chartres.   325
He never courted men in station,
Nor persons held in admiration;
Of no man's greatness was afraid,
Because he sought for no man's aid.
Though trusted long in great affairs   330
He gave himself no haughty airs:
Without regarding private ends,
Spent all his credit for his friends;
And only chose the wise and good;

No flatt'rers; no allies in blood: 335
But succoured virtue in distress,
And seldom failed of good success;
As numbers in their hearts must own,
Who, but for him, had been unknown.
     'With princes kept a due decorum,   340
But never stood in awe before 'em.
He followed David's lesson just:
"In princes never put thy trust";
And, would you make him truly sour,
Provoke him with a slave in pow'r.   345
The Irish senate if you named,
With what impatience he declaimed!
Fair Liberty was all his cry,
For her he stood prepared to die;
For her he boldly stood alone;   350
For her he oft exposed his own.
Two kingdoms, just as faction led,
Had set a price upon his head;
But not a traitor could be found
To sell him for six hundred pound.   355
   'Had he but spared his tongue and pen
He might have rose like other men:
But pow'r was never in his thought,
And wealth he valued not a groat:
Ingratitude he often found,   360
And pitied those who meant the wound:
But kept the tenor of his mind,
To merit well of human kind:
Nor made a sacrifice of those
Who still were true, to please his foes.   365
He laboured many a fruitless hour
To reconcile his friends in pow'r;
Saw mischief by a faction brewing,
While they pursued each other's ruin.
But, finding vain was all his care,   370
He left the Court in mere despair.
   'And, oh! how short are human schemes!
Here ended all our golden dreams.
What St John's skill in state affairs,
What Ormond's valour, Oxford's cares,   375
To save their sinking country lent,
Was all destroyed by one event.

Too soon that precious life[13] was ended,
On which alone our weal depended.
When up a dangerous faction starts,
With wrath and vengeance in their hearts;
By solemn League and Cov'nant bound,
To ruin, slaughter, and confound;
To turn religion to a fable,
And make the government a Babel;
Pervert the law, disgrace the gown,
Corrupt the senate, rob the crown;
To sacrifice old England's glory,
And make her infamous in story:
When such a tempest shook the land,
How could unguarded virtue stand?
* 'With horror, grief, despair, the Dean*
Beheld the dire destructive scene:
His friends in exile, or the tower,
Himself within the frown of power,
Pursued by base envenomed pens,
Far to the land of slaves and fens;
A servile race in folly nursed,
Who truckle most when treated worst.
* 'By innocence and resolution,*
He bore continual persecution,
While numbers to preferment rose,
Whose merits were, to be his foes;
When ev'n his own familiar friends,
Intent upon their private ends,
Like renegadoes now he feels,
Against him lifting up their heels.
* 'The Dean did by his pen defeat*
An infamous destructive cheat;
Taught fools their int'rest how to know,
And gave them arms to ward the blow.
Envy hath owned it was his doing,
To save that helpless land from ruin;
While they who at the steerage stood,
And reaped the profit, sought his blood.
* 'To save them from their evil fate,*
In him was held a crime of state.
A wicked monster on the bench,

380

385

390

395

400

405

410

415

---

[13] Queen Anne's

Whose fury blood could never quench,
As vile and profligate a villain,   420
As modern Scroggs, or old Tressilian,[14]
Who long all justice had discarded,
Nor feared he God, nor man regarded,
Vowed on the Dean his rage to vent,
And make him of his zeal repent;   425
But Heav'n his innocence defends,
The grateful people stand his friends.
Not strains of law, nor judge's frown,
Nor topics brought to please the crown,
Nor witness hired, nor jury picked,   430
Prevail to bring him in convict.
    'In exile, with a steady heart,
He spent his life's declining part;
Where folly, pride, and faction sway,
Remote from St John, Pope, and Gay.   435
    'His friendships there, to few confined,
Were always of the middling kind;
No fools of rank, a mongrel breed,
Who fain would pass for lords indeed:
Where titles gave no right or power   440
And peerage is a withered flower;
He would have held it a disgrace,
If such a wretch had known his face.
On rural squires, that kingdom's bane,
He vented oft his wrath in vain;   445
Biennial squires to market brought;
Who sell their souls and votes for nought;
The nation stripped, go joyful back,
To rob the church, their tenants rack,
Go snacks with thieves and rapparees,[15]   450
And keep the peace to pick up fees;
In ev'ry job to have a share,
A jail or barrack to repair;
And turn the tax for public roads,
Commodious to their own abodes.   455
    'Perhaps I may allow, the Dean

----

[14] [Swift's note] 'Scroggs was Chief Justice under King Charles the Second: his judgement always varied in State Trials, according to directions from Court. Tressilian was a wicked judge, hanged above three hundred years ago.'
[15] A name given the highwaymen in Ireland, originally the name for the Irish soldiers who went out in small patrols to plunder the Protestants.

Had too much satire in his vein;
And seemed determined not to starve it,
Because no age could more deserve it.
Yet malice never was his aim;   460
He lashed the vice, but spared the name;
No individual could resent,
Where thousands equally were meant.
His satire points at no defect,
But what all mortals may correct;   465
For he abhorred that senseless tribe
Who call it humour when they gibe.
He spared a hump, or crooked nose,
Whose owners set not up for beaux.
True genuine dulness moved his pity,   470
Unless it offered to be witty.
Those who their ignorance confessed
He ne'er offended with a jest;
But laughed to hear an idiot quote
A verse from Horace, learned by rote.   475
  'He knew a hundred pleasant stories
With all the turns of Whigs and Tories:
Was cheerful to his dying day;
And friends would let him have his way.
  'He gave the little wealth he had   480
To build a house for fools and mad;
And showed by one satiric touch,
No nation wanted it so much.
That kingdom he hath left his debtor,
I wish it soon may have a better.'   485

Isaac Watts (1674–1748)

12. Submission to Afflictive Providences

Job i. 21

Naked as from the earth we came,
    And crept to life at first,
We to the earth return again,
    And mingle with our dust.

The dear delights we here enjoy   5
   And fondly call our own
Are but short favours borrowed now
   To be repaid anon.

'Tis God that lifts our comforts high,
   Or sinks 'em in the grave.   10
He gives, and (blessed be his Name)
   He takes but what he gave.

Peace, all our angry passions then!
   Let each rebellious sigh
Be silent at his sovereign will,   15
   And every murmur die.

If smiling Mercy crown our lives
   Its praises shall be spread,
And we'll adore the justice too
   That strikes our comforts dead.   20

13. Crucifixion to the World by the Cross of Christ

Galatians vi. 14

When I survey the wondrous cross
On which the prince of glory died,
My richest gain I count but loss,
And pour contempt on all my pride.

Forbid it, Lord, that I should boast,   5
Save in the death of Christ my God;
All the vain things that charm me most,
I sacrifice them to his blood.

See from his head, his hands, his feet,
Sorrow and love flow mingled down;   10
Did e'er such love and sorrow meet?
Or thorns compose so rich a crown?

His dying crimson like a robe
Spreads o'er his body on the tree,

Then am I dead to all the globe,   15
And all the globe is dead to me.

   Were the whole realm of nature mine
That were a present far too small;
Love so amazing, so divine
Demands my soul, my life, my all.   20

14. The Church the Garden of Christ

We are a garden walled around,
Chosen and made peculiar ground;
A little spot inclosed by grace
Out of the world's wide wilderness.

Like trees of myrrh and spice we stand,   5
Planted by God the Father's hand;
And all his springs in Sion flow,
To make the young plantation grow.

Awake, O heavenly wind, and come,
Blow on this garden of perfume;   10
Spirit Divine, descend and breathe
A gracious gale on plants beneath.

Make our best spices flow abroad
To entertain our Saviour-God:
And faith, and love, and joy appear,   15
And every grace be active here.

Let my beloved come, and taste
His pleasant fruits at his own Feast.
I come, my Spouse, I come, he cries,
With love and pleasure in his eyes.   20

Our Lord into his garden comes,
Well pleased to smell our poor perfumes,
And calls us to a feast divine,
Sweeter than honey, milk, or wine.

Eat of the Tree of Life, my friends,   25
The blessings that my Father sends;
Your taste shall all my dainties prove,
And drink abundance of my love.

Jesus, we will frequent thy board,
And sing the bounties of our Lord: 30
But the rich food on which we live
Demands more praise than tongues can give.

15. The Nativity of Christ

Luke i 3 etc, Luke ii. 1 etc.

Behold, the grace appears,
   The promise is fulfiled;
Mary the wondrous virgin bears,
   And Jesus is the child.

The Lord, the highest God,   5
   Calls him his only Son;
He bids him rule the lands abroad,
   And gives him David's throne.

O'er Jacob shall he reign
   With a peculiar sway;   10
The nations shall his grace obtain,
   His kingdom ne'er decay.

To bring the glorious news
   A heavenly form appears;
He tells the shepherds of their joys,   15
   And banishes their fears.

'Go, humble swains,' said he,
   'To David's city fly;
The promised infant born to-day
   Doth in a manger lie.   20

'With looks and hearts serene,
   Go visit Christ your King;'

And straight a flaming troop was seen;
   The shepherds heard them sing:

  'Glory to God on high,   25
    And heavenly peace on earth,
Good-will to men, to angels joy,
    At the Redeemer's birth!'

  In worship so divine
    Let saints employ their tongues,   30
With the celestial host we join,
    And loud repeat their songs:

  'Glory to God on high,
    And heavenly peace on earth,
Good-will to men, to angels joy,   35
    At our Redeemer's birth.'

16. The Rich Sinner Dying

Psalm xlix. 6, Ecclesiastes viii. 8, Job iii. 14, 15

  In vain the wealthy mortals toil,
And heap their shining dust in vain,
Look down and scorn the humble poor,
And boast their lofty hills of gain.

  Their golden cordials cannot ease   5
Their painéd hearts or aching heads,
Nor fright nor bribe approaching death
From glittering roofs and downy beds.

  The lingering, the unwilling soul
The dismal summons must obey,   10
And bid a long and sad farewell
To the pale lump of lifeless clay.

  Thence they are huddled to the grave,
Where kings and slaves have equal thrones;
Their bones without distinction lie   15
Amongst the heap of meaner bones.

17. The Banquet of Love

Song of Solomon ii. 1-4, 6, 7.

Behold the Rose of Sharon here,
The Lily which the valleys bear;
Behold the Tree of Life, that gives
Refreshing fruit and healing leaves.

Amongst the thorns so lilies shine;   5
Amongst wild gourds the noble vine;
So in mine eyes my Saviour proves
Amidst a thousand meaner loves.

Beneath his cooling shade I sat
To shield me from the burning heat;   10
Of heavenly fruit he spreads a feast
To feed my eyes and please my taste.

Kindly he brought me to the place
Where stands the banquet of his grace,
He saw me faint, and o'er my head   15
The banner of his love he spread.

With living bread and generous wine
He cheers this sinking heart of mine;
And opening his own heart to me,
He shows his thoughts, how kind they be.   20

O never let my Lord depart,
Lie down and rest upon my heart;
I charge my sins not once to move,
Nor stir, nor wake, nor grieve my love.

18. Man Frail, and God Eternal

Psalm 90 v 1-5

Our God, our help in ages past,
 Our hope for years to come,

Our shelter from the stormy blast,
 And our eternal home.

Under the shadow of thy throne   5
 Thy saints have dwelt secure;
Sufficient is thine arm alone,
 And our defence is sure.

Before the hills in order stood,
 Or earth received her frame,   10
From everlasting thou art God,
 To endless years the same.

Thy word commands our flesh to dust,
 'Return, ye sons of men':
All nations rose from earth at first,   15
 And turn to earth again.

A thousand ages in thy sight
 Are like an evening gone;
Short as the watch that ends the night
 Before the rising sun.   20

The busy tribes of flesh and blood,
 With all their lives and cares,
Are carried downwards by thy flood,
 And lost in following years.

Time like an ever-rolling stream   25
 Bears all its sons away;
They fly forgotten as a dream
 Dies at the opening day.

Like flowery fields the nations stand
 Pleased with the morning light;   30
The flowers beneath the mower's hand
 Lie withering ere 'tis night.

Our God, our help in ages past,
 Our hope for years to come,
Be thou our guard while troubles last,   35
 And our eternal home.

19. A Prospect of Heaven Makes Death Easy

There is a land of pure delight
  Where saints immortal reign
Infinite day excludes the night
  And pleasures banish pain.

There everlasting spring abides,   5
  And never-withering flowers:
Death like a narrow sea divides
  This heavenly land from ours.

Sweet fields beyond the swelling flood
  Stand dressed in living green: 10
So to the Jews old Canaan stood,
  While Jordan rolled between.

But timorous mortals start and shrink
  To cross this narrow sea,
And linger shivering on the brink   15
  And fear to launch away.

O could we make our doubts remove,
  These gloomy doubts that rise,
And see the Canaan that we love
  With unbeclouded eyes,   20

Could we but climb where Moses stood,
  And view the landscape o'er
Not Jordan's stream, nor Death's cold flood,
  Should fright us from the shore.

20. The Day of Judgement: An Ode

Attempted in English Saphics

When the fierce north-wind with his airy forces
Rears up the Baltic to a foaming fury;
And the red lightning with a storm of hail comes
  Rushing amain down;

How the poor sailors stand amazed and tremble,   5
While the hoarse thunder, like a bloody trumpet,
Roars a loud onset to the gaping waters
    Quick to devour them.

Such shall the noise be, and the wild disorder
(If things eternal may be like these earthly),   10
Such the dire terror when the great Archangel
    Shakes the creation;

Tears the strong pillars of the vault of Heaven,
Breaks up old marble, the repose of princes,
Sees the graves open, and the bones arising,   15
    Flames all around them.

Hark, the shrill outcries of the guilty wretches!
Lively bright horror and amazing anguish
Stare through their eyelids, while the living worm lies
    Gnawing within them.   20

Thoughts, like old vultures, prey upon their heart-strings,
And the smart twinges, when the eye beholds the
Lofty Judge frowning, and a flood of vengeance
    Rolling afore him.

Hopeless immortals! how they scream and shiver,   25
While devils push them to the pit wide-yawning
Hideous and gloomy, to receive them headlong
    Down to the centre!

Stop here, my fancy: (all away, ye horrid
Doleful ideas!) come, arise to Jesus,   30
How He sits God-like! and the saints around Him
    Throned, yet adoring!

O may I sit there when He comes triumphant,
Dooming the nations! then ascend to glory,
While our Hosannas all along the passage   35
    Shout the Redeemer.

Thomas Parnell (1679–1718)

21. An Elegy, To an Old Beauty

In vain, poor Nymph, to please our youthful sight
You sleep in cream and frontlets all the night,
Your face with patches soil, with paint repair,
Dress with gay gowns, and shade with foreign hair.
If truth in spite of manners must be told,   5
Why, really fifty-five is something old.
    Once you were young; or one, whose life's so long
She might have born my mother, tells me wrong.
And once (since envy's dead before you die),
The women own, you played a sparkling eye,   10
Taught the light foot a modish little trip,
And pouted with the prettiest purple lip.
    To some new charmer are the roses fled,
Which blew, to damask all thy cheek with red;
Youth calls the graces there to fix their reign,   15
And airs by thousands fill their easy train.
So parting summer bids her flow'ry prime
Attend the sun to dress some foreign clime,
While with'ring seasons in succession, here,
Strip the gay gardens, and deform the year.   20
    But thou (since Nature bids) the world resign,
'Tis now thy daughter's daughter's time to shine.
With more address (or such as pleases more)
She runs her female exercises o'er,
Unfurls or closes, raps or turns the fan,   25
And smiles, or blushes at the creature man.
With quicker life, as gilded coaches pass,
In sideling courtesy she drops the glass.
    With better strength, on visit-days she bears
To mount her fifty flights of ample stairs.   30
Her mien, her shape, her temper, eyes and tongue
Are sure to conquer – for the rogue is young;
And all that's madly wild, or oddly gay,
We call it only pretty Fanny's way.
    Let time that makes you homely, make you sage,   35

The sphere of wisdom is the sphere of age.
'Tis true, when beauty dawns with early fire,
And hears the flatt'ring tongues of soft desire,
If not from virtue, from its gravest ways
The soul with pleasing avocation strays.   40
But beauty gone, 'tis easier to be wise;
As harpers better, by the loss of eyes.
    Henceforth retire, reduce your roving airs,
Haunt less the plays, and more the public pray'rs,
Reject the Mechlin head, and gold brocade,   45
Go pray, in sober Norwich crêpe arrayed.
Thy pendent diamonds let thy Fanny take,
(Their trembling lustre shows how much you shake);
Or bid her wear thy necklace rowed with pearl,
You'll find your Fanny an obedient girl.   50
    So for the rest, with less incumbrance hung,
You walk through life, unmingled with the young;
And view the shade and substance as you pass
With joint endeavour trifling at the glass,
Or folly drest, and rambling all her days,   55
To meet her counterpart, and grow by praise:
Yet still sedate yourself, and gravely plain,
You neither fret, nor envy at the vain.
    'Twas thus (if man with woman we compare)
The wise Athenian crossed a glittering fair,   60
Unmoved by tongues and sights, he walked the place,
Through tape, toys, tinsel, gimp, perfume, and lace;
Then bends from Mars's Hill his awful eyes,
And 'What a world I never want?' he cries;
But cries unheard: for folly will be free.   65
So parts the buzzing gaudy crowd, and he:
As careless he for them, as they for him;
He wrapt in wisdom, and they whirled by whim.

Edward Young (1683–1765)

22. from *Night Thoughts on Life, Death, and Immortality in Nine Nights*

The Complaint

HUMBLY INSCRIBED TO THE RIGHT HONOURABLE ARTHUR ONSLOW, ESQ.,
SPEAKER OF THE HOUSE OF COMMONS.

Tired Nature's sweet restorer, balmy Sleep!
He, like the world, his ready visit pays
Where Fortune smiles; the wretched he forsakes;
Swift on his downy pinion flies from woe,
And lights on lids unsullied with a tear.   5
   From short (as usual) and disturbed repose
I wake: how happy they who wake no more!
Yet that were vain, if dreams infest the grave.
I wake, emerging from a sea of dreams
Tumultuous; where my wrecked desponding thought,   10
From wave to wave of fancied misery,
At random drove, her helm of reason lost:
Though now restored, 'tis only change of pain,
(A bitter change!) severer for severe.
The Day too short for my distress; and Night,   15
E'en in the zenith of her dark domain,
Is sunshine to the colour of my fate.
   Night, sable goddess! from her ebon throne,
In rayless majesty, now stretches forth
Her leaden sceptre o'er a slumbering world.   20
Silence, how dead! and darkness, how profound!
Nor eye, nor listening ear, an object finds;
Creation sleeps. 'Tis as the general pulse
Of life stood still, and Nature made a pause;
An awful pause! prophetic of her end.   25
And let her prophecy be soon fulfilled:
Fate! drop the curtain; I can lose no more.
   Silence and Darkness! solemn sisters! twins
From ancient Night, who nurse the tender thought

To reason, and on reason build resolve,   30
(That column of true majesty in man),
Assist me: I will thank you in the grave;
The grave your kingdom: *there* this frame shall fall
A victim sacred to your dreary shrine.
But what are ye? –   35
            Thou, who didst put to flight
Primeval Silence, when the morning stars,
Exulting, shouted o'er the rising ball; –
O Thou, whose Word from solid darkness struck
That spark, the sun! strike wisdom from my soul;   40
My soul, which flies to Thee, her trust, her treasure,
As misers to their gold, while others rest.
   Through this opaque of Nature and of soul,
This double night, transmit one pitying ray,
To lighten and to cheer. O lead my mind,   45
(A mind that fain would wander from its woe),
Lead it through various scenes of life and death;
And from each scene the noblest truths inspire.
Nor less inspire my conduct than my song:
Teach my best reason, reason; my best will   50
Teach rectitude; and fix my firm resolve
Wisdom to wed, and pay her long arrear:
Nor let the phial of thy vengeance, poured
On this devoted head, be poured in vain.
   The bell strikes *one*. We take no note of time   55
But from its loss. To give it then a tongue
Is wise in man. As if an angel spoke,
I feel the solemn sound. If heard aright,
It is the knell of my departed hours.
Where are they? With the years beyond the flood.   60
It is the signal that demands despatch:
How much is to be done! My hopes and fears
Start up alarmed, and o'er life's narrow verge
Look down – on what? A fathomless abyss,
A dread eternity! how surely *mine!*   65
And can eternity belong to me,
Poor pensioner on the bounties of an hour?
   How poor, how rich, how abject, how august,
How complicate, how wonderful is man!
How passing wonder He who made him such!   70
Who centred in our make such strange extremes!
From different natures marvellously mixed,

Connexion exquisite of distant worlds!
Distinguished link in being's endless chain!
Midway from nothing to the Deity! 75
A beam ethereal, sullied and absorbed!
Though sullied and dishonoured, still divine!
Dim miniature of greatness absolute!
An heir of glory! a frail child of dust!
Helpless immortal! insect *infinite*! 80
A worm! a god! – I tremble at myself,
And in myself am lost! At home a stranger,
Thought wanders up and down, surprised, aghast,
And wondering at her own. How reason reels!
O what a miracle to man is man, 85
Triumphantly distressed! what joy! what dread!
Alternately transported and alarmed!
What can preserve my life? or what destroy?
An angel's arm can't snatch me from the grave;
Legions of angels can't confine me there. 90
   'Tis past conjecture; all things rise in proof:
While o'er my limbs Sleep's soft dominion spread,
What though my soul fantastic measures trod
O'er fairy fields; or mourned along the gloom
Of pathless woods; or, down the craggy steep 95
Hurled headlong, swam with pain the mantled pool;
Or scaled the cliff; or danced on hollow winds,
With antic shapes, wild natives of the brain?
   Her ceaseless flight, though devious, speaks her nature
Of subtler essence than the trodden clod; 100
Active, aërial, towering, unconfined,
Unfettered with her gross companion's fall.
E'en silent Night proclaims my soul immortal:
E'en silent Night proclaims eternal day.
For human weal, Heaven husbands all events; 105
Dull sleep instructs, nor sport vain dreams in vain.
   Why then *their* loss deplore that are not lost?
Why wanders wretched thought their tombs around
In infidel distress? Are angels there?
Slumbers, raked up in dust, ethereal fire? 110
They live! they greatly live a life on earth
Unkindled, unconceived; and from an eye
Of tenderness let heavenly pity fall
On me, more justly numbered with the dead.
   This is the desert, this the solitude: 115

How populous, how vital is the grave!
This is creation's melancholy vault,
The vale funereal, the sad cypress-gloom;
The land of apparitions, empty shades!
All, all on earth is shadow, all beyond   120
Is substance; the reverse is Folly's creed:
How solid all, where change shall be no more!
  This is the bud of being, the dim dawn,
The twilight of our day, the vestibule:
Life's theatre as yet is shut, and Death,   125
Strong Death, alone can heave the massy bar,
This gross impediment of clay remove,
And make us embryos of existence free.
From real life but little more remote
Is he, not yet a candidate for light,   130
The future embryo, slumb'ring in his sire.
Embryos we must be till we burst the shell,
Yon ambient azure shell, and spring to life,
The life of gods (O transport!) and of man.
  Yet man (fool man!) *here* buries all his thoughts;   135
Inters celestial hopes without one sigh;
Prisoner of earth, and pent beneath the moon,
Here pinions all his wishes; winged by Heaven
To fly at infinite; and reach it there
Where seraphs gather immortality,   140
On life's fair tree, fast by the throne of God.
What golden joys ambrosial clustering glow
In His full beam, and ripen for the just,
Where momentary ages are no more!
Where time, and pain, and chance, and death expire!   145
And is it in the flight of threescore years
To push eternity from human thought,
And smother souls immortal in the dust?
A soul immortal, spending all her fires,
Wasting her strength in strenuous idleness,   150
Thrown into tumult, raptured, or alarmed,
At aught this scene can threaten, or indulge,
Resembles ocean into tempest wrought,
To waft a feather, or to drown a fly.
  Where falls this censure? It o'erwhelms myself.   155
How was my heart incrusted by the world!
O how self-fettered was my grovelling soul!
How, like a worm, was I wrapt round and round

In silken thought, which reptile Fancy spun,
Till darkened Reason lay quite clouded o'er 160
With soft conceit of endless comfort here,
Nor yet put forth her wings to reach the skies!
   Night visions may befriend (as sung above):
Our *waking* dreams are fatal. How I dreamt
Of things impossible! (could sleep do more?) 165
Of joys perpetual in perpetual change!
Of stable pleasures on the tossing wave!
Eternal sunshine in the storms of life!
How richly were my noon-tide trances hung
With gorgeous tapestries of pictured joys! 170
Joy behind joy, in endless perspective!
Till at Death's toll, whose restless iron tongue
Calls daily for his millions at a meal,
Starting I woke, and found myself undone.
Where now my frenzy's pompous furniture? 175
The cobwebbed cottage, with its ragged wall
Of mouldering mud, is royalty to me!
The spider's most attenuated thread
Is cord, is cable, to man's tender tie
On earthly bliss; it breaks at every breeze. 180
   O ye blest scenes of permanent delight!
Full above measure! lasting beyond bound!
A perpetuity of bliss *is* bliss.
Could you, so rich in rapture, fear an end,
That ghastly thought would drink up all your joy, 185
And quite unparadise the realms of light.
Safe are you lodged above these rolling spheres;
The baleful influence of whose giddy dance
Sheds sad vicissitude on all beneath.
Here teems with revolutions every hour, 190
And rarely for the better; or the best
More mortal than the common births of fate.
Each moment has its sickle, emulous
Of Time's enormous scythe, whose ample sweep
Strikes empires from the root; each moment plays 195
His little weapon in the narrower sphere
Of sweet domestic comfort, and cuts down
The fairest bloom of sublunary bliss.
   Bliss! sublunary bliss! – proud words, and vain!
Implicit treason to divine decree! 200
A bold invasion of the rights of Heaven!

I clasped the phantoms, and I found them air.
O had I weighed it ere my fond embrace,
What darts of agony had missed my heart!
    Death! great proprietor of all! 'tis thine   205
To tread out empire, and to quench the stars. [...]

John Gay (1685–1732)

23. Sweet William's Farewell to Black-eyed Susan: a Ballad

All in the Downs the fleet was moored,
    The streamers waving in the wind,
When black-eyed Susan came aboard.
    Oh! where shall I my true love find!
Tell me, ye jovial sailors, tell me true,   5
If my sweet William sails among the crew.

William, who high upon the yard,
    Rocked with the billow to and fro,
Soon as her well-known voice he heard,
    He sighed and cast his eyes below: 10
The cord slides swiftly through his glowing hands,
And, (quick as lightning), on the deck he stands.

So the sweet lark, high-poised in air,
    Shuts close his pinions to his breast,
(If, chance, his mate's shrill call he hear)   15
    And drops at once into her nest.
The noblest Captain in the British fleet,
Might envy William's lip those kisses sweet.

O Susan, Susan, lovely dear,
    My vows shall ever true remain;   20
Let me kiss off that falling tear,
    We only part to meet again.
Change, as ye list, ye winds; my heart shall be
The faithful compass that still points to thee.

Believe not what the landmen say,   25
    Who tempt with doubts thy constant mind:
They'll tell thee, sailors, when away,
    In ev'ry port a mistress find.
Yes, yes, believe them when they tell thee so,
For thou art present wheresoe'er I go.   30

If to far India's coast we sail,
    Thy eyes are seen in di'monds bright,
Thy breath is Africk's spicy gale,
    Thy skin is ivory, so white.
Thus ev'ry beauteous object that I view,   35
Wakes in my soul some charm of lovely Sue.

Though battle call me from thy arms,
    Let not my pretty Susan mourn;
Though cannons roar, yet safe from harms,
    William shall to his Dear return.   40
Love turns aside the balls that round me fly,
Lest precious tears should drop from Susan's eye.

The boatswain gave the dreadful word,
    The sails their swelling bosom spread,
No longer must she stay aboard: 45
    They kissed, she sighed, he hung his head;
Her less'ning boat, unwilling rows, to land:
Adieu, she cries! and waved her lily hand.

24. Newgate's Garland

*being a new Ballad, showing how Mr Jonathan Wild's Throat was cut from Ear to Ear
with a Penknife, by Mr Blake, alias Blueskin, the bold Highwayman, as he stood at his
Trial in the Old Bailey*

Ye gallants of Newgate, whose fingers are nice,
In diving in pockets, or cogging of dice,
Ye sharpers so rich, who can buy off the noose,
Ye honester poor rogues, who die in your shoes,
    Attend and draw near,   5
    Good news ye shall hear,
    How Jonathan's throat was cut from ear to ear;

How Blueskin's sharp penknife hath set you at ease,
And every man round me may rob, if he please.

When to the Old Bailey this Blueskin was led,   10
He held up his hand, his indictment was read,
Loud rattled his chains, near him Jonathan stood,
For full forty pounds was the price of his blood.
    Then hopeless of life,
    He drew his penknife,   15
    And made a sad widow of Jonathan's wife.
But forty pounds paid her, her grief shall appease,
And every man round me may rob, if he please.

Some say there are courtiers of highest renown,
Who steal the king's gold, and leave him but a crown;   20
Some say there are peers, and some Parliament men,
Who meet once a year to rob courtiers again:
    Let them all take their swing,
    To pillage the king,
    And get a blue ribbon instead of a string.   25
Now Blueskin's sharp penknife hath set you at ease,
And every man round me may rob, if he please.

Knaves of old, to hide guilt by their cunning inventions,
Called briberies grants, and plain robberies pensions;
Physicians and lawyers (who take their degrees   30
To be learned rogues) called their pilfering, fees;
    Since this happy day,
    Now ev'ry man may
    Rob (as safe as in office) upon the highway.
For Blueskin's sharp penknife hath set you at ease,   35
And every man round me may rob, if he please.

Some cheat in the customs, some rob the excise,
But he who robs both is esteemèd most wise.
Church-wardens, too prudent to hazard the halter,
As yet only venture to steal from the altar: 40
    But now to get gold,
    They may be more bold,
    And rob on the highway, since Jonathan's cold.
For Blueskin's sharp penknife hath set you at ease,
And every man round me may rob, if he please.   45

Some by public revenues, which passed through their hands,
Have purchased clean houses, and bought dirty Lands,
Some to steal from a charity think it no sin,
Which, at home (says the proverb) does always begin;
   But, if ever you be   50
   Assigned a trustee,
   Treat not orphans like masters of the chancery.
But take to the highway, and more honestly seize,
For every man round me may rob, if he please.

What a pother has here been with wood and his brass,   55
Who would modestly make a few half-pennies pass!
The patent is good, and the precedent's old.
For Diomede changèd his copper for gold:
   But if Ireland despise
   Thy new half-pennies,[16]   60
   With more safety to rob on the road I advise.
For Blueskin's sharp penknife hath set thee at ease,
And every man round me may rob, if he please.

25. Mr Pope's Welcome from Greece upon his having finished his translation of Homer's *Iliad*

Long hast thou, friend! been absent from thy soil,
   Like patient Ithacus at siege of Troy;
I have been witness of thy six years' toil,
   Thy daily labours, and thy night's annoy,
Lost to thy native land, with great turmoil,   5
   On the wide sea, oft threat'ning to destroy:
Methinks with thee I've trod Sigæan ground,
And heard the shores of Hellespont resound.

Did I not see thee when thou first sett'st sail
   To seek adventures fair in Homer's land?   10
Did I not see thy sinking spirits fail,
   And wish thy bark had never left the strand?
Ev'n in mid ocean often didst thou quail,
   And oft lift up thy holy eye and hand,
Praying the Virgin dear, and saintly choir,   15

---

[16] Refers to the same theme as Swift's *The Drapier's Letters*, see note on p. 135 above.

Back to the port to bring thy bark entire.

Cheer up, my friend, thy dangers now are o'er;
    Methinks – nay, sure the rising coasts appear;
Hark how the guns salute from either shore,
    As thy trim vessel cuts the Thames so fair: 20
Shouts answ'ring shouts, from Kent and Essex roar,
    And bells break loud through ev'ry gust of air:
Bonfires do blaze, and bones and cleavers ring,
As at the coming of some mighty king.

Now pass we Gravesend with a friendly wind,   25
    And Tilbury's white fort, and long Blackwall;
Greenwich, where dwells the friend of human kind,
    More visited than or her park or hall,
Withers the good, and (with him ever joined)
    Facetious Disney, greet thee first of all: 30
I see his chimney smoke, and hear him say,
Duke! that's the room for Pope, and that for Gay.

Come in, my friends, here shall ye dine and lie,
    And here shall breakfast, and here dine again;
And sup, and breakfast on, (if ye comply)   35
    For I have still some dozens of champagne:
His voice still lessens as the ship sails by;
    He waves his hand to bring us back in vain;
For now I see, I see proud London's spires;
Greenwich is lost, and Deptford dock retires.   40

Oh, what a concourse swarms on yonder quay!
    The sky re-echoes with new shouts of joy:
By all this show, I ween, 'tis Lord May'r's day;
    I hear the voice of trumpet and hautboy: –
No, now I see them near – oh, these are they   45
    Who come in crowds to welcome thee from Troy.
Hail to the bard whom long as lost we mourned,
From siege, from battle, and from storm returned!

Of goodly dames, and courteous knights, I view
    The silken petticoat, and broidered vest;   50
Yea Peers, and mighty Dukes, with ribbands blue,
    (True blue, fair emblem of unstainèd breast).
Others I see, as noble, and more true,

By no court-badge distinguished from the rest:
First see I Methuen, of sincerest mind,   55
As Arthur grave, as soft as womankind.

What lady's that, to whom he gently bends?
    Who knows not her? ah! those are Wortley's[17] eyes:
How art thou honoured, numbered with her friends?
    For she distinguishes the good and wise.   60
The sweet-tongued Murray near her side attends.
    Now to my heart the glance of Howard flies;
Now Harvey, fair of face, I mark full well,
With thee, youth's youngest daughter, sweet Lepell.

I see two lovely sisters, hand in hand,   65
    The fair-haired Martha, and Teresa brown;
Madge Bellenden, the tallest of the land;
    And smiling Mary, soft and fair as down.
Yonder I see the cheerful Duchess stand,
    For friendship, zeal, and blithesome humours known.   70
Whence that loud shout in such a hearty strain?
Why, all the Hamiltons are in her train.

See next the decent Scudamore advance,
    With Winchelsea, still meditating song:
With her perhaps Miss Howe came there by chance,   75
    Nor knows with whom, nor why she comes along.
Far off from these see Santlow, famed for dance;
    And frolic Bicknell, and her sister young;
With other names, by me not to be named,
Much loved in private, not in public famed!   80

But now behold the female band retire,
    And the shrill music of their voice is stilled!
Methinks I see famed Buckingham admire,
    That in Troy's ruins thou hast not been killed;
Sheffield, who knows to strike the living lyre,   85
    With hand judicious, like thy Homer skilled.
Bathurst impetuous hastens to the coast,
Whom you and I strive who shall love the most.

---

[17] Lady Mary Wortley Montagu, with whom Pope later spectacularly fell out, and with her all the society beauties of the city, an opportunity for gracious flattery and celebration; they are followed by men of influence and power.

See generous Burlington, with goodly Bruce,
  (But Bruce comes wafted in a soft sedan),   90
Dan Prior next, beloved by every muse,
  And friendly Congreve, unreproachful man!
(Oxford by Cunningham hath sent excuse).
  See hearty Watkins come with cup and can;
And Lewis, who has never friend forsaken;   95
And Laughton whisp'ring asks – Is Troy town taken?

Earl Warwick comes, of free and honest mind;
  Bold, gen'rous Craggs, whose heart was ne'er disguised:
Ah why, sweet St John, cannot I thee find?
  St John for ev'ry social virtue prized. –   100
Alas! to foreign climates he's confined,
  Or else to see thee here I well surmised:
Thou too, my Swift, dost breathe Boeotian air;
When wilt thou bring back wit and humour here?

Harcourt I see for eloquence renowned,   105
  The mouth of justice, oracle of law!
Another Simon is beside him found,
  Another Simon, like as straw to straw.
How Lansdown smiles, with lasting laurel crowned!
  What mitred prelate there commands our awe?   110
See Rochester approving nods his head,
And ranks one modern with the mighty dead.

Carlton and Chandois thy arrival grace;
  Hanmer, whose eloquence th' unbiased sways;
Harley, whose goodness opens in his face,   115
  And shows his heart the seat where virtue stays.
Ned Blount advances next, with busy pace,
  In haste, but saunt'ring, hearty in his ways:
I see the friendly Carylls come by dozens,
Their wives, their uncles, daughters, sons, and cousins.   120

Arbuthnot there I see, in physick's art,
  As Galen learned, or famed Hippocrate;
Whose company drives sorrow from the heart,
  As all disease his med'cines dissipate:
Kneller amid the triumph bears his part,   125
  Who could (were mankind lost) anew create:
What can th' extent of his vast soul confine?

A painter, critic, engineer, divine!

Thee Jervas hails, robust and debonair,
 Now have we conquered Homer, friends, he cries: 130
Dartneuf, grave joker, joyous Ford is there,
 And wond'ring Maine, so fat with laughing eyes:
(Gay, Maine, and Cheney, boon companions dear,
 Gay fat, Maine fatter, Cheney huge of size,)
Yea Dennis, Gildon, (hearing thou hast riches,)   135
And honest, hatless Cromwell, with red breeches.

O Wanley, whence com'st thou with shortened hair,
 And visage from thy shelves with dust besprent?
'*Forsooth* (quoth he) *from placing Homer there,*
 For ancients to compyle is myne entente: 140
Of ancients only hath Lord Harley care;
 But hither me hath my meeke lady sent: –
In manuscript of Greeke rede we thilke same,
But book yprint best plesyth myn gude dame.'

Yonder I see, among th' expecting crowd,   145
 Evans with laugh jocose, and tragic Young;
High-buskined Booth, grave Mawbert, wand'ring Frowd,
 And Titcomb's belly waddles slow along.
See Digby faints at Southern talking loud,
 Yea Steele and Tickell mingle in the throng;   150
Tickell whose skiff (in partnership they say)
Set forth for Greece, but foundered in the way.

Lo the two Doncastles in Berkshire known!
 Lo Bickford, Fortescue, of Devon land!
Lo Tooker, Eckershall, Sykes, Rawlinson!   155
 See hearty Morley takes thee by the hand!
Ayrs, Graham, Buckridge, joy thy voyage done;
 But who can count the leaves, the stars, the sand?
Lo Stonor, Fenton, Caldwell, Ward and Broome!
Lo thousands more, but I want rhyme and room!   160

How loved! how honoured thou! yet be not vain;
 And sure thou art not, for I hear thee say,
All this, my friends, I owe to Homer's strain,
 On whose strong pinions I exalt my lay.
What from contending cities did he gain;   165

And what rewards his grateful country pay?
None, none were paid – why then all this for me?
These honours, Homer, had been just to thee.

26. *from* Trivia

or the Art of Walking the Streets of London

BOOK III: OF WALKING THE STREETS BY NIGHT

O Trivia, Goddess, leave these low abodes,
And traverse o'er the wide ethereal roads,
Celestial Queen, put on thy robes of light,
Now Cynthia named, fair regent of the Night.
At sight of thee the villain sheaths his sword,   5
Nor scales the wall, to steal the wealthy hoard.
O may thy silver lamp from heav'n's high bow'r
Direct my footsteps in the midnight hour!
   When night first bids the twinkling stars appear,
Or with her cloudy vest inwraps the air,   10
Then swarms the busy street; with caution tread,
Where the shop-windows falling threat thy head;
Now lab'rers home return, and join their strength
To bear the tott'ring plank, or ladder's length;
Still fix thy eyes intent upon the throng,   15
And as the passes open, wind along.
   Where the fair columns of St Clement stand,
Whose straitened bounds encroach upon the Strand;
Where the low penthouse bows the walker's head,
And the rough pavement wounds the yielding tread;   20
Where not a post protects the narrow space,
And strung in twines, combs dangle in thy face;
Summon at once thy courage, rouse thy care,
Stand firm, look back, be resolute, beware.
Forth issuing from steep lanes, the collier's steeds   25
Drag the black load; another cart succeeds,
Team follows team, crowds heaped on crowds appear,
And wait impatient, 'till the road grow clear.
Now all the pavement sounds with trampling feet,
And the mixt hurry barricades the street.   30
Entangled here, the waggon's lengthened team

Cracks the tough harness; here a pond'rous beam
Lies over-turned athwart; for slaughter fed
Here lowing bullocks raise their horned head.
Now oaths grow loud, with coaches coaches jar,   35
And the smart blow provokes the sturdy war;
From the high box they whirl the thong around,
And with the twining lash their shins resound:
Their rage ferments, more dang'rous wounds they try,
And the blood gushes down their painful eye.   40
And now on foot the frowning warriors light,
And with their pond'rous fists renew the fight;
Blow answers blow, their cheeks are smeared with blood,
'Till down they fall, and grappling roll in mud.
So when two boars, in wild Ytene bred,   45
Or on Westphalia's fatt'ning chestnuts fed,
Gnash their sharp tusks, and roused with equal fire.
Dispute the reign of some luxurious mire;
In the black flood they wallow o'er and o'er,
'Till their armed jaws distil with foam and gore.   50
    Where the mob gathers, swiftly shoot along,
Nor idly mingle in the noisy throng.
Lured by the silver hilt, amid the swarm,
The subtil artist will thy side disarm.
Nor is thy flaxen wig with safety worn;   55
High on the shoulder, in a basket born,
Lurks the sly boy; whose hand to rapine bred,
Plucks off the curling honours of thy head.
    Here dives the skulking thief with practised slight,
And unfelt fingers make thy pocket light.   60
Where's now thy watch, with all its trinkets, flown?
And thy late snuff-box is no more thy own.
But lo! his bolder theft some tradesman spies,
Swift from his prey the scudding lurcher flies;
Dext'rous he 'scapes the coach with nimble bounds,   65
Whilst ev'ry honest tongue *stop thief* resounds.
So speeds the wily fox, alarmed by fear,
Who lately filched the turkey's callow care;
Hounds following hounds grow louder as he flies,
And injured tenants join the hunter's cries.   70
Breathless he stumbling falls: Ill-fated boy!
Why did not honest work thy youth employ?
Seized by rough hands, he's dragged amid the rout,
And stretched beneath the pump's incessant spout:

Or plunged in miry ponds, he gasping lies, 75
Mud chokes his mouth, and plasters o'er his eyes.
    Let not the ballad-singer's shrilling strain
Amid the swarm thy list'ning ear detain:
Guard well thy pocket; for these Sirens stand
To aid the labours of the diving hand; 80
Confed'rate in the cheat, they draw the throng,
And cambric handkerchiefs reward the song.
But soon as coach or cart drives rattling on,
The rabble part, in shoals they backward run.
So Jove's loud bolts the mingled war divide, 85
And Greece and Troy retreat on either side.
    If the rude throng pour on with furious pace,
And hap to break thee from a friend's embrace,
Stop short; nor struggle through the crowd in vain,
But watch with careful eye the passing train. 90
Yet I (perhaps too fond) if chance the tide
Tumultuous bear my partner from my side,
Impatient venture back; despising harm,
I force my passage where the thickest swarm.
Thus his lost bride the Trojan sought in vain 95
Through night, and arms, and flames, and hills of slain.
Thus Nisus wandered o'er the pathless grove,
To find the brave companion of his love,
The pathless grove in vain he wanders o'er:
Euryalus, alas! is now no more. 100
    That walker, who regardless of his pace,
Turns oft to pore upon the damsel's face,
From side to side by thrusting elbows tost,
Shall strike his aching breast against the post;
Or water, dashed from fishy stalls, shall stain 105
His hapless coat with spurts of scaly rain.
But if unwarily he chance to stray,
Where twirling turnstiles intercept the way,
The thwarting passenger shall force them round,
And beat the wretch half breathless to the ground. 110
    Let constant vigilance thy footsteps guide,
And wary circumspection guard thy side;
Then shalt thou walk unharmed the dang'rous night,
Nor need th' officious link-boy's smoky light.
Thou never wilt attempt to cross the road, 115
Where alehouse benches rest the porter's load,
Grievous to heedless shins; no barrow's wheel,

That bruises oft the truant school-boy's heel,
Behind thee rolling, with insidious pace,
Shall mark thy stocking with a miry trace.   120
Let not thy vent'rous steps approach too nigh,
Where gaping wide, low steepy cellars lie;
Should thy shoe wrench aside, down, down you fall,
And overturn the scolding huckster's stall,
The scolding huckster shall not o'er thee moan,   125
But pence exact for nuts and pears o'erthrown.
    Though you through cleanlier alleys wind by day,
To shun the hurries of the public way,
Yet ne'er to those dark paths by night retire;
Mind only safety, and contemn the mire,   130
Then no impervious courts thy haste detain,
Nor sneering ale-wives bid thee turn again.
    Where Lincoln's Inn, wide space, is railed around,
Cross not with vent'rous step; there oft is found
The lurking thief, who while the day-light shone,   135
Made the walls echo with his begging tone:
That crutch which late compassion moved, shall wound
Thy bleeding head, and fell thee to the ground.
Though thou art tempted by the link-man's call,
Yet trust him not along the lonely wall;   140
In the mid-way he'll quench the flaming brand,
And share the booty with the pilf'ring band.
Still keep the public streets, where oily rays
Shot from the crystal lamp, o'erspread the ways.
    Happy Augusta! law-defended town!   145
Here no dark lanthorns shade the villain's frown;
No Spanish jealousies thy lanes infest,
Nor Roman vengeance stabs th' unwary breast;
Here tyranny ne'er lifts her purple hand,
But liberty and justice guard the land;   150
No bravos here profess the bloody trade,
Nor is the church the murd'rer's refuge made.
    Let not the chairman, with assuming stride,
Press near the wall, and rudely thrust thy side:
The laws have set him bounds; his servile feet   155
Should ne'er encroach where posts defend the street.
Yet who the footman's arrogance can quell,
Whose flambeau gilds the sashes of Pell-mell,
When in long rank a train of torches flame,
To light the midnight visits of the dame?   160

Others, perhaps, by happier guidance led,
May where the chairman rests, with safety tread;
Whene'er I pass, their poles unseen below,
Make my knee tremble with the jarring blow.
    If wheels bar up the road, where streets are crost,   165
With gentle words the coachman's ear accost:
He ne'er the threat, or harsh command obeys,
But with contempt the spattered shoe surveys.
Now man with utmost fortitude thy soul,
To cross the way where carts and coaches roll;   170
Yet do not in thy hardy skill confide,
Nor rashly risk the kennel's spacious stride;
Stay till afar the distant wheel you hear,
Like dying thunder in the breaking air;
Thy foot will slide upon the miry stone,   175
And passing coaches crush thy tortured bone,
Or wheels enclose the road; on either hand
Pent round with perils, in the midst you stand,
And call for aid in vain; the coachman swears,
And car-men drive, unmindful of thy prayers.   180
Where wilt thou turn? ah! whither wilt thou fly?
On ev'ry side the pressing spokes are nigh.
So sailors, while Carybdis' gulf they shun,
Amazed, on Scylla's craggy dangers run.
    Be sure observe where brown Ostrea stands,   185
Who boasts her shelly ware from Wallfleet sands;
There may'st thou pass, with safe unmiry feet,
Where the raised pavement leads athwart the street.
If where Fleet-ditch with muddy current flows,
You chance to roam; where oyster-tubs in rows   190
Are ranged beside the posts; there stay thy haste,
And with the sav'ry fish indulge thy taste:
The damsel's knife the gaping shell commands,
While the salt liquor streams between her hands.
    The man had sure a palate covered o'er   195
With brass or steel, that on the rocky shore
First broke the oozy oyster's pearly coat,
And risked the living morsel down his throat.
What will not lux'ry taste? Earth, sea, and air
Are daily ransacked for the bill of fare.   200
Blood stuffed in skins is British Christians' food,
And France robs marshes of the croaking brood;
Spongy morells in strong ragouts are found,

And in the soup the slimy snail is drowned.
    When from high spouts the dashing torrents fall,   205
Ever be watchful to maintain the wall;
For should'st thou quit thy ground, the rushing throng
Will with impetuous fury drive along;
All press to gain those honours thou hast lost,
And rudely shove thee far without the post.   210
Then to retrieve the shed you strive in vain,
Draggled all o'er, and soaked in floods of rain.
Yet rather bear the show'r, and toils of mud,
Than in the doubtful quarrel risk thy blood.
O think on Oedipus' detested state,   215
And by his woes be warned to shun thy fate.
    Where three roads joined, he met his sire unknown;
(Unhappy sire, but more unhappy son!)
Each claimed the way, their swords the strife decide,
The hoary monarch fell, he groaned and died!   220
Hence sprung the fatal plague that thinned thy reign,
Thy cursèd incest! and thy children slain!
Hence wert thou doomed in endless night to stray
Through Theban streets, and cheerless grope thy way.
    Contemplate, mortal, on thy fleeting years;   225
See, with black train the funeral pomp appears!
Whether some heir attends in sable state,
And mourns with outward grief a parent's fate;
Or the fair virgin, nipped in beauty's bloom,
A croud of lovers follow to her tomb.   230
Why is the hearse with 'scutcheons blazoned round,
And with the nodding plume of Ostrich crowned?
No: the dead know it not, nor profit gain;
It only serves to prove the living vain.
How short is life! how frail is human trust!   235
Is all this pomp for laying dust to dust?
    Where the nailed hoop defends the painted stall,
Brush not thy sweeping skirt too near the wall;
Thy heedless sleeve will drink the coloured oil,
And spot indelible thy pocket soil.   240
Has not wise nature strung the legs and feet
With firmest nerves, designed to walk the street?
Has she not given us hands, to grope aright,
Amidst the frequent dangers of the night?
And think'st thou not the double nostril meant,   245
To warn from oily woes by previous scent?

Who can the various city frauds recite,
With all the petty rapines of the night?
Who now the Guinea-dropper's bait regards,
Tricked by the sharper's dice, or juggler's cards? 250
Why should I warn thee ne'er to join the fray,
Where the sham-quarrel interrupts the way?
Lives there in these our days so soft a clown,
Braved by the bully's oaths, or threat'ning frown?
I need not strict enjoin the pocket's care, 255
When from the crowded play thou lead'st the fair;
Who has not here, or watch, or snuff-box lost,
Or handkerchiefs that India's shuttle boast?
    O! may thy virtue guard thee through the roads
Of Drury's mazy courts, and dark abodes, 260
The harlots guileful paths, who nightly stand,
Where Katherine Street descends into the Strand.
Say, vagrant Muse, their wiles and subtle arts,
To lure the strangers' unsuspecting hearts;
So shall our youth on healthful sinews tread, 265
And city cheeks grow warm with rural red.
    'Tis she who nightly strolls with saunt'ring pace,
No stubborn stays her yielding shape embrace;
Beneath the lamp her tawdry ribbons glare,
The new-scoured manteau, and the slattern air; 270
High-draggled petticoats her travels show,
And hollow cheeks with artful blushes glow;
With flatt'ring sounds she soothes the cred'lous ear,
My noble captain! charmer! love! my dear!
In riding-hood near tavern-doors she plies, 275
Or muffled pinners hide her livid eyes.
With empty bandbox she delights to range,
And feigns a distant errand from the 'Change;
Nay, she will oft the Quaker's hood profane,
And trudge demure the rounds of Drury-lane. 280
She darts from sars'net ambush wily leers,
Twitches thy sleeve, or with familiar airs
Her fan will pat thy cheek; these snares disdain,
Nor gaze behind thee, when she turns again.
    I knew a yeoman, who for thirst of gain, 285
To the great city drove from Devon's plain
His num'rous lowing herd; his herds he sold,
And his deep leathern pocket bagged with gold;
Drawn by a fraudful nymph, he gazed, he sighed;

Unmindful of his home, and distant bride,   290
She leads the willing victim to his doom,
Through winding alleys to her cobweb room.
Thence through the street he reels from post to post,
Valiant with wine, nor knows his treasure lost.
    The vagrant wretch th' assembled watchmen spies,   295
He waves his hanger, and their poles defies;
Deep in the Round House pent, all night he snores,
And the next morn in vain his fate deplores.
    Ah hapless swain, unused to pains and ills!
Can'st thou forego roast-beef for nauseous pills?   300
How wilt thou lift to Heav'n thy eyes and hands,
When the long scroll the surgeon's fees demands!
Or else (ye Gods avert that worst disgrace)
Thy ruined nose falls level with thy face,
Then shall thy wife thy loathsome kiss disdain,   305
And wholesome neighbours from thy mug refrain.
    Yet there are watchmen, who with friendly light
Will teach thy reeling steps to tread aright;
For sixpence will support thy helpless arm,
And home conduct thee, safe from nightly harm;   310
But if they shake their lanthorns, from afar
To call their breth'ren to confed'rate war
When rakes resist their pow'r; if hapless you
Should chance to wander with the scou'ring crew;
Though fortune yield thee captive, ne'er despair,   315
But seek the constable's consid'rate ear;
He will reverse the watchman's harsh decree,
Moved by the rhet'ric of a silver fee.
Thus would you gain some fav'rite courtier's word;
Fee not the petty clerks, but bribe my lord.   320
    Now is the time that rakes their revels keep;
Kindlers of riot, enemies of sleep.
His scattered pence the flying nicker flings,
And with the copper show'r the casement rings.
Who has not heard the scourer's midnight fame?   325
Who has not trembled at the Mohock's° name?   *aristocratic ruffians of the*
Was there a watchman took his hourly rounds,   *eighteenth century*
Safe from their blows, or new-invented wounds?   *(cf Mohawk)*
I pass their desp'rate deeds, and mischiefs done
Where from Snow Hill black steepy torrents run;   330
How matrons, hooped within the hoghead's womb,
Were tumbled furious thence, the rolling tomb

O'er the stones thunders, bounds from side to side.
So Regulus to save his country died.
    Where a dim gleam the paly lanthorn throws   335
O'er the mid pavement, heapy rubbish grows;
Or archèd vaults their gaping jaws extend,
Or the dark caves to common-shores descend.
Oft by the winds extinct the signal lies,
Or smothered in the glimmering socket dies,   340
E'er night has half rolled round her ebon throne;
In the wide gulf the shattered coach o'erthrown
Sinks with the snorting steeds; the reins are broke,
And from the crackling axle flies the spoke.
So when famed Eddystone's[18] far-shooting ray,   345
That led the sailor through the stormy way,
Was from its rocky roots by billows torn,
And the high turret in the whirlwind borne,
Fleets bulged their sides against the craggy land,
And pitchy ruines blackened all the strand.   350
    Who then through night would hire the harnessed steed,
And who would choose the rattling wheel for speed?
    But hark! distress with screaming voice draws nigh'r,
And wakes the slumb'ring street with cries of *Fire!*
At first a glowing red enwraps the skies,   355
And born by winds the scatt'ring sparks arise;
From beam to beam the fierce contagion spreads;
The spiry flames now lift aloft their heads,
Through the burst sash a blazing deluge pours,
And splitting tiles descend in rattling show'rs.   360
Now with thick crowds th' enlightened pavement swarms,
The fire-man sweats beneath his crookèd arms,
A leathern casque his vent'rous head defends,
Boldly he climbs where thickest smoke ascends;
Moved by the mother's streaming eyes and pray'rs,   365
The helpless infant through the flame he bears,
With no less virtue, than through hostile fire
The Dardan hero bore his aged sire.
See forceful engines spout their levelled streams,
To quench the blaze that runs along the beams;   370
The grappling hook plucks rafters from the walls,

---

[18] The famous lighthouse(s), some 14 miles south of Plymouth Hoe, warning ships off the notorious Eddystone reef. The second lighthouse structure was destroyed in the violent 1703 storm, with its builder, the rich merchant Henry Winstanley, inside.

And heaps on heaps the smoky ruin falls.
Blown by strong winds the fiery tempest roars,
Bears down new walls, and pours along the floors;
The heav'ns are all a-blaze, the face of night   375
Is covered with a sanguine dreadful light:
'Twas such a light involved thy tow'rs, O Rome,
The dire presage of mighty Cæsar's doom,
When the sun veiled in rust his mourning head,
And frightful prodigies the skies o'erspread.   380
Hark! the drum thunders! far, ye crowds, retire:
Behold! the ready match is tipped with fire,
The nitrous store is laid, the smutty train
With running blaze awakes the barrelled grain;
Flames sudden wrap the walls; with sullen sound   385
The shattered pile sinks on the smoky ground.
    So when the years shall have revolved the date,
Th' inevitable hour of Naples' fate,
Her sapped foundations shall with thunders shake,
And heave and toss upon the sulph'rous lake;   390
Earth's womb at once the fiery flood shall rend,
And in th' abyss her plunging tow'rs descend.
    Consider, reader, what fatigues I've known,
The toils, the perils of the wintry town;
What riots seen, what bustling crowds I bored,   395
How oft I crossed where carts and coaches roared;
Yet shall I bless my labours, if mankind
Their future safety from my dangers find.
Thus the bold traveller, (inured to toil,
Whose steps have printed Asia's desert soil,   400
The barb'rous Arabs haunt; or shiv'ring crossed
Dark Greenland's mountains of eternal frost;
Whom providence in length of years restores
To the wished harbour of his native shores)
Sets forth his journals to the public view,   405
To caution, by his woes, the wandring crew.
    And now complete my gen'rous labours lie,
Finished, and ripe for immortality.
Death shall entomb in dust this mould'ring frame,
But never reach th' eternal part, my fame.   410
When W* and G**, mighty names, are dead;
Or but at Chelsea under custards read;
When critics crazy bandboxes repair,
And tragedies, turned rockets, bounce in air;

High-raised on Fleet Street posts, consigned to fame,   415
This work shall shine, and walkers bless my name.

27. The Elephant and the Bookseller

Fable X

The man, who with undaunted toils
Sails unknown seas to unknown soils,
With various wonders feasts his sight:
What stranger wonders does he write!
We read, and in description view   5
Creatures which Adam never knew;
For, when we risk no contradiction,
It prompts the tongue to deal in fiction.
Those things that startle me or you,
I grant are strange; yet may be true.   10
Who doubts that elephants are found
For science and for sense renowned?
Borri records their strength of parts,
Extent of thought, and skill in arts;
How they perform the law's decrees,   15
And save the state the hang-man's fees,
And how by travel understand
The language of another land.
Let those, who question this report,
To Pliny's ancient page resort.   20
How learn'd was that sagacious breed!
Who now (like them) the Greek can read!
   As one of these, in days of yore,
Rummaged a shop of learning o'er,
Not like our modern dealers, minding   25
Only the margin's breadth and binding;
A book his curious eye detains,
Where, with exactest care and pains,
Were ev'ry beast and bird portrayed,
That e'er the search of man surveyed.   30
Their natures and their powers were writ
With all the pride of human wit;
The page he with attention spread,
And thus remarked on what he read.

'Man with strong reason is endowed;   35
A Beast scarce instinct is allowed:
But let this author's worth be tried,
'Tis plain that neither was his guide.
Can he discern the diffrent natures,
And weigh the pow'r of other creatures,   40
Who by the partial work hath shown
He knows so little of his own?
How falsely is the spaniel drawn!
Did Man from him first learn to fawn?
A dog proficient in the trade!   45
He, the chief flatt'rer nature made!
Go, man, the ways of courts discern,
You'll find a spaniel still might learn.
How can the fox's theft and plunder
Provoke his censure, or his wonder?   50
From courtiers' tricks, and lawyers' arts
The fox might well improve his parts.
The lion, wolf, and tiger's brood
He curses, for their thirst of blood;
But is not man to man a prey?   55
Beasts kill for hunger, men for pay.'
    The Bookseller, who heard him speak,
And saw him turn a page of Greek,
Thought, *what a genius have I found*!
Then thus addrest with bow profound.   60
    'Learn'd Sir, if you'd employ your pen
Against the senseless sons of men,
Or write the history of Siam,
No man is better pay than I am;
Or, since you're learn'd in Greek, let's see   65
Something against the Trinity.
    When wrinkling with a sneer his trunk,
'Friend', quoth the Elephant, 'you're drunk;
E'en keep your money, and be wise;
Leave man on man to criticise,   70
For that you ne'er can want a pen
Among the senseless sons of men,
They unprovoked will court the fray,
Envy's a sharper spur than pay,
No author ever spared a brother,   75
Wits are game-cocks to one another.'

Alexander Pope (1688–1744)

28. On Silence

Silence! coeval with eternity;
    Thou wert, e'er nature's self began to be,
'Twas one vast nothing, all, and all slept fast in thee.

Thine was the sway, e'er heav'n was formed, or earth,
    E'er fruitful thought conceived creation's birth,   5
Or midwife word gave aid, and spoke the infant forth.

Then various elements against thee joined,
    In one more various animal combined,
And framed the clam'rous race of busy human-kind.

The tongue moved gently first, and speech was low,   10
    'Till wrangling science taught it noise and show,
And wicked wit arose, thy most abusive foe.

But rebel wit deserts thee oft in vain;
    Lost in the maze of words, he turns again,
And seeks a surer state, and courts thy gentle reign.   15

Afflicted sense thou kindly dost set free,
    Oppressed with argumental tyranny,
And routed reason finds a safe retreat in thee.

With thee in private modest dulness lies,
    And in thy bosom lurks in thought's disguise;   20
Thou varnisher of fools, and cheat of all the wise!

Yet thy indulgence is by both confessed;
    Folly by thee lies sleeping in the breast,
And 'tis in thee at last that wisdom seeks for rest.

Silence, the knave's repute, the whore's good name,   25
    The only honour of the wishing dame;
Thy very want of tongue makes thee a kind of Fame.

But could'st thou seize some tongues that now are free,
How church and state would be obliged to thee!
At senate, and at bar, how welcome would'st thou be!   30

Yet speech, ev'n there, submissively withdraws
From rights of subjects, and the poor man's cause;
Then pompous silence reigns, and stills the noisy laws.

Past services of friends, good deeds of foes,
What fav'rites gain, and what the nation owes,   35
Fly the forgetful world, and in thy arms repose.

The country wit, religion of the town,
The courtier's learning, policy o'th' gown,
Are best by thee expressed, and shine in thee alone.

The parson's cant, the lawyer's sophistry,   40
Lord's quibble, critic's jest: all end in thee,
All rest in peace at last, and sleep eternally.

29. 'Women ben full of Ragerie'

an imitation of Chaucer

Women ben full of ragerie°,	*wantonness*
Yet swinken° nat sans secresie.	*toil*
Thilke° moral shall ye understond,	*this*
From schole-boy's tale of fayre Irelond°:	*[a proper name]*
Which to the fennes hath him betake,	5
To filch the gray ducke fro the lake.	
Right then, there passen by the way	
His aunt, and eke° her daughters tway.	*also*
Ducke in his trowses hath he hent°,	*shoved*
Not to be spied of ladies gent.	10
'But ho! our nephew,' (crieth one,)	
'Ho!' quoth another, 'Cozen John';	
And stoppen, and lough, and callen out, –	
This sely° clerk full low doth lout*:	*simple, bow*
They asken that, and talken this,	15
'Lo here is Coz,' and 'here is Miss.'	
But, as he glozeth with speeches soote°,	*sweet*

The ducke sore tickleth his erse roote:
Fore-piece and buttons all-to-brest,
Forth thrust a white neck, and red crest.   20
'Te-he,' cried ladies; clerke nought spake:
Miss stared; and gray ducke crieth *Quaake.*
'O Moder, Moder,' quoth the daughter,
'Be thilke same thing maids longe a'ter?'
'Bette is to pyne on coals and chalke,
Then trust on mon, whose yerde can *talke.*'   25

30. from *Essay on criticism*

   ... Of all the causes which conspire to blind
Man's erring judgement, and misguide the mind,
What the weak head with strongest bias rules,   205
Is pride, the never-failing vice of fools.
Whatever nature has in worth denied,
She gives in large recruits of needful pride;
For as in bodies, thus in souls we find
What wants in blood and spirits, swelled with wind: 210
Pride, where wit fails, steps in to our defence,
And fills up all the mighty void of sense.
If once right reason drives that cloud away,
Truth breaks upon us with resistless day.
Trust not yourself; but your defects to know,   215
Make use of ev'ry friend – and ev'ry foe.
   A little learning is a dang'rous thing;
Drink deep, or taste not the Piërian spring:
There shallow draughts intoxicate the brain,
And drinking largely sobers us again.   220
Fired at first sight with what the Muse imparts,
In fearless youth we tempt the heights of arts,
While from the bounded level of our mind,
Short views we take, nor see the lengths behind,
But more advanced, behold with strange surprise   225
New distant scenes of endless science rise!
So pleased at first the tow'ring Alps we try,
Mount o'er the vales, and seem to tread the sky,
Th' eternal snows appear already past,
And the first clouds and mountains seem the last: 230
But those attained, we tremble to survey

The growing labours of the lengthened way,
Th' increasing prospect tires our wand'ring eyes,
Hills peep o'er hills, and Alps on Alps arise!
    A perfect judge will read each work of wit,   235
With the same spirit that its author writ,
Survey the whole, nor seek slight faults to find
Where nature moves, and rapture warms the mind;
Nor lose, for that malignant dull delight,
The gen'rous pleasure to be charmed with wit.   240
But in such lays as neither ebb, nor flow,
Correctly cold, and regularly low,
That shunning faults, one quiet tenour keep;
We cannot blame indeed---but we may sleep.
In wit, as nature, what affects our hearts   245
Is not th' exactness of peculiar parts;
Tis not a lip, or eye, we beauty call,
But the joint force and full result of all.
Thus when we view some well-proportioned dome,
 (The world's just wonder, and ev'n thine, O Rome!)   250
No single parts unequally surprise,
All comes united to th' admiring eyes;
No monstrous height, or breadth, or length appear;
The whole at once is bold, and regular.
    Whoever thinks a faultless piece to see,   255
Thinks what ne'er was, nor is, nor e'er shall be.
In ev'ry work regard the writer's end,
Since none can compass more than they intend;
And if the means be just, the conduct true,
Applause, in spite of trivial faults, is due.   260
As men of breeding, sometimes men of wit,
T'avoid great errors, must the less commit.
Neglect the rules each verbal critic lays,
For not to know some trifles, is a praise.
Most critics, fond of some subservient art,   265
Still make the whole depend upon a part:
They talk of principles, but notions prize,
And all to one loved folly sacrifice ...

    ... Be thou the first true merit to befriend,
His praise is lost, who stays 'till all commend.
Short is the date, alas, of modern rhymes,
And 'tis but just to let 'em live betimes.
No longer now that golden age appears,   480

When patriarch-wits survived a thousand years:
Now length of fame (our second life) is lost,
And bare threescore is all ev'n that can boast:
Our sons their fathers failing language see,
And such as Chaucer is, shall Dryden be.   485
So when the faithful pencil has designed
Some bright idea of the master's mind,
Where a new world leaps out at his command,
And ready nature waits upon his hand;
When the ripe colours soften and unite,   490
And sweetly melt into just shade and light,
When mellowing years their full perfection give,
And each bold figure just begins to live;
The treach'rous colours the fair art betray,
And all the bright creation fades away! . . .   495

    . . . 'Tis best sometimes your censure to restrain,
And charitably let the dull be vain:
Your silence there is better than your spite,   600
For who can rail so long as they can write?
Still humming on, their drowsy course they keep,
And lashed so long, like tops, are lashed asleep.
False steps but help them to renew the race,
As after stumbling, jades will mend their pace.   605
What crowds of these, impenitently bold,
In sounds and jingling syllables grown old,
Still run on poets, in a raging vein,
Ev'n to the dregs and squeezings of the brain,
Strain out the last dull droppings of their sense,   610
And rhyme with all the rage of impotence.
    Such shameless bards we have; and yet 'tis true,
There are as mad, abandoned critics too.
The bookful blockhead, ignorantly read,
With loads of learned lumber in his head,   615
With his own tongue still edifies his ears,
And always list'ning to himself appears.
All books he reads, and all he reads assails,
From Dryden's *Fables* down to Durfey's *Tales*.
With him, most authors steal their works, or buy;   620
Garth did not write his own *Dispensary*.
Name a new play, and he's the poet's friend,
Nay showed his faults – but when would poets mend?
No place so sacred from such fops is barred,

Nor is Paul's church more safe than Paul's church-yard: 625
Nay, fly to altars; there they'll talk you dead;
For fools rush in where angels fear to tread.
Distrustful sense with modest caution speaks,
It still looks home, and short excursions makes;
But rattling nonsense in full vollies breaks,   630
And never shocked, and never turned aside,
Bursts out, resistless, with a thund'ring tide.
 But where's the man, who counsel can bestow,
Still pleased to teach, and yet not proud to know?
Unbiassed, or by favour, or by spite;   635
Not dully prepossessed, or blindly right;
Though learn'd, well-bred; and though well-bred, sincere;
Modestly bold, and humanly severe:
Who to a friend his faults can freely show,
And gladly praise the merit of a foe?   640
Blest with a taste exact, yet unconfined;
A knowledge both of books and human-kind;
Gen'rous converse; a soul exempt from pride;
And love to praise, with reason on his side?
 Such once were Critics; such the happy few,   645
Athens and Rome in better ages knew.
The mighty Stagirite° first left the shore,   *Aristotle*
Spread all his sails, and durst the deeps explore;
He steered securely, and discovered far,
Led by the light of the Mæonian Star.   650
Poets, a race long unconfined, and free,
Still fond and proud of savage liberty,
Received his laws; and stood convinced 'twas fit
Who conquered Nature, should preside o'er Wit.
 Horace still charms with graceful negligence,   655
And without method talks us into sense,
Will like a friend, familiarly convey
The truest notions in the easiest way.
He, who supreme in judgement, as in wit,
Might boldly censure, as he boldly writ,   660
Yet judged with coolness, though he sung with fire,
His precepts teach but what his works inspire.
Our critics take a contrary extreme,
They judge with fury, but they write with fle'me:
Nor suffers Horace more in wrong translations   665
By wits, than critics in as wrong quotations.
 See Dionysius Homer's thoughts refine,

And call new beauties forth from ev'ry line!
    Fancy and art in gay Petronius meet,
The scholar's learning, with the courtier's wit.   670
    In grave Quintilian's copious work, we find
The justest rules, and clearest method joined:
Thus useful arms in magazines we place,
All ranged in order, and disposed with grace;
Nor thus alone the curious eye to please,   675
But to be found, when need requires, with ease.
    Thee, bold Longinus! all the Nine inspire,
And bless their critic with a poet's fire.
An ardent judge, who zealous in his trust,
With warmth gives sentence, yet is always just;   680
Whose own example strengthens all his laws,
And is himself that great sublime he draws.
    Thus long succeeding critics justly reigned,
Licence repressed, and useful laws ordained.
Learning and Rome alike in empire grew,   685
And arts still followed where her eagles flew.
From the same foes, at last, both felt their doom,
And the same age saw learning fall, and Rome.
With tyranny, then superstition joined,
As that the body, this enslaved the mind;   690
Much was believed, but little understood,
And to be dull was construed to be good;
A second deluge learning thus o'er-run,
And the monks finished what the Goths begun.
    At length Erasmus, that great, injured name,   695
(The glory of the priesthood, and the shame!)
Stemmed the wild torrent of a barb'rous age,
And drove those holy Vandals off the stage.
    But see! each Muse, in Leo's golden days,
Starts from her trance, and trims her withered bays!   700
Rome's ancient genius, o'er its ruins spread,
Shakes off the dust, and rears his rev'rend head.
Then sculpture and her sister-arts revive;
Stones leaped to form, and rocks began to live;
With sweeter notes each rising temple rung;   705
A Raphael painted, and a Vida sung.
Immortal Vida! on whose honoured brow
The poet's bays and critic's ivy grow:
Cremona now shall ever boast thy name,
As next in place to Mantua, next in fame!   710

But soon by impious arms from Latium chased,
Their ancient bounds the banished Muses passed;
Thence arts o'er all the northern world advance;
But critic learning flourished most in France:
The rules, a nation born to serve, obeys;   715
And Boileau still in right of Horace sways.
But we, brave Britons, foreign laws despised,
And kept unconquered, and uncivilised,
Fierce for the liberties of wit, and bold,
We still defied the Romans, as of old.   720
Yet some there were, among the sounder few
Of those who less presumed, and better knew,
Who durst assert the juster ancient cause,
And here restored wit's fundamental laws.
Such was the Muse, whose rules and practice tell,   725
Nature's chief masterpiece is writing well.
Such was Roscommon[19] – not more learn'd than good,
With manners gen'rous as his noble blood;
To him the wit of Greece and Rome was known,
And ev'ry author's merit but his own.   730
Such late was Walsh[20], the Muse's judge and friend,
Who justly knew to blame or to commend;
To failings mild, but zealous for desert;
The clearest head, and the sincerest heart.
This humble praise, lamented Shade! receive,   735
This praise at least a grateful Muse may give:
The Muse, whose early voice you taught to sing,
Prescribed her heights, and pruned her tender wing,
(Her guide now lost) no more attempts to rise,
But in low numbers short excursions tries:
Content, if hence th' unlearn'd their wants may view,   740
The learn'd reflect on what before they knew:
Careless of censure, nor too fond of fame;
Still pleased to praise, yet not afraid to blame;
Averse alike to flatter, or offend;
Not free from faults, nor yet too vain to mend.   745

[19] Wentworth Dillon, the fourth Earl or Roscommon *(c.* 1633–1685) translated Horace's *Ars Poetica* into verse and composed an *Essay on Translated Verse*. He was Milton's first public advocate.

[20] Dryden valued the poet William Walsh (1663–1708) as a judge, and Walsh praised Pope's efforts.

31. Windsor Forest

To the Right Honourable George, Lord Lansdown

Non injussa cano: Te nostræ Vare myricæ
Te Nemus omne canet; nec Phoebo gratior ulla est
Quam sibi quæ Vari præscripsit pagina nomen.

Virgil, *Eclogue* VI, lines 9–12[21]

Thy forests, Windsor! and thy green retreats,
At once the Monarch's and the Muse's seats,
Invite my lays. Be present, sylvan maids!
Unlock your springs, and open all your shades.
Granville commands; your aid O Muses bring!   5
What Muse for Granville can refuse to sing?
   The groves of Eden, vanished now so long,
Live in description, and look green in song:
These, were my breast inspired with equal flame,
Like them in beauty, should be like in fame.   10
Here hills and vales, the woodland and the plain,
Here earth and water, seem to strive again;
Not Chaos-like together crushed and bruised,
But as the world, harmoniously confused:
Where order in variety we see,   15
And where, though all things differ, all agree.
Here waving groves a chequered scene display,
And part admit, and part exclude the day;
As some coy nymph her lover's warm address
Nor quite indulges, nor can quite repress.   20
There, interspersed in lawns and opening glades,
Thin trees arise that shun each other's shades.
Here in full light the russet plains extend;
There wrapped in clouds the bluish hills ascend.

---

[21] Pope compresses into three lines Virgil's four;
    Non iniussa cano. Si quis tamen haec quoque, si quis
    captus amore leget, te nostrae, Vare, myricae,
    te nemus omne canet; nec Phoebo gratior ulla est
    quam sibi quae Vari praescripsit pagina nomen . . .
C. H. Sisson's free translation reads:
    But I will sing of you, and bind
    Bearers to honour you, the grove
    Shall sing of you and bring you love.
    The name of Varus guarantees
    That everything I write shall please.

Ev'n the wild heath displays her purple dyes,   25
And 'midst the desert fruitful fields arise,
That crowned with tufted trees and springing corn,
Like verdant isles the sable waste adorn.
Let *India* boast her plants, nor envy we
The weeping amber or the balmy tree,   30
While by our oaks the precious loads are born,
And realms commanded which those trees adorn.
Not proud Olympus yields a nobler sight,
Though Gods assembled grace his tow'ring height,
Than what more humble mountains offer here,   35
Where, in their blessings, all those Gods appear.
See Pan with flocks, with fruits Pomona crowned,
Here blushing Flora paints th' enameled ground,
Here Ceres' gifts in waving prospect stand,
And nodding tempt the joyful reaper's hand;   40
Rich industry sits smiling on the plains,
And peace and plenty tell, a Stuart reigns.
   Not thus the land appeared in ages past,
A dreary desert and a gloomy waste,
To savage beasts and savage laws a prey,   45
And kings more furious and severe than they;
Who claimed the skies, dispeopled air and floods,
The lonely lords of empty wilds and woods:
Cities laid waste, they stormed the dens and caves,
 (For wiser brutes were backward to be slaves).   50
What could be free, when lawless beasts obeyed,
And ev'n the elements a tyrant swayed?
In vain kind seasons swelled the teeming grain,
Soft show'rs distilled, and suns grew warm in vain;
The swain with tears his frustrate labour yields,   55
And famished dies amidst his ripened fields.
What wonder then, a beast or subject slain
Were equal crimes in a despotic reign?
Both doomed alike, for sportive Tyrants bled,
But that the subject starved, the beast was fed.   60
Proud Nimrod first the bloody chase began,
A mighty hunter, and his prey was man:
Our haughty Norman boasts that barb'rous name,
And makes his trembling slaves the royal game.
The fields are ravished from th' industrious swains,   65
From men their cities, and from Gods their fanes:
The levelled towns with weeds lie covered o'er;

The hollow winds through naked temples roar;
Round broken columns clasping ivy twined;
O'er heaps of ruin stalked the stately hind;   70
The fox obscene to gaping tombs retires,
And savage howlings fill the sacred quires.
Awed by his nobles, by his commons cursed,
Th' oppressor ruled tyrannic where he durst,
Stretched o'er the poor and church his iron rod,   75
And served alike his vassals and his God.
Whom ev'n the Saxon spared, and bloody Dane,
The wanton victims of his sport remain:
But see, the man who spacious regions gave
A waste for beasts, himself denied a grave!   80
Stretched on the lawn, his second hope survey,
At once the chaser, and at once the prey:
Lo Rufus, tugging at the deadly dart,
Bleeds in the forest, like a wounded hart.
Succeeding monarchs heard the subjects' cries,   85
Nor saw displeased the peaceful cottage rise.
Then gath'ring flocks on unknown mountains fed,
O'er sandy wilds were yellow harvests spread,
The forests wondered at th' unusual grain,
And secret transport touched the conscious swain.   90
Fair Liberty, Britannia's goddess, rears
Her cheerful head, and leads the golden years.
   Ye vig'rous swains! while youth ferments your blood,
And purer spirits swell the sprightly flood,
Now range the hills, the thickest woods beset,   95
Wind the shrill horn, or spread the waving net.
When milder autumn summer's heat succeeds,
And in the new-shorn field the partridge feeds,
Before his lord the ready spaniel bounds,
Panting with hope, he tries the furrowed grounds;   100
But when the tainted gales the game betray,
Couched close he lies, and meditates the prey:
Secure they trust th' unfaithful field, beset,
Till hov'ring o'er 'em sweeps the swelling net.
Thus (if small things we may with great compare)   105
When Albion sends her eager sons to war,
Some thoughtless town, with ease and plenty blest,
Near, and more near, the closing lines invest;
Sudden they seize th' amazed, defenceless prize,
And high in air Britannia's standard flies.   110

See! from the brake the whirring pheasant springs,
And mounts exulting on triumphant wings:
Short is his joy; he feels the fiery wound,
Flutters in blood, and panting beats the ground.
Ah! what avail his glossy, varying dyes,   115
His purple crest, and scarlet-circled eyes,
The vivid green his shining plumes unfold,
His painted wings, and breast that flames with gold?
    Nor yet, when moist Arcturus clouds the sky,
The woods and fields their pleasing toils deny.   120
To plains with well-breathed beagles we repair,
And trace the mazes of the circling hare:
(Beasts, urged by us, their fellow-beasts pursue,
And learn of man each other to undo).
With slaught'ring guns th' unwearied fowler roves,   125
When frosts have whitened all the naked groves;
Where doves in flocks the leafless trees o'ershade,
And lonely woodcocks haunt the wat'ry glade.
He lifts the tube, and levels with his eye;
Strait a short thunder breaks the frozen sky: 130
Oft, as in airy rings they skim the heath,
The clam'rous lapwings feel the leaden death:
Oft, as the mounting larks their notes prepare,
They fall, and leave their little lives in air.
    In genial spring, beneath the quiv'ring shade,   135
Where cooling vapours breathe along the mead,
The patient fisher takes his silent stand,
Intent, his angle trembling in his hand;
With looks unmoved, he hopes the scaly breed,
And eyes the dancing cork, and bending reed.   140
Our plenteous streams a various race supply,
The bright-eyed perch with fins of Tyrian dye,
The silver eel, in shining volumes rolled,
The yellow carp, in scales bedropped with gold,
Swift trouts, diversified with crimson stains,   145
And pykes, the tyrants of the wat'ry plains.
    Now Cancer glows with Phoebus' fiery car;
The youth rush eager to the sylvan war,
Swarm o'er the lawns, the forest walks surround,
Rouse the fleet hart, and cheer the opening hound.   150
Th' impatient courser pants in ev'ry vein,
And pawing, seems to beat the distant plain;
Hills, vales, and floods appear already crossed,

And e'er he starts, a thousand steps are lost.
See! the bold youth strain up the threat'ning steep, 155
Rush through the thickets, down the valleys sweep,
Hang o'er their coursers' heads with eager speed,
And earth rolls back beneath the flying steed.
Let old Arcadia boast her ample plain,
Th' immortal huntress, and her virgin-train; 160
Nor envy, Windsor! since thy shades have seen
As bright a Goddess, and as chaste a Queen;
Whose care, like hers, protects the sylvan reign,
The earth's fair light, and empress of the main.
Here, as old bards have sung, Diana strayed, 165
Bathed in the springs, or sought the cooling shade;
Here armed with silver bows, in early dawn,
Her buskinned Virgins traced the dewy lawn.
Above the rest a rural nymph was famed,
Thy offspring, Thames! the fair Lodona named; 170
(Lodona's fate, in long oblivion cast,
The Muse shall sing, and what she sings shall last.)
Scarce could the Goddess from her nymph be known,
But by the crescent and the golden zone.
She scorned the praise of beauty, and the care, 175
A belt her waist, a fillet binds her hair,
A painted quiver on her shoulder sounds,
And with her dart the flying deer she wounds.
It chanced, as eager of the chase, the maid
Beyond the forest's verdant limits strayed, 180
Pan saw and loved, and burning with desire
Pursued her flight, her flight increased his fire.
Not half so swift the trembling doves can fly,
When the fierce eagle cleaves the liquid sky;
Not half so swiftly the fierce eagle moves, 185
When through the clouds he drives the trembling doves;
As from the god she flew with furious pace,
Or as the god, more furious, urged the chase.
Now fainting, sinking, pale, the nymph appears;
Now close behind, his sounding steps she hears; 190
And now his shadow reached her as she run,
His shadow lengthened by the setting sun;
And now his shorter breath, with sultry air,
Pants on her neck, and fans her parting hair.
In vain on father Thames she called for aid, 195
Nor could Diana help her injured maid.

Faint, breathless, thus she prayed, nor prayed in vain;
'Ah Cynthia! ah – though banished from thy train,
Let me, O let me, to the shades repair,
My native shades – there weep, and murmur there.'   200
She said, and melting as in tears she lay,
In a soft, silver stream dissolved away.
The silver stream her virgin coldness keeps,
For ever murmurs, and for ever weeps;
Still bears the name the hapless virgin bore,   205
And bathes the forest where she ranged before.
In her chaste current oft the Goddess laves,
And with celestial tears augments the waves.
Oft in her glass the musing shepherd spies
The headlong mountains and the downward skies,   210
The watry landscape of the pendant woods,
And absent trees that tremble in the floods;
In the clear azure gleam the flocks are seen,
And floating forests paint the waves with green.
Through the fair scene roll slow the ling'ring streams,   215
Then foaming pour along, and rush into the Thames.
    Thou too, great father of the British floods!
With joyful pride survey'st our lofty woods;
Where tow'ring oaks their spreading honours rear,
And future navies on thy shores appear.   220
Not Neptune's self from all his streams receives
A wealthier tribute, than to thine he gives.
No seas so rich, so gay no banks appear,
No lake so gentle, and no spring so clear.
Not fabled Po more swells the poet's lays,   225
While through the skies his shining current strays,
Than thine, which visits Windsor's famed abodes,
To grace the mansion of our earthly Gods:
Nor all his stars a brighter lustre show,
Than the fair nymphs that grace thy side below: 230
Here Jove himself, subdued by beauty still,
Might change Olympus for a nobler hill.
    Happy the man whom this bright court approves,
His sov'reign favours, and his country loves:
Happy next him, who to these shades retires,   235
Whom nature charms, and whom the Muse inspires;
Whom humbler joys of home-felt quiet please,
Successive study, exercise, and ease.
He gathers health from herbs the forest yields,

And of their fragrant physic spoils the fields: 240
With chymic art exalts the min'ral pow'rs,
And draws the aromatic souls of flow'rs:
Now marks the course of rolling orbs on high;
O'er figured worlds now travels with his eye:
Of ancient writ unlocks the learned store,   245
Consults the dead, and lives past ages o'er:
Or wand'ring thoughtful in the silent wood,
Attends the duties of the wise and good,
T' observe a mean, be to himself a friend,
To follow nature, and regard his end;   250
Or looks on heav'n with more than mortal eyes,
Bids his free soul expatiate in the skies,
Amid her kindred stars familiar roam,
Survey the region, and confess her home!
Such was the life great Scipio once admired,   255
Thus Atticus, and Trumbal thus retired.
　　Ye sacred Nine! that all my soul possess,
Whose raptures fire me, and whose visions bless,
Bear me, oh bear me to sequestered scenes,
The bow'ry mazes, and surrounding greens;   260
To Thames's banks which fragrant breezes fill,
Or where ye Muses sport on Cooper's Hill.
(On Cooper's Hill eternal wreaths shall grow,
While lasts the mountain, or while Thames shall flow.)
I seem through consecrated walks to rove,   265
I hear soft music die along the grove;
Led by the sound I roam from shade to shade,
By god-like poets venerable made:
Here his first lays majestic Denham sung;
There the last numbers flowed from Cowley's tongue.   270
O early lost! what tears the river shed,
When the sad pomp along his banks was led?
His drooping swans on ev'ry note expire,
And on his willows hung each Muse's lyre.
　　Since fate relentless stopped their heav'nly voice,   275
No more the forests ring, or groves rejoice;
Who now shall charm the shades, where Cowley strung
His living harp, and lofty Denham sung?
But hark! the groves rejoice, the forest rings!
Are these revived? or is it Granville sings?   280
　　'Tis yours, my Lord, to bless our soft retreats,
And call the Muses to their ancient seats;

To paint anew the flow'ry sylvan scenes,
To crown the forests with immortal greens,
Make Windsor-hills in lofty numbers rise,   285
And lift her turrets nearer to the skies;
To sing those honours you deserve to wear,
And add new lustre to her silver star.
   Here noble Surrey felt the sacred rage,
Surrey, the Granville of a former age;   290
Matchless his pen, victorious was his lance,
Bold in the lists, and graceful in the dance:
In the same shades the Cupids tuned his lyre,
To the same notes, of love, and soft desire:
Fair Geraldine, bright object of his vow,   295
Then filled the groves, as heav'nly Myra now.
   Oh would'st thou sing what heroes Windsor bore,
What kings first breathed upon her winding shore,
Or raise old warriors, whose adored remains
In weeping vaults her hallowed earth contains!   300
With Edward's acts adorn the shining page,
Stretch his long triumphs down through ev'ry age,
Draw monarchs chained, and Crecy's glorious field,
The lillies blazing on the regal shield.
Then, from her roofs when Verrio's colours fall,   305
And leave inanimate the naked wall,
Still in thy song should vanquished France appear,
And bleed for ever under Britin's spear.
   Let softer strains ill-fated Henry mourn,
And palms eternal flourish round his urn.   310
Here o'er the martyr-King the marble weeps,
And fast beside him, once-feared Edward sleeps:
Whom not th' extended Albion could contain,
From old Belerium to the northern main,
The grave unites; where ev'n the great find rest,   315
And blended lie th' oppressor and th' oppressed!
   Make sacred Charles's tomb for ever known,
(Obscure the place, and un-inscribed the stone)
Oh fact accurs'd! what tears has Albion shed,
Heav'ns, what new wounds! and how her old have bled?   320
She saw her sons with purple deaths expire,
Her sacred domes involved in rolling fire,
A dreadful series of intestine wars,
Inglorious triumphs, and dishonest scars.
At length great Anna said – 'Let discord cease!'   325

She said, the world obeyed, and all was peace!
    In that blest moment, from his oozy bed
Old father Thames advanced his rev'rend head.
His tresses dropped with dews, and o'er the stream
His shining horns diffused a golden gleam: 330
Graved on his urn, appeared the Moon that guides
His swelling waters, and alternate tides;
The figured streams in waves of silver rolled,
And on their banks Augusta rose in gold.
Around his throne the sea-born brothers stood,   335
Who swell with tributary urns his flood:
First the famed authors of his ancient name,
The winding Isis and the fruitful Thame:
The Kennet swift, for silver eels renowned;
The Loddon slow, with verdant alders crowned;   340
Cole, whose clear streams his flow'ry islands lave;
And chalky Wey, that rolls a milky wave:
The blue, transparent Vandalis appears;
The gulfy Lee his sedgy tresses rears;
And sullen Mole, that hides his diving flood;   345
And silent Darent, stained with Danish blood.
    High in the midst, upon his urn reclined,
(His sea-green mantle waving with the wind)
The God appeared: he turned his azure eyes
Where Windsor-domes and pompous turrets rise;   350
Then bowed and spoke; the winds forget to roar,
And the hushed waves glide softly to the shore.
    'Hail, sacred Peace! hail long-expected days,
That Thames's glory to the stars shall raise!
Though Tiber's streams immortal Rome behold,   355
Though foaming Hermus swells with tides of gold,
From heav'n itself though sev'n-fold Nilus flows,
And harvests on a hundred realms bestows;
These now no more shall be the Muse's themes,
Lost in my fame, as in the sea their streams.   360
Let Volga's banks with iron squadrons shine,
And groves of lances glitter on the Rhine,
Let barb'rous Ganges arm a servile train;
Be mine the blessings of a peaceful reign.
No more my sons shall dye with British blood   365
Red Iber's sands, or Ister's foaming flood;
Safe on my shore each unmolested swain
Shall tend the flocks, or reap the bearded grain;

The shady empire shall retain no trace
Of war or blood, but in the sylvan chase;   370
The trumpet sleep, while cheerful horns are blown,
And arms employed on birds and beasts alone.
Behold! th' ascending villa's on my side,
Project long shadows o'er the crystal tide.
Behold! Augusta's glitt'ring spires increase,   375
And temples rise, the beauteous works of Peace.
I see, I see where two fair cities bend
Their ample bow, a new Whitehall ascend!
There mighty nations shall enquire their doom,
The world's great oracle in times to come;   380
There kings shall sue, and suppliant states be seen
Once more to bend before a British queen.
    'Thy trees, fair Windsor! now shall leave their woods,
And half thy forests rush into my floods,
Bear Britain's thunder, and her cross display,   385
To the bright regions of the rising day;
Tempt icy seas, where scarce the waters roll,
Where clearer flames glow round the frozen pole;
Or under southern skies exalt their sails,
Led by new stars, and borne by spicy gales!   390
For me the balm shall bleed, and amber flow,
The coral redden, and the ruby glow,
The pearly shell its lucid globe infold,
And Phoebus warm the ripening ore to gold.
The time shall come, when free as seas or wind   395
Unbounded Thames shall flow for all mankind,
Whole nations enter with each swelling tide,
And seas but join the regions they divide;
Earth's distant ends our glory shall behold,
And the new world launch forth to seek the old.   400
Then ships of uncouth form shall stem the tide,
And feathered people crowd my wealthy side,
And naked youths and painted chiefs admire
Our speech, our colour, and our strange attire!
Oh stretch thy reign, fair Peace! from shore to shore,   405
'Till conquest cease, and slav'ry be no more;
'Till the freed Indians in their native groves
Reap their own fruits, and woo their sable loves,
Peru once more a race of kings behold,
And other Mexicos be roofed with gold.   410
Exiled by thee from earth to deepest hell,

In brazen bonds shall barb'rous discord dwell:
Gigantic pride, pale terror, gloomy care,
And mad ambition, shall attend her there:
There purple vengeance bathed in gore retires,   415
Her weapons blunted, and extinct her fires:
There hateful envy her own snakes shall feel,
And persecution mourn her broken wheel:
There faction roar, rebellion bite her chain,
And gasping furies thirst for blood in vain.'   420
    Here cease thy flight, nor with unhallowed lays
Touch the fair fame of Albion's golden days:
The thoughts of gods let Granville's verse recite,
And bring the scenes of opening fate to light.
My humble Muse, in unambitious strains,   425
Paints the green forests and the flow'ry plains,
Where Peace descending bids her olives spring,
And scatters blessings from her dove-like wing.
Ev'n I more sweetly pass my careless days,
Pleased in the silent shade with empty praise;   430
Enough for me, that to the list'ning swains
First in these fields I sung the sylvan strains.

32. Two or Three, or, A Receipt to make a Cuckold

Two or three visits, and two or three bows,
Two or three civil things, two or three vows,
Two or three kisses, with two or three sighs,
Two or three *Jesus's* – and *let me dies* –
Two or three squeezes, and two or three touses,   5
With two or three thousand pound lost at their houses,
Can never fail cuckolding two or three spouses.

33. from *The Rape of the Lock*

Canto I

> Nolueram, Belinda, tuos violare capillos;
> Sed iuvat, hoc precibus me tribuisse tuis.

Martial, *Epigrams* xii. 84 (II 1-2)[22]

---

[22] 'I was reluctant, Belinda [Martial's poem addresses Polytimus, an adolescent lad], to mess up your hair, but I am glad now that I harkened to your prayers.'

What dire offence from am'rous causes springs
What mighty contests rise from trivial things,
I sing – This verse to Caryll,[23] Muse! is due:
This, ev'n Belinda may vouchsafe to view:
Slight is the subject, but not so the praise,   5
If she inspire, and he approve my lays.
Say what strange motive, Goddess! could compel
A well-bred lord t' assault a gentle belle?
    O say what stranger cause, yet unexplored,
Could make a gentle belle reject a lord?   10
In tasks so bold, can little men engage,
And in soft bosoms dwells such mighty rage?
    Sol through white curtains shot a tim'rous ray,
And oped those eyes that must eclipse the day;
Now lap-dogs give themselves the rousing shake,   15
And sleepless lovers, just at twelve, awake:
Thrice rung the bell, the slipper knocked the ground,
And the pressed watch returned a silver sound.
Belinda still her downy pillow pressed,
Her guardian sylph prolonged the balmy rest;   20
'Twas he had summoned to her silent bed
The morning dream that hovered o'er her head;
A youth more glitt'ring than a birthnight beau,
(That ev'n in slumber caused her cheek to glow)
Seemed to her ear his winning lips to lay,   25
And thus in whispers said, or seemed to say.
    'Fairest of mortals, thou distinguished care
Of thousand bright inhabitants of air!
If e'er one vision touched thy infant thought,
Of all the nurse and all the priest have taught,   30
Of airy elves by moonlight shadows seen,
The silver token, and the circled green,
Or virgins visited by angel pow'rs,
With golden crowns and wreaths of heav'nly flow'rs,
Hear and believe! thy own importance know,   35
Nor bound thy narrow views to things below.
Some secret truths from learned pride concealed,
To maids alone and children are revealed:
What though no credit doubting wits may give?
The fair and innocent shall still believe.   40

[23] One of Pope's and Gay's close friends, John Caryll (1625–1711), diplomat and dramatist, who suggested the subject of the poem to Pope.

Know then, unnumbered spirits round thee fly,
The light militia of the lower sky;
These, though unseen, are ever on the wing,
Hang o'er the box, and hover round the ring.
Think what an equipage thou hast in air,   45
And view with scorn two pages and a chair.
As now your own, our beings were of old,
And once enclosed in woman's beauteous mold;
Thence, by a soft transition, we repair
From earthly vehicles to these of air.   50
Think not, when woman's transient breath is fled,
That all her vanities at once are dead;
Succeeding vanities she still regards,
And though she plays no more, o'erlooks the cards.
Her joy in gilded chariots, when alive,   55
And love of ombre, after death survive.
For when the fair in all their pride expire,
To their first elements their souls retire;
The sprites of fiery termagants in flame
Mount up, and take a salamander's name.   60
Soft yielding minds to water glide away,
And sip with nymphs, their elemental tea.
The graver prude sinks downward to a gnome,
In search of mischief still on earth to roam.
The light coquettes in sylphs aloft repair,   65
And sport and flutter in the fields of air.
    'Know further yet; whoever fair and chaste
Rejects mankind, is by some sylph embraced:
For spirits, freed from mortal laws, with ease
Assume what sexes and what shapes they please.   70
What guards the purity of melting maids,
In courtly balls, and midnight masquerades,
Safe from the treach'rous friend, the daring spark,
The glance by day, the whisper in the dark,
When kind occasion prompts their warm desires,   75
When music softens, and when dancing fires?
'Tis but their sylph, the wise celestials know,
Though honour is the word with men below.
    'Some nymphs there are, too conscious of their face,
For life predestined to the gnomes' embrace.   80
These swell their prospects and exalt their pride,
When offers are disdained, and love denied:
Then gay ideas crowd the vacant brain,

While peers, and dukes, and all their sweeping train,
And garters, stars, and coronets appear,   85
And in soft sounds "Your Grace" salutes their ear.
'Tis these that early taint the female soul,
Instruct the eyes of young coquettes to roll,
Teach infant cheeks a bidden blush to know,
And little hearts to flutter at a beau.   90
    'Oft, when the world imagine women stray,
The sylphs through mystic mazes guide their way,
Through all the giddy circle they pursue,
And old impertinence expel by new.
What tender maid but must a victim fall   95
To one man's treat, but for another's ball?
When Florio speaks, what virgin could withstand,
If gentle Damon did not squeeze her hand?
With varying vanities, from ev'ry part,
They shift the moving toyshop of their heart;   100
Where wigs with wigs, with sword-knots sword-knots strive,
Beaux banish beaux, and coaches coaches drive.
This erring mortals levity may call,
Oh blind to truth! the sylphs contrive it all.
    'Of these am I, who thy protection claim,   105
A watchful sprite, and Ariel is my name.
Late, as I ranged the crystal wilds of air,
In the clear mirror of thy ruling star
I saw, alas! some dread event impend,
Ere to the main this morning sun descend,   110
But Heav'n reveals not what, or how, or where:
Warned by the sylph, oh pious maid beware!
This to disclose is all thy guardian can.
Beware of all, but most beware of man!'
    He said; when Shock, who thought she slept too long, 115
Leaped up, and waked his mistress with his tongue.
'Twas then, Belinda, if report say true,
Thy eyes first opened on a billet-doux;
Wounds, charms, and *ardours* were no sooner read,
But all the vision vanished from thy head.   120
    And now, unveiled, the toilet stands displayed,
Each silver vase in mystic order laid.
First, robed in white, the nymph intent adores
With head uncovered, the cosmetic pow'rs.
A heav'nly image in the glass appears,   125
To that she bends, to that her eyes she rears;

Th' inferior priestess, at her altar's side,
Trembling, begins the sacred rites of pride.
Unnumbered treasures ope at once, and here
The various off'rings of the world appear;   130
From each she nicely culls with curious toil,
And decks the goddess with the glitt'ring spoil.
This casket India's glowing gems unlocks,
And all Arabia breathes from yonder box.
The tortoise here and elephant unite,   135
Transformed to combs, the speckled and the white.
Here files of pins extend their shining rows,
Puffs, powders, patches, bibles, billet-doux.
Now awful beauty puts on all its arms;
The fair each moment rises in her charms,   140
Repairs her smiles, awakens ev'ry grace,
And calls forth all the wonders of her face;
Sees by degrees a purer blush arise,
And keener lightnings quicken in her eyes.
The busy sylphs surround their darling care;   145
These set the head, and those divide the hair,
Some fold the sleeve, whilst others plait the gown;
And Betty's praised for labours not her own.

Canto II

Not with more glories, in th' ethereal plain,
The sun first rises o'er the purpled main,
Than issuing forth, the rival of his beams
Launched on the bosom of the silver Thames.
Fair nymphs, and well-drest youths around her shone,   5
But ev'ry eye was fixed on her alone.
On her white breast a sparkling cross she wore,
Which Jews might kiss, and infidels adore.
Her lively looks a sprightly mind disclose,
Quick as her eyes, and as unfixed as those: 10
Favours to none, to all she smiles extends,
Oft she rejects, but never once offends.
Bright as the sun, her eyes the gazers strike,
And, like the sun, they shine on all alike.
Yet graceful ease, and sweetness void of pride,   15
Might hide her faults, if belles had faults to hide:
If to her share some female errors fall,
Look on her face, and you'll forget 'em all.

This nymph, to the destruction of mankind,
Nourished two locks which graceful hung behind   20
In equal curls, and well conspired to deck
With shining ringlets the smooth iv'ry neck.
Love in these labyrinths his slaves detains,
And mighty hearts are held in slender chains.
With hairy springes we the birds betray,   25
Slight lines of hair surprise the finny prey,
Fair tresses man's imperial race insnare,
And beauty draws us with a single hair.
   Th' advent'rous baron the bright locks admired,
He saw, he wished, and to the prize aspired;   30
Resolved to win, he meditates the way,
By force to ravish, or by fraud betray;
For when success a lover's toil attends,
Few ask, if fraud or force attained his ends.
   For this, ere Phoebus rose, he had implored   35
Propitious heav'n, and ev'ry power adored,
But chiefly love – to love an altar built,
Of twelve vast French romances, neatly gilt.
There lay three garters, half a pair of gloves,
And all the trophies of his former loves.   40
With tender billet-doux he lights the pyre,
And breathes three am'rous sighs to raise the fire.
Then prostrate falls, and begs with ardent eyes
Soon to obtain, and long possess the prize:
The pow'rs gave ear, and granted half his pray'r,   45
The rest, the winds dispersed in empty air.
   But now secure the painted vessel glides,
The sunbeams trembling on the floating tides,
While melting music steals upon the sky,
And softened sounds along the waters die.   50
Smooth flow the waves, the zephyrs gently play,
Belinda smiled, and all the world was gay.
All but the sylph – with careful thoughts oppressed,
Th' impending woe sat heavy on his breast.
He summons straight his denizens of air;   55
The lucid squadrons round the sails repair:
Soft o'er the shrouds aerial whispers breathe,
That seemed but zephyrs to the train beneath.
Some to the sun their insect wings unfold,
Waft on the breeze, or sink in clouds of gold.   60
Transparent forms, too fine for mortal sight,

Their fluid bodies half dissolved in light.
Loose to the wind their airy garments flew,
Thin glitt'ring textures of the filmy dew;
Dipped in the richest tincture of the skies,   65
Where light disports in ever-mingling dyes,
While ev'ry beam new transient colours flings,
Colours that change whene'er they wave their wings.
Amid the circle, on the gilded mast,
Superior by the head, was Ariel placed: 70
His purple pinions op'ning to the sun,
He raised his azure wand, and thus begun.
    'Ye sylphs and sylphids, to your chief give ear,
Fays, fairies, genii, elves, and daemons hear!
Ye know the spheres and various tasks assigned   75
By laws eternal to th' aerial kind.
Some in the fields of purest aether play,
And bask and whiten in the blaze of day.
Some guide the course of wand'ring orbs on high,
Or roll the planets through the boundless sky.   80
Some less refined, beneath the moon's pale light
Pursue the stars that shoot athwart the night;
Or suck the mists in grosser air below,
Or dip their pinions in the painted bow,
Or brew fierce tempests on the wintry main,   85
Or o'er the glebe distil the kindly rain.
Others on earth o'er human race preside,
Watch all their ways, and all their actions guide:
Of these the chief the care of nations own,
And guard with arms divine the British throne.   90
    'Our humbler province is to tend the fair,
Not a less pleasing, tho' less glorious care.
To save the powder from too rude a gale,
Nor let th' imprisoned essences exhale;
To draw fresh colours from the vernal flow'rs,   95
To steal from rainbows ere they drop in show'rs
A brighter wash; to curl their waving hairs,
Assist their blushes, and inspire their airs;
Nay oft, in dreams, invention we bestow,
To change a flounce, or add a furbelow!   100
    'This day, black omens threat the brightest fair
That e'er deserved a watchful spirit's care;
Some dire disaster, or by force, or slight,
But what, or where, the fates have wrapped in night.

Whether the nymph shall break Diana's law,   105
Or some frail China jar receive a flaw,
Or stain her honour, or her new brocade,
Forget her pray'rs, or miss a masquerade,
Or lose her heart, or necklace, at a ball;
Or whether heav'n has doomed that Shock must fall.   110
Haste then ye spirits! to your charge repair;
The flutt'ring fan be Zephyretta's care;
The drops to thee, Brillante, we consign;
And, Momentilla, let the watch be thine;
Do thou, Crispissa, tend her fav'rite lock;   115
Ariel himself shall be the guard of Shock.
　　'To fifty chosen sylphs, of special note,
We trust th' important charge, the petticoat:
Oft have we known that sev'nfold fence to fail,
Tho' stiff with hoops, and armed with ribs of whale.   120
Form a strong line about the silver bound,
And guard the wide circumference around.
　　'Whatever spirit, careless of his charge,
His post neglects, or leaves the fair at large,
Shall feel sharp vengeance soon o'ertake his sins,   125
Be stopped in vials, or transfixed with pins;
Or plunged in lakes of bitter washes lie,
Or wedged whole ages in a bodkin's eye:
Gums and pomatums shall his flight restrain,
While clogged he beats his silken wings in vain;   130
Or alom-styptics with contracting pow'r
Shrink his thin essence like a rivelled flower.
Or, as Ixion fixed, the Wretch shall feel
The giddy motion of the whirling mill,
In fumes of burning chocolate shall glow,   135
And tremble at the sea that froths below!'
　　He spoke; the spirits from the sails descend;
Some, orb in orb, around the nymph extend,
Some thrid the mazy ringlets of her hair,
Some hang upon the pendants of her ear;   140
With beating hearts the dire event they wait,
Anxious, and trembling for the birth of fate.

34. Eloisa to Abelard

The Argument: Abelard and Eloisa flourished in the twelfth century; they were two of the most distinguished persons of their age in learning and beauty, but for nothing more famous than for their unfortunate passion. After a long course of calamities, they retired each to a several convent, and consecrated the remainder of their days to religion. It was many years after this separation, that a letter of Abelard's to a friend, which contained the history of his misfortune, fell into the hands of Eloisa. This awakening all her tenderness, occasioned those celebrated letters (out of which the following is partly extracted) which give so lively a picture of the struggles of grace and nature, virtue and passion. [A.P.]

In these deep solitudes and awful cells,
Where heav'nly-pensive, contemplation dwells,
And ever-musing melancholy reigns;
What means this tumult in a Vestal's veins?
Why rove my thoughts beyond this last retreat?   5
Why feels my heart its long-forgotten heat?
Yet, yet I love! – From Abelard, it came,
And Eloïsa yet must kiss the name.
    Dear fatal name! rest ever unrevealed,
Nor pass these lips in holy silence sealed: 10
Hide it, my heart, within that close disguise,
Where mixed with God's, his loved Idea lies:
Oh write it not, my hand – the name appears
Already written – wash it out, my tears!
In vain lost Eloïsa weeps and prays,   15
Her heart still dictates, and her hand obeys.
    Relentless walls! whose darksome round contains
Repentant sighs, and voluntary pains:
Ye rugged rocks! which holy knees have worn;
Ye grots and caverns shagged with horrid thorn!   20
Shrines! where their vigils pale-eyed virgins keep,
And pitying saints, whose statues learn to weep!
Though cold like you, unmoved and silent grown,
I have not yet forgot my self to stone.
Heav'n claims me all in vain, while he has part,   25
Still rebel nature holds out half my heart;
Nor pray'rs nor fasts its stubborn pulse restrain,
Nor tears, for ages, taught to flow in vain.
    Soon as thy letters trembling I unclose,
That well-known name awakens all my woes.   30
Oh name for ever sad! for ever dear!
Still breathed in sighs, still ushered with a tear.

I tremble too where'er my own I find,
Some dire misfortune follows close behind.
Line after line my gushing eyes o'erflow,   35
Led through a sad variety of woe:
Now warm in love, now with'ring in thy bloom,
Lost in a convent's solitary gloom!
There stern Religion quenched th' unwilling flame,
There died the best of passions, Love and Fame.   40
    Yet write, oh write me all, that I may join
Griefs to thy griefs, and echo sighs to thine.
Nor foes nor fortune take this pow'r away;
And is my Abelard less kind than they?
Tears still are mine, and those I need not spare,   45
Love but demands what else were shed in pray'r;
No happier task these faded eyes pursue;
To read and weep is all they now can do.
    Then share thy pain, allow that sad relief;
Ah, more than share it! give me all thy grief.   50
Heav'n first taught letters for some wretch's aid,
Some banished lover, or some captive maid;
They live, they speak, they breathe what love inspires,
Warm from the soul, and faithful to its fires,
The virgin's wish without her fears impart,   55
Excuse the blush, and pour out all the heart,
Speed the soft intercourse from soul to soul,
And waft a sigh from Indus to the Pole.
    Thou know'st how guiltless first I met thy flame,
When love approached me under friendship's name;   60
My fancy formed thee of angelic kind,
Some emanation of th' all-beauteous mind.
Those smiling eyes, attemp'ring ev'ry ray,
Shone sweetly lambent with celestial day.
Guiltless I gazed; heav'n listened while you sung;   65
And truths divine came mended from that tongue.
From lips like those what precept failed to move?
Too soon they taught me 'twas no sin to love;
Back through the paths of pleasing sense I ran,
Nor wished an angel whom I loved a man.   70
Dim and remote the joys of saints I see;
Nor envy them that heav'n I lose for thee.
    How oft, when prest to marriage, have I said,
Curse on all laws but those which love has made?
Love, free as air, at sight of human ties,   75

Spreads his light wings, and in a moment flies.
Let wealth, let honour, wait the wedded dame,
August her deed, and sacred be her fame;
Before true passion all those views remove,
Fame, wealth, and honour! what are you to Love? 80
The jealous God, when we profane his fires,
Those restless passions in revenge inspires,
And bids them make mistaken mortals groan,
Who seek in love for ought but love alone.
Should at my feet the world's great master fall, 85
Himself, his throne, his world, I'd scorn 'em all:
Not Cæsar's empress would I deign to prove;
No, make me mistress to the man I love;
If there be yet another name, more free,
More fond than mistress, make me that to thee! 90
Oh happy state! when souls each other draw,
When love is liberty, and nature, law:
All then is full, possessing, and possessed,
No craving void left aching in the breast;
Ev'n thought meets thought e'er from the lips it part, 95
And each warm wish springs mutual from the heart.
This sure is bliss (if bliss on earth there be)
And once the lot of Abelard and me.
   Alas how changed! what sudden horrors rise!
A naked lover bound and bleeding lies! 100
Where, where was Eloïse? her voice, her hand,
Her poniard, had opposed the dire command.
Barbarian stay! that bloody stroke restrain;
The crime was common, common be the pain.
I can no more; by shame, by rage suppressed, 105
Let tears, and burning blushes speak the rest.
   Can'st thou forget that sad, that solemn day,
When victims at yon altar's foot we lay?
Can'st thou forget what tears that moment fell,
When, warm in youth, I bade the world farewell? 110
As with cold lips I kissed the sacred veil,
The shrines all trembled, and the lamps grew pale:
Heav'n scarce believed the conquest it surveyed,
And saints with wonder heard the vows I made.
Yet then, to those dread altars as I drew, 115
Not on the Cross my eyes were fixed, but you:
Not grace, or zeal, love only was my call,
And if I lose thy love, I lose my all.

Come! with thy looks, thy words, relieve my woe;
Those still at least are left thee to bestow.   120
Still on that breast enamoured let me lie,
Still drink delicious poison from thy eye,
Pant on thy lip, and to thy heart be pressed;
Give all thou can'st – and let me dream the rest.
Ah no! instruct me other joys to prize,   125
With other beauties charm my partial eyes,
Full in my view set all the bright abode,
And make my soul quit Abelard for God.
    Ah think at least thy flock deserves thy care,
Plants of thy hand, and children of thy pray'r.   130
From the false world in early youth they fled,
By thee to mountains, wilds, and deserts led.
You raised these hallowed walls; the desert smiled,
And Paradise was opened in the wild.
No weeping orphan saw his father's stores   135
Our shrines irradiate, or emblaze the floors;
No silver saints, by dying misers given,
Here bribed the rage of ill-requited heav'n;
But such plain roofs as piety could raise,
And only vocal with the Maker's praise.   140
In these lone walls (their day's eternal bound)
These moss-grown domes with spiry turrets crowned,
Where awful arches make a noon-day night,
And the dim windows shed a solemn light;
Thy eyes diffused a reconciling ray,   145
And gleams of glory brightened all the day.
But now no face divine contentment wears,
'Tis all blank sadness, or continual tears.
See how the force of others' pray'rs I try,
(Oh pious fraud of am'rous charity!)   150
But why should I on others' pray'rs depend?
Come thou, my father, brother, husband, friend!
Ah let thy handmaid, sister, daughter move,
And, all those tender names in one, thy love!
The darksome pines that o'er yon' rocks reclined   155
Wave high, and murmur to the hollow wind,
The wand'ring streams that shine between the hills,
The grots that echo to the tinkling rills,
The dying gales that pant upon the trees,
The lakes that quiver to the curling breeze;   160
No more these scenes my meditation aid,

Or lull to rest the visionary maid.
But o'er the twilight groves, and dusky caves,
Long-sounding isles, and intermingled graves,
Black melancholy sits, and round her throws   165
A death-like silence, and a dread repose:
Her gloomy presence saddens all the scene,
Shades ev'ry flow'r, and darkens ev'ry green,
Deepens the murmur of the falling floods,
And breathes a browner horror on the woods.   170
    Yet here for ever, ever must I stay;
Sad proof how well a lover can obey!
Death, only death, can break the lasting chain;
And here ev'n then, shall my cold dust remain,
Here all its frailties, all its flames resign,   175
And wait, 'till 'tis no sin to mix with thine.
    Ah wretch! believed the spouse of God in vain,
Confessed within the slave of love and man.
Assist me heav'n! but whence arose that pray'r?
Sprung it from piety, or from despair?   180
Ev'n here, where frozen chastity retires,
Love finds an altar for forbidden fires.
I ought to grieve, but cannot what I ought;
I mourn the lover, not lament the fault;
I view my crime, but kindle at the view,   185
Repent old pleasures, and solicit new;
Now turned to heav'n, I weep my past offence,
Now think of thee, and curse my innocence.
Of all affliction taught a lover yet,
'Tis sure the hardest science, to forget!   190
How shall I lose the sin, yet keep the sense,
And love th' offender, yet detest th' offence?
How the dear object from the crime remove,
Or how distinguish penitence from love?
Unequal task! a passion to resign,   195
For hearts so touched, so pierced, so lost as mine.
Ere such a soul regains its peaceful state,
How often must it love, how often hate!
How often hope, despair, resent, regret,
Conceal, disdain – do all things but forget.   200
But let heav'n seize it, all at once 'tis fired,
Not touched, but rapt; not wakened, but inspired!
Oh come! oh teach me nature to subdue,
Renounce my love, my life, my self – and you.

Fill my fond heart with God alone, for he   205
Alone, can rival, can succeed to thee.
   How happy is the blameless Vestal's lot!
The world forgetting, by the world forgot:
Eternal sun-shine of the spotless mind!
Each pray'r accepted, and each wish resigned;   210
Labour and rest, that equal periods keep;
'Obedient slumbers that can wake and weep'[24];
Desires composed, affections ever even;
Tears that delight, and sighs that waft to heav'n.
Grace shines around her with serenest beams,   215
And whisp'ring angels prompt her golden dreams.
For her the Spouse prepares the bridal ring,
For her white virgins Hymenæeals sing,
For her th' unfading rose of Eden blooms,
And wings of seraphs shed divine perfumes,   220
To sounds of heav'nly harps she dies away,
And melts in visions of eternal day.
   Far other dreams my erring soul employ,
Far other raptures, of unholy joy:
When at the close of each sad, sorrowing day,   225
Fancy restores what vengeance snatched away,
Then conscience sleeps, and leaving nature free,
All my loose soul unbounded springs to thee.
O cursed, dear horrors of all-conscious night!
How glowing guilt exalts the keen delight!   230
Provoking dæmons all restraint remove,
And stir within me ev'ry source of love.
I hear thee, view thee, gaze o'er all thy charms,
And round thy phantom glue my clasping arms.
I wake: – no more I hear, no more I view,   235
The phantom flies me, as unkind as you.
I call aloud; it hears not what I say;
I stretch my empty arms; it glides away.
To dream once more I close my willing eyes;
Ye soft illusions, dear deceits, arise!   240
Alas, no more! – methinks we wand'ring go
Through dreary wastes, and weep each other's woe,
Where round some mould'ring tow'r pale ivy creeps,
And low-browed rocks hang nodding o'er the deeps.
Sudden you mount, you beckon from the skies;   245

---

[24] from Richard Crashaw

Clouds interpose, waves roar, and winds arise.
I shriek, start up, the same sad prospect find,
And wake to all the griefs I left behind.
　　For thee the fates, severely kind, ordain
A cool suspense from pleasure and from pain; 250
Thy life a long, dead calm of fixed repose;
No pulse that riots, and no blood that glows.
Still as the sea, e'er winds were taught to blow,
Or moving spirit bade the waters flow;
Soft as the slumbers of a saint forgiv'n, 255
And mild as opening gleams of promised heav'n.
　　Come Abelard! for what hast thou to dread?
The torch of Venus burns not for the dead.
Nature stands checked; religion disapproves;
Ev'n thou art cold – yet Eloïsa loves. 260
Ah hopeless, lasting flames! like those that burn
To light the dead, and warm th' unfruitful urn.
　　What scenes appear, where-e'er I turn my view!
The dear ideas where I fly, pursue,
Rise in the grove, before the altar rise, 265
Stain all my soul, and wanton in my eyes!
I waste the matin lamp in sighs for thee,
Thy image steals between my God and me,
Thy voice I seem in ev'ry hymn to hear,
With ev'ry bead I drop too soft a tear. 270
When from the censer clouds of fragrance roll,
And swelling organs lift the rising soul,
One thought of thee puts all the pomp to flight,
Priests, tapers, temples, swim before my sight:
In seas of flame my plunging soul is drowned, 275
While altars blaze, and angels tremble round.
　　While prostrate here in humble grief I lie,
Kind, virtuous drops just gath'ring in my eye,
While praying, trembling, in the dust I roll,
And dawning grace is opening on my soul: 280
Come, if thou dar'st, all charming as thou art!
Oppose thy self to heav'n; dispute my heart;
Come, with one glance of those deluding eyes,
Blot out each bright idea of the skies;
Take back that grace, those sorrows, and those tears; 285
Take back my fruitless penitence and pray'rs;
Snatch me, just mounting, from the blest abode;
Assist the fiends, and tear me from my God!

No, fly me, fly me! far as pole from pole;
Rise Alps between us! and whole oceans roll!   290
Ah, come not, write not, think not once of me,
Nor share one pang of all I felt for thee.
Thy oaths I quit, thy memory resign;
Forget, renounce me, hate whate'er was mine.
Fair eyes, and tempting looks (which yet I view!)   295
Long loved, adored ideas, all adieu!
O grace serene! oh virtue heav'nly fair!
Divine oblivion of low-thoughted care!
Fresh blooming hope, gay daughter of the sky!
And faith, our early immortality!   300
Enter, each mild, each amicable guest;
Receive, and wrap me in eternal rest!
   See in her cell sad Eloïsa spread,
Propped on some tomb, a neighbour of the dead!
In each low wind methinks a spirit calls,   305
And more than echoes talk along the walls.
Here, as I watched the dying lamps around,
From yonder shrine I heard a hollow sound.
'Come, sister, come!' (it said, or seemed to say)
'Thy place is here, sad sister, come away!   310
Once like thy self, I trembled, wept, and prayed,
Love's victim then, though now a sainted maid:
But all is calm in this eternal sleep,
Here grief forgets to groan, and love to weep,
Ev'n superstition loses ev'ry fear: 315
For God, not man, absolves our frailties here.'
  I come, I come! prepare your roseate bow'rs,
Celestial palms, and ever-blooming flow'rs.
Thither, where sinners may have rest, I go,
Where flames refined in breasts seraphic glow. 320
Thou, Abelard! the last sad office pay,
And smooth my passage to the realms of day;
See my lips tremble, and my eye-balls roll,
Suck my last breath, and catch the flying soul!
Ah no – in sacred vestments may'st thou stand, 325
The hallowed taper trembling in thy hand,
Present the Cross before my lifted eye,
Teach me at once, and learn of me to die.
Ah then, thy once loved Eloïsa see!
It will be then no crime to gaze on me.   330
See from my cheek the transient roses fly!

See the last sparkle languish in my eye!
'Till ev'ry motion, pulse, and breath, be o'er;
And ev'n my Abelard beloved no more.
O death all-eloquent! you only prove   335
What dust we dote on, when 'tis man we love.
    Then too, when fate shall thy fair frame destroy,
(That cause of all my guilt, and all my joy)
In trance ecstatic may thy pangs be drowned,
Bright clouds descend, and angels watch thee round,   340
From opening skies may streaming glories shine,
And saints embrace thee with a love like mine.
    May one kind grave unite each hapless name,
And graft my love immortal on thy fame!
Then, ages hence, when all my woes are o'er,   345
When this rebellious heart shall beat no more;
If ever chance two wand'ring lovers brings
To Paraclete's white walls and silver springs,
O'er the pale marble shall they join their heads,
And drink the falling tears each other sheds;   350
Then sadly say, with mutual pity moved,
'Oh may we never love as these have loved!'
From the full quire when loud Hosannas rise,
And swell the pomp of dreadful sacrifice,
Amid that scene, if some relenting eye   355
Glance on the stone where our cold relics lie,
Devotion's self shall steal a thought from heav'n,
One human tear shall drop, and be forgiv'n.
And sure if fate some future bard shall join
In sad similitude of griefs to mine,   360
Condemned whole years in absence to deplore,
And image charms he must behold no more;
Such if there be, who loves so long, so well;
Let him our sad, our tender story tell;
The well-sung woes will sooth my pensive ghost;   365
He best can paint 'em, who shall feel 'em most.

35. On Authors and Booksellers

What Authors lose, their Booksellers have won,
So Pimps grow rich, while Gallants are undone.

36. from *An Essay on Man*

To Henry St John L. Bolingbroke

Epistle I

Awake, my St John! leave all meaner things
To low ambition, and the pride of kings.
Let us (since life can little more supply
Than just to look about us and to die)
Expatiate free o'er all this scene of man: 5
A mighty maze! but not without a plan;
A wild, where weeds and flow'rs promiscuous shoot,
Or garden, tempting with forbidden fruit.
Together let us beat this ample field,
Try what the open, what the covert yield,   10
The latent tracts, the giddy heights explore
Of all who blindly creep, or sightless soar,
Eye nature's walks, shoot folly as it flies,
And catch the manners living as they rise,
Laugh where we must, be candid where we can,   15
But vindicate the ways of God to man.[25]
     Say first, of God above, or man below,
What can we reason, but from what we know?
Of man, what see we but his station here,
From which to reason, or to which refer?   20
Through worlds unnumbered though the God be known,
'Tis ours to trace him only in our own.
He who through vast immensity can pierce,
See worlds on worlds compose one universe,
Observe how system into system runs,   25
What other plannets and what other suns,
What varied being peoples ev'ry star,
May tell why heav'n made all things as they are.
But of this frame the bearings, and the ties,
The strong connections, nice dependencies,   30
Gradations just, has thy pervading soul
Looked through? or can a part contain the whole?
     Is the great chain, that draws all to agree,
And drawn supports, upheld by God, or thee?
     Presumptuous man! the reason wouldst thou find   35
Why formed so weak, so little and so blind!

---

[25] Pope insistently associates his poem with Milton's *Paradise Lost*.

First, if thou can'st, the harder reason guess
Why formed no weaker, blinder, and no less?
Ask of thy mother earth, why oaks are made
Taller or stronger than the weeds they shade?   40
Or ask of yonder argent fields above,
Why Jove's satellites are less than Jove?
   Of systems possible, if 'tis confessed
That wisdom infinite must form the best,
Where all must full or not coherent be,   45
And all that rises, rise in due degree;
Then, in the scale of life and sense, 'tis plain
There must be, somewhere, such a rank as man;
And all the question (wrangle e're so long)
Is only this, if God has placed him wrong?   50
   Respecting man, whatever wrong we call,
May, must be right, as relative to all.
In human works, though laboured on with pain,
A thousand movements scarce one purpose gain;
In God's, one single can its end produce,   55
Yet serves to second too some other use.
So man, who here seems principal alone,
Perhaps acts second to some sphere unknown,
Touches some wheel, or verges to some goal;
'Tis but a part we see, and not a whole.   60
   When the proud steed shall know why man restrains
His fiery course, or drives him o'er the plains;
When the dull ox, why now he breaks the clod,
Is now a victim, and now Egypt's god;
Then shall man's pride and dulness comprehend   65
His actions', passions', being's use and end;
Why doing, suff'ring, checked, impelled; and why
This hour a slave, the next a deity.
   Then say not man's imperfect, heav'n in fault;
Say rather, man's as perfect as he ought;   70
His being measured to his state and place,
His time a moment, and a point his space.
If to be perfect in a certain sphere,
What matter, soon or late, or here or there?
The blest today is as completely so,   75
As who began a thousand years ago.
   Heav'n from all creatures hides the book of fate,
All but the page prescribed, their present state,
From brutes what men, from men what spirits know,

Or who could suffer being here below?   80
The lamb thy riot dooms to bleed to day,
Had he thy reason, would he skip and play?
Pleased to the last, he crops the flow'ry food,
And licks the hand just raised to shed his blood.
Oh blindness to the future! kindly giv'n,   85
That each may fill the circle marked by heav'n,
Who sees with equal eye, as God of all,
A hero perish, or a sparrow fall,
Atoms, or Systems, into ruin hurled,
And now a bubble burst, and now a world.   90
　　Hope humbly then; with trembling pinions soar;
Wait the great teacher, Death, and God adore!
What future bliss, he gives not thee to know,
But gives that hope to be thy blessing now.
Hope springs eternal in the human breast;   95
Man never *is*, but always *to be* blest;
The soul, uneasy, and confined from home,
Rests and expatiates in a life to come.
　　Lo! the poor Indian, whose untutored mind
Sees God in clouds, or hears him in the wind;   100
His soul proud science never taught to stray
Far as the solar walk, or milky way;
Yet simple nature to his hope has giv'n
Behind the cloud-topped hill, an humbler heav'n,
Some safer world, in depth of woods embraced,   105
Some happier island in the watry waste,
Where slaves once more their native land behold,
No fiends torment, no Christians thirst for gold!
To *be*, contents his natural desire,
He asks no angel's wing, nor seraph's fire,   110
But thinks, admitted to that equal sky,
His faithful dog shall bear him company.
　　Go, wiser thou! and in thy scale of sense
Weigh thy opinion against providence:
Call imperfection what thou fancy'st such,   115
Say, here he gives too little, there too much;
Destroy all creatures for thy sport or gust,
Yet cry, if man's unhappy, God's unjust,
If man alone engross not heav'n's high care,
Alone made perfect here, immortal there: 120
Snatch from his hand the balance and the rod,
Re-judge his justice, be the God of God!

In pride, in reas'ning pride, our error lies;
All quit their sphere, and rush into the skies.
Pride still is aiming at the blest abodes,   125
Men would be angels, angels would be gods.
Aspiring to be gods, if angels fell,
Aspiring to be angels, men rebel:
And who but wishes to invert the laws
Of order, sins against th' eternal cause.   130
    Ask for what end the heav'nly bodies shine,
Earth for whose use? Pride answers, 'Tis for mine:
For me kind nature wakes her genial pow'r,
Suckles each herb, and spreads out ev'ry flow'r;
Annual for me, the grape, the rose renew   135
The juice nectareous, and the balmy dew;
For me, the mine a thousand treasures brings;
For me, health gushes from a thousand springs;
Seas roll to waft me, suns to light me rise:
My footstool earth, my canopy the skies.'   140
    But errs not nature from this gracious end,
From burning suns when livid deaths descend,
When earthquakes swallow, or when tempests sweep
Towns to one grave, or nations to the deep?
'No' ('tis replied) 'the first Almighty cause   145
Acts not by partial, but by gen'ral laws;
Th' exceptions few; some change since all began,
And what created perfect?' – Why then man?
If the great end be human happiness,
Then nature deviates; and can man do less?   150
As much that end a constant course requires
Of show'rs and sunshine, as of man's desires,
As much eternal springs and cloudless skies,
As men for ever temp'rate, calm, and wise.
If plagues or earthquakes break not heav'n's design,   155
Why then a Borgia, or a Catiline?
Who knows but he, whose hand the lightn'ing forms,
Who heaves old Ocean, and who wings the storms,
Pours fierce ambition in a Caesar's mind,
Or turns young Ammon loose to scourge mankind?   160
From pride, from pride, our very reas'ning springs;
Account for moral, as for nat'ral things:
Why charge we heav'n in those, in these acquit?
In both, to reason right is to submit.
    Better for us, perhaps, it might appear,   165

Were there all harmony, all virtue here;
That never air or ocean felt the wind;
That never passion discomposed the mind:
But all subsists by elemental strife;
And passions are the elements of life.   170
The gen'ral order, since the whole began
Is kept in nature, and is kept in man.
    What would this man? Now upward will he soar,
And little less than angel, would be more;
Now looking downward, just as grieved appears.   175
To want the strength of bulls, the fur of bears.
Made for his use all creatures if he call,
Say what their use, had he the pow'rs of all?
Nature to these, without profusion kind,
The proper organs, proper pow'rs assigned;   180
Each seeming want compensated of course,
Here with degrees of swiftness, there of force;
All in exact proportion to the state,
Nothing to add, and nothing to abate.
Each beast, each insect, happy in its own,   185
Is heav'n unkind to man, and man alone?
Shall he alone whom rational we call,
Be pleased with nothing, if not blessed with all?
    The bliss of man (could pride that blessing find)
Is not to act or think beyond mankind;   190
No pow'rs of body or of soul to share,
But what his nature and his state can bear.
Why has not man a microscopic eye?
For this plain reason, man is not a fly.
Say what the use, were finer optics giv'n,   195
T'inspect a mite, not comprehend the heav'n?
Or touch, if tremblingly alive all o'er,
To smart and agonise at ev'ry pore?
Or quick effluvia darting through the brain,
Die of a rose in aromatic pain?   200
If nature thundered in his op'ning ears,
And stunned him with the music of the spheres,
How would he wish, that heav'n had left him still
The whispering zephyr, and the purling rill?
Who finds not providence all good and wise,   205
Alike in what it gives and what it denies?
    Far as creation's ample range extends,
The scale of sensual, mental pow'rs ascends:

Mark how it mounts, to man's imperial race
From the green myriads in the peopled grass!   210
What modes of sight betwixt each wide extreme,
The mole's dim curtain, and the lynx's beam:
Of smell, the headlong lioness between,
And hound sagacious on the tainted green:
Of hearing, from the life that fills the flood,   215
To that which warbles through the vernal wood:
The spider's touch, how exquisitely fine,
Feels at each thread, and lives along the line:
In the nice bee, what sense so subtly true
From pois'nous herbs extracts the healing dew.   220
How instinct varies, in the grov'ling swine,
Compared, half reas'ning elephant, with thine;
'Twixt that, and reason, what a nice barrier,
For ever sep'rate, yet for ever near;
Remembrance and reflection how allied;   225
What thin partitions sense from thought divide:
And middle natures, how they long to join,
Yet never pass th' insuperable line!
Without this just gradation, could they be
Subjected these to those, or all to thee?   230
The pow'rs of all subdued by thee alone,
Is not thy reason all those pow'rs in one?
    See, through this air, this ocean, and this earth,
All matter quick, and bursting into birth.
Above, how high progressive life may go!   235
Around how wide! how deep extend below!
Vast chain of being, which from God began,
Nature's æthereal, human, angel, man,
Beast, bird, fish, insect! what no eye can see,
No glass can reach! from infinite to thee,   240
From thee to nothing! – On superior pow'rs
Were we to press, inferior might on ours:
Or in the full creation leave a void,
Where, one step broken, the great scale's destroyed;
From nature's chain whatever link you strike,   245
Tenth or ten thousandth, breaks the chain alike.
    And if each system in gradation roll,
Alike essential to th' amazing whole;
The least confusion but in one, not all
That system only, but the whole must fall.   250
Let earth unbalanced from her orbit fly,

Planets and suns rush lawless through the sky,
Let ruling angels from their spheres be hurled,
Being on being wrecked, and world on world,
Heav'n's whole foundations to their centre nod,   255
And nature tremble to the throne of God:
All this dread order break – For whom? For thee?
Vile worm! – Oh madness! pride! impiety!
   What if the foot, ordained the dust to tread,
Or hand to toil, aspired to be the head?   260
What if the head, the eye or ear repined
To serve mere engines to the ruling mind?
Just as absurd, for any part to claim
To be another in this gen'ral frame:
Just as absurd, to mourn the task or pains   265
The great directing mind of all ordains.
   All are but parts of one stupendous whole,
Whose body nature is, and God the soul;
That, changed through all, and yet in all the same,
Great in the earth, as in the æthereal frame,   270
Warms in the sun, refreshes in the breeze,
Glows in the stars, and blossoms in the trees,
Lives through all life, extends through all extent,
Spreads undivided, operates unspent,
Breathes in our soul, informs our mortal part,   275
As full, as perfect, in a hair as heart,
As full, as perfect in vile man that mourns,
As the rapt Seraph that adores and burns;
To him, no high, no low, no great, no small:
He fills, he bounds, connects, and equals all.   280
   Cease then, nor order imperfection name:
Our proper bliss depends on what we blame.
Know thy own point; this kind, this due degree
Of blindness, weakness, heav'n bestows on thee.
Submit – in this, or any other sphere,   285
Secure to be as blest as thou can'st bear:
Safe in the hand of one disposing Pow'r,
Or in the natal, or the mortal hour.
All nature is but art, unknown to thee;
All chance, direction which thou can'st not see: 290
All discord, harmony not understood:
All partial evil, universal good:
And spite of pride, in erring reason's spite,
One truth is clear, 'Whatever *is*, is *right*.'

37. An Epistle to Dr Arbuthnot

'Neque sermonibus Vulgi dederis te, nec in praemiis humanis spem posueris rerum tuarum: suis te oportet illecebris ipsa virtus trahat ad verum decus. Quid de te alii loquantur, ipsi videant, sed loquentur tamen.'[26]

Cicero, *De Re Publica* vi. 23

'Shut, shut the door, good John!' fatigued I said,
'Tie up the knocker, say I'm sick, I'm dead.'
The Dog-star rages! nay 'tis past a doubt,
All Bedlam, or Parnassus, is let out:
Fire in each eye, and papers in each hand,   5
They rave, recite, and madden round the land.
    What walls can guard me, or what shades can hide?
They pierce my thickets, through my grot they glide,
By land, by water, they renew the charge,
They stop the chariot, and they board the barge.   10
No place is sacred, not the church is free,
Ev'n Sunday shines no Sabbath day to me:
Then from the Mint walks forth the man of rhyme,
Happy! to catch me, just at dinner time.
    Is there a parson, much be-mused in beer,   15
A maudlin poetess, a rhyming peer,
A clerk, foredoomed his father's soul to cross,
Who pens a stanza when he should engross?
Is there, who locked from ink and paper, scrawls
With desp'rate charcoal round his darkened walls?   20
All fly to *Twik'nam* and in humble strain
Apply to me, to keep them mad or vain.
Arthur, whose giddy son neglects the laws,
Imputes to me and my damned works the cause:
Poor Cornus sees his frantic wife elope,   25
And curses wit, and poetry, and Pope.
    Friend to my life, (which did not you prolong,
The world had wanted many an idle song)
What drop or nostrum can this plague remove?
Or which must end me, a fool's wrath or love?   30
A dire dilemma! either way I'm sped,
If foes, they write, if friends, they read me dead.
Seized and tied down to judge, how wretchèd I,

---

[26] '... you will no longer harken to the gossip of common folk nor expect human recompense for your acts; virtue, by means of her own devices, should carry you to true distinction. What others say about you is their concern; true or false, they'll prattle anyway.'

Who can't be silent, and who will not lie;
To laugh, were want of goodness and of grace,   35
And to be grave, exceeds all pow'r of face.
I sit with sad civility, I read
With honest anguish, and an aching head;
And drop at last, but in unwilling ears,
This saving counsel, 'Keep your piece nine years.'   40
   'Nine years!' cries he, who high in Drury Lane,
Lulled by soft zephyrs through the broken pane,
Rhymes e'er he wakes, and prints before Term ends,
Obliged by hunger, and request of friends:
'The piece you think is incorrect? Why take it,   45
I'm all submission, what you'd have it, make it.'
   Three things another's modest wishes bound,
My friendship, and a prologue, and ten pound.
   Pitholeon sends to me: 'You know his Grace,
I want a patron; ask him for a place.'   50
Pitholeon libelled me – 'but here's a letter
Informs you, sir, 'twas when he knew no better.
Dare you refuse him? Curll invites to dine!
He'll write a journal, or he'll turn divine.'
   Bless me! a packet. – ''Tis a stranger sues,   55
A virgin tragedy, an orphan muse.'
If I dislike it, 'Furies, death and rage!'
If I approve, 'commend it to the stage.'
There (thank my stars) my whole commission ends,
The Players and I are, luckily, no friends.   60
Fired that the house reject him, ''Sdeath I'll print it
And shame the fools – your int'rest, sir, with Lintot.'
Lintot, dull rogue! will think your price too much.
'Not sir, if *you* revise it, and retouch.'
All my demurs but double his attacks,   65
At last he whispers, 'Do, and we go snacks.'
Glad of a quarrel, straight I clap the door,
'Sir, let me see your works and you no more.'
   'Tis sung, when Midas' ears began to spring,
(Midas, a sacred person and a king)   70
His very minister who spied them first,
(Some say his queen) was forced to speak, or burst.
And is not mine, my friend, a sorer case,
When ev'ry coxcomb perks them in my face,
'Good friend forbear! you deal in dang'rous things,   75
You'd never name queens, ministers or kings;

Keep close to ears, and those let asses prick,
''Tis nothing' – Nothing? if they bite and kick?
Out with it, Dunciad! let the secret pass,
That secret to each fool, that he's an ass: 80
The truth once told, (and wherefore should we lie?)
The queen of Midas slept, and so may I.
    You think this cruel? take it for a rule,
No creature smarts so little as a fool.
Let peals of laughter, Codrus! round thee break,   85
Thou unconcerned can'st hear the mighty crack:
Pit, box, and gall'ry in convulsions hurled,
Thou stand'st unshook amidst a bursting world.
Who shames a scribbler? break one cobweb through,
He spins the slight, self-pleasing thread anew;   90
Destroy his fib, or sophistry; in vain,
The creature's at his dirty work again;
Throned in the centre of his thin designs,
Proud of a vast extent of flimsy lines.
Whom have I hurt? has poet yet, or peer,   95
Lost the arched eye-brow, or Parnassian sneer?
And has not Colly still his lord, and whore?
His butchers Henley, his free-masons Moore?
Does not one table Bavius still admit?
Still to one bishop Phillips seem a wit?   100
Still Sappho – 'Hold! for God-sake – you'll offend:
No names – be calm – learn prudence of a friend:
I too could write, and I am twice as tall,
But foes like these!' – One flatt'rers worse than all;
Of all mad creatures, if the learn'd aright,   105
It is the slaver kills, and not the bite.
A fool quite angry is quite innocent;
Alas! 'tis ten times worse when they repent.
    One dedicates in high heroic prose,
And ridicules beyond a hundred foes;   110
One from all Grub Street will my fame defend,
And, more abusive, calls himself my friend.
This prints my Letters, or expects a bribe,
And others roar aloud, 'Subscribe, subscribe.'
    There are, who to my person pay their court,   115
I cough like Horace, and though lean, am short,
Ammon's great son one shoulder had too high,
Such Ovid's nose, and Sir! you have an Eye –
Go on, obliging creatures, make me see

All that disgraced my betters, met in me.   120
Say for my comfort, languishing in bed,
'Just so immortal Maro held his head:'
And when I die, be sure you let me know,
Great Homer died three thousand years ago.
   Why did I write? what sin to me unknown   125
Dipped me in ink, my parents, or my own?
As yet a child, nor yet a fool to fame,
I lisped in numbers, for the numbers came.
I left no calling for this idle trade.
No duty broke, no father disobeyed.   130
The Muse but served to ease some friend, not Wife,
To help me through this long disease, my life,
To second, Arbuthnot! thy art and care,
And teach, the being you preserved, to bear.
   But why then publish? Granville the polite,   135
And knowing Walsh, would tell me I could write,
Well-natured Garth inflamed with early praise,
And Congreve loved, and Swift endured my lays;
The courtly Talbot, Somers, Sheffield read,
Ev'n mitred Rochester would nod the head,   140
And St John's self (great Dryden's friend before)
With open arms received one poet more.
Happy my studies, when by these approved!
Happier their author, when by these beloved!
From these the world will judge of men and books,   145
Not from the Burnets, Oldmixons, and Cooks.
   Soft were my numbers, who could take offence
While pure description held the place of sense?
Like gentle Fanny's was my flow'ry theme,
A painted mistress, or a purling stream.   150
Yet then did Gildon draw his venal quill;
I wished the man a dinner, and sate still:
Yet then did Dennis rave in furious fret;
I never answered, I was not in debt:
If want provoked, or madness made them print,   155
I waged no war with Bedlam or the Mint.
   Did some more sober critics come abroad?
If wrong, I smiled; if right, I kissed the rod.
Pains, reading, study, are their just pretence,
And all they want is spirit, taste, and sense.   160
Comma's and points they set exactly right.
And 'twere a sin to rob them of their mite.

Yet ne'er one sprig of laurel graced these ribalds,
From slashing Bentley down to piddling Tibalds.
Each wight who reads not, and but scans and spells,   165
Each word-catcher that lives on syllables,
Ev'n such small critics some regard may claim,
Preserved in Milton's or in Shakespeare's name.
Pretty! in amber to observe the forms
Of hairs, or straws, or dirt, or grubs, or worms!   170
The things, we know, are neither rich nor rare,
But wonder how the devil they got there?
    Were others angry? I excused them too;
Well might they rage, I gave them but their due.
A man's true merit 'tis not hard to find,   175
But each man's secret standard in his mind,
That casting-weight pride adds to emptiness,
This, who can gratify? For who can guess?
The Bard whom pilf'red pastorals renown,
Who turns a Persian tale for half a crown,   180
Just writes to make his barrenness appear,
And strains from hard-bound brains eight lines a year:
He, who still wanting though he lives on theft,
Steals much, spends little, yet has nothing left:
And he, who now to sense, now nonsense leaning,   185
Means not, but blunders round about a meaning:
And he, whose fustian's so sublimely bad,
It is not poetry, but prose run mad:
All these, my modest satire bad translate,
And owned, that nine such poets made a Tate.   190
How did they fume, and stamp, and roar, and chafe?
And swear, not Addison himself was safe.
    Peace to all such! but were there one whose fires
True genius kindles, and fair fame inspires,
Blest with each talent, and each art to please,   195
And born to write, converse, and live with ease:
Should such a man, too fond to rule alone,
Bear, like the Turk, no brother near the throne,
View him with scornful, yet with jealous eyes,
And hate for arts that caused himself to rise;   200
Damn with faint praise, assent with civil leer,
And without sneering, teach the rest to sneer;
Willing to wound, and yet afraid to strike,
Just hint a fault, and hesitate dislike;
Alike reserved to blame, or to commend,   205

A tim'rous foe, and a suspicious friend;
Dreading ev'n fools, by flatterers besieged,
And so obliging that he ne'er obliged;
Like Cato, give his little Senate laws,
And sit attentive to his own applause;   210
While wits and templers ev'ry sentence raise,
And wonder with a foolish face of praise:
Who but must laugh if such a man there be?
Who would not weep, if Atticus were he?
    What though my Name stood rubric on the walls?   215
Or plastered posts, with claps in capitals?
Or smoking forth, a hundred hawkers load,
On wings of winds came flying all abroad,
I sought no homage from the race that write;
I kept, like Asian monarchs, from their sight: 220
Poems I heeded (now be-rhymed so long)
No more than thou, great George! a birth-day song.
I ne'er with wits nor witlings passed my days,
To spread about the itch of verse and praise;
Nor like a puppy daggled through the town,   225
To fetch and carry sing-song up and down;
Nor at rehearsals sweat, and mouthed, and cried,
With handkerchief and orange at my side;
But sick of fops, and poetry, and prate,
To Bufo left the whole Castalian state.   230
    Proud, as Apollo on his forkèd hill,
Sate full-blown Bufo puffed by ev'ry quill;
Fed with soft dedication all day long,
Horace and he went hand in hand in song.
His library, (where busts of poets dead   235
And a true Pindar stood without a head)
Received of wits an undistinguished race,
Who first his judgement asked, and then a place:
Much they extolled his pictures, much his seat,
And flattered ev'ry day, and some days eat: 240
Till grown more frugal in his riper days,
He paid some bards with port, and some with praise,
To some a dry rehearsal was assigned,
And others (harder still) he paid in kind.
Dryden alone (what wonder?) came not nigh,   245
Dryden alone escaped this judging eye.
But still the great have kindness in reserve,
He helped to bury whom he helped to starve.

May some choice Patron bless each gray goose quill!
May ev'ry Bavius have his Bufo still!   250
So, when a statesman wants a day's defence,
Or envy holds a whole week's war with sense,
Or simple pride for flatt'ry makes demands,
May dunce by dunce be whistled off my hands!
Blessed be the great, for those they take away,   255
And those they left me – for they left me Gay.
Left me to see neglected genius bloom,
Neglected die! and tell it on his tomb;
Of all thy blameless life the sole return
My verse, and Queensb'ry weeping o'er thy urn!   260
Oh, let me live my own, and die so too!
('To live and die is all I have to do'[27])
Maintain a poet's dignity and ease,
And see what friends, and read what books I please,
Above a patron, though I condescend   265
Sometimes to call a minister my friend.
I was not born for courts or great affairs,
I pay my debts, believe, and say my pray'rs;
Can sleep without a poem in my head,
Nor know, if Dennis be alive or dead.   270
    Why am I asked, 'What next shall see the light?'
Heav'ns! was I born for nothing but to write?
Has life no joys for me? or, to be grave,
Have I no friend to serve, no soul to save?
'I found him close with Swift' – 'Indeed? no doubt'   275
(Cries prating Balbus) 'something will come out.'
'Tis all in vain, deny it as I will.
'No, such a genius never can lie still.'
And then for mine obligingly mistakes
The first lampoon Sir Will or Bubo makes,   280
Poor guiltless I! and can I choose but smile,
When ev'ry coxcomb knows me by my style?
    Cursed be the verse, how well soe'er it flow,
That tends to make one worthy man my foe,
Give virtue scandal, innocence a fear,   285
Or from the soft-eyed virgin steal a tear!
But he who hurts a harmless neighbour's peace,
Insults fall'n worth, or beauty in distress,
Who loves a lie, lame slander helps about,

[27] from Denham *Of Prudence*, II 93f

Who writes a libel, or who copies out: 290
That fop, whose pride affects a patron's name,
Yet absent, wounds an author's honest fame;
Who can your merit selfishly approve,
And show the sense of it without the love;
Who has the vanity to call you friend, 295
Yet wants the honour injured to defend;
Who tells whate'er you think, whate'er you say,
And, if he lie not, must at least betray;
Who to the Dean and silver bell can swear,
And sees at Cannon's what was never there; 300
Who reads, but with a lust to misapply,
Make satire a lampoon, and fiction, lie.
A lash like mine no honest man shall dread,
But all such babbling blockheads in his stead.
    Let Sporus tremble – 'What? that thing of silk, 305
Sporus, that mere white curd of Ass's milk?
Satire or sense alas! can Sporus feel?
Who breaks a butterfly upon a wheel?'
Yet let me flap this bug with gilded wings,
This painted child of dirt, that stinks and stings; 310
Whose buzz the witty and the fair annoys,
Yet wit ne'er tastes, and beauty ne'er enjoys,
So well-bred spaniels civilly delight
In mumbling of the game they dare not bite.
Eternal smiles his emptiness betray, 315
As shallow streams run dimpling all the way.
Whether in florid impotence he speaks,
And, as the prompter breathes, the puppet squeaks;
Or at the ear of Eve, familiar toad,
Half froth, half venom, spits himself abroad, 320
In puns, or politics, or tales, or lies,
Or spite, or smut, or rhymes, or blasphemies.
His wit all see-saw between that and this,
Now high, now low, now master up, now miss,
And he himself one vile antithesis. 325
Amphibious thing! that acting either part,
The trifling head, or the corrupted heart,
Fop at the toilet, flatt'rer at the board,
Now trips a lady, and now struts a lord.
Eve's tempter thus the Rabbins have expressed, 330
A cherub's face, a reptile all the rest,
Beauty that shocks you, parts that none can trust,

Wit that can creep, and pride that licks the dust.
    Not fortune's worshipper, nor fashion's fool,
Nor lucre's madman, nor ambition's tool,   335
Not proud, nor servile; be one poet's praise
That, if he pleased, he pleased by manly ways;
That flatt'ry, ev'n to kings, he held a shame,
And thought a lie in verse or prose the same:
That not in fancy's maze he wandered long,   340
But stooped to truth, and moralised his song:
That not for fame, but virtue's better end,
He stood the furious foe, the timid friend,
The damning critic, half approving wit,
The coxcomb hit, or fearing to be hit;   345
Laughed at the loss of friends he never had,
The dull, the proud, the wicked, or the mad;
The distant threats of vengeance on his head,
The blow unfelt, the tear he never shed;
The tale revived, the lie so oft o'erthrown,   350
Th' imputed trash, and dulness not his own,
The morals blackened when the writings scape,
The libelled person, and the pictured shape;
Abuse on all he loved, or loved him, spread,
A friend in exile, or a father, dead;   355
The whisper, that to greatness still too near,
Perhaps, yet vibrates on his sovereign's ear –
Welcome for thee, fair virtue! all the past:
For thee, fair virtue! welcome even the last!
    'But why insult the poor, affront the great?'   360
A knave's a knave, to me, in ev'ry state:
Alike my scorn, if he succeed or fail,
Sporus at court, or Japhet in a jail,
A hireling scribbler, or a hireling peer,
Knight of the post corrupt, or of the shire,   365
If on a pillory, or near a throne,
He gain his prince's ear, or lose his own.
    Yet soft by nature, more a dupe than wit,
Sapho can tell you how this man was bit:
This dreaded sat'rist Dennis will confess   370
Foe to his pride, but friend to his distress:
So humble, he has knocked at Tibbald's door,
Has drunk with Cibber, nay has rhymed for Moore:
Full ten years slandered, did he once reply?
Three thousand suns went down on Welsted's lie: 375

To please a mistress, one aspersed his life;
He lashed him not, but let her be his wife:
Let Budgel charge low Grub Street on his quill,
And write whate'er he pleased, except his will;
Let the two Curlls of Town and Court, abuse   380
His father, mother, body, soul, and muse.
Yet why? that father held it for a rule
It was a sin to call our neighbour fool,
That harmless mother thought no wife a whore;
Hear this, and spare his family, James Moore!   385
Unspotted names, and memorable long,
If there be force in virtue, or in song.
    Of gentle blood (part shed in honour's cause,
While yet in Britain honour had applause)
Each parent sprang – 'What fortune, pray?' – Their own,   390
And better got than Bestia's from the Throne.
Born to no pride, inheriting no strife,
Nor marrying discord in a noble wife,
Stranger to civil and religious rage,
The good man walked innoxious through his age: 395
No courts he saw, no suits would ever try,
Nor dared an oath, nor hazarded a lie:
Unlearn'd, he knew no schoolman's subtle art,
No language, but the language of the heart,
By nature honest, by experience wise,   400
Healthy by temp'rance, and by exercise,
His life, though long, to sickness past unknown,
His death was instant, and without a groan.
Oh grant me thus to live, and thus to die!
Who sprung from kings shall know less joy than I.   405
    O friend! may each domestic bliss be thine!
Be no unpleasing Melancholy mine:
Me, let the tender office long engage
To rock the cradle of reposing age,
With lenient arts extend a mother's breath,   410
Make languor smile, and smooth the bed of death,
Explore the thought, explain the asking eye,
And keep a while one parent from the sky!
On cares like these if length of days attend,
May heav'n, to bless those days, preserve my friend,   415
Preserve him social, cheerful, and serene,
And just as rich as when he served a Queen.
Whether that blessing be denied or giv'n,
Thus far was right, the rest belongs to Heav'n.

38. Engraved on the Collar of a Dog which I gave to his Royal Highness

I am his Highness' dog at Kew;
Pray tell me, Sir, whose dog are you?

39. from *The Dunciad*

Book IV

[Pope's Argument to Book IV] The poet being, in this book, to declare the completion of the prophecies mentioned at the end of the former, makes a new invocation, as the greater poets are wont, when some high and worthy matter is to be sung. He shows the Goddess coming in her majesty, to destroy order and science, and to substitute the Kingdom of the Dull upon earth. How she leads captive the Sciences, and silenceth the Muses, and what they be who succeed in their stead. All her children, by a wonderful attraction, are drawn about her, and bear along with them divers others, who promote her empire by connivance, weak resistance, or discouragement of arts; such as half-wits, tasteless admirers, vain pretenders, the flatterers of dunces, or the patrons of them. All these crowd round her; one of them offering to approach her is driven back by a rival, but she commends and encourages both. The first who speak in form are the geniuses of the schools, who assure her of their care to advance her cause, by confining youth to words, and keeping them out of the way of real knowledge. Their address, and her gracious answer; with her charge to them and the universities. The universities appear by their proper deputies, and assure her that the same method is observed in the progress of education. The speech of Aristarchus on this subject. They are driven off by a band of young gentlemen returned from travel with their tutors; one of whom delivers to the Goddess, in a polite oration, an account of the whole conduct and fruits of their travels: presenting to her at the same time a young nobleman perfectly accomplished. She receives him graciously, and endues him with the happy quality of want of shame. She sees loitering about her a number of indolent persons abandoning all business and duty, and dying with laziness: to these approaches the Antiquary Annius, entreating her to make them virtuosos, and assign them over to him: but Mummius, another antiquary, complaining of his fraudulent proceeding, she finds a method to reconcile their difference. Then enter a troop of people fantastically adorned, offering her strange and exotic presents: amongst them, one stands forth and demands justice on another, who had deprived him of one of the greatest curiosities in nature: but he justifies himself so well, that the Goddess gives them both her approbation. She recommends to them to find proper employment for the indolents before-mentioned, in the study of butterflies, shells, birds' nests, moss, etc., but with particular caution, not to proceed beyond trifles, to any useful or extensive views of Nature, or of the Author of Nature. Against the last of these apprehensions, she is secured by a hearty address from the minute philosophers

and freethinkers, one of whom speaks in the name of the rest. The youth, thus instructed and principled, are delivered to her in a body, by the hands of Silenus, and then admitted to taste the cup of the Magus, her High Priest, which causes a total oblivion of all obligations, divine, civil, moral, or rational. To these her adepts she sends priests, attendants, and comforters, of various kinds; confers on them orders and degrees; and then dismissing them with a speech, confirming to each his privileges, and telling what she expects from each, concludes with a yawn of extraordinary virtue. The progress and effects whereof on all orders of men, and the consummation of all, in the restoration of Night and Chaos, conclude the poem.

Yet, yet a moment, one dim ray of light
Indulge, dread Chaos, and eternal Night!
Of darkness visible so much be lent,
As half to show, half veil, the deep intent.
Ye pow'rs! whose mysteries restored I sing,   5
To whom time bears me on his rapid wing,
Suspend a while your force inertly strong,
Then take at once the poet and the song.
   Now flamed the Dog Star's unpropitious ray,
Smote ev'ry brain, and withered every bay;   10
Sick was the sun, the owl forsook his bow'r.
The moon-struck prophet felt the madding hour:
Then rose the seed of Chaos, and of Night,
To blot out order, and extinguish light,
Of dull and venal a new world to mould,   15
And bring Saturnian days of lead and gold.
   She mounts the throne: her head a cloud concealed,
In broad effulgence all below revealed;
'Tis thus aspiring Dulness ever shines)
Soft on her lap her laureate son reclines.   20
   Beneath her footstool, Science groans in chains,
And Wit dreads exile, penalties, and pains.
There foamed rebellious Logic, gagged and bound,
There, stripped, fair Rhet'ric languished on the ground;
His blunted arms by Sophistry are borne,   25
And shameless Billingsgate her robes adorn.
Morality, by her false guardians drawn,
Chicane in furs, and Casuistry in lawn,
Gasps, as they straiten at each end the cord,
And dies, when Dulness gives her page the word.   30
Mad Mathesis alone was unconfined,
Too mad for mere material chains to bind,
Now to pure space lifts her ecstatic stare,

Now running round the circle, finds it square.
But held in tenfold bonds the Muses lie,   35
Watched both by Envy's and by Flatt'ry's eye:
There to her heart sad Tragedy addressed
The dagger wont to pierce the tyrant's breast;
But sober History restrained her rage,
And promised vengeance on a barb'rous age.   40
There sunk Thalia, nerveless, cold, and dead,
Had not her sister Satire held her head:
Nor couldst thou, Chesterfield! a tear refuse,
Thou wept'st, and with thee wept each gentle Muse.
    When lo! a harlot form soft sliding by,   45
With mincing step, small voice, and languid eye;
Foreign her air, her robe's discordant pride
In patchwork flutt'ring, and her head aside:
By singing peers upheld on either hand,
She tripped and laughed, too pretty much to stand;   50
Cast on the prostrate Nine a scornful look,
Then thus in quaint recitativo spoke.
    'O Cara! Cara! silence all that train:
Joy to great Chaos! let division reign:
Chromatic tortures soon shall drive them hence,   55
Break all their nerves, and fritter all their sense:
One trill shall harmonize joy, grief, and rage,
Wake the dull church, and lull the ranting stage;
To the same notes thy sons shall hum, or snore,
And all thy yawning daughters cry, *encore*.   60
Another Phoebus, thy own Phoebus, reigns,
Joys in my jigs, and dances in my chains.
But soon, ah soon rebellion will commence,
If music meanly borrows aid from sense.
Strong in new arms, lo! giant Handel stands,   65
Like bold Briareus, with a hundred hands;
To stir, to rouse, to shake the soul he comes,
And Jove's own thunders follow Mars's drums.
Arrest him, Empress, or you sleep no more –'
She heard, and drove him to th' Hibernian shore.   70
    And now had Fame's posterior trumpet blown,
And all the nations summoned to the throne.
The young, the old, who feel her inward sway,
One instinct seizes, and transports away.
None need a guide, by sure attraction led,   75
And strong impulsive gravity of head:

None want a place, for all their centre found,
Hung to the Goddess, and cohered around.
Not closer, orb in orb, conglobed are seen
The buzzing bees about their dusky queen.   80
  The gath'ring number, as it moves along,
Involves a vast involuntary throng,
Who gently drawn, and struggling less and less,
Roll in her vortex, and her pow'r confess.
Not those alone who passive own her laws,   85
But who, weak rebels, more advance her cause.
Whate'er of dunce in college or in town
Sneers at another, in toupee or gown;
Whate'er of mongrel no one class admits,
A wit with dunces, and a dunce with wits.   90
  Nor absent they, no members of her state,
Who pay her homage in her sons, the Great;
Who false to Phoebus, bow the knee to Baal;
Or, impious, preach his word without a call.
Patrons, who sneak from living worth to dead,   95
Withhold the pension, and set up the head;
Or vest dull Flatt'ry in the sacred gown;
Or give from fool to fool the laurel crown.
And (last and worst) with all the cant of wit,
Without the soul, the Muse's hypocrite.   100
  There marched the bard and blockhead, side by side,
Who rhymed for hire, and patronised for pride.
Narcissus, praised with all a Parson's pow'r,
Looked a white lily sank beneath a show'r.
There moved Montalto with superior air;   105
His stretched-out arm displayed a volume fair;
Courtiers and patriots in two ranks divide,
Through both he passed, and bowed from side to side:
But as in graceful act, with awful eye
Composed he stood, bold Benson thrust him by: 110
On two unequal crutches propped he came,
Milton's on this, on that one Johnston's name.
The decent knight retired with sober rage,
Withdrew his hand, and closed the pompous page.
But (happy for him as the times went then)   115
Appeared Apollo's may'r and aldermen,
On whom three hundred gold-capped youths await,
To lug the pond'rous volume off in state.
  When Dulness, smiling – 'Thus revive the wits!

But murder first, and mince them all to bits;   120
As er'st Medea (cruel, so to save!)
A new edition of old Aeson gave;
Let standard authors, thus, like trophies born,
Appear more glorious as more hacked and torn,
And you, my Critics! in the chequered shade,   125
Admire new light through holes yourselves have made.
   'Leave not a foot of verse, a foot of stone,
A page, a grave, that they can call their own;
But spread, my sons, your glory thin or thick,
On passive paper, or on solid brick.   130
So by each bard an Alderman shall sit,
A heavy lord shall hang at ev'ry wit,
And while on Fame's triumphal car they ride,
Some slave of mine be pinioned to their side.'
   Now crowds on crowds around the Goddess press,   135
Each eager to present their first address.
Dunce scorning dunce beholds the next advance,
But fop shows fop superior complaisance,
When lo! a spectre rose, whose index hand
Held forth the virtue of the dreadful wand;   140
His beavered brow a birchen garland wears,
Dropping with infant's blood, and mother's tears.
O'er every vein a shudd'ring horror runs;
Eton and Winton shake through all their sons.
All flesh is humbled, Westminster's bold race   145
Shrink, and confess the genius of the place:
The pale boy-senator yet tingling stands,
And holds his breeches close with both his hands.
   Then thus. 'Since man from beast by words is known,
Words are man's province, words we teach alone.   150
When reason doubtful, like the Samian letter,
Points him two ways, the narrower is the better.
Placed at the door of learning, youth to guide,
We never suffer it to stand too wide.
To ask, to guess, to know, as they commence,   155
As fancy opens the quick springs of sense,
We ply the memory, we load the brain,
Bind rebel Wit, and double chain on chain,
Confine the thought, to exercise the breath;
And keep them in the pale of words till death.   160
Whate'er the talents, or howe'er designed,
We hang one jingling padlock on the mind:

A poet the first day, he dips his quill;
And what the last? A very poet still.
Pity! the charm works only in our wall,   165
Lost, lost too soon in yonder house or hall.
There truant Wyndham every Muse gave o'er,
There Talbot sunk, and was a wit no more!
How sweet an Ovid, Murray was our boast!
How many Martials were in Pult'ney lost!   170
Else sure some bard, to our eternal praise,
In twice ten thousand rhyming nights and days,
Had reached the work, and all that mortal can;
And South beheld that masterpiece of Man.'
'Oh' (cried the Goddess) 'for some pedant reign!   175
Some gentle James, to bless the land again;
To stick the doctor's chair into the throne,
Give law to words, or war with words alone,
Senates and courts with Greek and Latin rule,
And turn the council to a grammar school!   180
For sure, if Dulness sees a grateful day,
'Tis in the shade of arbitrary sway.
O! if my sons may learn one earthly thing,
Teach but that one, sufficient for a king;
That which my priests, and mine alone, maintain,   185
Which as it dies, or lives, we fall, or reign:
May you, may Cam and Isis, preach it long!
'"The right divine of kings to govern wrong".'
   Prompt at the call, around the Goddess roll
Broad hats, and hoods, and caps, a sable shoal: 190
Thick and more thick the black blockade extends,
A hundred head of Aristotle's friends.
Nor wert thou, Isis! wanting to the day,
Though Christ Church long kept prudishly away.
Each staunch polemic, stubborn as a rock,   195
Each fierce logician, still expelling Locke,
Came whip and spur, and dashed through thin and thick
On German Crousaz, and Dutch Burgersdyck.
As many quit the streams that murm'ring fall
To lull the sons of Marg'ret and Clare Hall,   200
Where Bentley late tempestuous wont to sport
In troubled waters, but now sleeps in port.
Before them marched that awful aristarch;
Ploughed was his front with many a deep remark:
His hat, which never vailed to human pride,   205

Walker with rev'rence took, and laid aside.
Low bowed the rest: he, kingly, did but nod;
So upright Quakers please both man and God.
'Mistress! dismiss that rabble from your throne:
Avaunt – is Aristarchus yet unknown?   210
Thy mighty scholiast, whose unwearied pains
Made Horace dull, and humbled Milton's strains.
Turn what they will to verse, their toil is vain,
Critics like me shall make it prose again.
Roman and Greek grammarians! know your better: 215
Author of something yet more great than letter;
While tow'ring o'er your alphabet, like Saul,
Stands our digamma, and o'ertops them all.
'Tis true, on words is still our whole debate,
Disputes of *me* or *te*, of *aut* or *at*,   220
To sound or sink in *cano*, O or A,
Or give up Cicero to C or K.
Let Friend affect to speak as Terence spoke,
And Alsop never but like Horace joke:
For me, what Virgil, Pliny may deny,   225
Manilius or Solinus shall supply:
For Attic Phrase in Plato let them seek,
I poach in Suidas for unlicensed Greek.
In ancient sense if any needs will deal,
Be sure I give them fragments, not a meal;   230
What Gellius or Stobaeus hashed before,
Or chewed by blind old Scholiasts o'er and o'er.
The critic eye, that microscope of wit,
Sees hairs and pores, examines bit by bit:
How parts relate to parts, or they to whole,   235
The body's harmony, the beaming soul,
Are things which Kuster, Burman, Wasse shall see,
When man's whole frame is obvious to a flea.
    'Ah, think not, mistress! more true dulness lies
In Folly's cap, than Wisdom's grave disguise.   240
Like buoys, that never sink into the flood,
On learning's surface we but lie and nod.
Thine is the genuine head of many a house,
And much divinity without a Νοῦς.
Nor could a Barrow work on every block,   245
Nor has one Atterbury spoiled the flock.
See! still thy own, the heavy canon roll,
And metaphysic smokes involve the pole.

For thee we dim the eyes, and stuff the head
With all such reading as was never read: 250
For thee explain a thing till all men doubt it,
And write about it, Goddess, and about it:
So spins the silkworm small its slender store,
And labours till it clouds itself all o'er.
   'What though we let some better sort of fool   255
Thrid ev'ry science, run through ev'ry school?
Never by tumbler through the hoops was shown
Such skill in passing all, and touching none.
He may indeed (if sober all this time)
Plague with dispute, or persecute with rhyme.   260
We only furnish what he cannot use,
Or wed to what he must divorce, a Muse:
Full in the midst of Euclid dip at once,
And petrify a genius to a dunce:
Or set on metaphysic ground to prance,   265
Show all his paces, not a step advance.
With the same cement ever sure to bind,
We bring to one dead level ev'ry mind.
Then take him to develop, if you can,
And hew the block off, and get out the man.   270
But wherefore waste I words? I see advance
Whore, pupil, and laced governor from France.
Walker! our hat' – nor more he deigned to say,
But, stern as Ajax' spectre, strode away.[...]

   'O! would the sons of men once think their eyes
And reason giv'n them but to study *flies*!
See nature in some partial narrow shape,   455
And let the Author of the whole escape:
Learn but to trifle; or, who most observe,
To wonder at their Maker, not to serve.'
   'Be that my task' (replies a gloomy clerk,
Sworn foe to myst'ry, yet divinely dark;   460
Whose pious hope aspires to see the day
When moral evidence shall quite decay,
And damns implicit faith, and holy lies,
Prompt to impose, and fond to dogmatise):
   'Let others creep by timid steps, and slow,   465
On plain experience lay foundations low,
By common sense to common knowledge bred,
And last, to nature's cause through nature led.

All-seeing in thy mists, we want no guide,
Mother of arrogance, and source of pride!   470
We nobly take the high priori road,
And reason downward, till we doubt of God:
Make nature still encroach upon his plan;
And shove him off as far as e'er we can:
Thrust some mechanic cause into his place;   475
Or bind in matter, or diffuse in space.
Or, at one bound o'erleaping all his laws,
Make God man's image, man the final cause,
Find virtue local, all relation scorn
See all in *self*, and but for self be born: 480
Of naught so certain as our reason still,
Of naught so doubtful as of soul and will.
Oh hide the God still more! and make us see
Such as Lucretius drew, a god like thee:
Wrapped up in self, a god without a thought,   485
Regardless of our merit or default.
Or that bright image to our fancy draw,
Which Theocles in raptured vision saw,
While through poetic scenes the genius roves,
Or wanders wild in academic groves;   490
That nature our society adores,
Where Tindal dictates, and Silenus snores.'
   Roused at his name up rose the boozy sire,
And shook from out his pipe the seeds of fire;
Then snapped his box, and stroked his belly down: 495
Rosy and rev'rend, though without a gown.
Bland and familiar to the throne he came,
Led up the youth, and called the Goddess *Dame.*
Then thus, 'From priestcraft happily set free,
Lo! ev'ry finished son returns to thee: 500
First slave to words, then vassal to a name,
Then dupe to party; child and man the same;
Bounded by nature, narrowed still by art,
A trifling head, and a contracted heart.
Thus bred, thus taught, how many have I seen,   505
Smiling on all, and smiled on by a queen.
Marked out for honours, honoured for their birth,
To thee the most rebellious things on earth:
Now to thy gentle shadow all are shrunk,
All melted down, in pension, or in punk°!   *whore* 510
So K***°, so B*** * sneaked into the grave,   *Kent, Berkeley*

A monarch's half, and half a harlot's slave.
Poor W***° nipped in folly's broadest bloom,   *Warwick [?]*
Who praises now? his chaplain on his tomb.
Then take them all, oh take them to thy breast!   515
Thy Magus, Goddess, shall perform the rest.'
　　With that, a wizard old° his cup* extends;   *Walpole [?], [of self-love]*
Which whoso tastes, forgets his former friends,
Sire, ancestors, himself. One casts his eyes
Up to a star, and like Endymion dies: 520
A feather, shooting from another's head,
Extracts his brain, and principle is fled,
Lost is his God, his country, ev'rything;
And nothing left but homage to a king!
The vulgar herd turn off to roll with hogs,   525
To run with horses, or to hunt with dogs;
But, sad example! never to escape
Their infamy, still keep the human shape.
　　But she, good Goddess, sent to ev'ry child
Firm impudence, or stupefaction mild;   530
And straight succeeded, leaving shame no room,
Cibberian forehead, or Cimmerian gloom.
　　Kind self-conceit to some her glass applies,
Which no one looks in with another's eyes:
But as the flatt'rer or dependant paint,   535
Beholds himself a patriot, chief, or saint.
　　On others int'rest her gay liv'ry flings,
Int'rest that waves on parti-coloured wings:
Turned to the sun, she casts a thousand dyes,
And, as she turns, the colours fall or rise.   540
　　Others the siren sisters warble round,
And empty heads console with empty sound.
No more, alas! the voice of Fame they hear,
The balm of Dulness trickling in their ear.
Great C**, H**, P**, R**, K*,[28]
Why all your toils? your sons have learned to sing.   545
How quick ambition hastes to ridicule!
The sire is made a peer, the son a fool.
　　On some, a priest succinct in amice° white   *[a chef's hat]*
Attends; all flesh is nothing in his sight!   550
Beeves, at his touch, at once to jelly turn,

---

[28] Cowper, Harcourt, Parker, Raymond, King (the first four were Lord Chancellors, the last a Lord Chief Justice).

And the huge boar is shrunk into an urn:
The board with specious miracles he loads,
Turns hares to larks, and pigeons into toads.
Another (for in all what one can shine?)   555
Explains the *seve* and *verdeur* of the vine.
What cannot copious sacrifice atone?
Thy truffles, Perigord! thy hams, Bayonne!
With French libation, and Italian strain,
Wash Bladen white, and expiate Hays's stain.   560
Knight lifts the head, for what are crowds undone
To three essential partridges in one?[29]
Gone ev'ry blush, and silent all reproach,
Contending princes mount them in their coach.
    Next, bidding all draw near on bended knees,   565
The Queen confers her titles and degrees.
Her children first of more distinguished sort,
Who study Shakespeare at the Inns of Court,
Impale a glowworm, or vertú profess,
Shine in the dignity of F.R.S.°   *Fellow of the Royal Society* 570
Some, deep Freemasons, join the silent race
Worthy to fill Pythagoras's place:
Some botanists, or florists at the least,
Or issue members of an annual feast.
Nor passed the meanest unregarded, one   575
Rose a Gregorian, one a Gormogon.
The last, not least in honour or applause,
Isis and Cam made doctors of her laws.
    Then, blessing all, 'Go, Children of my care!
To practice now from theory repair.   580
All my commands are easy, short, and full:
My sons! be proud, be selfish, and be dull.
Guard my prerogative, assert my throne:
This nod confirms each privilege your own.
The cap and switch be sacred to his grace;   585
With staff and pumps the Marquis lead the race;
From stage to stage the licensed Earl may run,
Paired with his fellow-charioteer the sun;
The learned Baron butterflies design,
Or draw to silk Arachne's subtle line;   590
The Judge to dance his brother Sergeant call;

[29] Gamesters and cheats; and Knight the cashier for the South-sea Company, who absconded to Paris.

The Senator at cricket urge the ball;
The Bishop stow (pontific luxury!)
An hundred souls of turkeys in a pie;
The sturdy Squire to Gallic masters stoop,   595
And drown his lands and manors in a *soupe.*
Others import yet nobler arts from France,
Teach kings to fiddle, and make senates dance.
Perhaps more high some daring son may soar,
Proud to my list to add one monarch more;   600
And nobly conscious, princes are but things
Born for first ministers, as slaves for kings,
Tyrant supreme! shall three Estates command,
And MAKE ONE MIGHTY DUNCIAD OF THE LAND!'
    More she had spoke, but yawned – All nature nods: 605
What mortal can resist the yawn of gods?
Churches and chapels instantly it reached;
(St James's first, for leaden Gilbert preached)
Then catched the schools; the Hall scarce kept awake;
The Convocation gaped, but could not speak: 610
Lost was the nation's sense, nor could be found,
While the long solemn unison went round:
Wide, and more wide, it spread o'er all the realm;
E'en Palinurus nodded at the helm:
The vapour mild o'er each committee crept;   615
Unfinished treaties in each office slept;
And chiefless armies dozed out the campaign;
And navies yawned for orders on the main.
    O Muse! relate (for you can tell alone,
Wits have short memories, and dunces none),   620
Relate, who first, who last resigned to rest;
Whose heads she partly, whose completely blessed;
What charms could faction, what ambition lull,
The venal quiet, and entrance the dull;
Till drowned was sense, and shame, and right, and wrong –   625
O sing, and hush the nations with thy song!
      *   *   *   *
    In vain, in vain – the all-composing hour
Resistless falls: the Muse obeys the pow'r.
She comes! she comes! the sable throne behold
Of Night primeval, and of Chaos old!   630
Before her, Fancy's gilded clouds decay,
And all its varying rainbows die away.
Wit shoots in vain its momentary fires,

The meteor drops, and in a flash expires.
As one by one, at dread Medea's strain,   635
The sick'ning stars fade off th' ethereal plain;
As Argus' eyes by Hermes' wand oppressed,
Closed one by one to everlasting rest;
Thus at her felt approach, and secret might,
Art after art goes out, and all is night.   640
See skulking Truth to her old cavern fled,
Mountains of casuistry heaped o'er her head!
Philosophy, that leaned on heav'n before,
Shrinks to her second cause, and is no more.
Physic of Metaphysic begs defence,   645
And Metaphysic calls for aid on Sense!
See Mystery to Mathematics fly!
In vain! they gaze, turn giddy, rave, and die.
Religion, blushing, veils her sacred fires,
And, unawares, Morality expires.   650
Nor public flame, nor private, dares to shine;
Nor human spark is left, nor glimpse divine!
Lo! thy dread empire, Chaos! is restored;
Light dies before thy uncreating word:
Thy hand, great Anarch! lets the curtain fall;   655
And universal Darkness buries all.

40. Intended for Sir Isaac Newton in Westminster-Abbey

Nature and nature's laws lay hid in night:
God said, *Let Newton be!* and all was light.

James Thomson (1700–1748)

41. Hymn on Solitude

Hail, mildly pleasing Solitude,
Companion of the wise and good;
But, from whose holy, piercing eye,
The herd of fools, and villains fly.

Oh! how I love with thee to walk,   5
And listen to thy whisper'd talk,
Which innocence and truth imparts,
And melts the most obdurate hearts.

A thousand shapes you wear with ease,
And still in every shape you please.   10
Now wrapt in some mysterious dream,
A lone philosopher you seem;
Now quick from hill to vale you fly,
And now you sweep the vaulted sky;
A shepherd next, you haunt the plain,   15
And warble forth your oaten strain.
A lover now, with all the grace
Of that sweet passion in your face:
Then, calm'd to friendship, you assume
The gentle looking Hertford's bloom,   20
As, with her Musidora, she
(Her Musidora fond of thee)
Amid the long-withdrawing vale,
Awakes the rival'd nightingale.

Thine is the balmy breath of morn,   25
Just as the dew-bent rose is born;
And while meridian fervours beat,
Thine is the woodland dumb retreat;
But chief, when evening scenes decay,
And the faint landscape swims away,   30
Thine is the doubtful soft decline,
And that best hour of musing thine.

Descending angels bless thy train,
The virtues of the sage, and swain;
Plain Innocence in white array'd   35
Before thee lifts her fearless head;
Religion's beams around thee shine,
And cheer thy glooms with light divine:
About thee sports sweet Liberty;
And wrapt Urania sings to thee.   40

Oh, let me pierce thy secret cell!
And in thy deep recesses dwell;
Perhaps from Norwood's oak-clad hill,

When meditation has her fill,
I just may cast my careless eyes,   45
Where London's spiry turrets rise,
Think of its crimes, its cares, its pain,
Then shield me in the woods again.

42. Rule, Britannia! (with variations)

When Britain first, at Heaven's command,
    Arose from out the azure main,
This was the charter of the land,
    And guardian angels sung this strain:
        'Rule, Britannia, rule the waves;   5
        Britons never will be slaves.'

The nations, not so bless'd as thee,
    Must, in their turns, to tyrants fall;
While thou shalt flourish great and free,
    The dread and envy of them all.   10
        'Rule,' &c.

Still more majestic shalt thou rise,
    More dreadful from each foreign stroke;
As the loud blast that tears the skies
    Serves but to root thy native oak.   15
        'Rule,' &c.

Thee haughty tyrants ne'er shall tame:
    All their attempts to bend thee down
Will but arouse thy generous flame,
    But work their woe, and thy renown.   20
        'Rule,' &c.

To thee belongs the rural reign;
    Thy cities shall with commerce shine:
All thine shall be the subject main:
    And every shore it circles thine.   25
        'Rule,' &c.

The Muses, still with freedom found,
    Shall to thy happy coast repair:

Bless'd isle! with matchless beauty crown'd,
   And manly hearts to guard the fair: 30
      'Rule, Britannia, rule the waves,
      Britons never will be slaves.'

43. *from* Autumn

INSCRIBED TO THE RIGHT HONOURABLE ARTHUR ONSLOW, ESQ., SPEAKER OF
THE HOUSE OF COMMONS

*Thomson's Argument: The subject proposed. Addressed to Mr Onslow. A prospect of the
Fields ready for Harvest. Reflections in praise of Industry raised by that view. Reaping. A
Tale relative to it. A Harvest Storm. Shooting and Hunting; their barbarity. A ludicrous
account of Foxhunting. A view of an Orchard. Wall Fruit. A Vineyard. A description of
Fogs, frequent in the latter part of Autumn; whence a digression, inquiring into the rise of
Fountains and Rivers. Birds of season considered, that now shift their Habitation. The
prodigious number of them that cover the Northern and Western Isles of Scotland. Hence
a view of the Country. A prospect of the discoloured, fading Woods. After a gentle dusky
day, Moonlight. Autumnal Meteors. Morning: to which succeeds a calm, pure, sunshiny
Day, such as usually shuts up the season. The Harvest being gathered in, the Country
dissolved in joy. The whole concludes with a Panegyric on a philosophical Country Life.*

Crown'd with the sickle and the wheaten sheaf,
While Autumn, nodding o'er the yellow plain,
Comes jovial on; the Doric reed once more,
Well pleased, I tune. Whate'er the wintry frost
Nitrous prepared; the various blossom'd Spring   5
Put in white promise forth; and Summer-suns
Concocted strong, rush boundless now to view,
Full, perfect all, and swell my glorious theme. [...]

When the bright Virgin gives the beauteous days,
And Libra weighs in equal scales the year;
From Heaven's high cope the fierce effulgence shook   25
Of parting Summer, a serener blue,
With golden light enliven'd, wide invests
The happy world. Attemper'd suns arise,
Sweet-beam'd, and shedding oft through lucid clouds
A pleasing calm; while broad, and brown, below   30
Extensive harvests hang the heavy head.
Rich, silent, deep, they stand; for not a gale

Rolls its light billows o'er the bending plain:
A calm of plenty! till the ruffled air
Falls from its poise, and gives the breeze to blow.   35
Rent is the fleecy mantle of the sky;
The clouds fly different; and the sudden sun
By fits effulgent gilds the illumined field,
And black by fits the shadows sweep along.
A gaily chequer'd heart-expanding view,   40
Far as the circling eye can shoot around,
Unbounded tossing in a flood of corn.
These are thy blessings, Industry! rough power!
Whom labour still attends, and sweat, and pain;
Yet the kind source of every gentle art,   45
And all the soft civility of life:
Raiser of human kind! by Nature cast,
Naked, and helpless, out amid the woods
And wilds, to rude inclement elements;
With various seeds of art deep in the mind   50
Implanted, and profusely pour'd around
Materials infinite, but idle all.
Still unexerted, in the unconscious breast,
Slept the lethargic powers; Corruption still,
Voracious, swallow'd what the liberal hand   55
Of bounty scatter'd o'er the savage year:
And still the sad barbarian, roving, mix'd
With beasts of prey; or for his acorn-meal
Fought the fierce tusky boar; a shivering wretch!
Aghast, and comfortless, when the bleak north,   60
With Winter charged, let the mix'd tempest fly,
Hail, rain, and snow, and bitter-breathing frost:
Then to the shelter of the hut he fled;
And the wild season, sordid, pined away.
For home he had not; home is the resort   65
Of love, of joy, of peace and plenty, where,
Supporting and supported, polish'd friends,
And dear relations mingle into bliss.
But this the rugged savage never felt,
E'en desolate in crowds; and thus his days   70
Roll'd heavy, dark, and unenjoy'd along:
A waste of time! till Industry approach'd,
And roused him from his miserable sloth:
His faculties unfolded; pointed out,
Where lavish Nature the directing hand   75

Of art demanded; show'd him how to raise
His feeble force by the mechanic powers,
To dig the mineral from the vaulted earth,
On what to turn the piercing rage of fire,
On what the torrent, and the gather'd blast;   80
Gave the tall ancient forest to his axe;
Taught him to chip the wood, and hew the stone,
Till by degrees the finish'd fabric rose;
Tore from his limbs the blood-polluted fur,
And wrapt them in the woolly vestment warm,   85
Or bright in glossy silk, and flowing lawn;
With wholesome viands fill'd his table, pour'd
The generous glass around, inspired to wake
The life-refining soul of decent wit:
Nor stopp'd at barren bare necessity;   90
But still advancing bolder, led him on
To pomp, to pleasure, elegance, and grace;
And, breathing high ambition through his soul,
Set science, wisdom, glory, in his view,
And bade him be the Lord of all below.   95
Then gathering men their natural powers combined,
And form'd a Public; to the general good
Submitting, aiming, and conducting all.
For this the Patriot-Council met, the full,
The free, and fairly represented Whole;   100
For this they plann'd the holy guardian laws,
Distinguish'd orders, animated arts,
And with joint force Oppression chaining, set
Imperial Justice at the helm; yet still
To them accountable: nor slavish dream'd   105
That toiling millions must resign their weal,
And all the honey of their search, to such
As for themselves alone themselves have raised.

Hence every form of cultivated life
In order set, protected, and inspired,   110
Into perfection wrought. Uniting all,
Society grew numerous, high, polite,
And happy. Nurse of art! the city rear'd
In beauteous pride her tower-encircled head;
And, stretching street on street, by thousands drew,   115
From twining woody haunts, or the tough yew
To bows strong-straining, her aspiring sons.

Then Commerce brought into the public walk
The busy merchant; the big warehouse built;
Raised the strong crane; choked up the loaded street   120
With foreign plenty; and thy stream, O Thames,
Large, gentle, deep, majestic, king of floods!
Chose for his grand resort. On either hand,
Like a long wintry forest, groves of masts   125
Shot up their spires; the bellying sheet between
Possess'd the breezy void; the sooty hulk
Steer'd sluggish on; the splendid barge along
Row'd, regular, to harmony; around,
The boat, light-skimming, stretch'd its oary wings;   130
While deep the various voice of fervent toil
From bank to bank increased; whence ribb'd with oak,
To bear the British thunder, black, and bold,
The roaring vessel rush'd into the main.

Then too the pillar'd dome, magnific, heaved   135
Its ample roof and Luxury within
Pour'd out her glittering stores: the canvass smooth,
With glowing life protuberant, to the view
Embodied rose; the statue seem'd to breathe,
And soften into flesh; beneath the touch   140
Of forming art, imagination-flush'd.
All is the gift of Industry; whate'er
Exalts, embellishes, and renders life
Delightful. Pensive Winter cheer'd by him
Sits at the social fire, and happy hears   145
The excluded tempest idly rave along;
His harden'd fingers deck the gaudy Spring;
Without him Summer were an arid waste;
Nor to the Autumnal months could thus transmit
Those full, mature, immeasurable stores,   150
That, waving round, recall my wandering song. [...]

Here the rude clamour of the sportsman's joy,
The gun fast-thundering, and the winded horn,
Would tempt the muse to sing the rural game:
How in his mid-career the spaniel struck,
Stiff, by the tainted gale, with open nose,   370
Outstretch'd and finely sensible, draws full,
Fearful and cautious, on the latent prey;
As in the sun the circling covey bask

Their varied plumes, and watchful every way,
Through the rough stubble turn the secret eye.   375
Caught in the meshy snare, in vain they beat
Their idle wings, entangled more and more:
Nor on the surges of the boundless air,
Though borne triumphant, are they safe; the gun,
Glanced just, and sudden, from the fowler's eye,   380
O'ertakes their sounding pinions: and again,
Immediate, brings them from the towering wing,
Dead to the ground; or drives them wide dispersed,
Wounded, and wheeling various, down the wind.
These are not subjects for the peaceful Muse,   385
Nor will she stain with such her spotless song;
Then most delighted, when she social sees
The whole mix'd animal-creation round
Alive and happy. 'Tis not joy to her,
The falsely cheerful barbarous game of death,   390
This rage of pleasure, which the restless youth
Awakes, impatient, with the gleaming morn:
When beasts of prey retire, that all night long,
Urged by necessity, had ranged the dark,
As if their conscious ravage shunn'd the light,   395
Ashamed. Not so the steady tyrant Man,
Who with the thoughtless insolence of power
Inflamed, beyond the most infuriate wrath
Of the worst monster that e'er roam'd the waste,
For sport alone pursues the cruel chase,   400
Amid the beamings of the gentle days.
Upbraid, ye ravening tribes, our wanton rage,
For hunger kindles you, and lawless want;
But lavish fed, in Nature's bounty roll'd,
To joy at anguish, and delight in blood,   405
Is what your horrid bosoms never knew.

Poor is the triumph o'er the timid hare!
Scared from the corn, and now to some lone seat
Retired: the rushy fen; the ragged furze,
Stretch'd o'er the stony heath; the stubble chapt;   410
The thistly lawn; the thick entangled broom;
Of the same friendly hue, the wither'd fern;
The fallow ground laid open to the sun,
Concoctive; and the nodding sandy bank,
Hung o'er the mazes of the mountain brook.   415

Vain is her best precaution; though she sits
Conceal'd, with folded ears; unsleeping eyes,
By Nature raised to take the horizon in;
And head couch'd close betwixt her hairy feet,
In act to spring away. The scented dew   420
Betrays her early labyrinth; and deep,
In scatter'd sullen openings, far behind,
With every breeze she hears the coming storm.
But nearer, and more frequent, as it loads
The sighing gale, she springs amazed, and all   425
The savage soul of game is up at once:
The pack full-opening, various; the shrill horn
Resounded from the hills; the neighing steed,
Wild for the chase; and the loud hunter's shout;
O'er a weak, harmless, flying creature, all   430
Mix'd in mad tumult, and discordant joy.

The stag too, singled from the herd, where long
He ranged the branching monarch of the shades,
Before the tempest drives. At first, in speed
He, sprightly, puts his faith; and, roused by fear,   435
Gives all his swift aërial soul to flight;
Against the breeze he darts, that way the more
To leave the lessening murderous cry behind:
Deception short! though fleeter than the winds
Blown o'er the keen-air'd mountain by the north,   440
He bursts the thickets, glances through the glades,
And plunges deep into the wildest wood;
If slow, yet sure, adhesive to the track
Hot-steaming, up behind him come again
The inhuman rout, and from the shady depth   445
Expel him, circling through his every shift.
He sweeps the forest oft; and sobbing sees
The glades, mild opening to the golden day;
Where, in kind contest, with his butting friends
He wont to struggle, or his loves enjoy.   450
Oft in the full-descending flood he tries
To lose the scent, and lave his burning sides:
Oft seeks the herd; the watchful herd, alarm'd,
With selfish care avoid a brother's woe.
What shall he do? His once so vivid nerves,   455
So full of buoyant spirit, now no more
Inspire the course; but fainting breathless toil,

Sick, seizes on his heart: he stands at bay;
And puts his last weak refuge in despair.
The big round tears run down his dappled face;   460
He groans in anguish: while the growling pack,
Blood-happy, hang at his fair jutting chest,
And mark his beauteous chequer'd sides with gore.

Of this enough. But if the sylvan youth,
Whose fervent blood boils into violence,   465
Must have the chase; behold, despising flight,
The roused up lion, resolute, and slow,
Advancing full on the protended spear,
And coward band, that circling wheel aloof.
Slunk from the cavern, and the troubled wood,   470
See the grim wolf; on him his shaggy foe
Vindictive fix, and let the ruffian die:
Or, growling horrid, as the brindled boar
Grins fell destruction, to the monster's heart
Let the dart lighten from the nervous arm.   475

These Britain knows not; give, ye Britons, then
Your sportive fury, pitiless, to pour
Loose on the nightly robber of the fold;
Him, from his craggy winding haunts unearth'd,
Let all the thunder of the chase pursue.   480
Throw the broad ditch behind you; o'er the hedge
High bound, resistless; nor the deep morass
Refuse, but through the shaking wilderness
Pick your nice way; into the perilous flood
Bear fearless, of the raging instinct full;   485
And as you ride the torrent, to the banks
Your triumph sound sonorous, running round,
From rock to rock, in circling echoes tossed;
Then scale the mountains to their woody tops;
Rush down the dangerous steep; and o'er the lawn,   490
In fancy swallowing up the space between,
Pour all your speed into the rapid game.
For happy he! who tops the wheeling chase;
Has every maze evolved, and every guile
Disclosed; who knows the merits of the pack;   495
Who saw the villain seized, and dying hard,
Without complaint, though by a hundred mouths
Relentless torn: O glorious he, beyond

His daring peers! when the retreating horn
Calls them to ghostly halls of gray renown,   500
With woodland honours graced; the fox's fur,
Depending decent from the roof: and spread
Round the drear walls, with antic figures fierce,
The stag's large front: he then is loudest heard,
When the night staggers with severer toils,   505
With feats Thessalian Centaurs never knew,
And their repeated wonders shake the dome.

But first the fuel'd chimney blazes wide;
The tankards foam; and the strong table groans
Beneath the smoking sirloin, stretch'd immense   510
From side to side; in which, with desperate knife,
They deep incision make, and talk the while
Of England's glory, ne'er to be defaced
While hence they borrow vigour: or amain
Into the pasty plunged, at intervals,   515
If stomach keen can intervals allow,
Relating all the glories of the chase.
Then sated Hunger bids his Brother Thirst
Produce the mighty bowl; the mighty bowl,
Swell'd high with fiery juice, steams liberal round   520
A potent gale, delicious, as the breath
Of Maia to the love-sick shepherdess,
On violets diffused, while soft she hears
Her panting shepherd stealing to her arms.
Nor wanting is the brown October, drawn,   525
Mature and perfect, from his dark retreat
Of thirty years; and now his honest front
Flames in the light refulgent, not afraid
E'en with the vineyard's best produce to vie.
To cheat the thirsty moments. Whist a while   530
Walks his dull round beneath a cloud of smoke,
Wreath'd, fragrant, from the pipe; or the quick dice,
In thunder leaping from the box, awake
The sounding gammon: while romp-loving miss
Is haul'd about, in gallantry robust. [...]   535

Hence from the busy joy-resounding fields,   630
In cheerful error, let us tread the maze
Of Autumn, unconfined; and taste, revived,
The breath of orchard big with bending fruit,

Obedient to the breeze and beating ray,
From the deep-loaded bough a mellow shower   635
Incessant melts away. The juicy pear
Lies, in a soft profusion, scatter'd round.
A various sweetness swells the gentle race;
By Nature's all-refining hand prepared;
Of temper'd sun, and water, earth, and air,   640
In ever changing composition mix'd.
Such, falling frequent through the chiller night,
The fragrant stores, the wide projected heaps
Of apples, which the lusty-handed Year,
Innumerous, o'er the blushing orchard shakes.   645
A various spirit, fresh, delicious, keen,
Dwells in their gelid pores; and, active, points
The piercing cider for the thirsty tongue:
Thy native theme, and boon inspirer too,
Philips, Pomona's bard, the second thou   650
Who nobly durst, in rhyme-unfetter'd verse,
With British freedom sing the British song:
How, from Silurian vats, high sparkling wines
Foam in transparent floods; some strong, to cheer
The wintry revels of the labouring hind;   655
And tasteful some, to cool the summer hours.

In this glad season, while his sweetest beams
The sun sheds equal o'er the meeken'd day;
Oh lose me in the green delightful walks
Of Dodington, thy seat, serene and plain;   660
Where simple Nature reigns; and every view,
Diffusive, spreads the pure Dorsetian downs,
In boundless prospect; yonder shagg'd with wood,
Here rich with harvest, and there white with flocks!
Meantime the grandeur of thy lofty dome,   665
Far splendid, seizes on the ravish'd eye.
New beauties rise with each revolving day;
New columns swell; and still the fresh Spring finds
New plants to quicken, and new groves to green.
Full of thy genius all! the Muses' seat: 670
Where in the secret bower, and winding walk,
For virtuous Young and thee they twine the bay.
Here wandering oft, fired with the restless thirst
Of thy applause, I solitary court
The inspiring breeze: and meditate the book   675

Of Nature ever open; aiming thence,
Warm from the heart, to learn the moral song.
Here, as I steal along the sunny wall,
Where Autumn basks, with fruit empurpled deep,
My pleasing theme continual prompts my thought: 680
Presents the downy peach; the shining plum:
The ruddy, fragrant nectarine; and dark,
Beneath his ample leaf, the luscious fig.
The vine too here her curling tendrils shoots;
Hangs out her clusters, glowing to the south;   685
And scarcely wishes for a warmer sky. [...]

Amazing scene! Behold! the glooms disclose;
I see the rivers in their infant beds!
Deep, deep I hear them, labouring to get free;
I see the leaning strata, artful ranged;
The gaping fissures to receive the rains,   815
The melting snows, and ever dripping fogs.
Strow'd bibulous above I see the sands,
The pebbly gravel next, the layers then
Of mingled moulds, of more retentive earths
The gutter'd rocks and mazy-running clefts;   820
That, while the stealing moisture they transmit,
Retard its motion, and forbid its waste.
Beneath the incessant weeping of these drains,
I see the rocky siphons stretch'd immense,
The mighty reservoirs, of harden'd chalk,   825
Or stiff compacted clay, capacious form'd:
O'erflowing thence, the congregated stores,
The crystal treasures of the liquid world,
Through the stirr'd sands a bubbling passage burst;
And welling out, around the middle steep,   830
Or from the bottoms of the bosom'd hills,
In pure effusion flow. United, thus,
The exhaling sun, the vapour-burden'd air,
The gelid mountains, that to rain condensed
These vapours in continual current draw,   835
And send them, o'er the fair-divided earth,
In bounteous rivers to the deep again,
A social commerce hold, and firm support
The full-adjusted harmony of things.

When Autumn scatters his departing gleams,   840

Warn'd of approaching Winter, gather'd, play
The swallow-people; and toss'd wide around,
O'er the calm sky, in convolution swift,
The feather'd eddy floats: rejoicing once,
Ere to their wintry slumbers they retire;   845
In clusters clung, beneath the mouldering bank,
And where, unpierced by frost, the cavern sweats.
Or rather into warmer climes convey'd,
With other kindred birds of season, there
They twitter cheerful, till the vernal months   850
Invite them welcome back: for, thronging, now
Innumerous wings are in commotion all. [...]

Thus solitary, and in pensive guise,
Oft let me wander o'er the russet mead,   975
And through the sadden'd grove, where scarce is heard
One dying strain, to cheer the woodman's toil.
Haply some widow'd songster pours his plaint,
Far, in faint warblings, through the tawny copse:
While congregated thrushes, linnets, larks,   980
And each wild throat, whose artless strains so late
Swell'd all the music of the swarming shades,
Robb'd of their tuneful souls, now shivering sit
On the dead tree, a dull despondent flock;
With not a brightness waving o'er their plumes,   985
And nought save chattering discord in their note.
O let not, aim'd from some inhuman eye,
The gun the music of the coming year
Destroy; and harmless, unsuspecting harm,
Lay the weak tribes a miserable prey,   990
In mingled murder, fluttering on the ground!

The pale-descending year, yet pleasing still,
A gentler mood inspires; for now the leaf
Incessant rustles from the mournful grove;
Oft startling such as, studious, walk below,   995
And slowly circles through the waving air.
But should a quicker breeze amid the boughs
Sob, o'er the sky the leafy deluge streams;
Till choked, and matted with the dreary shower,
The forest walks, at every rising gale,   1000
Roll wide the wither'd waste, and whistle bleak.
Fled is the blasted verdure of the fields;

And, shrunk into their beds, the flowery race
Their sunny robes resign. E'en what remain'd
Of stronger fruits falls from the naked tree;   1005
And woods, fields, gardens, orchards, all around
The desolated prospect thrills the soul.

He comes! he comes! in every breeze the Power
Of Philosophic Melancholy comes!
His near approach the sudden starting tear,   1010
The glowing cheek, the mild dejected air,
The soften'd feature, and the beating heart,
Pierced deep with many a virtuous pang, declare.
O'er all the soul his sacred influence breathes!
Inflames imagination; through the breast   1015
Infuses every tenderness; and far
Beyond dim earth exalts the swelling thought.
Ten thousand thousand fleet ideas, such
As never mingled with the vulgar dream,
Crowd fast into the mind's creative eye.   1020
As fast the correspondent passions rise,
As varied, and as high: Devotion raised
To rapture, and divine astonishment;
The love of Nature unconfined, and, chief,
Of human race; the large ambitious wish,   1025
To make them blest; the sigh for suffering worth
Lost in obscurity; the noble scorn
Of tyrant pride; the fearless great resolve;
The wonder which the dying patriot draws,
Inspiring glory through remotest time;   1030
The awaken'd throb for virtue, and for fame;
The sympathies of love, and friendship dear;
With all the social offspring of the heart.

Oh! bear me then to vast embowering shades,
To twilight groves, and visionary vales;   1035
To weeping grottos, and prophetic glooms;
Where angel forms athwart the solemn dusk,
Tremendous sweep, or seem to sweep along;
And voices more than human, through the void
Deep sounding, seize the enthusiastic ear?   1040

Or is this gloom too much? Then lead, ye powers,
That o'er the garden and the rural seat

Preside, which shining through the cheerful hand
In countless numbers blest Britannia sees;
O lead me to the wide extended walks, 1045
The fair majestic paradise of Stowe!
Not Persian Cyrus on Ionia's shore
E'er saw such sylvan scenes; such various art
By genius fired, such ardent genius tamed
By cool judicious art; that, in the strife, 1050
All beauteous Nature fears to be outdone.
And there, O Pitt, thy country's early boast,
There let me sit beneath the shelter'd slopes,
Or in that Temple where, in future times,
Thou well shalt merit a distinguish'd name; 1055
And, with thy converse blest, catch the last smiles
Of Autumn beaming o'er the yellow woods.
While there with thee the enchanted round I walk,
The regulated wild, gay Fancy then
Will tread in thought the groves of attic land; 1060
Will from thy standard taste refine her own,
Correct her pencil to the purest truth
Of Nature, or, the unimpassion'd shades
Forsaking, raise it to the human mind.
Or if hereafter she, with juster hand, 1065
Shall draw the tragic scene, instruct her, thou,
To mark the varied movements of the heart,
What every decent character requires,
And every passion speaks: O through her strain
Breathe thy pathetic eloquence! that moulds 1070
The attentive senate, charms, persuades, exalts,
Of honest Zeal the indignant lightning throws,
And shakes Corruption on her venal throne.
While thus we talk, and through Elysian vales
Delighted rove, perhaps a sigh escapes: 1075
What pity, Cobham, thou thy verdant files
Of order'd trees shouldst here inglorious range,
Instead of squadrons flaming o'er the field,
And long embattled hosts! when the proud foe,
The faithless vain disturber of mankind, 1080
Insulting Gaul, has roused the world to war;
When keen, once more, within their bounds to press
Those polish'd robbers, those ambitious slaves,
The British youth would hail thy wise command,
Thy temper'd ardour and thy veteran skill. 1085

The western sun withdraws the shorten'd day;
And humid Evening, gliding o'er the sky,
In her chill progress, to the ground condensed
The vapours throws. Where creeping waters ooze,
Where marshes stagnate, and where rivers wind,   1090
Cluster the rolling fogs, and swim along
The dusky-mantled lawn. Meanwhile the Moon
Full-orb'd, and breaking through the scatter'd clouds,
Shows her broad visage in the crimson'd east.
Turn'd to the sun direct, her spotted disk,   1095
Where mountains rise, umbrageous dales descend,
And caverns deep, as optic tube descries,
A smaller earth, gives us his blaze again,
Void of its flame, and sheds a softer day.
Now through the passing cloud she seems to stoop,   1100
Now up the pure cerulean rides sublime.
Wide the pale deluge floats, and streaming mild
O'er the sky'd mountain to the shadowy vale,
While rocks and floods reflect the quivering gleam,
The whole air whitens with a boundless tide   1105
Of silver radiance, trembling round the world. [...]

Oh, knew he but his happiness, of men
The happiest he! who far from public rage,   1240
Deep in the vale, with a choice few retired,
Drinks the pure pleasures of the Rural Life.
What though the dome be wanting, whose proud gate,
Each morning, vomits out the sneaking crowd
Of flatterers false, and in their turn abused?   1245
Vile intercourse! what though the glittering robe
Of every hue reflected light can give,
Or floating loose, or stiff with mazy gold,
The pride and gaze of fools! oppress him not?
What though, from utmost land and sea purvey'd,   1250
For him each rarer tributary life
Bleeds not, and his insatiate table heaps
With luxury, and death? What though his bowl
Flames not with costly juice; nor sunk in beds,
Oft of gay care, he tosses out the night,   1255
Or melts the thoughtless hours in idle state?
What though he knows not those fantastic joys
That still amuse the wanton, still deceive;

A face of pleasure, but a heart of pain;
Their hollow moments undelighted all?   1260
Sure peace is his; a solid life, estranged
To disappointment, and fallacious hope:
Rich in content, in Nature's bounty rich,
In herbs and fruits; whatever greens the Spring,
When heaven descends in showers; or bends the bough,   1265
When Summer reddens, and when Autumn beams;
Or in the wintry glebe whatever lies
Conceal'd, and fattens with the richest sap:
These are not wanting; nor the milky drove,
Luxuriant, spread o'er all the lowing vale;   1270
Nor bleating mountains; nor the chide of streams,
And hum of bees, inviting sleep sincere
Into the guiltless breast, beneath the shade,
Or thrown at large amid the fragrant hay;
Nor aught besides of prospect, grove, or song,   1275
Dim grottos, gleaming lakes, and fountain clear.
Here too dwells simple Truth; plain Innocence;
Unsullied Beauty; sound unbroken Youth,
Patient of labour, with a little pleased;
Health ever blooming; unambitious Toil;   1280
Calm Contemplation, and poetic Ease. [...]

When Autumn's yellow lustre gilds the world,
And tempts the sickled swain into the field,
Seized by the general joy, his heart distends
With gentle throes; and, through the tepid gleams   1330
Deep musing, then he best exerts his song.
E'en Winter wild to him is full of bliss.
The mighty tempest, and the hoary waste,
Abrupt and deep, stretch'd o'er the buried earth,
Awake to solemn thought. At night the skies,   1335
Disclosed, and kindled, by refining frost,
Pour every lustre on the exalted eye.
A friend, a book, the stealing hours secure,
And mark them down for wisdom. With swift wing
O'er land and sea imagination roams;   1340
Or truth, divinely breaking on his mind,
Elates his being, and unfolds his powers;
Or in his breast heroic virtue burns.
The touch of kindred too and love he feels;
The modest eye, whose beams on his alone   1345

Ecstatic shine; the little strong embrace
Of prattling children, twined around his neck,
And emulous to please him, calling forth
The fond parental soul. Nor purpose gay,
Amusement, dance, or song, he sternly scorns;   1350
For happiness and true philosophy
Are of the social, still, and smiling kind.
This is the life which those who fret in guilt,
And guilty cities, never knew; the life,
Led by primeval ages, uncorrupt,   1355
When Angels dwelt, and God himself, with Man!

Oh Nature! all-sufficient! over all!
Enrich me with the knowledge of thy works!
Snatch me to Heaven; thy rolling wonders there,
World beyond world, in infinite extent,   1360
Profusely scatter'd o'er the blue immense,
Show me; their motions, periods, and their laws
Give me to scan; through the disclosing deep
Light my blind way: the mineral strata there;
Thrust, blooming, thence the vegetable world;   1365
O'er that the rising system, more complex,
Of animals; and higher still, the mind,
The varied scene of quick-compounded thought,
And where the mixing passions endless shift;
These ever open to my ravish'd eye;   1370
A search, the flight of time can ne'er exhaust!
But if to that unequal; if the blood,
In sluggish streams about my heart, forbid
That best ambition; under closing shades,
Inglorious, lay me by the lowly brook,   1375
And whisper to my dreams. From Thee begin,
Dwell all on Thee, with Thee conclude my song;
And let me never, never stray from Thee!

Charles Wesley (1707–1788)

44. A Morning Hymn

Christ, whose glory fills the skies,
   Christ, the true, the only light,
Sun of righteousness, arise,
   Triumph o'er the shades of night:
Day-spring from on high, be near: 5
Day-star, in my heart appear.

Dark and cheerless is the morn
   Unaccompanied by Thee,
Joyless is the day's return
   Till Thy mercy's beams I see;   10
Till they inward light impart,
Glad my eyes, and warm my heart,

Visit then this soul of mine,
   Pierce the gloom of sin, and grief,
Fill me, Radiance Divine,   15
   Scatter all my unbelief,
More and more Thyself display,
Shining to the perfect day.

45. 'O Thou eternal victim, slain'

Hebrews ix. 25.

O Thou eternal victim slain
A sacrifice for guilty man,
By the eternal Spirit made
An offering in the sinner's stead;
Our everlasting Priest art thou,   5
And plead'st thy death for sinners now.

Thy offering still continues, new,
Thy vesture keeps its bloody hue,
Thou stand'st the ever-slaughtered Lamb,
Thy priesthood still remains the same;   10
Thy years, O God, can never fail,
Thy goodness is unchangeable.

O that our faith may never move,
But stand unshaken as thy love!
Sure evidence of things unseen,   15
Now let it pass the years between,
And view Thee bleeding on the Tree,
My God, who dies for me, for me!

46. The Whole Armour of God

　　Soldiers of Christ, arise
　　And put your armour on,
Strong in the strength which God supplies
　　Through His eternal Son
　　Strong in the Lord of hosts,   5
　　And in His mighty power,
Who in the strength of Jesus trusts
　　Is more than conqueror.

　　Stand then in His great might,
　　With all His strength endued,   10
But take, to arm you for the fight,
　　The panoply of God;
　　That, having all things done,
　　And all your conflicts passed,
Ye may o'ercome through Christ alone   15
　　And stand entire at last.

　　Stand then against your foes,
　　In close and firm array;
Legions of wily fiends oppose
　　Throughout the evil day;   20
　　But meet the sons of night,
　　And mock their vain design,
Armed in the arms of heavenly light,
　　Of righteousness divine.

Leave no unguarded place, 25
No weakness of the soul,
Take every virtue, every grace,
     And fortify the whole;
     Indissolubly joined,
     To battle all proceed; 30
But arm yourselves with all the mind
     That was in Christ, your Head.

     Let truth the girdle be
     That binds your armour on,
In faithful firm sincerity 35
     To Jesus cleave alone;
     Let faith and love combine
     To guard your valiant breast,
The plate be righteousness divine,
     Imputed and imprest. 40

     Still let your feet be shod,
     Ready His will to do,
Ready in all the ways of God
     His glory to pursue:
     Ruin is spread beneath, 45
     The Gospel greaves put on,
And safe through all the snares of death
     To life eternal run.

     But, above all, lay hold
     On faith's victorious shield; 50
Armed with that adamant and gold,
     Be sure to win the field;
     If faith surround your heart,
     Satan shall be subdued,
Repelled his every fiery dart, 55
     And quenched with Jesu's blood.

     Jesus hath died for you!
     What can His love withstand?
Believe, hold fast your shield, and who
     Shall pluck you from His hand? 60
     Believe that Jesus reigns,
     All power to Him is giv'n:
Believe, till freed from sin's remains,
     Believe yourselves to Heav'n.

Your rock can never shake: 65
   Hither, He saith, come up!
The helmet of salvation take,
   The confidence of hope:
   Hope for his perfect love,
   Hope for his people's rest,   70
Hope to sit down with Christ above
   And share the marriage feast.

   Brandish in faith 'til then
   The spirit's two-edged sword,
Hew all the snares of fiends and men   75
   In pieces with the word:
   'Tis written. This applied
   Baffles their strength and art;
Spirit and soul with this divide,
   And joints and marrow part.   80

To keep your armour bright,
   Attend with constant care,
Still walking in your Captain's sight,
   And watching unto prayer.
   Ready for all alarms,   85
   Steadfastly set your face,
And always exercise your arms,
   And use your every grace.

   Pray, without ceasing, pray,
   (Your Captain gives the word)   90
His summons cheerfully obey
   And call upon the Lord;
   To God your every want
   In instant prayer display,
Pray always; pray and never faint;   95
   Pray, without ceasing, pray!

   In fellowship, alone,
   To God with faith draw near;
Approach His courts, besiege His throne
   With all the powers of prayer: 100
   Go to His temple, go,
   Nor from His altar move;

Let every house His worship know,
  And every heart His love.

To God your spirits dart,   105
  Your souls in words declare,
Or groan, to Him Who reads the heart,
  Th' unutterable prayer:
  His mercy now implore,
  And now show forth His praise,   110
In shouts, or silent awe, adore
  His miracles of grace.

Pour out your souls to God,
  And bow them with your knees,
And spread your hearts and hands abroad,   115
  And pray for Zion's peace;
  Your guides and brethren bear
  For ever on your mind;
Extend the arms of mighty prayer,
  Ingrasping all mankind.   120

From strength to strength go on,
  Wrestle, and fight, and pray,
Tread all the powers of darkness down
  And win the well fought day.
  Still let the Spirit cry   125
  In all His soldiers, 'Come'
Till Christ the Lord descends from high
  And takes the conquerors home.

47. **Free Grace**

And can it be, that I should gain
  An interest in the Saviour's blood?
Died He for me? – who caused His pain!
  For me? – who Him to death pursued.
Amazing love! how can it be   5
That Thou, my God, shouldst die for me?

'Tis mystery all! th' Immortal dies!
  Who can explore His strange design?

In vain the first-born seraph tries
　　To sound the depths of love divine.   10
'Tis mercy all! Let earth adore;
Let angel minds enquire no more.

He left His Father's throne above,
　　(So free, so infinite His grace!)
Emptied Himself of all but love,   15
　　And bled for Adam's helpless race:
'Tis mercy all, immense and free!
For, O my God! it found out me!

Long my imprisoned spirit lay,
　　Fast bound in sin and nature's night: 20
Thine eye diffused a quick'ning ray;
　　I woke; the dungeon flamed with light;
My chains fell off, my heart was free,
I rose, went forth, and followed Thee.

Still the small inward voice I hear,   25
　　That whispers all my sins forgiven;
Still the atoning blood is near,
　　That quenched the wrath of hostile heaven:
I feel the life His wounds impart;
I feel my Saviour in my heart.   30

No condemnation now I dread,
　　Jesus, and all in Him, is mine:
Alive in Him, my living head,
　　And clothed in righteousness divine,
Bold I approach th' eternal throne,   35
And claim the crown, through Christ, my own.

48. Wrestling with Jacob

Come, O Thou Traveller unknown,
　　Whom still I hold, but cannot see,
My company before is gone,
　　And I am left alone with Thee;
With Thee all night I mean to stay,   5
And wrestle till the break of day.

I need not tell Thee who I am,
   My misery or sin declare,
Thyself hast called me by my name,
   Look on Thy hands, and read it there;   10
But who, I ask Thee, who art Thou?
Tell me Thy name, and tell me now.

In vain Thou strugglest to get free,
   I never will unloose my hold;
Art thou the Man that died for me?   15
   The secret of Thy love unfold;
Wrestling I will not let Thee go
Till I Thy name, Thy nature know.

Wilt Thou not yet to me reveal
   Thy new, unutterable name?   20
Tell me, I still beseech Thee, tell;
   To know it now resolved I am;
Wrestling I will not let Thee go
Till I Thy name, Thy nature know.

'Tis all in vain to hold Thy tongue,   25
   Or touch the hollow of my thigh;
Though every sinew be unstrung,
   Out of my arms Thou shalt not fly;
Wrestling I will not let Thee go
Till I Thy name, Thy nature know.   30

What though my shrinking flesh complain,
   And murmur to contend so long,
I rise superior to my pain,
   When I am weak then I am strong;
And when my all of strength shall fail,   35
I shall with the God-man prevail.

My strength is gone, my nature dies,
   I sink beneath Thy weighty hand,
Faint to revive, and fall to rise;
   I fall, and yet by faith I stand,   40
I stand, and will not let Thee go,
Till I Thy name, Thy nature know.

Yield to me now; for I am weak,
   But confident in self-despair:
Speak to my heart, in blessings speak,   45
   Be conquered by my instant prayer;
Speak, or Thou never hence shalt move,
And tell me if Thy name is Love.

'Tis Love! 'tis Love! Thou died'st for me;
   I hear Thy whisper in my heart: 50
The morning breaks, the shadows flee:
   Pure universal love Thou art;
To me, to all Thy bowels move;
Thy nature, and Thy name is Love.

My prayer hath power with God; the grace   55
   Unspeakable I now receive,
Through faith I see Thee face to face;
   I see Thee face to face, and live:
In vain I have not wept and strove;
Thy nature, and Thy name is Love.   60

I know Thee, Saviour, who Thou art,
   Jesus, the feeble sinner's Friend;
Nor wilt Thou with the night depart,
   But stay, and love me to the end;
Thy mercies never shall remove;   65
Thy nature, and Thy name is Love.

The Sun of Righteousness on me
   Hath rose with healing in His wings;
Withered my nature's strength, from Thee
   My soul its life and succour brings;
My help is all laid up above;   70
Thy nature, and Thy name is Love.

Contented now upon my thigh
   I halt, till life's short journey end;
All helplessness, all weakness, I   75
   On Thee alone for strength depend,
Nor have I power from Thee to move;
Thy nature, and Thy name is Love.

Lame as I am, I take the prey,
    Hell, earth, and sin with ease o'ercome;   80
I leap for joy, pursue my way,
    And as a bounding hart fly home,
Through all eternity to prove,
Thy nature, and Thy name is Love.

49. 'Love Divine, all loves excelling'

Love Divine, all loves excelling,
    Joy of heaven, to earth come down,
Fix in us Thy humble dwelling,
    All Thy faithful mercies crown:
Jesu, Thou art all compassion,   5
    Pure, unbounded love Thou art,
Visit us with Thy salvation,
    Enter every trembling heart.

Breathe, O breathe Thy loving Spirit,
    Into every troubled breast,   10
Let us all in Thee inherit,
    Let us find that second rest:
Take away our power of sinning,
    Alpha and omega be,
End of faith as its Beginning,   15
    Set our hearts at liberty.

Come, almighty to deliver,
    Let us all Thy life receive;
Suddenly return, and never,
    Never more Thy temples leave.   20
Thee we would be always blessing,
    Serve Thee as Thy hosts above,
Pray, and praise Thee without ceasing,
    Glory in Thy perfect love.

Finish then Thy new creation,   25
    Pure, and spotless let us be,
Let us see Thy great salvation,
    Perfectly restored in Thee:
Changed from glory into glory,

Till in heaven we take our place,   30
Till we cast our crowns before Thee,
   Lost in wonder, love, and praise!

Samuel Johnson (1709–1784)

50. The Vanity of Human Wishes

In imitation of the Tenth Satire of Juvenal

Let observation, with extensive view,
survey mankind, from China to Peru;
Remark each anxious toil, each eager strife,
And watch the busy scenes of crowded life;
Then say how hope and fear, desire and hate,   5
O'erspread with snares the clouded maze of fate,
Where wav'ring man, betrayed by vent'rous pride,
To tread the dreary paths without a guide,
As treach'rous phantoms in the mist delude,
Shuns fancied ills, or chases airy good.   10
How rarely reason guides the stubborn choice,
Rules the bold hand, or prompts the suppliant voice,
How nations sink, by darling schemes oppressed,
When vengeance listens to the fool's request.
Fate wings with ev'ry wish th' afflictive dart,   15
Each gift of nature, and each grace of art,
With fatal heat impetuous courage glows,
With fatal sweetness elocution flows,
Impeachment stops the speaker's pow'rful breath,
And restless fire precipitates on death.   20
But scarce observed the knowing and the bold,
Fall in the gen'ral massacre of gold;
Wide-wasting pest! that rages unconfined,
And crowds with crimes the records of mankind;
For gold his sword the hireling ruffian draws,   25
For gold the hireling judge distorts the laws;
Wealth heaped on wealth, nor truth nor safety buys,
The dangers gather as the treasures rise.
   Let hist'ry tell where rival kings command,

And dubious title shakes the madded land,   30
When statues glean the refuse of the sword,
How much more safe the vassal than the lord,
Low skulks the hind beneath the rage of pow'r,
And leaves the wealthy traitor in the Tow'r,
Untouched his cottage, and his slumbers sound,   35
Though confiscation's vultures hover round.
    The needy traveler, serene and gay,
Walks the wild heath, and sings his toil away.
Does envy seize thee? crush th' upbraiding joy,
Increase his riches and his peace destroy,   40
New fears in dire vicissitude invade,
The rustling brake alarms, and quiv'ring shade,
Nor light nor darkness bring his pain relief,
One shows the plunder, and one hides the thief.
    Yet still one gen'ral cry the skies assails,   45
And gain and grandeur load the tainted gales;
Few know the toiling statesman's fear or care,
Th' insidious rival and the gaping heir.
    Once more, Democritus, arise on earth,
With cheerful wisdom and instructive mirth,   50
See motley life in modern trappings dressed,
And feed with varied fools th' eternal jest:
Thou who could'st laugh where want enchained caprice,
Toil crushed conceit, and man was of a piece;
Where wealth unloved without a mourner died;   55
And scarce a sycophant was fed by pride;
Where ne'er was known the form of mock debate,
Or seen a new-made mayor's unwieldy state;
Where change of fav'rites made no change of laws,
And senates heard before thy judged a cause;   60
How would'st thou shake at Britain's modish tribe,
Dart the quick taunt, and edge the piercing gibe?
Attentive truth and nature to decry,
And pierce each scene with philosophic eye.
To thee were solemn toys or empty show,   65
The robes of pleasure and the veils of woe:
All aid the farce, and all thy mirth maintain,
Whose joys are causeless, or whose griefs are vain.
    Such was the scorn that filled the sage's mind,
Renewed at ev'ry glance on humankind;   70
How just that scorn ere yet thy voice declare,
Search every state, and canvass ev'ry prayer.

Unnumbered suppliants crowd Preferment's gate;
Athirst for wealth, and burning to be great;
Delusive Fortune hears th' incessant call, 75
They mount, they shine, evaporate, and fall.
On ev'ry stage the foes of peace attend,
Hate dogs their flight, and insult mocks their end.
Love ends with hope, the sinking statesman's door
Pours in the morning worshipper no more; 80
For growing names the weekly scribbler lies,
To growing wealth the dedicator flies,
From every room descends the painted face,
That hung the bright Palladium of the place,
And smoked in kitchens, or in auctions sold, 85
To better features yields the frame of gold;
For now no more we trace in ev'ry line
Heroic worth, benevolence divine:
The form distorted justifies the fall,
And detestation rids th' indignant wall. 90
    But will not Britain hear the last appeal,
Sign her foes doom, or guard her fav'rites zeal;
Through Freedom's sons no more remonstrance rings,
Degrading nobles and controlling kings;
Our supple tribes repress their patriot throats, 95
And ask no questions but the price of votes;
With weekly libels and septennial ale,
Their wish is full to riot and to rail.
    In full-blown dignity, see Wolsey stand,
Law in his voice, and fortune in his hand: 100
To him the church, the realm, their pow'rs consign,
Through him the rays of regal bounty shine,
Still to new heights his restless wishes tow'r,
Claim leads to claim, and pow'r advances pow'r;
'Till conquest unresisted ceased to please, 105
And rights submitted, left him none to seize.
At length his sov'reign frowns – the train of state
Mark the keen glance, and watch the sign to hate.
Where'er he turns he meets a stranger's eye,
His suppliants scorn him, and his followers fly; 110
At once is lost the pride of awful state,
The golden canopy, the glitt'ring plate,
The regal palace, the luxurious board,
The liv'ried army, and the menial lord.
With age, with cares, with maladies oppressed, 115

He seeks the refuge of monastic rest.
Grief aids disease, remembered folly stings,
And his last sighs reproach the faith of kings.
　　Speak thou, whose thoughts at humble peace repine,
Shall Wolsey's wealth, with Wolsey's end be thine? 　　　　120
Or liv'st thou now, with safer pride content,
The wisest justice on the banks of Trent?
For why did Wolsey near the steeps of fate,
On weak foundations raise th' enormous weight?
Why but to sink beneath Misfortune's blow, 　　　　　　　125
With louder ruin to the gulfs below?
　　What gave great Villiers to th' assassin's knife,
And fixed disease on Harley's closing life?
What murdered Wentworth, and what exiled Hyde,
By kings protected, and to kings allied? 　　　　　　　　130
What but their wish indulged in courts to shine,
And pow'r too great to keep, or to resign?
　　When first the college rolls receive his name,
The young enthusiast quits his ease for fame;
Through all his veins the fever of renown 　　　　　　　135
Spreads from the strong contagion of the gown;
O'er Bodley's dome his future labours spread,
And Bacon's mansion trembles o'er his head.
Are these thy views? proceed illustrious youth,
And virtue guard thee to the throne of Truth! 　　　　　140
Yet should thy soul indulge the gen'rous heat,
'Till captive Science yields her last retreat;
Should Reason guide thee with her brightest ray,
And pour on misty Doubt resistless day;
Should no false Kindness lure to loose delight, 　　　　145
Nor Praise relax, nor Difficulty fright;
Should tempting Novelty thy cell refrain,
And Sloth effuse her opiate fumes in vain;
Should Beauty blunt on fops her fatal dart,
Nor claim the triumph of a lettered heart; 　　　　　　150
Should no Disease thy torpid veins invade,
Nor Melancholy's phantoms haunt thy shade;
Yet hope not life from grief or danger free,
Nor think the doom of man reversed for thee:
Deign on the passing world to turn thine eyes, 　　　　155
And pause awhile from letters, to be wise;
There mark what ills the scholar's life assail,
Toil, envy, want, the patron, and the jail.

See nations slowly wise, and meanly just,
To buried merit raise the tardy bust.   160
If dreams yet flatter, once again attend,
Hear Lydiat's life, and Galileo's end.
    Nor deem, when Learning her last prize bestows,
The glitt'ring eminence exempt from woes;
See when the vulgar 'scape, despised or awed,   165
Rebellion's vengeful talons seize on Laud.
From meaner minds, though smaller fines content
The plundered palace or sequestered rent;
Marked out by dangerous parts he meets the shock,
And fatal Learning leads him to the block: 170
Around his tomb let Art and Genius weep,
But hear his death, ye blockheads, hear and sleep.
    The festal blazes, the triumphal show,
The ravished standard, and the captive foe,
The senate's thanks, the gazette's pompous tale,   175
With force resistless o'er the brave prevail.
Such bribes the rapid Greek o'er Asia whirled,
For such the steady Romans shook the world;
For such in distant lands the Britons shine,
And stain with blood the Danube or the Rhine;   180
This pow'r has praise, that virtue scarce can warm,
'Till fame supplies the universal charm.
Yet Reason frowns on War's unequal game,
Where wasted nations raise a single name,
And mortgaged states their grandsires' wreaths regret, 185
From age to age in everlasting debt;
Wreaths which at last the dear-bought right convey
To rust on medals, or on stones decay.
    On what foundation stands the warrior's pride,
How just his hopes let Swedish Charles decide;   190
A frame of adamant, a soul of fire,
No dangers fright him, and no labours tire;
O'er love, o'er fear extends his wide domain,
Unconquered lord of pleasure and of pain;
No joys to him pacific sceptres yield,   195
War sounds the trump, he rushes to the field;
Behold surrounding kings their pow'r combine,
And one capitulate, and one resign;
Peace courts his hand, but spreads her charms in vain;
'Think nothing gained,' he cries, 'till nought remain, 200
On Moscow's walls till Gothic standards fly,

And all be mine beneath the polar sky.'
The march begins in military state,
And nations on his eye suspended wait;
Stern Famine guards the solitary coast,   205
And Winter barricades the realm of Frost;
He comes, not want and cold his course delay; –
Hide, blushing Glory, hide Pultowa's day:
The vanquished hero leaves his broken bands,
And shows his miseries in distant lands;   210
Condemned a needy supplicant to wait,
While ladies interpose, and slaves debate.
But did not Chance at length her error mend?
Did no subverted empire mark his end?
Did rival monarchs give the fatal wound?   215
Or hostile millions press him to the ground?
His fall was destined to a barren strand,
A petty fortress, and a dubious hand;
He left the name, at which the world grew pale,
To point a moral, or adorn a tale.   220
All times their scenes of pompous woes afford,
From Persia's tyrant to Bavaria's lord.
In gay hostility, and barb'rous pride,
With half mankind embattled at his side,
Great Xerxes comes to seize the certain prey,   225
And starves exhausted regions in his way;
Attendant Flatt'ry counts his myriads o'er,
'Till counted myriads sooth his pride no more;
Fresh praise is tried 'till madness fires his mind,
The waves he lashes, and enchains the wind;   230
New pow'rs are claimed, new pow'rs are still bestowed,
'Till rude resistance lops the spreading god;
The daring Greeks deride the martial show,
And heap their valleys with the gaudy foe;
Th' insulted sea with humbler thoughts he gains,   235
A single skiff to speed his flight remains;
Th' incumbered oar scarce leaves the dreaded coast
Through purple billows and a floating host.
    The bold Bavarian, in a luckless hour,
Tries the dread summits of Caesarean pow'r,   240
With unexpected legions bursts away,
And sees defenceless realms receive his sway;
Short sway! fair Austria spreads her mournful charms,
The queen, the beauty, sets the world in arms;

From hill to hill the beacons rousing blaze 245
Spreads wide the hope of plunder and of praise;
The fierce Croatian, and the wild Hussar,
And all the sons of ravage crowd the war;
The baffled prince in honour's flatt'ring bloom
Of hasty greatness finds the fatal doom, 250
His foes' derision, and his subjects' blame,
And steals to death from anguish and from shame.
    Enlarge my life with multitude of days,
In health, in sickness, thus the suppliant prays;
Hides from himself his state, and shuns to know, 255
That life protracted is protracted woe.
Time hovers o'er, impatient to destroy,
And shuts up all the passages of joy:
In vain their gifts the bounteous seasons pour,
The fruit autumnal, and the vernal flow'r, 260
With listless eyes the dotard views the store,
He views, and wonders that they please no more;
Now pall the tasteless meats, and joyless wines,
And Luxury with sighs her slave resigns.
Approach, ye minstrels, try the soothing strain, 265
And yield the tuneful lenitives of pain:
No sounds alas would touch th' impervious ear,
Though dancing mountains witness Orpheus near,
Nor lute nor lyre his feeble pow'rs attend,
Nor sweeter music of a virtuous friend, 270
But everlasting dictates crowd his tongue,
Perversely grave or positively wrong.
The still returning tale, and ling'ring jest,
Perplex the fawning niece and pampered guest,
While growing hopes scarce awe the gath'ring sneer, 275
And scarce a legacy can bribe to hear;
The watchful guests still hint the last offence,
The daughter's petulance, the son's expense,
Improve his heady rage with treach'rous skill,
And mould his passions 'till they make his will. 280
    Unnumbered maladies his joints invade,
Lay siege to life and press the dire blockade,
But unextinguished Av'rice still remains,
And dreaded losses aggravate his pains;
He turns, with anxious heart and crippled hands, 285
His bonds of debt, and mortgages of lands;
Or views his coffers with suspicious eyes,

Unlocks his gold, and counts it 'till he dies.
   But grant, the virtues of a temp'rate prime
Bless with an age exempt from scorn or crime;   290
An age that melts in unperceived decay,
And glides in modest innocence away;
Whose peaceful day Benevolence endears,
Whose night congratulating Conscience cheers;
The gen'ral fav'rite, as the gen'ral friend;   295
Such age there is, and who could wish its end?
   Yet ev'n on this her load Misfortune flings,
To press the weary minutes' flagging wings:
New sorrow rises as the day returns,
A sister sickens or a daughter mourns.   300
Now kindred merit fills the sable bier,
Now lacerated friendship claims a tear.
Year chases year, decay pursues decay,
Still drops some joy from with'ring life away;
New forms arise, and diff'rent views engage,   305
Superfluous lags the vet'ran on the stage,
'Till pitying Nature signs the last release,
And bids afflicted Worth retire to peace.
   But few there are whom hours like these await,
Who set unclouded in the gulfs of Fate.   310
From Lydia's monarch should the search descend,
By Solon cautioned to regard his end,
In life's last scene what prodigies surprise,
Fears of the brave, and follies of the wise?
From Marlb'rough's eyes the streams of dotage flow,   315
And Swift expires a driv'ler and a show.
   The teeming mother, anxious for her race,
Begs for each birth the fortune of a face:
Yet Vane could tell what ills from beauty spring;
And Sedley cursed the form that pleased a king.   320
Ye nymphs of rosy lips and radiant eyes,
Whom Pleasure keeps too busy to be wise,
Whom Joys with soft varieties invite,
By day the frolic, and the dance by night,
Who frown with vanity, who smile with art,   325
And ask the latest fashion of the heart,
What care, what rules your heedless charms shall save,
Each nymph your rival, and each youth your slave?
Against your fame with fondness hate combines,
The rival batters, and the lover mines.   330

With distant voice neglected Virtue calls,
Less heard and less, the faint remonstrance falls;
Tired with contempt, she quits the slipp'ry reign,
And Pride and Prudence take her seat in vain.
In crowd at once, where none the pass defend,   335
The harmless Freedom, and the private Friend.
The guardians yield, by force superior plied;
By Int'rest, Prudence; and by Flatt'ry, Pride.
Now beauty falls betrayed, despised, distressed,
And hissing Infamy proclaims the rest.   340
    Where then shall Hope and Fear their objects find?
Must dull Suspense corrupt the stagnant mind?
Must helpless man, in ignorance sedate,
Roll darkling down the torrent of his fate?
Must no dislike alarm, no wishes rise,   345
No cries attempt the mercies of the skies?
Inquirer, cease, petitions yet remain,
Which heav'n may hear, nor deem religion vain.
Still raise for good the supplicating voice,
But leave to heav'n the measure and the choice.   350
Safe in his pow'r, whose eyes discern afar
The secret ambush of a specious pray'r.
Implore his aid, in his decisions rest,
Secure whate'er he gives, he gives the best.
Yet when the sense of sacred presence fires,   355
And strong devotion to the skies aspires,
Pour forth thy fervours for a healthful mind,
Obedient passions, and a will resigned;
For love, which scarce collective man can fill;
For patience sov'reign o'er transmuted ill;   360
For faith that panting for a happier seat,
Counts death kind Nature's signal of retreat:
These goods for man the laws of heav'n ordain,
These goods he grants, who grants the pow'r to gain;
With these celestial Wisdom calms the mind,   365
And makes the happiness she does not find.

51. London: A Poem

In imitation of the Third Satire of Juvenal

> – *Quis ineptæ*
> *Tam patiens urbis, tam ferreus ut teneat se?*[30]

Juvenal, *Satire* I, 30–1

Though grief and fondness in my breast rebel,
When injured Thales bids the town farewell,
Yet still my calmer thoughts his choice commend,
I praise the hermit, but regret the friend;
Who now resolves, from vice and London far,   5
To breathe in distant fields a purer air,
And, fixed on Cambria's solitary shore,
Give to St David one true Briton more
    For who would leave, unbribed, Hibernia's land,
Or change the rocks of Scotland for the Strand?   10
There none are swept by sudden fate away,
But all whom hunger spares, with age decay:
Here malice, rapine, accident, conspire,
And now a rabble rages, now a fire;
Their ambush here relentless ruffians lay,   15
And here the fell attorney prowls for prey;
Here falling houses thunder on your head,
And here a female atheist talks you dead.
    While Thales waits the wherry that contains
Of dissipated wealth the small remains,   20
On Thames's bank in silent thought we stood,
Where Greenwich smiles upon the silver flood.
Struck with the seat that gave Eliza birth,
We kneel, and kiss the consecrated earth;
In pleasing dreams the blissful age renew,   25
And call Britannia's glories back to view;
Behold her cross triumphant on the main,
The guard of commerce, and the dread of Spain.
Ere masquerades debauched, excise oppressed,
Or English honour grew a standing jest.   30
    A transient calm the happy scenes bestow,
And for a moment lull the sense of woe.
At length awaking with contemptuous frown,
Indignant Thales eyes the neighb'ring town.

---

[30] 'For who can be so patient of this awful city, who so resolute as to keep his counsel?'

Since worth, he cries, in these degen'rate days   35
Wants ev'n the cheap reward of empty praise;
In those cursed walls, devote to vice and gain,
Since unrewarded science toils in vain;
Since hope but sooths to double my distress,
And ev'ry moment leaves my little less;   40
While yet my steady steps no staff sustains,
And life still vig'rous revels in my veins;
Grant me, kind heaven, to find some happier place,
Where honesty and sense are no disgrace;
Some pleasing bank where verdant osiers play,   45
Some peaceful vale with nature's painting gay;
Where once the harassed Briton found repose,
And safe in poverty defied his foes;
Some secret cell, ye pow'rs, indulgent give:
Let — live here, for — has learned to live.   50
Here let those reign, whom pensions can incite
To vote a patriot black, a courtier white;
Explain their country's dear-bought rights away,
And plead for pirates in the face of day;
With slavish tenets taint our poisoned youth,   55
And lend a lie the confidence of truth.
    Let such raise palaces, and manors buy,
Collect a tax, or farm a lottery,
With warbling eunuchs fill a licensed stage,
And lull to servitude a thoughtless age.   60
    Heroes, proceed! what bounds your pride shall hold?
What check restrain your thirst of pow'r and gold?
Behold rebellious virtue quite o'erthrown,
Behold our fame, our wealth, our lives your own.
To such, a groaning nation's spoils are giv'n,   65
When public crimes inflame the wrath of heav'n:
But what, my friend, what hope remains for me,
Who start at theft, and blush at perjury?
Who scarce forbear, though Britain's court he sing,
To pluck a titled poet's borrowed wing;   70
A statesman's logic unconvinced can hear,
And dare to slumber o'er the Gazetteer;
Despise a fool in half his pension dressed,
And strive in vain to laugh at H — y's jest.
    Others with softer smiles, and subtler art,   75
Can sap the principles, or taint the heart;
With more address a lover's note convey,

Or bribe a virgin's innocence away.
Well may they rise, while I, whose rustic tongue
Ne'er knew to puzzle right, or varnish wrong,   80
Spurned as a beggar, dreaded as a spy,
Live unregarded, unlamented die,
   For what but social guilt the friend endears?
Who shares Orgilio's° crimes, his fortune shares: *the proud man*
But thou, should tempting villainy present,   85
All Marlb'rough hoarded, or all Villiers spent,
Turn from the glitt'ring bribe thy scornful eye,
Nor sell for gold, what gold could never buy,
The peaceful slumber, self-approving day,
Unsullied fame, and conscience ever gay.   90
   The cheated nation's happy fav'rites see;
Mark whom the great caress, who frown on me.
London! the needy villain's gen'ral home,
The common sewer of Paris and of Rome,
With eager thirst, by folly or by fate,   95
Sucks in the dregs of each corrupted state.
Forgive my transports on a theme like this,
I cannot bear a French metropolis.
   Illustrious Edward! from the realms of day,
The land of heroes and of saints survey;   100
Nor hope the British lineaments to trace,
The rustic grandeur, or the surly grace,
But lost in thoughtless ease, and empty show,
Behold the warrior dwindled to a beau;
Sense, freedom, piety, refined away,   105
Of France the mimic, and of Spain the prey.
   All that at home no more can beg or steal,
Or like a gibbet better than a wheel;
Hissed from the stage, or hooted from the court,
Their air, their dress, their politics import;   110
Obsequious, artful, voluble and gay,
On Britain's fond credulity they prey.
No gainful trade their industry can 'scape,
They sing, they dance, clean shoes, or cure a clap;
All sciences a fasting Monsieur knows,   115
And bid him go to hell, to hell he goes.
   Ah! what avails it, that, from slav'ry far,
I drew the breath of life in English air;
Was early taught a Briton's right to prize,
And lisp the tales of Henry's victories;   120

If the gulled conqueror receives the chain,
And flattery subdues when arms are vain?
    Studious to please, and ready to submit,
The supple Gaul was born a parasite:
Still to his int'rest true, where-e'er he goes,   125
Wit, bravery, worth, his lavish tongue bestows;
In ev'ry face a thousand graces shine,
From ev'ry tongue flows harmony divine.
These arts in vain our rugged natives try,
Strain out with faltering diffidence a lie,   130
And gain a kick for awkward flattery.
    Besides, with justice this discerning age
Admires their wond'rous talents for the stage:
Well may they venture on the mimic's art,
Who play from morn to night a borrowed part;   135
Practised their master's notions to embrace,
Repeat his maxims, and reflect his face;
With ev'ry wild absurdity comply,
And view each object with another's eye;
To shake with laughter ere the jest they hear,   140
To pour at will the counterfeited tear,
And as their patron hints the cold or heat,
To shake in dog-days, in December sweat.
How, when competitors like these contend,
Can surly virtue hope to fix a friend?   145
Slaves that with serious impudence beguile,
And lie without a blush, without a smile;
Exalt each trifle, ev'ry vice adore,
Your taste in snuff, your judgement in a whore;
Can Balbo's° eloquence applaud, and swear   *the stammerer* 150
He gropes his breeches with a monarch's air.
    For arts like these preferred, admired, caressed,
They first invade your table, then your breast;
Explore your secrets with insidious art,
Watch the weak hour, and ransack all the heart;   155
Then soon your ill-placed confidence repay,
Commence your lords, and govern or betray.
    By numbers here from shame or censure free,
All crimes are safe, but hated poverty.
This, only this, the rigid law pursues,   160
This, only this, provokes the snarling Muse.
The sober trader at a tattered cloak,
Wakes from his dream, and labours for a joke;

With brisker air the silken courtiers gaze,
And turn the varied taunt a thousand ways. 165
Of all the griefs that harass the distressed;
Sure the most bitter is a scornful jest;
Fate never wounds more deep the gen'rous heart,
Than when a blockhead's insult points the dart.
    Has heaven reserved, in pity to the poor, 170
No pathless waste or undiscovered shore?
No secret island in the boundless main?
No peaceful desert yet unclaimed by Spain?
Quick let us rise, the happy seats explore,
And bear oppression's insolence no more. 175
    This mournful truth is ev'ry where confessed,
Slow rises worth, by poverty depressed:
But here more slow, where all are slaves to gold,
Where looks are merchandise, and smiles are sold;
Where won by bribes, by flatteries implored, 180
The groom retails the favours of his lord.
    But hark! th' affrighted crowd's tumultuous cries
Roll through the streets and thunder to the skies:
Raised from some pleasing dream of wealth and power,
Some pompous palace or some blissful bow'r, 185
Aghast you start, and scarce with aching sight
Sustain th' approaching fire's tremendous light;
Swift from pursuing horrors take your way,
And leave your little all to flames a prey;
Then through the world a wretched vagrant roam, 190
For where can starving merit find a home?
In vain your mournful narrative disclose,
While all neglect, and most insult your woes.
    Should heaven's just bolts Orgilio's wealth confound,
And spread his flaming palace on the ground, 195
Swift o'er the land the dismal rumour flies,
And public mournings pacify the skies;
The laureate tribe in servile verse relate,
How virtue wars with persecuting fate;
With well-feigned gratitude the pensioned band 200
Refund the plunder of the beggared land.
See! while he builds, the gaudy vassals come,
And crowd with sudden wealth the rising dome;
The price of boroughs and of souls restore;
And raise his treasures higher than before. 205
Now blessed with all the baubles of the great,

The polished marble, and the shining plate,
Orgilio sees the golden pile aspire,
And hopes from angry heav'n another fire.
   Could'st thou resign the park and play content, 210
For the fair banks of Severn or of Trent;
There might'st thou find some elegant retreat,
Some hireling senator's deserted seat;
And stretch thy prospects o'er the smiling land,
For less than rent the dungeons of the Strand; 215
There prune thy walks, support thy drooping flow'rs,
Direct thy rivulets, and twine thy bow'rs;
And, while thy beds a cheap repast afford,
Despise the dainties of a venal lord.
There ev'ry bush with nature's music rings, 220
There ev'ry breeze bears health upon its wings;
On all thy hours security shall smile,
And bless thine evening walk and morning toil.
   Prepare for death, if here at night you roam,
And sign your will before you sup from home. 225
Some fiery fop, with new commission vain,
Who sleeps on brambles till he kills his man;
Some frolic drunkard, reeling from a feast,
Provokes a broil, and stabs you for a jest.
Yet ev'n these heroes, mischievously gay, 230
Lords of the street, and terrors of the way;
Flushed as they are with folly, youth and wine,
Their prudent insults to the poor confine;
Afar they mark the flambeau's bright approach,
And shun the shining train, and golden coach. 235
   In vain, these dangers past, your doors you close,
And hope the balmy blessings of repose:
Cruel with guilt and daring with despair,
The midnight murd'rer bursts the faithless bar;
Invades the sacred hour of silent rest, 240
And plants, unseen, a dagger in your breast.
   Scarce can our fields, such crowds at Tyburn die,
With hemp the gallows and the fleet supply.
Propose your schemes, ye senatorian band,
Whose ways and means support the sinking land; 245
Lest ropes be wanting in the tempting spring,
To rig another convoy for the king.
   A single jail, in Alfred's golden reign,
Could half the nation's criminals contain;

Fair Justice then, without constraint adored,   250
Held high the steady scale, but sheathed the sword;
No spies were paid, no special juries known,
Blest age! but ah! how diff'rent from our own!
    Much could I add, but see the boat at hand,
The tide retiring calls me from the land: 255
Farewell! – When youth, and health, and fortune spent,
Thou fly'st for refuge to the wilds of Kent;
And tired like me with follies and with crimes,
In angry numbers warn'st succeeding times;
Then shall thy friend, nor thou refuse his aid,   260
Still foe to vice, forsake his Cambrian shade;
In virtue's cause once more exert his rage,
Thy satire point, and animate thy page.

52. Prologue Spoken by Mr Garrick

at the opening of the theatre in Drury Lane, 1747

When learning's triumph o'er her barb'rous foes
First reared the stage, immortal Shakespeare rose;
Each change of many-coloured life he drew,
Exhausted worlds, and then imagined new:
Existence saw him spurn her bounded reign,   5
And panting time toiled after him in vain:
His pow'rful strokes presiding truth impressed,
And unresisted passion stormed the breast.
    Then Jonson came, instructed from the school,
To please in method, and invent by rule;   10
His studious patience, and laborious art,
By regular approach assailed the heart;
Cold approbation gave the ling'ring bays,
For those who durst not censure, scarce could praise.
A mortal born, he met the general doom,   15
But left, like Egypt's kings, a lasting tomb.
    The wits of Charles found easier ways to fame,
Nor wished for Jonson's art, or Shakespeare's flame;
Themselves they studied, as they felt, they writ;
Intrigue was plot, obscenity was wit.   20
Vice always found a sympathetic friend;
They pleased their age, and did not aim to mend.

Yet bards like these aspired to lasting praise,
And proudly hoped to pimp in future days.
Their cause was gen'ral, their supports were strong,   25
Their slaves were willing, and their reign was long;
Till shame regained the post that sense betrayed,
And virtue called oblivion to her aid.
    Then, crushed by rules, and weakened as refined,
For years the pow'r of tragedy declined;   30
From bard to bard the frigid caution crept,
Till declamation roared, while passion slept.
Yet still did Virtue deign the stage to tread,
Philosophy remained, though Nature fled.
But forced at length her ancient reign to quit,   35
She saw great Faustus lay the ghost of Wit:
Exulting folly hailed the joyful day,
And pantomime and song confirmed her sway.
But who the coming changes can presage,
And mark the future periods of the stage?   40
Perhaps if skill could distant times explore,
New Behns, new Durfeys, yet remain in store.
Perhaps, where Lear has raved, and Hamlet died,
On flying cars new sorcerers may ride.
Perhaps (for who can guess th' effects of chance?)   45
Here Hunt may box, or Mahomet may dance.°   *Hunt was a lightweight boxer;*
Hard is his lot, that here by fortune placed,   *Mahomet a celebrated*
Must watch the wild vicissitudes of taste;   *rope-dancer.*
With every meteor of caprice must play,
And chase the new-blown bubbles of the day.   50
Ah! let not censure term our fate our choice;
The stage but echoes back the public voice,
The drama's laws the drama's patrons give,
For we that live to please, must please to live.
    Then prompt no more the follies you decry,   55
As tyrants doom their tools of guilt to die;
'Tis yours this night to bid the reign commence
Of rescued nature, and reviving sense;
To chase the charms of sound, the pomp of show,
For useful mirth, and salutary woe;   60
Bid scenic virtue form the rising age,
And truth diffuse her radiance from the stage.

Thomas Gray (1716–1771)

53. Lines on Beech Trees

And, as they bow their hoary tops, relate
In murmuring sounds the dark decrees of fate;
While visions, as poetic eyes avow,
Cling to each leaf and swarm on every bough.

54. Translation from Dante

Inferno canto xxxiii 1–78

From his dire food the grisly felon raised
His gore-dyed lips, which on the clottered locks
Of the half-devoured head he wiped, and thus
Began: 'Would'st thou revive the deep despair,
The anguish, that, unuttered, natheless wrings   5
My inmost heart? Yet if the telling may
Beget the traitor's infamy, whom thus
I ceaseless gnaw insatiate, thou shalt see me
At once give loose to utterance and to tears.
    'I know not who thou art nor on what errand   10
Sent hither; but a Florentine my ear,
Won by thy tongue, declares thee. Know, thou see'st
In me Count Ugolino, and Ruggieri,
Pisa's perfidious prelate, this: now hear
My wrongs and from them judge of my revenge.   15
    'That I did trust him, that I was betrayed
By trusting, and by treachery slain, it recks not
That I advise thee; that which yet remains
To thee and all unknown (a horrid tale),
The bitterness of death, I shall unfold.   20
Attend, and say if he have injured me.
    'Through a small crevice opening, what scant light
That grim and antique tower admitted (since
Of me the Tower of Famine hight, and known

To many a wretch) already 'gan the dawn   25
To send. The whilst I slumbering lay, a sleep
Prophetic of my woes with direful hand
Oped the dark veil of fate. I saw methought
Toward Pisa's mount, that intercepts the view
Of Lucca, chased by hell-hounds gaunt and bloody   30
A wolf full-grown; with fleet and equal speed
His young ones ran beside him. Lanfranc there
And Sigismundo and Gualandi rode
Amain, my deadly foes, headed by this
The deadliest: he their chief, the foremost he   35
Flashed to pursue and cheer the eager cry.
Nor long endured the chase: the panting sire,
Of strength bereft, his helpless offspring soon
O'erta'en beheld, and in their trembling flanks
The hungry pack their sharp-set fangs embrued.   40
   'The morn had scarce commenced when I awoke:
My children (they were with me) sleep as yet
Gave not to know their sum of misery,
But yet in low and uncompleted sounds
I heard 'em wail for bread. Oh! thou art cruel,   45
Or thou dost mourn to think what my poor heart
Foresaw, foreknew; oh! if thou weep not now,
Where are thy tears? Too soon they had aroused them,
Sad with the fears of sleep, and now the hour
Of timely food approached; when, at the gate   50
Below, I heard the dreadful clank of bars
And fastening bolts. Then on my children's eyes
Speechless my sight I fixed, nor wept, for all
Within was stone. They wept, unhappy boys,
They wept; and first my little dear Anselmo   55
Cried, 'Father, why do you gaze so sternly?
What would you have?' Yet wept I not or answered
All that whole day or the succeeding night,
Till a new sun arose with weakly gleam
And wan, such as mought entrance find within   60
That house of woe. But oh! when I beheld
My sons, and in four faces saw my own
Despair reflected, either hand I gnawed
For anguish, which they construed hunger. Straight
Arising all they cried, 'Far less shall be   65
Our sufferings, sir, if you resume your gift;
These miserable limbs with flesh you clothed;

Take back what once was yours.' I swallowed down
My struggling sorrow, nor to heighten theirs.
That day and yet another, mute we sat   70
And motionless. O earth, could'st thou not gape
Quick to devour me? Yet a fourth day came,
When Gaddo, at my feet outstretched, imploring
In vain my help, expired; ere the sixth morn
Had dawned, my other three before my eyes   75
Died one by one. I saw 'em fall; I heard
Their doleful cries. For three days more I groped
About among their cold remains (for then
Hunger had reft my eyesight), often calling
On their dear names, that heard me now no more;   80
The fourth, what sorrow could not, famine did.'
    He finished; then with unrelenting eye
Askance he turned him, hasty to renew
The hellish feast, and rent his trembling prey.

55. Propertius, *Elegies* II. I

To Maecenas

You ask why thus my loves I still rehearse,
Whence the soft strain and ever-melting verse:
From Cynthia all that in my numbers shines;
She is my genius, she inspires the lines;
No Phoebus else, no other muse I know;   5
She tunes my easy rhyme and gives the lay to flow.
If the loose curls around her forehead play,
Or lawless o'er the ivory margin stray;
If the thin Coan web her shape reveal,
And half disclose those limbs it should conceal;   10
Of those loose curls, that ivory front, I write,
Of the dear web whole volumes I indite.
Or if to music she the lyre awake,
That the soft subject of my song I make,
And sing with what a careless grace she flings   15
Her artful hand across the sounding strings.
If sinking into sleep she seem to close
Her languid lids, I favour her repose
With lulling notes, and thousand beauties see

That slumber brings to aid my poetry. 20
When less averse and yielding to desires,
She half accepts and half rejects my fires;
While to retain the envious lawn she tries,
And struggles to elude my longing eyes;
The fruitful muse from that auspicious night 25
Dates the long *Iliad* of the amorous fight.
In brief, whate'er she do, or say, or look,
'Tis ample matter for a lover's book;
And many a copious narrative you'll see,
Big with important nothing's history. 30
    Yet would the tyrant Love permit me raise
My feeble voice to sing the victor's praise,
To paint the hero's toil, the ranks of war,
The laurelled triumph and the sculptured car,
No giant-race, no tumult of the skies, 35
No mountain-structure in my verse should rise;
Nor tale of Thebes or Ilium there should be,
Or how the Persian trod the indignant sea;
Not Marius' Cimbrian wreaths would I relate,
Nor lofty Carthage struggling with her fate. 40
Here should Augustus great in arms appear,
And thou, Maecenas, be my second care;
Here Mutina from flames and famine free,
And there the ensanguined wave of Sicily,
And sceptred Alexandria's captive shore, 45
And sad Philippi red with Roman gore.
Then, while the vaulted skies loud Ios rend,
In golden chains should loaded monarchs bend,
And hoary Nile with pensive aspect seem
To mourn the glories of his sevenfold stream, 50
While prows, that late in fierce encounter met,
Move through the sacred way and vainly threat.
Thee too the muse should consecrate to fame,
And with his garlands weave thy ever-faithful name;
But nor Callimachus' enervate strain 55
May tell of Jove and Phlegra's blasted plain,
Nor I with unaccustomed vigour trace
Back to its source divine the Julian race.
Sailors to tell of seas and winds delight,
The shepherd of his flocks, the soldier of the fight; 60
A milder warfare I in verse display;
Each in his proper art should waste the day.

Nor thou my gentle calling disapprove:
To die is glorious in the bed of love.
Happy the youth, and not unknown to fame,   65
Whose heart has never felt a second flame.
Oh, might that envied happiness be mine!
To Cynthia all my wishes I confine;
Or if, alas! it be my fate to try
Another love, the quicker let me die.   70
But she, the mistress of my faithful breast,
Has oft the charms of constancy confessed,
Condemns her fickle sex's fond mistake,
And hates the tale of Troy for Helen's sake.
Me from myself the soft enchantress stole: 75
Ah! let her ever my desires control.
Or if I fall the victim of her scorn,
From her loved door may my pale corpse be borne.
The power of herbs can other harms remove,
And find a cure for every ill but love.   80
The Lemnian's hurt Machaon could repair,
Heal the slow chief and send again to war;
To Chiron Phoenix owed his long-lost sight,
And Phoebus' son recalled Androgeon to the light.
Here arts are vain, even magic here must fail,   85
The powerful mixture and the midnight spell.
The hand that can my captive heart release
And to this bosom give its wonted peace,
May the long thirst of Tantalus allay,
Or drive the infernal vulture from his prey.   90
For ills unseen what remedy is found,
Or who can probe the undiscovered wound?
The bed avails not or the leech's care,
Nor changing skies can hurt nor sultry air.
'Tis hard the elusive symptoms to explore: 95
Today the lover walks, tomorrow is no more;
A train of mourning friends attend his pall,
And wonder at the sudden funeral.
    When then my fates that breath they gave shall claim,
When the short marble but preserves a name,   100
A little verse, my all that shall remain,
Thy passing courser's slackened speed retain
(Thou envied honour of thy poet's days,
Of all our youth the ambition and the praise!);
Then to my quiet urn awhile draw near,   105

And say, while o'er the place you drop a tear,
Love and the fair were of his life the pride;
He lived while she was kind, and, when she frowned, he died.

56. Ode on the Spring

Lo! where the rosy-bosomed hours,
    Fair Venus' train, appear,
Disclose the long-expecting flowers,
    And wake the purple year!
The Attic warbler pours her throat,   5
Responsive to the cuckoo's note,
The untaught harmony of spring:
While whispering pleasure as they fly,
Cool zephyrs through the clear blue sky
    Their gathered fragrance fling.   10

Where'er the oak's thick branches stretch
    A broader browner shade;
Where'er the rude and moss-grown beech
    O'er-canopies the glade,
Beside some water's rushy brink   15
With me the Muse shall sit, and think
(At ease reclined in rustic state)
How vain the ardour of the crowd,
How low, how little are the proud,
    How indigent the great!   20

Still is the toiling hand of care;
    The panting herds repose.
Yet hark, how through the peopled air
    The busy murmur glows!
The insect youth are on the wing,   25
Eager to taste the honeyed spring,
And float amid the liquid noon:
Some lightly o'er the current skim,
Some show their gaily-gilded trim
    Quick-glancing to the sun.   30

To contemplation's sober eye
    Such is the race of man:

And they that creep, and they that fly,
    Shall end where they began.
Alike the busy and the gay   35
But flutter through life's little day,
In fortune's varying colours dressed:
Brushed by the hand of rough mischance,
Or chilled by age, their airy dance
    They leave, in dust to rest.   40

Methinks I hear in accents low
    The sportive kind reply:
Poor moralist! and what art thou?
    A solitary fly!
Thy joys no glittering female meets,   45
No hive hast thou of hoarded sweets,
No painted plumage to display:
On hasty wings thy youth is flown;
Thy sun is set, thy spring is gone –
    We frolic, while 'tis May.   50

57. Ode on a Distant Prospect of Eton College

Anthropos: ikane prophasis eis to dustuxein.

Ye distant spires, ye antique towers,
    That crown the watery glade,
Where grateful Science still adores
    Her Henry's holy shade;
And ye that from the stately brow   5
Of Windsor's heights the expanse below
Of grove, of lawn, of mead survey,
Whose turf, whose shade, whose flowers among
Wanders the hoary Thames along
    His silver-winding way.   10

Ah, happy hills, ah, pleasing shade,
    Ah, fields beloved in vain,
Where once my careless childhood strayed,
    A stranger yet to pain!
I feel the gales, that from ye blow,   15
A momentary bliss bestow,

As waving fresh their gladsome wing,
My weary soul they seem to soothe,
And, redolent of joy and youth,
   To breathe a second spring.   20

Say, Father Thames, for thou hast seen
   Full many a sprightly race
Disporting on thy margent green
   The paths of pleasure trace,
Who foremost now delight to cleave   25
With pliant arm thy glassy wave?
The captive linnet which enthrall?
What idle progeny succeed
To chase the rolling circle's speed,
   Or urge the flying ball?   30

While some on earnest business bent
   Their murmuring labours ply
'Gainst graver hours, that bring constraint
   To sweeten liberty:
Some bold adventurers disdain   35
The limits of their little reign,
And unknown regions dare descry:
Still as they run they look behind,
They hear a voice in every wind,
   And snatch a fearful joy.   40

Gay hope is theirs by fancy fed,
   Less pleasing when possessed;
The tear forgot as soon as shed,
   The sunshine of the breast:
Theirs buxom health of rosy hue,   45
Wild wit, invention ever-new,
And lively cheer of vigour born;
The thoughtless day, the easy night,
The spirits pure, the slumbers light,
   That fly the approach of morn.   50

Alas, regardless of their doom,
   The little victims play!
No sense have they of ills to come,
   Nor care beyond today:
Yet see how all around 'em wait   55

The ministers of human fate,
And black Misfortune's baleful train!
Ah, show them where in ambush stand
To seize their prey the murtherous band!
    Ah, tell them, they are men! 60

These shall the fury Passions tear,
    The vultures of the mind,
Disdainful Anger, pallid Fear,
    And Shame that skulks behind;
Or pining Love shall waste their youth, 65
Or Jealousy with rankling tooth,
That inly gnaws the secret heart,
And Envy wan, and faded Care,
Grim-visaged comfortless Despair,
    And Sorrow's piercing dart. 70

Ambition this shall tempt to rise,
    Then whirl the wretch from high,
To bitter Scorn a sacrifice,
    And grinning Infamy.
The stings of Falsehood those shall try, 75
And hard Unkindness' altered eye,
That mocks the tear it forced to flow;
And keen Remorse with blood defiled,
And moody Madness laughing wild
    Amid severest woe. 80

Lo, in the vale of years beneath
    A grisly troop are seen,
The painful family of Death,
    More hideous than their Queen:
This racks the joints, this fires the veins, 85
That every labouring sinew strains,
Those in the deeper vitals rage:
Lo, Poverty, to fill the band,
That numbs the soul with icy hand,
    And slow-consuming Age. 90

To each his sufferings: all are men,
    Condemned alike to groan;
The tender for another's pain,
    The unfeeling for his own.

Yet ah! why should they know their fate? 95
Since sorrow never comes too late,
And happiness too swiftly flies.
Thought would destroy their paradise.
No more; where ignorance is bliss,
　　'Tis folly to be wise. 100

58. Ode to Adversity

Daughter of Jove, relentless power,
Thou tamer of the human breast,
Whose iron scourge and torturing hour,
The bad affright, afflict the best!
Bound in thy adamantine chain 5
The proud are taught to taste of pain,
And purple tyrants vainly groan
With pangs unfelt before, unpitied and alone.

When first thy sire to send on earth
Virtue, his darling child, designed, 10
To thee he gave the heavenly birth,
And bade to form her infant mind.
Stern rugged nurse! thy rigid lore
With patience many a year she bore:
What sorrow was, thou bad'st her know, 15
And from her own she learned to melt at others' woe.

Scared at thy frown terrific, fly
Self-pleasing folly's idle brood,
Wild laughter, noise, and thoughtless joy,
And leave us leisure to be good. 20
Light they disperse, and with them go
The summer friend, the flattering foe;
By vain prosperity received,
To her they vow their truth and are again believed.

Wisdom in sable garb arrayed, 25
Immersed in rapturous thought profound,
And melancholy, silent maid
With leaden eye that loves the ground,
Still on thy solemn steps attend:

Warm charity, the general friend,   30
With Justice to herself severe,
And Pity, dropping soft the sadly-pleasing tear.

Oh, gently on thy suppliant's head,
Dread goddess, lay thy chastening hand!
Not in thy Gorgon terrors clad,   35
Nor circled with the vengeful band
(As by the impious thou art seen)
With thundering voice and threatening mien,
With screaming horror's funeral cry,
Despair and fell disease and ghastly poverty.   40

Thy form benign, oh Goddess, wear,
Thy milder influence impart,
Thy philosophic train be there
To soften, not to wound my heart.
The generous spark extinct revive,   45
Teach me to love and to forgive,
Exact my own defects to scan,
What others are to feel, and know myself a man.

59. Ode on the Death of a Favourite Cat

Drowned in a Tub of Gold Fishes

'Twas on a lofty vase's side,
Where China's gayest art had dyed
 The azure flowers, that blow;
Demurest of the tabby kind,
The pensive Selima reclined,   5
 Gazed on the lake below.

Her conscious tail her joy declared;
The fair round face, the snowy beard,
 The velvet of her paws,
Her coat that with the tortoise vies,   10
Her ears of jet and emerald eyes,
 She saw; and purred applause.

Still had she gazed; but 'midst the tide
Two angel forms were seen to glide,
   The genii of the stream: 15
Their scaly armour's Tyrian hue
Through richest purple to the view
   Betrayed a golden gleam.

The hapless nymph with wonder saw:
A whisker first and then a claw,   20
   With many an ardent wish,
She stretched in vain to reach the prize.
What female heart can gold despise?
   What cat's averse to fish?

Presumptuous maid! with looks intent   25
Again she stretched, again she bent,
   Nor knew the gulf between.
(Malignant Fate sat by and smiled)
The slippery verge her feet beguiled,
   She tumbled headlong in.   30

Eight times emerging from the flood
She mewed to every watery god,
   Some speedy aid to send.
No dolphin came, no Nereid stirred:
Nor cruel Tom nor Susan heard.   35
   A favourite has no friend!

From hence, ye beauties, undeceived,
Know, one false step is ne'er retrieved,
   And be with caution bold.
Not all that tempts your wandering eyes   40
And heedless hearts is lawful prize;
   Nor all that glisters gold.

60. The Alliance of Education and Government a fragment

Essay I

As sickly plants betray a niggard earth,
Whose barren bosom starves her generous birth,
Nor genial warmth nor genial juice retains
Their roots to feed and fill their verdant veins;
And as in climes, where winter holds his reign,   5
The soil, though fertile, will not teem in vain,
Forbids her gems to swell, her shades to rise,
Nor trusts her blossoms to the churlish skies:
So draw mankind in vain the vital airs,
Unformed, unfriended, by those kindly cares   10
That health and vigour to the soul impart,
Spread the young thought and warm the opening heart.
So fond Instruction on the growing powers
Of nature idly lavishes her stores,
If equal Justice with unclouded face   15
Smile not indulgent on the rising race,
And scatter with a free though frugal hand
Light golden showers of plenty o'er the land:
But Tyranny has fixed her empire there,
To check their tender hopes with chilling fear,   20
And blast the blooming promise of the year.
   This spacious animated scene survey
From where the rolling orb, that gives the day,
His sable sons with nearer course surrounds,
To either pole and life's remotest bounds.   25
How rude so e'er the exterior form we find,
Howe'er opinion tinge the varied mind,
Alike to all the kind impartial heaven
The sparks of truth and happiness has given:
With sense to feel, with memory to retain,   30
They follow pleasure and they fly from pain;
Their judgement mends the plan their fancy draws,
The event presages and explores the cause.
The soft returns of gratitude they know,
By fraud elude, by force repel the foe;   35
While mutual wishes, mutual woes, endear
The social smile and sympathetic tear.
   Say then, through ages by what fate confined
To different climes seem different souls assigned?

Here measured laws and philosophic ease 40
Fix and improve the polished arts of peace.
There Industry and Gain their vigils keep,
Command the winds and tame the unwilling deep.
Here force and hardy deeds of blood prevail;
There languid pleasure sighs in every gale. 45
Oft o'er the trembling nations from afar
Has Scythia breathed the living cloud of war;
And, where the deluge burst, with sweepy sway
Their arms, their kings, their gods were rolled away.
As oft have issued, host impelling host, 50
The blue-eyed myriads from the Baltic coast.
The prostrate south to the destroyer yields
Her boasted titles and her golden fields:
With grim delight the brood of winter view
A brighter day and heavens of azure hue, 55
Scent the new fragrance of the breathing rose,
And quaff the pendent vintage, as it grows.
Proud of the yoke and pliant to the rod,
Why yet does Asia dread a monarch's nod,
While European freedom still withstands 60
The encroaching tide, that drowns her lessening lands,
And sees far off with an indignant groan
Her native plains and empires once her own?
Can opener skies and suns of fiercer flame
O'erpower the fire that animates our frame, 65
As lamps, that shed at ev'n a cheerful ray,
Fade and expire beneath the eye of day?
Need we the influence of the northern star
To string our nerves and steel our hearts to war?
And, where the face of nature laughs around, 70
Must sickening Virtue fly the tainted ground?
Unmanly thought! what seasons can control,
What fancied zone can circumscribe the Soul,
Who, conscious of the source from whence she springs,
By Reason's light on Resolution's wings, 75
Spite of her frail companion, dauntless goes
O'er Libya's deserts and through Zembla's snows?
She bids each slumbering energy awake,
Another touch, another temper take,
Suspends the inferior laws that rule our clay: 80
The stubborn elements confess her sway;
Their little wants, their low desires, refine,

And raise the mortal to a height divine.
   Not but the human fabric from the birth
Imbibes a flavour of its parent earth: 85
As various tracts enforce a various toil,
The manners speak the idiom of their soil.
An iron-race the mountain-cliffs maintain,
Foes to the gentler genius of the plain:
For where unwearied sinews must be found   90
With sidelong plough to quell the flinty ground,
To turn the torrent's swift-descending flood,
To brave the savage rushing from the wood,
What wonder if, to patient valour trained,
They guard with spirit what by strength they gained;   95
And while their rocky ramparts round they see,
The rough abode of want and liberty,
(As lawless force from confidence will grow)
Insult the plenty of the vales below?
What wonder in the sultry climes, that spread   100
Where Nile redundant o'er his summer-bed
From his broad bosom life and verdure flings,
And broods o'er Egypt with his watery wings,
If with adventurous oar and ready sail,
The dusky people drive before the gale,   105
Or on frail floats to distant cities ride,
That rise and glitter o'er the ambient tide.

61. Elegy Written in a Country Churchyard

The curfew tolls the knell of parting day,
The lowing herd wind slowly o'er the lea,
The ploughman homeward plods his weary way,
And leaves the world to darkness and to me.

Now fades the glimmering landscape on the sight,   5
And all the air a solemn stillness holds,
Save where the beetle wheels his droning flight,
And drowsy tinklings lull the distant folds;

Save that from yonder ivy-mantled tower
The moping owl does to the moon complain   10

Of such as, wandering near her secret bower,
Molest her ancient solitary reign.

Beneath those rugged elms, that yew-tree's shade,
Where heaves the turf in many a mouldering heap,
Each in his narrow cell for ever laid,   15
The rude forefathers of the hamlet sleep.

The breezy call of incense-breathing morn,
The swallow twittering from the straw-built shed,
The cock's shrill clarion or the echoing horn,
No more shall rouse them from their lowly bed.   20

For them no more the blazing hearth shall burn,
Or busy housewife ply her evening care:
No children run to lisp their sire's return,
Nor climb his knees the envied kiss to share.

Oft did the harvest to their sickle yield,   25
Their furrow oft the stubborn glebe has broke;
How jocund did they drive their team afield!
How bowed the woods beneath their sturdy stroke!

Let not ambition mock their useful toil,
Their homely joys and destiny obscure;   30
Nor grandeur hear, with a disdainful smile,
The short and simple annals of the poor.

The boast of heraldry, the pomp of power,
And all that beauty, all that wealth e'er gave,
Awaits alike the inevitable hour.   35
The paths of glory lead but to the grave.

Nor you, ye proud, impute to these the fault,
If memory o'er their tomb no trophies raise,
Where through the long-drawn aisle and fretted vault
The pealing anthem swells the note of praise.   40

Can storied urn or animated bust
Back to its mansion call the fleeting breath?
Can honour's voice provoke the silent dust,
Or flattery soothe the dull cold ear of death?

Perhaps in this neglected spot is laid   45
Some heart once pregnant with celestial fire;
Hands that the rod of empire might have swayed,
Or waked to ecstasy the living lyre.

But knowledge to their eyes her ample page
Rich with the spoils of time did ne'er unroll;   50
Chill penury repressed their noble rage,
And froze the genial current of the soul.

Full many a gem of purest ray serene
The dark unfathomed caves of ocean bear:
Full many a flower is born to blush unseen   55
And waste its sweetness on the desert air.

Some village Hampden that with dauntless breast
The little tyrant of his fields withstood;
Some mute inglorious Milton here may rest,
Some Cromwell guiltless of his country's blood.   60

Th' applause of list'ning senates to command,
The threats of pain and ruin to despise,
To scatter plenty o'er a smiling land,
And read their history in a nation's eyes,

Their lot forbade: nor circumscribed alone   65
Their growing virtues, but their crimes confined;
Forbade to wade through slaughter to a throne,
And shut the gates of mercy on mankind,

The struggling pangs of conscious truth to hide,
To quench the blushes of ingenuous shame,   70
Or heap the shrine of luxury and pride
With incense kindled at the muse's flame.

Far from the madding crowd's ignoble strife
Their sober wishes never learned to stray;
Along the cool sequestered vale of life   75
They kept the noiseless tenor of their way.

Yet e'en these bones from insult to protect
Some frail memorial still erected nigh,

With uncouth rhymes and shapeless sculpture decked,
Implores the passing tribute of a sigh. 80

Their name, their years, spelt by th' unlettered muse,
The place of fame and elegy supply:
And many a holy text around she strews,
That teach the rustic moralist to die.

For who to dumb forgetfulness a prey, 85
This pleasing anxious being e'er resigned,
Left the warm precincts of the cheerful day,
Nor cast one longing lingering look behind?

On some fond breast the parting soul relies,
Some pious drops the closing eye requires; 90
Ev'n from the tomb the voice of nature cries,
Ev'n in our ashes live their wonted fires.

For thee who, mindful of th' unhonoured dead,
Dost in these lines their artless tale relate;
If chance, by lonely contemplation led, 95
Some kindred spirit shall inquire thy fate,

Haply some hoary-headed swain may say,
'Oft have we seen him at the peep of dawn
Brushing with hasty steps the dews away
To meet the sun upon the upland lawn. 100

'There at the foot of yonder nodding beech
That wreathes its old fantastic roots so high,
His listless length at noontide would he stretch,
And pore upon the brook that babbles by.

'Hard by yon wood, now smiling as in scorn, 105
Muttering his wayward fancies he would rove,
Now drooping, woeful wan, like one forlorn,
Or crazed with care, or crossed in hopeless love.

'One morn I missed him on the customed hill,
Along the heath and near his favourite tree; 110
Another came; nor yet beside the rill,
Nor up the lawn, nor at the wood was he;

'The next with dirges due in sad array
Slow through the church-way path we saw him borne.
Approach and read (for thou can'st read) the lay,   115
Graved on the stone beneath yon aged thorn.'

THE EPITAPH

Here rests his head upon the lap of earth
A youth to fortune and to fame unknown.
Fair science frowned not on his humble birth,
And melancholy marked him for her own.   120

Large was his bounty and his soul sincere,
Heaven did a recompense as largely send:
He gave to misery all he had, a tear,
He gained from heaven ('twas all he wished) a friend.

No farther seek his merits to disclose,   125
Or draw his frailties from their dread abode,
(There they alike in trembling hope repose)
The bosom of his Father and his God.

62. The Progress of Poesy

A Pindaric Ode

   I.1
Awake, Aeolian lyre, awake,
And give to rapture all thy trembling strings.
From Helicon's harmonious springs
A thousand rills their mazy progress take:
The laughing flowers, that round them blow,   5
Drink life and fragrance as they flow.
Now the rich stream of music winds along,
Deep, majestic, smooth, and strong,
Through verdant vales and Ceres' golden reign:
Now rolling down the steep amain,   10
Headlong, impetuous, see it pour:
The rocks and nodding groves rebellow to the roar.

I.2

Oh! Sovereign of the willing soul,
Parent of sweet and solemn-breathing airs,
Enchanting shell! the sullen cares   15
And frantic passions hear thy soft control.
On Thracia's hills the lord of war
Has curbed the fury of his car,
And dropped his thirsty lance at thy command.
Perching on the sceptered hand   20
Of Jove, thy magic lulls the feathered king
With ruffled plumes and flagging wing:
Quenched in dark clouds of slumber lie
The terror of his beak and lightnings of his eye.

I.3

Thee the voice, the dance, obey,   25
Tempered to thy warbled lay.
O'er Idalia's velvet-green
The rosy-crownèd loves are seen
On Cytherea's day
With antic sports and blue-eyed pleasures,   30
Frisking light in frolic measures;
Now pursuing, now retreating,
Now in circling troops they meet:
To brisk notes in cadence beating
Glance their many-twinkling feet.   35
Slow melting strains their queen's approach declare:
Where'er she turns the graces homage pay.
With arms sublime, that float upon the air,
In gliding state she wins her easy way:
O'er her warm cheek and rising bosom move   40
The bloom of young desire and purple light of love.

II.1

Man's feeble race what ills await,
Labour, and penury, the racks of pain,
Disease, and sorrow's weeping train,
And death, sad refuge from the storms of fate!   45
The fond complaint, my song, disprove,
And justify the laws of Jove.
Say, has he given in vain the heavenly muse?
Night and all her sickly dews,
Her spectres wan and birds of boding cry,   50

He gives to range the dreary sky:
Till down the eastern cliffs afar
Hyperion's march they spy and glittering shafts of war.

II.2
In climes beyond the solar road,
Where shaggy forms o'er ice-built mountains roam,   55
The muse has broke the twilight-gloom
To cheer the shivering native's dull abode.
And oft, beneath the odorous shade
Of Chile's boundless forests laid,
She deigns to hear the savage youth repeat   60
In loose numbers wildly sweet
Their feather-cinctured chiefs and dusky loves.
Her track, where'er the goddess roves,
Glory pursue and generous shame,
The unconquerable mind and freedom's holy flame.   65

II. 3
Woods that wave o'er Delphi's steep,
Isles that crown the Aegean deep,
Fields that cool Ilissus laves,
Or where Maeander's amber waves
In lingering lab'rinths creep,   70
How do your tuneful echoes languish,
Mute but to the voice of anguish?
Where each old poetic mountain
Inspiration breathed around:
Every shade and hallowed fountain   75
Murmured deep a solemn sound:
Till the sad nine in Greece's evil hour
Left their Parnassus for the Latian plains.
Alike they scorn the pomp of tyrant-power,
And coward vice that revels in her chains.   80
When Latium had her lofty spirit lost,
They sought, oh Albion! next thy sea-encircled coast.

III. 1
Far from the sun and summer-gale,
In thy green lap was nature's darling laid,
What time, where lucid Avon strayed,   85
To him the mighty mother did unveil
Her awful face: the dauntless child

Stretched forth his little arms and smiled.
'This pencil take,' (she said) 'whose colours clear
Richly paint the vernal year: 90
Thine too these golden keys, immortal boy!
This can unlock the gates of joy;
Of horror that and thrilling fears,
Or ope the sacred source of sympathetic tears.'

III.2
Nor second he, that rode sublime   95
Upon the seraph-wings of ecstasy,
The secrets of the abyss to spy.
He passed the flaming bounds of place and time:
The living throne, the sapphire-blaze,
Where angels tremble while they gaze,   100
He saw; but blasted with excess of light,
Closed his eyes in endless night.
Behold, where Dryden's less presumptuous car,
Wide o'er the fields of glory, bear
Two coursers of ethereal race,   105
With necks in thunder clothed, and long-resounding pace.

III.3
Hark, his hands the lyre explore!
Bright-eyed fancy hovering o'er
Scatters from her pictured urn
Thoughts that breathe and words that burn.   110
But ah! 'tis heard no more –
Oh! lyre divine, what daring spirit
Wakes thee now? Though he inherit
Nor the pride nor ample pinion,
That the Theban eagle bear   115
Sailing with supreme dominion
Through the azure deep of air:
Yet oft before his infant eyes would run
Such forms as glitter in the muse's ray
With orient hues, unborrowed of the sun: 120
Yet shall he mount and keep his distant way
Beyond the limits of a vulgar fate,
Beneath the good how far – but far above the great.

63. The Fatal Sisters[33]

An Ode

Now the storm begins to lower,
(Haste, the loom of hell prepare,)
Iron-sleet of arrowy shower
Hurtles in the darkened air.

Glittering lances are the loom,   5
Where the dusky warp we strain,
Weaving many a soldier's doom,
Orkney's woe, and Randver's bane.

See the grisly texture grow,
('Tis of human entrails made,)   10
And the weights that play below,
Each a gasping warrior's head.

Shafts for shuttles, dipped in gore,
Shoot the trembling cords along.
Sword, that once a monarch bore,   15
Keep the tissue close and strong!

Mista black, terrific maid,
Sangrida and Hilda see,
Join the wayward work to aid:
'Tis the woof of victory.   20

Ere the ruddy sun be set,
Pikes must shiver, javelins sing,
Blade with clattering buckler meet,
Hauberk crash and helmet ring.

---

[33] Gray's prefatory note to the poem: 'In the eleventh century Sigurd, Earl of the Orkney-Islands, went with a fleet of ships and a considerable body of troops into Ireland, to the assistance of Sictryg with the silken beard, who was then making war on his father-in-law Brian, King of Dublin: the Earl and all his forces were cut to pieces, and Sictryg was in danger of a total defeat; but the enemy had a greater loss by the death of Brian, their King, who fell in the action. On Christmas day, the day of the battle, a Native of Caithness in Scotland saw at a distance a number of persons on horseback riding full speed towards a hill, and seeming to enter into it. Curiosity led him to follow them, till looking through an opening in the rocks he saw twelve gigantic figures resembling women: they were all employed about a loom; and as they wove, they sung the following dreadful song; which when they had finished, they tore the web into twelve pieces, and (each taking her portion) galloped six to the north and as many to the south.

(Weave the crimson web of war) 25
Let us go and let us fly,
Where our friends the conflict share,
Where they triumph, where they die.

As the paths of fate we tread,
Wading through the ensanguined field: 30
Gondula and Geira, spread
O'er the youthful King your shield.

We the reins to slaughter give,
Ours to kill and ours to spare:
Spite of danger he shall live. 35
(Weave the crimson web of war.)

They, whom once the desert-beach
Pent within its bleak domain,
Soon their ample sway shall stretch
O'er the plenty of the plain. 40

Low the dauntless earl is laid,
Gored with many a gaping wound:
Fate demands a nobler head;
Soon a king shall bite the ground.

Long his loss shall Eirin weep, 45
Ne'er again his likeness see;
Long her strains in sorrow steep,
Strains of immortality!

Horror covers all the heath,
Clouds of carnage blot the sun. 50
Sisters, weave the web of death;
Sisters, cease. The work is done.

Hail the task, and hail the hands!
Songs of joy and triumph sing!
Joy to the victorious bands; 55
Triumph to the younger King.

Mortal, thou that hear'st the tale,
Learn the tenor of our song.
Scotland, through each winding vale
Far and wide the notes prolong.   60

Sisters, hence with spurs of speed:
Each her thundering faulchion wield;
Each bestride her sable steed.
Hurry, hurry to the field.

64. Caradoc

Have ye seen the tusky boar,
Or the bull, with sullen roar,
On surrounding foes advance?
So Caradoc bore his lance.

65. Conan

Conan's name, my lay, rehearse,
Build to him the lofty verse,
Sacred tribute of the bard,
Verse, the hero's sole reward.
As the flame's devouring force;   5
As the whirlwind in its course;
As the thunder's fiery stroke,
Glancing on the shivered oak;
Did the sword of Conan mow
The crimson harvest of the foe.   10

William Collins (1721–1759)

66. Ode to Evening

If aught of oaten stop, or pastoral song,
May hope, chaste Eve, to soothe thy modest ear,
    Like thy own solemn springs,
    Thy springs and dying gales;

O nymph reserved, while now the bright-haired sun   5
Sits in yon western tent, whose cloudy skirts,
   With brede ethereal wove,
   O'erhang his wavy bed:
Now air is hushed, save where the weak-eyed bat
With short shrill shriek flits by on leathern wing,   10
   Or where the beetle winds
   His small but sullen horn,
As oft he rises, 'midst the twilight path
Against the pilgrim borne in heedless hum:
   Now teach me, maid composed,   15
   To breathe some softened strain,
Whose numbers, stealing through thy darkening vale,
May not unseemly with its stillness suit,
   As musing slow, I hail
   Thy genial loved return!   20
For when thy folding star arising shows
His paly circlet, at his warning lamp
   The fragrant hours, and elves
   Who slept in buds the day,
And many a nymph who wreathes her brows with sedge,   25
And sheds the freshening dew, and, lovelier still,
   The pensive pleasures sweet,
   Prepare thy shadowy car:
Then lead, calm vot'ress, where some sheety lake
Cheers the lone heath, or some time-hallowed pile,   30
   Or upland fallows grey
   Reflect its last cool gleam.
Or if chill blustering winds, or driving rain,
Prevent my willing feet, be mine the hut
   That from the mountain's side   35
   Views wilds and swelling floods,
And hamlets brown, and dim-discovered spires,
And hears their simple bell, and marks o'er all
   Thy dewy fingers draw
   The gradual dusky veil.   40
While Spring shall pour his show'rs, as oft he wont,
And bathe thy breathing tresses, meekest Eve!
   While Summer loves to sport
   Beneath thy ling'ring light;
While sallow Autumn fills thy lap with leaves,   45
Or Winter, yelling through the troublous air,
   Affrights thy shrinking train,

And rudely rends thy robes:
So long, sure-found beneath they sylvan shed,
Shall fancy, friendship, science, rose-lipped health   50
   Thy gentlest influence own,
   And hymn thy favourite name!

67. Agib and Secander; or, The Fugitives

Persian Eclogue the Fourth

SCENE *a Mountain in Circassia,* TIME Midnight

   In fair Circassia, where, to love inclined,
Each swain was blest, for every maid was kind!
At that still hour, when awful midnight reigns,
And none but wretches haunt the twilight plains;
What time the moon had hung her lamp on high,   5
And passed in radiance through the cloudless sky:
Sad o'er the dews two brother shepherds fled,
Where wildering fear and desperate sorrow led.
Fast as they pressed their flight, behind them lay
Wide ravaged plains and valleys stole away.   10
Along the mountain's bending sides they ran,
Till faint and weak Secander thus began.

SECANDER

O stay thee, Agib, for my feet deny,
No longer friendly to my life, to fly.
Friend of my heart, O turn thee and survey,   15
Trace our sad flight through all its length of way!
And first review that long-extended plain,
And yon wide groves, already passed with pain!
Yon ragged cliff whose dangerous path we tried,
And last this lofty mountain's weary side!   20

AGIB

Weak as thou art, yet hapless must thou know
The toils of flight, or some severer woe!
Still as I haste, the Tartar shouts behind,
And shrieks and sorrows load the saddening wind:

In rage of heart, with ruin in his hand,   25
He blasts our harvests and deforms our land.
Yon citron grove, whence first in fear we came,
Droops its fair honours to the conquering flame:
Far fly the swains, like us, in deep despair,
And leave to ruffian bands their fleecy care.   30

SECANDER

Unhappy land, whose blessings tempt the sword,
In vain, unheard, thou call'st thy Persian Lord!
In vain thou court'st him, helpless to thine aid,
To shield the shepherd and protect the maid.
Far off in thoughtless indolence resigned,   35
Soft dreams of love and pleasure soothe his mind:
Midst fair sultanas lost in idle joy,
No wars alarm him and no fears annoy.

AGIB

Yet these green hills, in summer's sultry heat,
Have lent the monarch oft a cool retreat.   40
Sweet to the sight is Zabran's flowery plain,
And once by maids and shepherds loved in vain!
No more the virgins shall delight to rove
By Sargis' banks or Irwan's shady grove:
On Tarkie's mountain catch the cooling gale,   45
Or breathe the sweets of Aly's flowery vale:
Fair scenes! but ah! no more with peace possessed,
With ease alluring and with plenty blest.
No more the shepherds' whitening tents appear,
Nor the kind products of a bounteous year;   50
No more the date with snowy blossoms crowned,
But Ruin spreads her baleful fires around.

SECANDER

In vain Circassia boasts her spicy groves,
For ever famed for pure and happy loves;
In vain she boasts her fairest of the fair,   55
Their eyes' blue languish and their golden hair!
Those eyes in tears their fruitless grief must send;
Those hairs the Tartar's cruel hand shall rend.

AGIB

Ye Georgian swains that piteous learn from far
Circassia's ruin and the waste of war: 60
Some weightier arms than crooks and staves prepare,
To shield your harvests and defend your fair:
The Turk and Tartar like designs pursue,
Fixed to destroy and steadfast to undo.
Wild as his land, in native deserts bred,   65
By lust incited or by malice led,
The villain-Arab, as he prowls for prey,
Oft marks with blood and wasting flames the way;
Yet none so cruel as the Tartar foe,
To death inured and nursed in scenes of woe.   70

   He said, when loud along the vale was heard
A shriller shriek and nearer fires appeared:
The affrighted shepherds through the dews of night,
Wide o'er the moonlight hills, renewed their flight.

68. Ode Occasioned by the Death of Mr Thomson

Haec tibi semper erunt, et cum solennia vota
reddemus Nymphis, et cum lustrabimus agros. . . .
– Amavit nos quoque Daphnis.[34]

                               Virgil, Eclogues v, II. 74–5,52

In yonder grave a Druid lies,
   Where slowly winds the stealing wave!
The year's best sweets shall duteous rise
   To deck its poet's sylvan grave!

In yon deep bed of whispering reeds   5
   His airy harp shall now be laid,
That he, whose heart in sorrow bleeds,
   May love through life the soothing shade.

Then maids and youths shall linger here,

[34] 'These ceremonies will be for ever dedicated to you, first when each year we renew our vows to the nymphs, and then when we reconsecrate the fields ...' 'And us, too, Daphnis loved.'

And, while its sounds at distance swell,   10
Shall sadly seem in pity's ear
    To hear the woodland pilgrim's knell.

Remembrance oft shall haunt the shore
    When Thames in summer wreaths is dressed,
And oft suspend the dashing oar   15
    To bid his gentle spirit rest!

And oft as ease and health retire
    To breezy lawn or forest deep,
The friend shall view yon whitening spire,
    And 'mid the varied landscape weep.   20

But thou, who own'st that earthy bed,
  · Ah! what will every dirge avail?
Or tears, which love and pity shed
    That mourn beneath the gliding sail!

Yet lives there one, whose heedless eye   25
    Shall scorn thy pale shrine glimmering near?
With him, sweet bard, may fancy die,
    And joy desert the blooming year.

But thou, lorn stream, whose sullen tide
    No sedge-crowned sisters now attend,   30
Now waft me from the green hill's side,
    Whose cold turf hides the buried friend!

And see, the fairy valleys fade,
    Dun night has veiled the solemn view!
– Yet once again, dear parted shade,   35
    Meek nature's child, again adieu!

The genial meads, assigned to bless
    Thy life, shall mourn thy early doom,
Their hinds and shepherd-girls shall dress
    With simple hands thy rural tomb.   40

Long, long, thy stone and pointed clay
    Shall melt the musing Briton's eyes:
'O! vales and wild woods', shall he say,
    'In yonder grave your Druid lies!'

Mary Leapor (1722–1746)

66. An Epistle to a Lady

In vain, dear madam, yes in vain you strive;
Alas! to make your luckless Mira thrive,
For Tycho and Copernicus agree,
No golden planet bent its rays on me.
'Tis twenty winters, if it is no more; 5
To speak the truth it may be twenty four.
As many springs their 'pointed space have run,
Since Mira's eyes first opened on the sun.
  Twas when the flocks on slabby hillocks lie,
And the cold fishes rule the wat'ry sky: 10
But though these eyes the learnèd page explore,
And turn the pond'rous volumes o'er and o'er,
I find no comfort from their systems flow,
But am dejected more as more I know.
Hope shines a while, but like a vapour flies, 15
(The fate of all the curious and the wise)
For, Ah! cold Saturn triumphed on that day,
And frowning Sol denied his golden ray.
  You see I'm learnèd, and I show't the more,
That none may wonder when they find me poor. 20
Yet Mira dreams, as slumb'ring poets may,
And rolls in treasures till the breaking day:
While books and pictures in bright order rise,
And painted parlours swim before her eyes:
Till the shrill clock impertinently rings, 25
And the soft visions move their shining wings:
Then Mira wakes, – her pictures are no more,
And through her fingers slides the vanished ore.
Convinced too soon, her eye unwilling falls
On the blue curtains and the dusty walls: 30
She wakes, alas! to business and to woes,
To sweep her kitchen, and to mend her clothes.
  But see pale sickness with her languid eyes,
At whose appearance all delusion flies:
The world recedes, its vanities decline, 35

Clorinda's features seem as faint as mine!
Gay robes no more the aching sight admires,
Wit grates the ear, and melting music tires:
Its wonted pleasures with each sense decay,
Books please no more, and paintings fade away,   40
The sliding joys in misty vapours end:
Yet let me still, Ah! let me grasp a friend:
And when each joy, when each loved object flies,
Be you the last that leaves my closing eyes.
    But how will this dismantled soul appear,   45
When stripped of all it lately held so dear,
Forced from its prison of expiring clay,
Afraid and shiv'ring at the doubtful way.
    Yet did these eyes a dying parent see,
Loosed from all cares except a thought for me,   50
Without a tear resign her short'ning breath,
And dauntless meet the ling'ring stroke of death.
Then at th' Almighty's sentence shall I mourn:
'Of dust thou art, to dust shalt thou return.'
Or shall I wish to stretch the line of fate,   55
That the dull years may bear a longer date,
To share the follies of succeeding times
With more vexations and with deeper crimes:
Ah no – though heav'n brings near the final day,
For such a life I will not, dare not pray;   60
But let the tear for future mercy flow,
And fall resigned beneath the mighty blow.
Nor I alone – for through the spacious ball,
With me will numbers of all ages fall:
And the same day that Mira yields her breath,   65
Thousands may enter through the gates of death.

70. Mira's Will

IMPRIMIS – My departed shade I trust
To heav'n – My body to the silent dust;
My name to public censure I submit,
To be disposed of as the world thinks fit;
My vice and folly let oblivion close,   5
The world already is o'erstocked with those;
My wit I give, as misers give their store,

To those who think they had enough before.
   Bestow my patience to compose the lives
Of slighted virgins and neglected wives;   10
To modish lovers I resign my truth,
My cool reflection to unthinking youth;
And some good-nature give ('tis my desire)
To surly husbands, as their needs require;
And first discharge my funeral – and then   15
To the small poets I bequeath my pen.
   Let a small sprig (true emblem of my rhyme)
Of blasted laurel on my hearse recline;
Let some grave wight, that struggles for renown,
By chanting dirges through a market-town,   20
With gentle step precede the solemn train;
A broken flute upon his arm shall lean.
Six comic poets may the corpse surround,
And all free-holders, if they can be found:
Then follow next the melancholy throng,   25
As shrewd instructors, who themselves are wrong.
The virtuoso, rich in sun-dried weeds,
The politician, whom no mortal heeds,
The silent lawyer, chambered all the day,
And the stern soldier that receives no pay.   30
But stay – the mourners should be first our care,
Let the freed 'prentice lead the miser's heir;
Let the young relict wipe her mournful eye,
And widowed husbands o'er their garlic cry.
   All this let my executors fulfil,   35
And rest assured that this is Mira's will,
Who was, when she these legacies designed,
In body healthy, and composed in mind.

Christopher Smart (1722–1771)

71. A Song to David

'David the Son of Jesse said, and the Man who was raised up on High, the Anointed of the God of Jacob, and the sweet Psalmist of Israel, said, The Spirit of the Lord spake by Me, and His Word was in my Tongue.'

Samuel xxiii. 1, 2

O thou, that sit'st upon a throne,
With harp of high majestic tone,
   To praise the King of kings;
And voice of heav'n-ascending swell,
Which, while its deeper notes excell,   5
   Clear, as a clarion, rings:

To bless each valley, grove and coast,
And charm the cherubs to the post
   Of gratitude in throngs;
To *keep* the days on Zion's mount,   10
And send the year to his account,
   With dances and with songs:

O Servant of God's holiest charge,
The minister of praise at large,
   Which thou may'st now receive;   15
From thy blest mansion hail and hear,
From topmost eminence appear
   To this the wreath I weave.

Great, valiant, pious, good, and clean,
Sublime, contemplative, serene,   20
   Strong, constant, pleasant, wise!
Bright effluence of exceeding grace;
Best man! – the swiftness and the race,
   The peril, and the prize!

Great – from the lustre of his crown,   25
From Samuel's horn and God's renown,
   Which is the people's voice;
For all the host, from rear to van,
Applauded and embraced the man –
   The man of God's own choice.   30

Valiant – the word and up he rose –
The fight – he triumphed o'er the foes,
   Whom God's just laws abhor;
And armed in gallant faith he took
Against the boaster, from the brook,   35
   The weapons of the war.

Pious – magnificent and grand;
'Twas he the famous temple planned:
   (The seraph in his soul)
Foremost to give his Lord his dues,   40
Foremost to bless the welcome news,
   And foremost to condole.

Good – from Jehudah's genuine vein,
From God's best nature good in grain,
   His aspect and his heart;   45
To pity, to forgive, to save,
Witness En-gedi's conscious cave,
   And Shimei's blunted dart.

Clean – if perpetual prayer be pure,
And love, which could itself inure   50
   To fasting and to fear –
Clean in his gestures, hands, and feet,
To smite the lyre, the dance compleat,
   To play the sword and spear.

Sublime – invention ever young,   55
Of vast conception, tow'ring tongue,
   To God th' eternal theme;
Notes from yon exaltations caught,
Unrivalled royalty of thought,
   O'er meaner strains supreme.   60

Contemplative – on God to fix
His musings, and above the six
   The sabbath-day he blest;
'Twas then his thoughts self-conquest pruned,
And heavenly melancholy tuned,   65
  · To bless and bear the rest.

Serene – to sow the seeds of peace,
Rememb'ring, when he watched the fleece,
   How sweetly Kidron purled –
To further knowledge, silence vice,   70
And plant perpetual paradise
   When God had calmed the world.

Strong – in the Lord, who could defy
Satan, and all his powers that lie

In sempiternal night; 75
And hell, and horror, and despair
Were as the lion and the bear
    To his undaunted might.

Constant – in love to God THE TRUTH,
Age, manhood, infancy, and youth – 80
    To Jonathan his friend
Constant, beyond the verge of death;
And Ziba, and Mephibosheth,
    His endless fame attend.

Pleasant – and various as the year; 85
Man, soul, and angel, without peer,
    Priest, champion, sage and boy;
In armour, or in ephod clad,
His pomp, his piety was glad;
    Majestic was his joy. 90

Wise – in recovery from his fall,
Whence rose his eminence o'er all,
    Of all the most reviled;
The light of Israel in his ways,
Wise are his precepts, prayer and praise, 95
    And counsel to his child.

His muse, bright angel of his verse,
Gives balm for all the thorns that pierce,
    For all the pangs that rage;
Blest light, still gaining on the gloom, 100
The more than Michal of his bloom,
    Th' Abishag of his age.

He sung of God – the mighty source
Of all things – the stupendous force
    On which all strength depends; 105
From whose right arm, beneath whose eyes,
All period, pow'r, and enterprise
    Commences, reigns, and ends.

Angels – their ministry and meed,
Which to and fro with blessings speed, 110
    Or with their citterns wait;

Where Michael with his millions bows,
Where dwells the seraph and his spouse,
   The cherub and her mate.

Of man – the semblance and effect   115
Of God and Love – the Saint elect
   For infinite applause –
To rule the land, the briny broad,
To be laborious in his laud,
   And heroes in his cause.   120

The world – the clust'ring spheres he made,
The glorious light, the soothing shade,
   Dale, champaign, grove, and hill;
The multitudinous abyss,
Where secrecy remains in bliss,   125
   And wisdom hides her skill.

Trees, plants, and flow'rs – of virtuous root;
Gem yielding blossom, yielding fruit,
   Choice gums and precious balm;
Bless ye the nosegay in the vale,   130
And with the sweetners of the gale
   Enrich the thankful psalm.

Of fowl – e'en ev'ry beak and wing
Which cheer the winter, hail the spring,
   That live in peace or prey;   135
They that make music, or that mock,
The quail, the brave domestic cock,
   The raven, swan, and jay.

Of fishes – ev'ry size and shape,
Which nature frames of light escape,   140
   Devouring man to shun:
The shells are in the wealthy deep,
The shoals upon the surface leap,
   And love the glancing sun.

Of beasts – the beaver plods his task;   145
While the sleek tigers roll and bask,
   Nor yet the shades arouse:
Her cave the mining coney scoops;

Where o'er the mead the mountain stoops,
    The kids exult and browse.   150

Of gems – their virtue and their price,
Which hid in earth from man's device,
    Their darts of lustre sheathe;
The jasper of the master's stamp,
The topaz blazing like a lamp   155
    Among the mines beneath.

Blest was the tenderness he felt
When to his graceful harp he knelt,
    And did for audience call;
When Satan with his hand he quelled,   160
And in serene suspense he held
    The frantic throes of Saul.

His furious foes no more maligned
As he such melody divined,
    And sense and soul detained;   165
Now striking strong, now soothing soft,
He sent the godly sounds aloft,
    Or in delight refrained.

When up to heav'n his thoughts he piled,
From fervent lips fair Michal smiled,   170
    As blush to blush she stood;
And chose herself the queen, and gave
Her utmost from her heart, 'so brave,
    'And plays his hymns so good.'

The pillars of the Lord are seven,   175
Which stand from earth to topmost heav'n;
    His wisdom drew the plan
His WORD accomplished the design,
From brightest gem to deepest mine,
    From CHRIST enthroned to man.   180

Alpha, the cause of causes, first
In station, fountain, whence the burst
    Of light, and blaze of day;
Whence bold attempt, and brave advance,

Have motion, life, and ordinance,   185
   And heav'n itself its stay.

Gamma supports the glorious arch
On which angelic legions march,
   And is with sapphires paved;
Thence the fleet clouds are sent adrift,   190
And thence the painted folds, that lift
   The crimson veil, are waved.

Eta with living sculpture breathes,
With verdant carvings, flow'ry wreathes
   Of never-wasting bloom;   195
In strong relief his goodly base
All instruments of labour grace,
   The trowel, spade, and loom.

Next Theta stands to the Supreme –
Who formed, in number, sign, and scheme,   200
   Th' illustrious lights that are;
And one addressed his saffron robe,
And one, clad in a silver globe,
   Held rule with ev'ry star.

Iota's tuned to choral hymns   205
Of those that fly, while he that swims
   In thankful safety lurks;
And foot, and chapitre, and niche,
The various histories enrich
   Of God's recorded works.   210

Sigma presents the social droves,
With him that solitary roves,
   And man of all the chief;
Fair on whose face, and stately frame,
Did God impress his hallowed name,   215
   For ocular belief.

OMEGA! GREATEST and the BEST,
Stands sacred to the day of rest,
   For gratitude and thought;
Which blessed the world upon his pole,   220
And gave the universe his goal,

And closed th' infernal draught.

O DAVID, scholar of the Lord!
Such is thy science, whence reward
   And infinite degree;   225
O strength, O sweetness, lasting ripe!
God's harp thy symbol, and thy type
   The lion and the bee!

There is but One who ne'er rebelled,
But One by passion unimpelled,   230
   By pleasures uninticed;
He from himself his semblance sent,
Grand object of his own content,
   And saw the God in CHRIST.

Tell them I am, JEHOVA said   235
To MOSES; while earth heard in dread,
   And smitten to the heart,
At once above, beneath, around,
All nature, without voice or sound,
Replied, O Lord, THOU ART.   240

Thou art – to give and to confirm,
For each his talent and his term;
   All flesh thy bounties share:
Thou shalt not call thy brother fool;
The porches of the Christian school   245
   Are meekness, peace, and pray'r.

Open, and naked of offence,
Man's made of mercy, soul, and sense;
   God armed the snail and wilk;
Be good to him that pulls thy plough;   250
Due food and care, due rest, allow
   For her that yields thee milk.

Rise up before the hoary head,
And God's benign commandment dread,
   Which says thou shalt not die: 255
'Not as I will, but as thou wilt,'
Prayed He whose conscience knew no guilt;
   With whose blessed pattern vie.

Use all thy passions! – love is thine,
And joy, and jealousy divine; 260
   Thine hope's eternal fort,
And care thy leisure to disturb,
With fear concupiscence to curb,
   And rapture to transport.

Act simply, as occasion asks; 265
Put mellow wine in seasoned casks;
   Till not with ass and bull:
Remember thy baptismal bond;
Keep from commixtures foul and fond,
   Nor work thy flax with wool. 270

Distribute: pay the Lord his tithe,
And make the widow's heart-strings blithe;
   Resort with those that weep:
As you from all and each expect,
For all and each thy love direct, 275
   And render as you reap.

The slander and its bearer spurn,
And propagating praise sojourn
   To make thy welcome last;
Turn from old Adam to the New; 280
By hope futurity pursue;
   Look upwards to the past.

Control thine eye, salute success,
Honour the wiser, happier bless,
   And for thy neighbour feel; 285
Grudge not of Mammon and his leaven,
Work emulation up to heaven
   By knowledge and by zeal.

O DAVID, highest in the list
Of worthies, on God's ways insist, 290
   The genuine word repeat:
Vain are the documents of men,
And vain the flourish of the pen
   That keeps the fool's conceit.

PRAISE above all – for praise prevails;   295
Heap up the measure, load the scales,
    And good to goodness add:
The gen'rous soul her saviour aids,
But peevish obloquy degrades;
    The Lord is great and glad.   300

For ADORATION all the ranks
Of angels yield eternal thanks,
    And DAVID in the midst;
With God's good poor, which, last and least
In man's esteem, thou to thy feast,   305
    O blessed bride-groom, bid'st.

For ADORATION seasons change,
And order, truth, and beauty range,
    Adjust, attract, and fill:
The grass the polyanthus cheques;   310
And polished porphyry reflects,
    By the descending rill.

Rich almonds colour to the prime
For ADORATION; tendrils climb,
    And fruit-trees pledge their gems;   315
And Ivis° with her gorgeous vest   *hummingbird* [Smart]
Builds for her eggs her cunning nest,
    And bell-flowers bow their stems.

With vinous syrup cedars spout;
From rocks pure honey gushing out,   320
    For ADORATION springs:
All scenes of painting crowd the map
Of nature; to the mermaid's pap
    The scaled infant clings.

The spotted ounce and playsome cubs   325
Run rustling 'mongst the flow'ring shrubs,
    And lizards feed the moss;
For ADORATION beasts embark,
While waves upholding halcyon's ark
    No longer roar and toss.   330

While Israel sits beneath his fig,
With coral root and amber sprig
   The weaned advent'rer sports;
Where to the palm the jasmin cleaves,
For ADORATION 'mongst the leaves
   The gale his peace reports. 335

Increasing days their reign exalt,
Nor in the pink and mottled vault
   Th' opposing spirits tilt;
And, by the coasting reader spied, 340
The silverlings and crusions glide
   For ADORATION gilt.

For ADORATION rip'ning canes
And cocoa's purest milk detains
   The western pilgrim's staff; 345
Where rain in clasping boughs inclosed,
And vines with oranges disposed,
   Embow'r the social laugh.

Now labour his reward receives,
For ADORATION counts his sheaves 350
   To peace, her bounteous prince;
The nectarine his strong tint imbibes,
And apples of ten thousand tribes,
   And quick peculiar quince.

The wealthy crops of whit'ning rice, 355
'Mongst thyine woods and groves of spice,
   For ADORATION grow;
And, marshalled in the fencèd land,
The peaches and pomègranates stand,
   Where wild carnations blow. 360

The laurels with the winter strive;
The crocus burnishes alive
   Upon the snow-clad earth:
For ADORATION myrtles stay
To keep the garden from dismay, 365
   And bless the sight from dearth.

The pheasant shows his pompous neck;
And ermine, jealous of a speck,

With fear eludes offence:
The sable, with his glossy pride,   370
For ADORATION is descried,
   Where frosts the wave condense.

The cheerful holly, pensive yew,
And holy thorn, their trim renew;
   The squirrel hoards his nuts: 375
All creatures batten o'er their stores,
And careful nature all her doors
   For ADORATION shuts.

For ADORATION, DAVID's psalms
Lift up the heart to deeds of alms;   380
   And he, who kneels and chants,
Prevails his passions to control,
Finds meat and med'cine to the soul,
   Which for translation pants.

For ADORATION, beyond match,   385
The scholar bullfinch aims to catch
   The soft flute's iv'ry touch;
And, careless on the hazel spray,
The daring redbreast keeps at bay
   The damsel's greedy clutch.   390

For ADORATION, in the skies,
The Lord's philosopher espies
   The Dog, the Ram, and Rose;
The planets ring, Orion's sword;
Nor is his greatness less adored   395
   In the vile worm that glows.

For ADORATION on the strings°   *Aeolian lays* [Smart]
The western breezes work their wings,
   The captive ear to sooth. –
Hark! 'tis a voice – how still, and small –   400
That makes the cataracts to fall,
   Or bids the sea be smooth.

For ADORATION, incense comes
From bezoar, and Arabian gums;
   And on the civet's fur.   405

But as for prayer, or e're it faints,
Far better is the breath of saints
   Than galbanum and myrrh.

For ADORATION from the down,
Of dam'sons to th'anana's crown,   410
   God sends to tempt the taste;
And while the luscious zest invites,
The sense, that in the scene delights,
   Commands desire be chaste.

For ADORATION, all the paths   415
Of grace are open, all the baths
   Of purity refresh; ·
And all the rays of glory beam
To deck the man of God's esteem,
   Who triumphs o'er the flesh.   420

For ADORATION, in the dome
Of Christ the sparrows find an home;
   And on his olives perch:
The swallow also dwells with thee,
O man of God's humility,   425
   Within his Saviour CHURCH.

Sweet is the dew that falls betimes,
And drops upon the leafy limes;
   Sweet Hermon's fragrant air:
Sweet is the lilly's silver bell,   430
And sweet the wakeful tapers smell
   That watch for early pray'r.

Sweet the young nurse with love intense,
Which smiles o'er sleeping innocence;
   Sweet when the lost arrive: 435
Sweet the musician's ardour beats,
While his vague mind's in quest of sweets,
   The choicest flow'rs to hive.

Sweeter in all the strains of love,
The language of thy turtle dove,   440
   Paired to thy swelling chord;
Sweeter with ev'ry grace endued,

The glory of thy gratitude,
   Respired unto the Lord.

Strong is the horse upon his speed;   445
Strong in pursuit the rapid glede,
   Which makes at once his game:
Strong the tall ostrich on the ground;
Strong through the turbulent profound
   Shoots xiphias° to his aim.   *the sword-fish* [Smart] 450

Strong is the lion – like a coal
His eye-ball – like a bastion's mole
   His chest against the foes:
Strong, the gier-eagle on his sail,
Strong against tide, th' enormous whale   455
   Emerges as he goes.

But stronger still, in earth and air,
And in the sea, the man of pray'r;
   And far beneath the tide;
And in the seat to faith assigned,   460
Where ask is have, where seek is find,
   Where knock is open wide.

Beauteous the fleet before the gale;
Beauteous the multitudes in mail,
   Ranked arms and crested heads: 465
Beauteous the garden's umbrage mild,
Walk, water, meditated wild,
   And all the bloomy beds.

Beauteous the moon full on the lawn;
And beauteous, when the veil's withdrawn,   470
   The virgin to her spouse:
Beauteous the temple decked and filled,
When to the heav'n of heav'n's they build
   Their heart-directed vows.

Beauteous, yea beauteous more than these,   475
The shepherd king upon his knees,
   For his momentous trust;
With wish of infinite conceit,

For man, beast, mute, the small and great,
   And prostrate dust to dust.   480

Precious the bounteous widow's mite;
And precious, for extreme delight,
   The largess from the churl:
Precious the ruby's blushing blaze,
And alba's blest imperial rays,   485
   And pure cerulean pearl.

Precious the penitential tear;
And precious is the sigh sincere,
   Acceptable to God:
And precious are the winning flow'rs,   490
In gladsome Israel's feast of bow'rs,
   Bound on the hallowed sod.

More precious that diviner part
Of David, ev'n the Lord's own heart,
   Great, beautiful, and new: 495
In all things where it was intent,
In all extremes in each event,
   Proof – answ'ring true to true.

Glorious the sun in mid career;
Glorious th' assembled fires appear;   500
   Glorious the comet's train:
Glorious the trumpet and alarm;
Glorious th' almighty stretched-out arm;
   Glorious th' enraptured main:

Glorious the northern lights astream;   505
Glorious the song, when God's the theme;
   Glorious the thunder's roar:
Glorious hosanna from the den;
Glorious the catholic amen;
   Glorious the martyr's gore: 510

Glorious – more glorious is the crown
Of Him that brought salvation down
   By meekness, called thy Son;
Thou at stupendous truth believed,
And now the matchless deed's achieved,   515
   DETERMINED, DARED, and DONE.

72. from *Jubilate Agno*

72. from *Fragment A*

Rejoice in God, O ye Tongues; give the glory to the Lord, and the Lamb.

Nations, and languages, and every Creature, in which is the breath of Life.

Let man and beast appear before him, and magnify his name together.

Let Noah and his company approach the throne of Grace, and do homage to the Ark of their Salvation.

Let Abraham present a Ram, and worship the God of his Redemption.   5

Let Isaac, the Bridegroom, kneel with his Camels, and bless the hope of his pilgrimage.

Let Jacob, and his speckled Drove adore the good Shepherd of Israel.

Let Esau offer a scape Goat for his seed, and rejoice in the blessing of God his father.

Let Nimrod, the mighty hunter, bind a Leopard to the altar, and consecrate his spear to the Lord.

Let Ishmael dedicate a Tyger, and give praise for the liberty, in which the Lord has let him at large.   10

Let Balaam appear with an Ass, and bless the Lord his people and his creatures for a reward eternal.

Let Anah, the son of Zibion, lead a Mule to the temple, and bless God, who amerces the consolation of the creature for the service of Man.

Let Daniel come forth with a Lion, and praise God with all his might through faith in Christ Jesus.

Let Naphthali with an Hind give glory in the goodly words of Thanksgiving.

Let Aaron, the high priest, sanctify a Bull, and let him go free to the Lord and Giver of Life.   15

Let the Levites of the Lord take the Beavers of the brook alive into the Ark of the Testimony.

Let Eleazar with the Ermine serve the Lord decently and in purity.

Let Ithamar minister with a Chamois, and bless the name of Him, which clotheth the naked.

Let Gershom with an Pygarg (Hart) bless the name of Him, who feedeth the hungry.

Let Merari praise the wisdom and power of God with the Coney, who scoopeth the rock, and archeth in the sand.   20

Let Kohath serve with the Sable, and bless God in the ornaments of the Temple.

Let Jehoida bless God with an Hare, whose mazes are determined for the health of the body and to parry the adversary.

Let Ahitub humble himself with an Ape before Almighty God, who is the maker of variety and pleasantry.

Let Abiathar with a Fox praise the name of the Lord, who balances craft
against strength and skill against number.

Let Moses, the Man of God, bless with a Lizard, in the sweet majesty of
good-nature, and the magnanimity of meekness.   25

Let Joshua praise God with an Unicorn – the swiftness of the Lord, and
the strength of the Lord, and the spear of the Lord mighty in battle.

Let Caleb with an Ounce praise the Lord of the Land of beauty and rejoice
in the blessing of his good Report.

Let Othniel praise God with the Rhinoceros, who put on his armour for
the reward of beauty in the Lord.

Let Tola bless with the Toad, which is the good creature of God, though his
virtue is in the secret, and his mention is not made.

Let Barak praise with the Pard – and great is the might of the faithful and
great is the Lord in the nail of Jael and in the sword of the Son of
Abinoam.   30

Let Gideon bless with the Panther – the Word of the Lord is invincible by
him that lappeth from the brook.

Let Jotham praise with the Urchin, who took up his parable and provided
himself for the adversary to kick against the pricks.

Let Boaz, the Builder of Judah, bless with the Rat, which dwelleth in
hardship and peril, that they may look to themselves and keep their
houses in order.

Let Obed-Edom with a Dormouse praise the Name of the Lord God his
Guest for increase of his store and for peace.

Let Abishai bless with the Hyaena – the terror of the Lord, and the
fierceness, of his wrath against the foes of the King and of Israel.   35

Let Ethan praise with the Flea, his coat of mail, his piercer, and his
vigour, which wisdom and providence have contrived to attract
observation and to escape it.

Let Heman bless with the Spider, his warp and his woof, his subtlety and
industry, which are good.

Let Chalcol praise with the Beetle, whose life is precious in the sight of
God, though his appearance is against him.

Let Darda with a Leech bless the Name of the Physician of body and
soul.

Let Mahol praise the Maker of Earth and Sea with the Otter, whom
God has given to dive and to burrow for his preservation.   40

Let David bless with the Bear – The beginning of victory to the Lord –
to the Lord the perfection of excellence – Hallelujah from the heart of
God, and from the hand of the artist inimitable, and from the echo of
the heavenly harp in sweetness magnifical and mighty.

Let Solomon praise with the Ant, and give the glory to the Fountain of all
Wisdom.

Let Romamti-ezer bless with the Ferret – The Lord is a rewarder of them, that diligently seek him.

Let Samuel, the Minister from a child, without ceasing praise with the Porcupine, which is the creature of defence and stands upon his arms continually.

Let Nathan with the Badger bless God for his retired fame, and privacy inaccessible to slander.   45

Let Joseph, who from the abundance of his blessing may spare to him, that lacketh, praise with the Crocodile, which is pleasant and pure, when he is interpreted, though his look is of terror and offence.

Let Esdras bless Christ Jesus with the Rose and his people, which is a nation of living sweetness.

Let Mephibosheth with the Cricket praise the God of cheerfulness, hospitality, and gratitude.

Let Shallum with the Frog bless God for the meadows of Canaan, the fleece, the milk and the honey.

Let Hilkiah praise with the Weasel, which sneaks for his prey in craft, and dwelleth at ambush.   50

Let Job bless with the Worm – the life of the Lord is in Humiliation, the Spirit also and the truth.

Let Elihu bless with the Tortoise, which is food for praise and thanksgiving.

Let Hezekiah praise with the Dromedary – the zeal for the glory of God is excellence, and to bear his burden is grace.

Let Zadok worship with the Mole – before honour is humility, and he that looketh low shall learn.

Let Gad with the Adder bless in the simplicity of the preacher and the wisdom of the creature.   55

Let Tobias bless Charity with his Dog, who is faithful, vigilant, and a friend in poverty.

Let Anna bless God with the Cat, who is worthy to be presented before the throne of grace, when he has trampled upon the idol in his prank.

Let Benaiah praise with the Asp – to conquer malice is nobler, than to slay the lion.

Let Barzillai bless with the Snail – a friend in need is as the balm of Gilead, or as the slime to the wounded bark.

Let Joab with the Horse worship the Lord God of Hosts.   60

Let Shemaiah bless God with the Caterpiller – the minister of vengeance is the harbinger of mercy.

Let Ahirnelech with the Locust bless God from the tyranny of numbers.

Let Cornelius with the Swine bless God, which purifyeth all things for the poor.

Let Araunah bless with the Squirrel, which is a gift of homage from the poor man to the wealthy and increaseth good will.

Let Bakbakkar bless with the Salamander, which feedeth upon ashes as
bread, and whose joy is at the mouth of the furnace. 65

Let Jabez bless with Tarantula, who maketh his bed in the moss, which
he feedeth, that the pilgrim may take heed to his way.

Let Jakim with the Satyr bless God in the dance.

Let Iddo praise the Lord with the Moth – the writings of man perish as the
garment, but the Book of God endureth for ever.

Let Nebuchadnezzar bless with the Grasshopper – the pomp and vanities
of the world are as the herb of the field, but the glory of the Lord
increaseth for ever.

Let Naboth bless with the Canker-worm – envy is cruel and killeth and
preyeth upon that which God has given to aspire and bear fruit. 70

Let Lud bless with the Elk, the strenuous asserter of his liberty, and the
maintainer of his ground.

Let Obadiah with the Palmer-worm bless God for the remnant that is left.

Let Agur bless with the Cockatrice – The consolation of the world is
deceitful, and temporal honour the crown of him that creepeth.

Let Ithiel bless with the Baboon, whose motions are regular in the wil-
derness, and who defendeth himself with a staff against the assailant.

Let Ucal bless with the Cameleon, which feedeth on the Flowers and
washeth himself in the dew. 75

Let Lemuel bless with the Wolf, which is a dog without a master, but the
Lord hears his cries and feeds him in the desert.

Let Hananiah bless with the Civet, which is pure from benevolence.

Let Azarias bless with the Reindeer, who runneth upon the waters, and
wadeth through the land in snow.

Let Mishael bless with the Stoat – the praise of the Lord gives propriety to
all things.

Let Savaran bless with the Elephant, who gave his life for his country that
he might put on immortality. 80

Let Nehemiah, the imitator of God, bless with the Monkey, who is
worked down from Man.

Let Manasses bless with the Wild-Ass – liberty begetteth insolence, but
necessity is the mother of prayer.

Let Jebus bless with the Camelopard, which is good to carry and to parry
and to kneel.

Let Huz bless with the Polypus – lively subtlety is acceptable to the Lord.

Let Buz bless with the Jackall – but the Lord is the Lion's provider. 85

Let Meshullam bless with the Dragon, who maketh his den in desolation
and rejoiceth amongst the ruins.

Let Enoch bless with the Rackoon, who walked with God as by the instinct.

Let Hashbadana bless with the Catamountain, who stood by the Pulpit of
God against the dissensions of the Heathen.

Let Ebed-Melech bless with the Mantiger, the blood of the Lord is sufficient to do away the offence of Cain, and reinstate the creature which is amerced.

Let A Little Child with a Serpent bless Him, who ordaineth strength in babes to the confusion of the Adversary. 90

Let Huldah bless with the Silkworm – the ornaments of the Proud are from the bowels of their Betters.

Let Susanna bless with the Butterfly – beauty hath wings, but chastity is the Cherub.

Let Sampson bless with the Bee, to whom the Lord hath given strength to annoy the assailant and wisdom to his strength.

Let Amasiah bless with the Chaffer – the top of the tree is for the brow of the champion, who has given the glory to God.

Let Hashum bless with the Fly, whose health is the honey of the air, but he feeds upon the thing strangled, and perisheth. 95

Let Malchiah bless with the Gnat – it is good for man and beast to mend their pace.

Let Pedaiah bless with the Humble-Bee, who loves himself in solitude and makes his honey alone.

Let Maaseiah bless with the Drone, who with the appearance of a Bee is neither a soldier nor an artist, neither a swordsman nor smith.

Let Urijah bless with the Scorpion, which is a scourge against the murmurers –the Lord keep it from our coasts.

Let Anaiah bless with the Dragon-fly, who sails over the pond by the wood-side and feedeth on the cresses. 100

Let Zorobabel bless with the Wasp, who is the Lord's architect, and buildeth his edifice in armour.

Let Jehu bless with the Hornet, who is the soldier of the Lord to extirpate abomination and to prepare the way of peace.

Let Mattithiah bless with the Bat, who inhabiteth the desolations of pride and flieth amongst the tombs.

Let Elias which is the innocency of the Lord rejoice with the Dove.

Let Asaph rejoice with the Nightingale – The musician of the Lord! and the watchman of the Lord! [...] 105

72b. from *Fragment B*

For I will consider my Cat Jeoffry. 695
For he is the servant of the Living God duly and daily serving him.
For at the first glance of the glory of God in the East he worships in his way.
For is this done by wreathing his body seven times round with elegant quickness.
For then he leaps up to catch the musk, which is the blessing of God upon his prayer.

For he rolls upon prank to work it in.   700
For having done duty and received blessing he begins to consider himself.
For this he performs in ten degrees.
For first he looks upon his fore-paws to see if they are clean.
For secondly he kicks up behind to clear away there.
For thirdly he works it upon stretch with the fore-paws extended.   705
For fourthly he sharpens his paws by wood.
For fifthly he washes himself.
For Sixthly he rolls upon wash.
For Seventhly he fleas himself, that he may not be interrupted upon the beat.
For Eighthly he rubs himself against a post.   710
For Ninthly he looks up for his instructions.
For Tenthly he goes in quest of food.
For having considered God and himself he will consider his neighbour.
For if he meets another cat he will kiss her in kindness.
For when he takes his prey he plays with it to give it chance.   715
For one mouse in seven escapes by his dallying.
For when his day's work is done his business more properly begins.
For he keeps the Lord's watch in the night against the adversary.
For he counteracts the powers of darkness by his electrical skin and glaring
   eyes.
For he counteracts the Devil, who is death, by brisking about the life.   720
For in his morning orisons he loves the sun and the sun loves him.
For he is of the tribe of Tiger.
For the Cherub Cat is a term of the Angel Tiger.
For he has the subtlety and hissing of a serpent, which in goodness he suppresses.
For he will not do destruction, if he is well-fed, neither will he spit without
   provocation.   725
For he purrs in thankfulness, when God tells him he's a good Cat.
For he is an instrument for the children to learn benevolence upon.
For every house is incomplete without him and a blessing is lacking in the
   spirit.
For the Lord commanded Moses concerning the cats at the departure of the
   Children of Israel from Egypt.
For every family had one cat at least in the bag.   730
For the English Cats are the best in Europe.
For he is the cleanest in the use of his fore-paws of any quadruped.
For the dexterity of his defence is an instance of the love of God to him
   exceedingly.
For he is the quickest to his mark of any creature.
For he is tenacious of his point.   735
For he is a mixture of gravity and waggery.
For he knows that God is his Saviour.

For there is nothing sweeter than his peace when at rest.

For there is nothing brisker than his life when in motion.

For he is of the Lord's poor and so indeed is he called by benevolence per-
petually – Poor Jeoffry! poor Jeoffry! the rat has bit thy throat.   740

For I bless the name of the Lord Jesus that Jeoffry is better.

For the divine spirit comes about his body to sustain it in complete cat.

For his tongue is exceeding pure so that it has in purity what it wants in music.

For he is docile and can learn certain things.

For he can set up with gravity which is patience upon approbation.   745

For he can fetch and carry, which is patience in employment.

For he can jump over a stick which is patience upon proof positive.

For he can spraggle upon waggle at the word of command.

For he can jump from an eminence into his master's bosom.

For he can catch the cork and toss it again.   750

For he is hated by the hypocrite and miser.

For the former is afraid of detection.

For the latter refuses the charge.

For he camels his back to bear the first notion of business.

For he is good to think on, if a man would express himself neatly.   755

For he made a great figure in Egypt for his signal services.

For he killed the Ichneumon-rat very pernicious by land.

For his ears are so acute that they sting again.

For from this proceeds the passing quickness of his attention.

For by stroking of him I have found out electricity.   760

For I perceived God's light about him both wax and fire.

For the Electrical fire is the spiritual substance, which God sends bodies both
of man and beast.

For God has blessed him in the variety of his movements.

For, though he cannot fly, he is an excellent clamberer.

For his motions upon the face of the earth are more than any other
quadruped.   765

For he can tread to all the measures upon the music.

For he can swim for life.

For he can creep.

72c. from *Fragment B*

Let Elizur rejoice with the Partridge, who
is a prisoner of state and is proud of
his keepers

Let Shedeur rejoice with Pyrausta, who
dwelleth in a medium of fire, which
God hath adapted for him.

Let Shelumiel rejoice with Olor, who is of
a goodly savour, and the very look of
him harmonises the mind.

Let Jael rejoice with the Plover, who
whistles for his live, and foils the
marksmen and their guns.

Let Raguel rejoice with the Cock of
Portugal – God send good Angels to
the allies of England!

Let Hobab rejoice with Necydalus, who is
the Greek of a Grub.

Let Zurishaddai with the Polish Cock
rejoice – The Lord restore peace to
Europe.

Let Zuar rejoice with the Guinea Hen –
The Lord add to his mercies in the
WEST!

Let Chesed rejoice with Strepsiceros,
whose weapons are the ornaments of
his peace.

Let Hagar rejoice with Gnesion, who is
the right sort of eagle, and towers the
highest.

Let Libni rejoice with the Redshank, who
migrates not but is translated to the
upper regions.

Let Nahshon rejoice with the Seabreese,
the Lord gives the sailors of his Spirit.

Let Helon rejoice with the Woodpecker –
the Lord encourage the propagation
of trees!

Let Amos rejoice with the Coote – prepare
to meet thy God, O Israel.

Let Ephah rejoice with Buprestis, the Lord
endue us with temperance and
humanity, till every cow have her mate!

Let Sarah rejoice with the Redwing, whose
harvest is in the frost and snow.

Let Rebekah rejoice with Iynx, who holds
his head on one side to deceive the
adversary.

Let Shuah rejoice with Boa, which is the
vocal serpent.

72c from *Fragment B*

*For l am not without authority in my
jeopardy, which I derive inevitably
from the glory of the name of the Lord.*

*For I bless God whose name is Jealous – and
there is a zeal to deliver us from
everlasting burnings.*

*For my existimation is good even amongst
the slanderers and my memory shall
arise for a sweet savour unto the Lord.*

*For I bless the PRINCE of PEACE and pray
that all the guns may be nailed up, save
such as are for the rejoicing days.*

*For I have abstained from the blood of the
grape and that even at the Lord's table.*

*For I have glorified God in GREEK and
LATIN, the consecrated languages
spoken by the Lord on earth.*

*For I meditate the peace of Europe amongst
family bickerings and domestic jars.*

*For the HOST is in the WEST – the Lord
make us thankful unto salvation.*

*For I preach the very GOSPEL of CHRIST
without comment and with this
weapon shall I slay envy.*

*For I bless God in the rising generation,
which is on my side.*

*For I have translated in the charity, which
makes things better and I shall be
translated myself at the last.*

*For he that walked upon the sea, hath pre-
pared the floods with the Gospel of peace.*

*For the merciful man is merciful to his beast,
and to the trees that give them shelter.*

*For he hath turned the shadow of death into
the morning, the Lord is his name.*

*For I am come home again, but there is
nobody to kill the calf or to pay the
music.*

*For the hour of my felicity, like the womb of
Sarah, shall come at the latter end.*

*For I should have availed myself of waggery,
had not malice been multitudinous.*

*For there are still serpents that can speak –
God bless my head, my heart and my
heel.*

Let Ehud rejoice with Onocrotalus;
    whose braying is for the glory of God,
    because he makes the best music in
    his power.
Let Shamgar rejoice with Otis, who looks
    about him for the glory of God, and
    sees the horizon complete at once.
Let Bohan rejoice with the Scythian Stag –
    he is beef and breeches against want
    and nakedness.
Let Achsah rejoice with the Pigeon who
    is an antidote to malignity and will
    carry a letter.
Let Tohu rejoice with the Grouse – the
    Lord further the cultivating of heaths
    and the peopling of deserts.
Let Hillel rejoice with Ammodytes, whose
    colour is deceitful and he plots
    against the pilgrim's feet.
Let Eli rejoice with Leucon – he is an
    honest fellow, which is a rarity.

Let Jemuel rejoice with Charadrius, who
    is from the HEIGHT and the sight
    of him is good for the jaundice.
Let Pharaoh rejoice with Anataria, whom
    God permits to prey upon the ducks
    to check their increase.
Let Lotan rejoice with Sauterelle. Blessed
    be the name of the Lord from the
    Lote-tree to the Palm.
Let Dishon rejoice with the Landrail, God
    give his grace to the society for
    preserving the game.
Let Hushim rejoice with the King's Fisher,
    who is of royal beauty, though
    plebeian size.
Let Machir rejoice with Convolvulus,
    from him to the ring of Saturn, which
    is the girth of Job; to the signet of
    God – from Job and his daughters
    BLESSED BE JESUS.
Let Atad bless with Eleos, the nightly
    Memorialist eleeson kurie.
Let Jamin rejoice with the Bittern –
    blessed be the name of Jesus for
    Denver Sluice, Ruston, and the
    draining of the fens.
Let Ohad rejoice with Byturos who eateth
    the vine and is a minister of
    temperance.

For I bless God that I am of the same seed
    as Ehud, Mutius Scaevola, and Colonel
    Draper.

For the word of God is a sword on my side –
    no matter what other weapon a stick or
    a straw.
For I have adventured myself in the name
    of the Lord, and he hath marked me for
    his own.
For I bless God for the Postmaster general
    and all conveyancers of letters under his
    care especially Allen and Shelvock.
For my grounds in New Canaan shall
    infinitely compensate for the flats and
    mains of Staindrop Moor.
For the praise of God can give to a mute fish
    the notes of a nightingale.

For I have seen the White Raven and
    Thomas Hall of Willingham and am
    my self a greater curiosity than both.
For I look up to heaven which is my prospect
    to escape envy by surmounting it.

For if Pharaoh had known Joseph, he would
    have blessed God and me for the
    illumination of the people.
For I pray God to bless improvements in
    gardening till London be a city of palm-
    trees.
For I pray to give his grace to the poor of
    England, that Charity be not offended
    and that Benevolence may increase.
For in my nature I quested for beauty, but
    God, God hath sent me to sea for pearls.

For there is a blessing from the STONE of
    JESUS which is founded upon hell to
    the precious jewel on the right hand of
    God.

For the nightly visitor is at the window of
    the impenitent, while I sing a psalm of
    my own composing.
For there is a note added to the scale, which
    the Lord hath made fuller, stronger and
    more glorious.
For I offer my goat as he browses the vine,
    bless the Lord from chambering and
    drunkenness.

Let Zohar rejoice with Cychramus who cometh with the quails on a particular affair.

Let Serah, the daughter of Asher, rejoice with Ceyx, who maketh his cabin in the Halcyon's hold.

Let Magdiel rejoice with Ascarides, which is the life of the bowels – the worm hath a part in our frame.

Let Becher rejoice with Oscen who terrifies the wicked, as trumpet and alarm the coward.

Let Shaul rejoice with Circos, who hath clumsy legs, but he can wheel it the better with his wings. –

Let Hamul rejoice with the Crystal, who is pure and translucent.

Let Ziphion rejoice with the Tit-Lark who is a groundling, but he raises the spirits.

Let Mibzar rejoice with the Cadess, as is their number, so are their names, blessed be the Lord Jesus for them all.

Let Jubal rejoice with Caecilia, the woman and the slow-worm praise the name of the Lord.

Let Arodi rejoice with the Royston Crow, there is a society of them at Trumpington and Cambridge.

Let Areli rejoice with the Criel, who is a dwarf that towereth above others.

Let Phuvah rejoice with Platycerotes, whose weapons of defence keep them innocent.

Let Shimron rejoice with the Kite, who is of more value than many sparrows.

Let Sered rejoice with the Wittal – a silly bird is wise unto his own preservation.

Let Elon rejoice with Attelabus, who is the Locust without wings.

Let Jahleel rejoice with the Woodcock, who liveth upon suction and is pure from his diet.

Let Shuni rejoice with the Gull, who is happy in not being good for food.

For there is a traveling for the glory of God without going to Italy or France.

For I bless the children of Asher for the evil I did them and the good I might have received at their hands.

For I rejoice like a worm in the rain in him that cherishes and from him that tramples.

For I am ready for the trumpet and alarm to fight, to die and to rise again.

For the banished of the Lord shall come about again, for so he hath prepared for them.

For sincerity is a jewel which is pure and transparent, eternal and inestimable.

For my hands and my feet are perfect as the sublimity of Naphtali and the felicity of Asher.

For the names and number of animals are as the name and number of the stars. –

For I pray the Lord Jesus to translate my MAGNIFICAT into verse and represent it.

For I bless the Lord Jesus from the bottom of Royston Cave to the top of King's Chapel.

For I am a little fellow, which is intitled to the great mess by the benevolence of God my father.

For I this day made over my inheritance to my mother in consideration of her infirmities.

For I this day made over my inheritance to my mother in consideration of her age.

For I this day made over my inheritance to my mother in consideration of her poverty.

For I bless the thirteenth of August, in which I had the grace to obey the voice of Christ in my conscience.

For I bless the thirteenth of August, in which I was willing to run all hazards for the sake of the name of the Lord.

For I bless the thirteenth of August, in which I was willing to be called a fool for the sake of Christ.

Let Ezbon rejoice with Musimon, who is from the ram and she-goat.

Let Barkos rejoice with the Black Eagle, which is the least of his species and the best-natured.

Let Bedan rejoice with Ossifrage – the bird of prey and the man of prayer.

Let Naomi rejoice with Pseudosphece who is between a wasp and a hornet.

Let Ruth rejoice with the Tumbler – it is a pleasant thing to feed him and be thankful.

Let Ram rejoice with the Fieldfare are, who is a good gift from God in the season of scarcity.

Let Manoah rejoice with Cerastes, who is a Dragon with horns.

Let Talmai rejoice with Alcedo, who makes a cradle for its young, which is rocked by the winds.

Let Bukki rejoice with the Buzzard, who is clever, with the reputation of a silly fellow.

Let Michal rejoice with Leucrocuta who is a mixture of beauty and magnanimity.

Let Abiah rejoice with Morphnus who is a bird of passage to the Heavens.

Let Hur rejoice with the Water-wag-tail, who is a neighbour, and loves to be looked at.

Let Dodo rejoice with the purple Worm, who is clothed sumptuously, though he fares meanly.

Let Ahio rejoice with the Merlin who is a cousin german of the hawk.

Let Joram rejoice with the Water-Rail, who takes his delight in the river.

Let Chileab rejoice with Ophion who is clean made, less than an hart, and a Sardinian.

Let Shephatiah rejoice with the little Owl, which is the winged Cat.

Let Ithream rejoice with the great Owl, who understandeth that which he professes.

Let Abigail rejoice with Lethophagus – God be gracious to the widows indeed.

For I lent my flocks and my herds and my lands at once unto the Lord.

For nature is more various than observation though observers be innumerable.

For Agricola is Geourgos.

For I pray God to bless POLLY in the blessing of Naomi and assign her to the house of DAVID.

For I am in charity with the French who are my foes and Moabites because of the Moabitish womnan.

For my Angel is always ready at a pinch to help me out and to keep me up.

For CHRISTOPHER must slay the Dragon with a PHEON's head.

For they have separated me and my bosom, whereas the right comes by setting us together.

For silly fellow! silly fellow! is against me and belongeth neither to me nor my family.

For he that scorneth the scorner hath condescended to my low estate.

For Abiah is the father of Joab and Joab of all Romans and English Men.

For they pass by me in their tour, and the good Samaritan is not yet come. –

For I bless God in the behalf of TRINITY COLLEGE in CAMBRIDGE and the society of PURPLES in LONDON –

For I have a nephew CHRISTOPHER to whom I implore the grace of God.

For I pray God praise the CAM – Mr HIGGS and Mr and Mrs WASHBOURNE as the drops of the dew.

For I pray God bless the king of Sardinia and make him an instrument of his peace.

For I am possessed of a cat, surpassing in beauty, from whom I take occasion to bless Almighty God.

For I pray God for the professors of the University of Cambridge to attend and to amend.

For the Fatherless Children and widows are never deserted of the Lord.

Let Anathoth bless with Saurix, who is a
bird of melancholy.

Let Shammua rejoice with the Vultur who
is strength and fierceness.

Let Shobab rejoice with Evech who is of
the goat kind which is meditation and
pleasantry.

Let Ittai the Gittite rejoice with the
Gerfalcon – amicus certus in re
incerta cernitur.

Let Ibhar rejoice with the Pochard – a
child born in prosperity is the chiefest
blessing of peace.

Let Elishua rejoice with Cantharis – God
send bread and milk to the children.

Let Chimham bless with Drepanis who is
a passenger from the sea to heaven.

Let Toi rejoice with Percnopteros which
haunteth the sugar-fens.

Let Nepheg rejoice with Cenchris which
is the spotted serpent.

Let Japhia rejoice with Buteo who hath
three testicles.

Let Gibeon rejoice with the Puttock, who
will shift for himself to the last
extremity.

Let Elishama rejoice with Mylaecos Isxete
xeira mulaiou alitridest. eudete
makra.

Let Elimelech rejoice with the Horn-Owl
who is of gravity and amongst my
friends in the tower.

Let Eliada rejoice with the Gier-eagle who
is swift and of great penetration.

Let Eliphalet rejoice with Erodius who is
God's good creature, which is
sufficient for him.

Let Jonathan, David's nephew, rejoice
with Oripelargus who is noble by his
ascent.

Let Sheva rejoice with the Hobby, who is
the service of the great.

Let Ahimaaz rejoice with the Silver-
Worm who is a living mineral.

*For I pray God be gracious to the house of
Stuart and consider their afflictions.*

*For I pray God be gracious to the seed of
Virgil, to Mr GOODMAN SMITH
of King's and Joseph STUD.*

*For I give God the glory that I am a son of
ABRAHAM a PRINCE of the house
of my fathers.*

*For my brethren have dealt deceitfully as a
brook, and as the stream of brooks that
pass away.*

*For I bless God for my retreat at
CANBURY, as it was the place of the
nativity of my children.*

*For I pray God to give them the food which
cannot earn for them any otherwise
than by prayer.*

*For I pray God bless the Chinese which are
of ABRAHAM and the Gospel grew
with them at the first.*

*For I bless God in the honey of the sugar-
cane and the milk of the cocoa.*

*For I bless God in the libraries of the learned
and for all the booksellers in the world.*

*For I bless God in the strength of my loins
and for the voice which he hath made
sonorous.*

*For 'tis no more a merit to provide for
oneself, but to quit all for the sake of
the Lord.*

*For there is no invention but the gift of God,
and no grace like the grace of gratitude.*

*For grey hairs are honourable and tell every
one of them to the glory of God.*

*For I bless the Lord Jesus for the memory of
GAY, POPE and SWIFT.*

*For all good words are from GOD, and all
others are cant.*

*For I am enobled by my ascent and the Lord
hath raised me above my Peers.*

*For I pray God bless my lord
CLARENDON and his seed for ever.*

*For there is silver in my mines and I bless
God that it is rather there than in my
coffers.*

Let Shobi rejoice with the Kastrel – blessed be the name JESUS in falconry and in the MALL.

Let Elkanah rejoice with Cymindis – the Lord illuminate us against the powers of darkness.

Let Ziba rejoice with Glottis whose tongue is wreathed in his throat.

Let Micah rejoice with the spotted Spider, who counterfeits death to effect his purposes.

Let Rizpah rejoice with the Eyed Moth who is beautiful in corruption.

Let Naharai, Joab's armour-bearer rejoice with Rock who is a bird of stupendous magnitude.

Let Abiezer, the Anethothite, rejoice with Phrynos who is the scaled frog.

Let Nachon rejoice with Pareas who is a serpent more innocent than others.

Let Lapidoth with Percnos – the Lord is the builder of the wall of CHINA – REJOICE.

Let Ahinoam rejoice with Prester – The seed of the woman hath bruised the serpent's head.

Let Phurah rejoice with Penelopes, the servant of Gideon with the fowl of the brook.

Let Jether, the son of Gideon, rejoice with Ecchetae which are musical grashoppers.

Let Hushai rejoice with the Ospray who is able to parry the eagle.

Let Eglah rejoice with Phalaris who is a pleasant object upon the water.

Let Haggith rejoice with the white Weasel who devoureth the honey and its maker.

Let Abital rejoice with Ptyas who is arrayed in green and gold.

Let Maacah rejoice with Dryophyte who was blessed of the Lord in the valley. [...]

For I blessed God in St James's Park till I routed all the company.

For the officers of the peace are at variance with me, and the watchman smites me with his staff

For I am the seed of the WELCH WOMAN and speak the truth from my heart.

For they lay wagers touching my life. – God be gracious to the winners.

For the piety of Rizpah is imitable in the Lord – wherefore I pray for the dead.

For the Lord is my ROCK and I am the bearer of his CROSS.

For I am like a frog in the brambles, but the Lord hath put his whole armor upon me.

For I was a Viper-catcher in my youth and the Lord delivered me from his venom.

For I rejoice that I attribute to God, what others vainly ascribe to feeble man.

For I am ready to die for his sake – who lay down his life for all mankind.

For the son of JOSHUA shall prevail against the servant of Gideon – Good men have their betters.

For my seed shall worship the Lord JESUS as numerous and musical as the grashoppers of Paradise.

For I pray God to turn the council of Ahitophel into foolishness.

For the learning of the Lord increases daily, as the sun is an improving angel.

For I pray God for a reformation amongst the women and the restoration of the veil.

For beauty is better to look upon than to meddle with and tis good for a man not to know a woman.

For the Lord Jesus made him a nosegay and blessed it and he blessed the inhabitants of flowers.

Oliver Goldsmith (1730?–1774)

73. The Description of an Author's Bedchamber

Where the Red Lion, flaring o'er the way,
Invites each passing stranger that can pay;
Where Calvert's butt and Parson's black champagne
Regale the drabs and bloods of Drury Lane;
There in a lonely room, from bailiffs snug,   5
The Muse found Scroggen stretched beneath a rug;
A window patched with paper lent a ray,
That dimly showed the state in which he lay;
The sanded floor that grits beneath the tread;
The humid wall with paltry pictures spread;   10
The royal game of goose was there in view,
And the twelve rules the royal martyr drew;
The Seasons framed with listing found a place,
And brave Prince William showed his lamp-black face:
The morn was cold, he views with keen desire   15
The rusty grate unconscious of a fire;
With beer and milk arrears the frieze was scored,
And five cracked teacups dressed the chimney board;
A nightcap decked his brows instead of bay,
A cap by night – a stocking all the day!   20

74. An Elegy on the Death of a Mad Dog

Good people all, of every sort,
    Give ear unto my song,
And if you find it wondrous short,
    It cannot hold you long

In lslington there was a man,   5
    Of whom the world might say
That still a godly race he ran,
    Whene'er he went to pray.

A kind and gentle heart he had,
   To comfort friends and foes;   10
The naked every day he clad,
   When he put on his clothes.

And in that town a dog was found,
   As many dogs there be,
Both mongrel, puppy, whelp and hound,   15
   And curs of low degree.

This dog and man at first were friends;
   But when a pique began,
The dog, to gain some private ends,
   Went mad and bit the man.   20

Around from all the neighbouring streets
   The wondering neighbours ran,
And swore the dog had lost his wits,
   To bite so good a man.

The wound it seemed both sore and sad   25
   To every Christian eye;
And while they swore the dog was mad,
   They swore the man would die.

But soon a wonder came to light,
   That showed the rogues they lied: 30
The man recovered of the bite,
   The dog it was that died.

75. Song from *The Vicar of Wakefield*

When lovely woman stoops to folly,
   And finds too late that men betray,
What charm can soothe her melancholy,
   What art can wash her guilt away?

The only art her guilt to cover,   5
   To hide her shame from every eye,
To give repentance to her lover,
   And wring his bosom – is, to die.

76. The Deserted Village

to Sir Joshua Reynolds

Sweet Auburn, loveliest village of the plain,
Where health and plenty cheered the labouring swain,
Where smiling spring its earliest visit paid,
And parting summer's lingering blooms delayed:
Dear lovely bowers of innocence and ease,   5
Seats of my youth, when every sport could please,
How often have I loitered o'er thy green,
Where humble happiness endeared each scene;
How often have I paused on every charm,
The sheltered cot, the cultivated farm,   10
The never-failing brook, the busy mill,
The decent church that topped the neighbouring hill,
The hawthorn bush, with seats beneath the shade,
For talking age and whispering lovers made.
How often have I blessed the coming day,   15
When toil remitting lent its turn to play,
And all the village train, from labour free,
Led up their sports beneath the spreading tree,
While many a pastime circled in the shade,
The young contending as the old surveyed;   20
And many a gambol frolicked o'er the ground,
And sleights of art and feats of strength went round.
And still as each repeated pleasure tired,
Succeeding sports the mirthful band inspired;
The dancing pair that simply sought renown,   25
By holding out to tire each other down;
The swain mistrustless of his smutted face,
While secret laughter tittered round the place;
The bashful virgin's sidelong looks of love,
The matron's glance that would those looks reprove: 30
These were thy charms, sweet village; sports like these,
With sweet succession, taught even toil to please;
These round thy bowers their cheerful influence shed,
These were thy charms – but all these charms are fled.
    Sweet smiling village, loveliest of the lawn,   35
Thy sports are fled and all thy charms withdrawn;
Amidst thy bowers the tyrant's hand is seen,
And desolation saddens all thy green:
One only master grasps the whole domain,

And half a tillage stints thy smiling plain: 40
No more thy glassy brook reflects the day,
But, choked with sedges, works its weedy way.
Along thy glades, a solitary guest,
The hollow-sounding bittern guards its nest;
Amidst thy desert walks the lapwing flies, 45
And tires their echoes with unvaried cries;
Sunk are thy bowers in shapeless ruin all,
And the long grass o'ertops the mouldering wall;
And trembling, shrinking from the spoiler's hand,
Far, far away, thy children leave the land. 50
    Ill fares the land, to hastening ills a prey,
Where wealth accumulates and men decay:
Princes and lords may flourish or may fade;
A breath can make them, as a breath has made;
But a bold peasantry, their country's pride, 55
When once destroyed, can never be supplied.
    A time there was, ere England's grief's began,
When every rood of ground maintained its man;
For him light labor spread her wholesome store,
Just gave what life required, but gave no more: 60
His best companions, innocence and health;
And his best riches, ignorance of wealth.
    But times are altered; trade's unfeeling train
Usurp the land and dispossess the swain;
Along the lawn, where scattered hamlets rose, 65
Unwieldy wealth and cumbrous pomp repose;
And every want to opulence allied,
And every pang that folly pays to pride.
These gentle hours that plenty bade to bloom,
Those calm desires that asked but little room, 70
Those healthful sports that graced the peaceful scene,
Lived in each look and brightened all the green;
These, far departing, seek a kinder shore,
And rural mirth and manners are no more.
    Sweet Auburn! Parent of the blissful hour, 75
Thy glades forlorn confess the tyrant's power.
Here as I take my solitary rounds,
Amidst thy tangling walks and ruined grounds,
And, many a year elapsed, return to view
Where once the cottage stood, the hawthorn grew, 80
Remembrance wakes with all her busy train,
Swells at my breast and turns the past to pain.

In all my wanderings round this world of care,
In all my griefs – and God has given my share –
I still had hopes my latest hours to crown,   85
Amidst these humble bowers to lay me down;
To husband out life's taper at the close,
And keep the flame from wasting by repose.
I still had hopes, for pride attends us still,
Amidst the swains to show my book-learned skill,   90
Around my fire an evening group to draw,
And tell of all I felt and all I saw;
And, as a hare, whom hounds and horns pursue,
Pants to the place from whence at first she flew,
I still had hopes, my long vexations past,   95
Here to return – and die at home at last.
    O blest retirement, friend to life's decline,
Retreats from care, that never must be mine,
How happy he who crowns in shades like these
A youth of labour with an age of ease;   100
Who quits a world where strong temptations try
And, since 'tis hard to combat, learns to fly.
For him no wretches, born to work and weep,
Explore the mine or tempt the dangerous deep;
No surly porter stands in guilty state   105
To spurn imploring famine from the gate;
But on he moves to meet his latter end,
Angels around befriending virtue's friend;
Bends to the grave with unperceived decay,
While resignation gently slopes the way;   110
And, all his prospects brightening to the last,
His heaven commences ere the world be past!
    Sweet was the sound, when oft at evening's close
Up yonder hill the village murmur rose;
There, as I passed with careless steps and slow,   115
The mingling notes came softened from below;
The swain responsive as the milkmaid sung,
The sober herd that lowed to meet their young;
The noisy geese that gabbled o'er the pool,
The playful children just let loose from school;   120
The watch-dog's voice that bayed the whispering wind,
And the loud laugh that spoke the vacant mind;
These all in sweet confusion sought the shade,
And filled each pause the nightingale had made.
But now the sounds of population fail,   125

No cheerful murmurs fluctuate in the gale,
No busy steps the grassgrown foot-way tread,
For all the bloomy flush of life is fled.
All but yon widowed, solitary thing
That feebly bends beside the plashy spring;   130
She, wretched matron, forced, in age, for bread,
To strip the brook with mantling cresses spread,
To pick her wintry faggot from the thorn,
To seek her nightly shed and weep till morn;
She only left of all the harmless train,   135
The sad historian of the pensive plain.
    Near yonder copse, where once the garden smiled,
And still where many a garden flower grows wild;
There, where a few torn shrubs the place disclose,
The village preacher's modest mansion rose.   140
A man he was to all the country dear,
And passing rich with forty pounds a year;
Remote from towns he ran his godly race,
Nor e'er had changed, nor wished to change, his place;
Unpractised he to fawn, or seek for power   145
By doctrines fashioned to the varying hour;
Far other aims his heart had learned to prize,
More skilled to raise the wretched than to rise.
His house was known to all the vagrant train,
He chid their wanderings, but relieved their pain;   150
The long-remembered beggar was his guest,
Whose beard descending swept his aged breast;
The ruined spendthrift, now no longer proud,
Claimed kindred there and had his claims allowed;
The broken soldier, kindly bade to stay,   155
Sat by his fire and talked the night away;
Wept o'er his wounds or tales of sorrow done,
Shouldered his crutch and showed how fields were won.
Pleased with his guests, the good man learned to glow,
And quite forgot their vices in their woe;   160
Careless their merits or their faults to scan,
His pity gave ere charity began.
    Thus to relieve the wretched was his pride,
And even his failings leaned to virtue's side;
But in his duty prompt at every call,   165
He watched and wept, he prayed and felt, for all.
And, as a bird each fond endearment tries
To tempt its new-fledged offspring to the skies,

He tried each art, reproved each dull delay,
Allured to brighter worlds and led the way.   170
    Beside the bed where parting life was laid,
And sorrow, guilt, and pain by turns dismayed,
The reverend champion stood. At his control,
Despair and anguish fled the struggling soul;
Comfort came down the trembling wretch to raise,   175
And his last faltering accents whispered praise.
    At church, with meek and unaffected grace,
His looks adorned the venerable place;
Truth from his lips prevailed with double sway,
And fools, who came to scoff, remained to pray.   180
The service past, around the pious man,
With steady zeal, each honest rustic ran;
Even children followed with endearing wile,
And plucked his gown, to share the good man's smile.
His ready smile a parent's warmth expressed,   185
Their welfare pleased him and their cares distressed;
To them his heart, his love, his griefs were given,
But all his serious thoughts had rest in Heaven.
As some tall cliff, that lifts its awful form,
Swells from the vale and midway leaves the storm,   190
Though round its breast the rolling clouds are spread,
Eternal sunshine settles on its head.
    Beside yon straggling fence that skirts the way,
With blossomed furze unprofitably gay,
There, in his noisy mansion, skilled to rule,   195
The village master taught his little school;
A man severe he was and stern to view;
I knew him well, and every truant knew;
Well had the boding tremblers learned to trace
The day's disasters in his morning face;   200
Full well they laughed, with counterfeited glee,
At all his jokes, for many a joke had he;
Full well the busy whisper, circling round,
Conveyed the dismal tidings when he frowned;
Yet he was kind, or, if severe in aught,   205
The love he bore to learning was in fault;
The village all declared how much he knew;
'Twas certain he could write and cipher too;
Lands he could measure, terms and tides presage,
And even the story ran that he could gauge.   210
In arguing too, the parson owned his skill,

For even though vanquished, he could argue still;
While words of learned length and thundering sound
Amazed the gazing rustics ranged around,
And still they gazed, and still the wonder grew,   215
That one small head could carry all he knew.
    But past is all his fame. The very spot,
Where many a time he triumphed, is forgot.
Near yonder thorn, that lifts its head on high,
Where once the signpost caught the passing eye,   220
Low lies that house where nutbrown draughts inspired,
Where greybeard mirth and smiling toil retired,
Where village statesmen talked with looks profound,
And news much older than their ale went round.
Imagination fondly stoops to trace   225
The parlour splendours of that festive place;
The white-washed wall, the nicely sanded floor,
The varnished clock that clicked behind the door;
The chest contrived a double debt to pay,
A bed by night, a chest of drawers by day;   230
The pictures placed for ornament and use,
The twelve good rules, the royal game of goose;
The hearth, except when winter chilled the day,
With aspen boughs and flowers and fennel gay;
While broken teacups, wisely kept for show,   235
Ranged o'er the chimney, glistened in a row.
    Vain, transitory splendours! Could not all
Reprieve the tottering mansion from its fall!
Obscure it sinks, nor shall it more impart
An hour's importance to the poor man's heart;   240
Thither no more the peasant shall repair
To sweet oblivion of his daily care;
No more the farmer's news, the barber's tale,
No more the woodman's ballad shall prevail;
No more the smith his dusky brow shall clear,   245
Relax his ponderous strength and lean to hear;
The host himself no longer shall be found
Careful to see the mantling bliss go round;
Nor the coy maid, half willing to be pressed,
Shall kiss the cup to pass it to the rest.   250
    Yes! let the rich deride, the proud disdain,
These simple blessings of the lowly train;
To me more dear, congenial to my heart,
One native charm than all the gloss of art;

Spontaneous joys, where nature has its play,   255
The soul adopts and owns their firstborn sway;
Lightly they frolic o'er the vacant mind,
Unenvied, unmolested, unconfined:
But the long pomp, the midnight masquerade,
With all the freaks of wanton wealth arrayed,   260
In these, ere triflers half their wish obtain,
The toiling pleasure sickens into pain;
And, even while fashion's brightest arts decoy,
The heart distrusting asks, if this be joy.
    Ye friends to truth, ye statesmen, who survey   265
The rich man's joys increase, the poor's decay,
'Tis yours to judge how wide the limits stand
Between a splendid and a happy land.
Proud swells the tide with loads of freighted ore,
And shouting Folly hails them from her shore;   270
Hoards, e'en beyond the miser's wish abound,
And rich men flock from all the world around.
Yet count our gains. This wealth is but a name
That leaves our useful products still the same.
Not so the loss. The man of wealth and pride   275
Takes up a space that many poor supplied;
Space for his lake, his park's extended bounds,
Space for his horses, equipage and hounds;
The robe that wraps his limbs in silken sloth
Has robbed the neighbouring fields of half their growth;   280
His seat, where solitary sports are seen,
Indignant spurns the cottage from the green;
Around the world each needful product flies,
For all the luxuries the world supplies:
While thus the land, adorned for pleasure all,   285
In barren splendour feebly waits the fall.
    As some fair female unadorned and plain,
Secure to please while youth confirms her reign,
Slights every borrowed charm that dress supplies,
Nor shares with art the triumph of her eyes;   290
But when those charms are passed, for charms are frail,
When time advances and when lovers fail,
She then shines forth, solicitous to bless,
In all the glaring impotence of dress:
Thus fares the land, by luxury betrayed,   295
In nature's simplest charms at first arrayed;
But verging to decline, its splendours rise,

Its vistas strike, its palaces surprise;
While scourged by famine from the smiling land,
The mournful peasant leads his humble band;   300
And while he sinks, without one arm to save,
The country blooms – a garden and a grave.
    Where then, ah where, shall poverty reside,
To scape the pressure of contiguous pride?
If to some common's fenceless limits strayed,   305
He drives his flock to pick the scanty blade,
Those fenceless fields the sons of wealth divide,
And even the bare-worn common is denied.
    If to the city sped – What waits him there?
To see profusion that he must not share;   310
To see ten thousand baneful arts combined
To pamper luxury and thin mankind;
To see those joys the sons of pleasure know
Extorted from his fellow creature's woe.
Here, while the courtier glitters in brocade,   315
There the pale artist plies the sickly trade;
Here, while the proud their long-drawn pomps display,
There the black gibbet glooms beside the way.
The dome where Pleasure holds her midnight reign
Here, richly decked, admits the gorgeous train;   320
Tumultuous grandeur crowds the blazing square,
The rattling chariots clash, the torches glare.
Sure scenes like these no troubles e'er annoy!
Sure these denote one universal joy!
Are these thy serious thoughts? – Ah, turn thine eyes   325
Where the poor, houseless, shivering female lies.
She once, perhaps, in village plenty blest,
Has wept at tales of innocence distressed;
Her modest looks the cottage might adorn,
Sweet as the primrose peeps beneath the thorn: 330
Now lost to all; her friends, her virtue fled,
Near her betrayer's door she lays her head,
And, pinched with cold and shrinking from the shower,
With heavy heart deplores that luckless hour,
When idly first, ambitious of the town,   335
She left her wheel and robes of country brown.
    Do thine, sweet Auburn, thine, the loveliest train,
Do thy fair tribes participate her pain?
Even now, perhaps, by cold and hunger led,
At proud men's doors they ask a little bread!   340

Ah, no. To distant climes, a dreary scene,
Where half the convex world intrudes between,
Through torrid tracts with fainting steps they go,
Where wild Altama murmurs to their woe.
Far different there from all that charmed before   345
The various terrors of that horrid shore:
Those blazing suns that dart a downward ray,
And fiercely shed intolerable day;
Those matted woods where birds forget to sing,
But silent bats in drowsy clusters cling;   350
Those poisonous fields with rank luxuriance crowned,
Where the dark scorpion gathers death around;
Where at each step the stranger fears to wake
The rattling terrors of the vengeful snake;
Where crouching tigers wait their hapless prey,   355
And savage men more murderous still than they;
While oft in whirls the mad tornado flies,
Mingling the ravaged landscape with the skies.
Far different these from every former scene,
The cooling brook, the grassy-vested green,   360
The breezy covert of the warbling grove,
That only sheltered thefts of harmless love.
    Good Heaven! what sorrows gloomed that parting day,
That called them from their native walks away;
When the poor exiles, every pleasure past,   365
Hung round their bowers and fondly looked their last,
And took a long farewell and wished in vain
For seats like these beyond the western main;
And shuddering still to face the distant deep,
Returned and wept, and still returned to weep.   370
The good old sire the first prepared to go
To new-found worlds, and wept for others' woe;
But for himself, in conscious virtue brave,
He only wished for worlds beyond the grave.
His lovely daughter, lovelier in her tears,   375
The fond companion of his helpless years,
Silent went next, neglectful of her charms,
And left a lover's for a father's arms.
With louder plaints the mother spoke her woes,
And blessed the cot where every pleasure rose;   380
And kissed her thoughtless babes with many a tear,
And clasped them close, in sorrow doubly dear;
Whilst her fond husband strove to lend relief

In all the silent manliness of grief.
 O luxury! thou cursed by Heaven's decree,   385
How ill exchanged are things like these for thee!
How do thy potions with insidious joy
Diffuse their pleasures only to destroy!
Kingdoms, by thee to sickly greatness grown,
Boast of a florid vigor not their own.   390
At every draught more large and large they grow,
A bloated mass of rank unwieldy woe;
Till sapped their strength and every part unsound,
Down, down they sink and spread a ruin round.
 Even now the devastation is begun,   395
And half the business of destruction done;
Even now, methinks, as pondering here I stand,
I see the rural virtues leave the land.
Down where yon anchoring vessel spreads the sail,
That idly waiting flaps with every gale,   400
Downward they move, a melancholy band,
Pass from the shore and darken all the strand.
Contented toil and hospitable care,
And kind connubial tenderness are there;
And piety, with wishes placed above,   405
And steady loyalty and faithful love.
And thou, sweet Poetry, thou loveliest maid,
Still first to fly where sensual joys invade;
Unfit, in these degenerate times of shame,
To catch the heart or strike for honest fame;   410
Dear charming nymph, neglected and decried,
My shame in crowds, my solitary pride;
Thou source of all my bliss and all my woe,
That found'st me poor at first and keep'st me so;
Thou guide by which the nobler arts excel,   415
Thou nurse of every virtue, fare thee well!
Farewell, and oh, where'er thy voice be tried,
On Torno's cliffs or Pambamarca's side,
Whether where equinoctial fervours glow,
Or winter wraps the polar world in snow,   420
Still let thy voice, prevailing over time,
Redress the rigours of the inclement clime;
Aid slighted truth; with thy persuasive strain
Teach erring man to spurn the rage of gain;
Teach him, that states of native strength possessed,   425
Though very poor, may still be very blest;

That trade's proud empire hastes to swift decay,
As ocean sweeps the laboured mole away;
While self-dependent power can time defy,
As rocks resist the billows and the sky.   430

William Cowper (1731–1800)

77. The Poplar Tree

The poplars are felled; farewell to the shade
And the whispering sound of the cool colonnade;
The winds play no longer and sing in the leaves,
Nor Ouse on his bosom their image receives.

Twelve years have elapsed since I first took a view   5
Of my favourite field, and the bank where they grew:
And now in the grass behold they are laid,
And the tree is my seat that once lent me a shade!

The blackbird has fled to another retreat
Where the hazels afford him a screen from the heat;   10
And the scene where his melody charmed me before
Resounds with his sweet-flowing ditty no more.

My fugitive years are all hasting away,
And I must ere long lie as lowly as they,
With a turf on my breast and a stone at my head,   15
Ere another such grove shall arise in its stead.

The change both my heart and my fancy employs;
I reflect on the frailty of man and his joys:
Short-lived as we are, yet our pleasures, we see,
Have a still shorter date, and die sooner than we.   20

78. Alexander Selkirk

I am monarch of all I survey;
   My right there is none to dispute;

From the centre all round to the sea
   I am lord of the fowl and the brute.
O Solitude! where are the charms
   That sages have seen in thy face?
Better dwell in the midst of alarms,
   Than reign in this horrible place.

I am out of humanity's reach,
   I must finish my journey alone,
Never hear the sweet music of speech;
   I start at the sound of my own.
The beasts that roam over the plain
   My form with indifference see;
They are so unacquainted with man,
   Their tameness is shocking to me.

Society, Friendship, and Love
   Divinely bestowed upon man,
Oh, had I the wings of a dove
   How soon would I taste you again!
My sorrows I then might assuage
   In the ways of religion and truth,
Might learn from the wisdom of age,
   And be cheered by the sallies of youth.

Ye winds that have made me your sport,
   Convey to this desolate shore
Some cordial endearing report
   Of a land I shall visit no more:
My friends, do they now and then send
   A wish or a thought after me?
O tell me I yet have a friend,
   Though a friend I am never to see.

How fleet is a glance of the mind!
   Compared with the speed of its flight,
The tempest itself lags behind,
   And the swift-wingéd arrows of light.
When I think of my own native land
   In a moment I seem to be there;
But alas! recollection at hand
   Soon hurries me back to despair.

But the sea-fowl is gone to her nest,
   The beast is laid down in his lair;
Even here is a season of rest,
   And I to my cabin repair.
There's mercy in every place,   45
   And mercy – encouraging thought! –
Gives even affliction a grace
   And reconciles man to his lot.

79. The Castaway

Obscurest night involved the sky,
   The Atlantic billows roared,
When such a destined wretch as I,
   Washed headlong from on board,
Of friends, of hope, of all bereft,   5
His floating home for ever left.

No braver chief could Albion boast
   Than he with whom he went,
Nor ever ship left Albion's coast
   With warmer wishes sent.   10
He loved them both, but both in vain,
Nor him beheld, nor her again.

Not long beneath the whelming brine,
   Expert to swim, he lay;
Nor soon he felt his strength decline,   15
   Or courage die away;
But waged with death a lasting strife,
Supported by despair of life.

He shouted: nor his friends had failed
   To check the vessel's course,   20
But so the furious blast prevailed,
   That, pitiless perforce,
They left their outcast mate behind,
And scudded still before the wind.

Some succour yet they could afford;   25
   And such as storms allow,

The cask, the coop, the floated cord,
   Delayed not to bestow.
But he (they knew) nor ship nor shore,
Whate'er they gave, should visit more.   30

Nor, cruel as it seemed, could he
   Their haste himself condemn,
Aware that flight, in such a sea,
   Alone could rescue them;
Yet bitter felt it still to die   35
Deserted, and his friends so nigh.

He long survives, who lives an hour
   In ocean, self-upheld;
And so long he, with unspent power,
   His destiny repelled;   40
And ever, as the minutes flew,
Entreated help, or cried 'Adieu!'

At length, his transient respite past,
   His comrades, who before
Had heard his voice in every blast,   45
   Could catch the sound no more;
For then, by toil subdued, he drank
The stifling wave, and then he sank.

No poet wept him; but the page
   Of narrative sincere,   50
That tells his name, his worth, his age,
   Is wet with Anson's tear:
And tears by bards or heroes shed
Alike immortalise the dead.

I therefore purpose not, or dream,   55
   Descanting on his fate,
To give the melancholy theme
   A more enduring date:
But misery still delights to trace
Its semblance in another's case.   60

No voice divine the storm allayed,
   No light propitious shone,

When, snatched from all effectual aid,
    We perished, each alone:
But I beneath a rougher sea,   65
And whelmed in deeper gulfs than he.

80. Loss of the Royal George

    Toll for the Brave!
The brave that are no more!
    All sunk beneath the wave
Fast by their native shore!
    Eight hundred of the brave   5
Whose courage well was tried,
    Had made the vessel heel
And laid her on her side.
    A land-breeze shook the shrouds
And she was overset;   10
    Down went the Royal George,
With all her crew complete.

    Toll for the brave!
Brave Kempenfelt is gone;
    His last sea-fight is fought,   15
His work of glory done.
    It was not in the battle;
No tempest gave the shock;
    She sprang no fatal leak,
She ran upon no rock.   20
    His sword was in its sheath,
His fingers held the pen,
    When Kempenfelt went down
With twice four hundred men.

    Weigh the vessel up   25
Once dreaded by our foes!
    And mingle with our cup
The tears that England owes.
    Her timbers yet are sound,
And she may float again   30
    Full charged with England's thunder,
And plough the distant main:

> But Kempenfelt is gone,
> His victories are o'er;
> > And he and his eight hundred 35
> Shall plough the wave no more.

81. To Mary

The twentieth year is well-nigh past
Since first our sky was overcast;
Ah would that this might be the last!
> My Mary!

Thy spirits have a fainter flow, 5
I see thee daily weaker grow –
'Twas my distress that brought thee low,
> My Mary!

Thy needles, once a shining store,
For my sake restless heretofore,
Now rust disused, and shine no more; 10
> My Mary!

For though thou gladly wouldst fulfil
The same kind office for me still,
Thy sight now seconds not thy will, 15
> My Mary!

But well thou play'd'st the housewife's part,
And all thy threads with magic art
Have wound themselves about this heart,
> My Mary! 20

Thy indistinct expressions seem
Like language uttered in a dream;
Yet me they charm, whate'er the theme,
> My Mary!

Thy silver locks, once auburn bright, 25
Are still more lovely in my sight
Than golden beams of orient light,
> My Mary!

For could I view nor them nor thee,
What sight worth seeing could I see?
The sun would rise in vain for me,
    My Mary!

30

Partakers of thy sad decline,
Thy hands their little force resign;
Yet, gently prest, press gently mine,
    My Mary!

35

And then I feel that still I hold
A richer store ten thousandfold
Than misers fancy in their gold,
    My Mary!

40

Such feebleness of limbs thou prov'st
That now at every step thou mov'st
Upheld by two; yet still thou lov'st,
    My Mary!

And still to love, though prest with ill,
In wintry age to feel no chill,
With me is to be lovely still,
    My Mary!

45

But ah! by constant heed I know
How oft the sadness that I show
Transforms thy smiles to looks of woe,
    My Mary!

50

And should my future lot be cast
With much resemblance of the past,
Thy worn-out heart will break at last –
    My Mary!

55

82. Epitaph on a Hare

Here lies, whom hound did ne'er pursue,
    Nor swifter greyhound follow,
Whose foot ne'er tainted morning dew,
    Nor ear heard huntsman's hallo';

Old Tiney, surliest of his kind,   5
    Who, nursed with tender care,
And to domestic bounds confined,
    Was still a wild Jack hare.

Though duly from my hand he took
    His pittance every night,   10
He did it with a jealous look,
    And, when he could, would bite.

His diet was of wheaten bread,
    And milk, and oats, and straw;
Thistles, or lettuces instead,   15
    With sand to scour his maw.

On twigs of hawthorn he regaled,
    On pippins' russet peel,
And, when his juicy salads failed,
    Sliced carrot pleased him well.   20

A Turkey carpet was his lawn,
    Whereon he loved to bound,
To skip and gambol like a fawn,
    And swing his rump around.

His frisking was at evening hours,   25
    For then he lost his fear,
But most before approaching showers,
    Or when a storm drew near.

Eight years and five round rolling moons
    He thus saw steal away,   30
Dozing out all his idle noons,
    And every night at play.

I kept him for his humour's sake,
    For he would oft beguile
My heart of thoughts that made it ache,   35
    And force me to a smile.

But now beneath his walnut shade
    He finds his long last home,

And waits, in snug concealment laid,
   Till gentler Puss shall come.   40

He, still more agèd, feels the shocks
   From which no care can save,
And, partner once of Tiney's box,
   Must soon partake his grave.

83. On the Death of Mrs Throckmorton's Bullfinch

Ye Nymphs, if e'er your eyes were red
With tears o'er hapless fav'rites shed,
   O, share Maria's grief!
Her favourite, even in his cage,
(What will not hunger's cruel rage?)   5
   Assassined by a thief.

Where Rhenus strays his vines among,
The egg was laid from which he sprung,
   And though by nature mute,
Or only with a whistle blessed,
Well-taught he all the sounds expressed   10
   Of flageolet or flute.

The honours of his ebon poll
Were brighter than the sleekest mole,
   His bosom of the hue   15
With which Aurora decks the skies,
When piping winds shall soon arise
   To sweep away the dew.

Above, below, in all the house,
Dire foe alike of bird and mouse,   20
   No cat had leave to dwell;
And Bully's cage supported stood
On props of smoothest-shaven wood,
   Large built and latticed well.

Well latticed, – but the grate, alas!   25
Not rough with wire of steel or brass,

For Bully's plumage sake,
But smooth with wands from Ouse's side,
With which, when neatly peeled and dried,
   The swains their baskets make.   30

Night veiled the pole: all seemed secure:
When, led by instinct sharp and sure,
   Subsistence to provide,
A beast forth sallied on the scout,
Long backed, long tailed, with whiskered snout,   35
   And badger-coloured hide.

He, entering at the study door,
Its ample area 'gan explore;
   And something in the wind
Conjectured, sniffing round and round,   40
Better than all the books he found,
   Food chiefly for the mind.

Just then, by adverse fate impressed,
A dream disturbed poor Bully's rest;
   In sleep he seemed to view   45
A rat fast clinging to the cage,
And, screaming at the sad presage,
   Awoke and found it true.

For, aided both by ear and scent,
Right to his mark the monster went, –   50
   Ah, Muse! forbear to speak
Minute the horrors that ensued;
His teeth were strong, the cage was wood, –
   He left poor Bully's beak.

O, had he made that too his prey!   55
That beak, whence issued many a lay
   Of such mellifluous tone,
Might have repaid him well, I wote,
For silencing so sweet a throat,
   Fast stuck within his own.   60

Maria weeps, – the Muses mourn; –
So, when by Bacchanalians torn,
   On Thracian Hebrus' side

The tree-enchanter Orpheus fell,
His head alone remained to tell   65
   The cruel death he died.

84. from *Olney Hymns*

84a. *Walking with God*

Genesis v. 24

Oh! for a closer walk with God;
   A calm and heavenly frame;
A light to shine upon the road
   That leads me to the Lamb!

Where is the blessedness I knew   5
   When first I saw the Lord?
Where is the soul-refreshing view
   Of Jesus and his word?

What peaceful hours I once enjoyed!
   How sweet their memory still!   10
But they have left an aching void,
   The world can never fill.

Return, O holy Dove, return,
   Sweet messenger of rest!
I hate the sins that made thee mourn,   15
   And drove thee from my breast.

The dearest idol I have known,
   Whate'er that idol be,
Help me to tear it from thy throne,
   And worship only Thee.   20

So shall my walk be close with God,
   Calm and serene my frame;
So purer light shall mark the road
   That leads me to the Lamb.

84b. *Jehovah-Shammah*

Ezekiel xlviii. 35

As birds their infant brood protect,
And spread their wings to shelter them,
Thus saith the Lord to his elect,
So will I guard Jerusalem.

And what then is Jerusalem,   5
This darling object of his care?
Where is its worth in God's esteem?
Who built it? who inhabits there?

Jehovah founded it in blood,
The blood of his incarnate Son;   10
There dwell the saints, once foes to God,
The sinners whom he calls his own.

There, though besieged on every side,
Yet much beloved, and guarded well,
From age to age they have defied   15
The utmost force of earth and hell.

Let earth repent, and hell despair,
This city has a sure defence;
Her name is called, 'The Lord is there',
And who has power to drive him thence?   20

84c. *Praise for the Fountain Opened*

Zechariah xiii. 1

There is a fountain filled with blood
    Drawn from Emmanuel's veins;
And sinners, plunged beneath that flood,
    Lose all their guilty stains.

The dying thief rejoiced to see   5
    That fountain in his day;
And there have I, as vile as he,
    Washed all my sins away.

Dear dying Lamb, thy precious blood
    Shall never lose its power,   10
Till all the ransomed church of God
    Be saved, to sin no more.

E'er since, by faith, I saw the stream
    Thy flowing wounds supply,
Redeeming love has been my theme,   15
    And shall be till I die.

Then in a nobler, sweeter song,
    I'll sing thy power to save;
When this poor lisping stammering tongue
    Lies silent in the grave.   20

Lord, I believe thou hast prepared
    (Unworthy though I be)
For me a blood-bought free reward,
    A golden harp for me!

'Tis strung and tuned for endless years,   25
    And formed by power divine,
To sound in God the Father's ears
    No other name but thine.

84d. *Old Testament Gospel*

Hebrews iv. 2

    Israel in ancient days
    Not only had a view
    Of Sinai in a blaze,
    But learned the Gospel too;
The types and figures were a glass,   5
In which they saw the Saviour's face.

    The paschal sacrifice
    And blood-besprinkled door,
    Seen with enlightened eyes,
    And once applied with power,   10
Would teach the need of other blood,
To reconcile an angry God.

The Lamb, the Dove, set forth
His perfect innocence,
Whose blood of matchless worth 15
Should be the soul's defence;
For he who can for sin atone,
Must have no failings of his own.

The scape-goat on his head
The people's trespass bore, 20
And to the desert led,
Was to be seen no more:
In him our Surety seemed to say,
'Behold, I bear your sins away.'

Dipt in his fellow's blood, 25
The living bird went free;
The type, well understood,
Expressed the sinner's plea;
Described a guilty soul enlarged,
And by a Saviour's death discharged. 30

Jesus, I love to trace,
Throughout the sacred page,
The footsteps of thy grace,
The same in every age!
O grant that I may faithful be 35
To clearer light vouchsafed to me!

84e. *The Shining Light*

My former hopes are fled,
My terror now begins;
I feel, alas! that I am dead
In trespasses and sins.

Ah, whither shall I fly? 5
I hear the thunder roar;
The Law proclaims destruction nigh,
And vengeance at the door.

When I review my ways,
I dread impending doom: 10
But sure a friendly whisper says,
'Flee from the wrath to come.'

I see, or think I see,
A glimmering from afar;
A beam of day, that shines for me,   15
To save me from despair.

Forerunner of the sun,
It marks the pilgrim's way;
I'll gaze upon it while I run,
And watch the rising day.   20

84f. *Light Shining out of Darkness*

God moves in a mysterious way
    His wonders to perform;
He plants his footsteps in the sea,
    And rides upon the storm.

Deep in unfathomable mines   5
    Of never-failing skill,
He treasures up his bright designs,
    And works his sovereign will.

Ye fearful saints, fresh courage take,
    The clouds ye so much dread   10
Are big with mercy, and shall break
    In blessings on your head.

Judge not the Lord by feeble sense,
    But trust him for his grace;
Behind a frowning providence   15
    He hides a smiling face.

His purposes will ripen fast,
    Unfolding every hour;
The bud may have a bitter taste,
    But sweet will be the flower.   20

Blind unbelief is sure to err,
    And scan his work in vain:
God is his own interpreter,
    And He will make it plain.

84g. *Mourning and Longing*

The Saviour hides his face!
  My spirit thirsts to prove
Renewed supplies of pardoning grace,
  And never-fading love.

The favoured souls who know   5
  What glories shine in him,
Pant for his presence as the roe
  Pants for the living stream.

What trifles tease me now!
  They swarm like summer flies;   10
They cleave to every thing I do,
  And swim before my eyes.

How dull the sabbath day,
  Without the sabbath's Lord!
How toilsome then to sing and pray,   15
  And wait upon the Word!

Of all the truths I hear,
  How few delight my taste!
I glean a berry here and there,
  But mourn the vintage past.   20

Yet let me (as I ought)
  Still hope to be supplied;
No pleasure else is worth a thought,
  Nor shall I be denied.

Though I am but a worm,   25
  Unworthy of his care,
The Lord will my desire perform,
  And grant me all my prayer.

84h. *Joy and Peace in Believing*

Sometimes a light surprises
  The Christian while he sings;
It is the Lord who rises
  With healing on his wings:

When comforts are declining,   5
    He grants the soul again
A season of clear shining,
    To cheer it after rain.

In holy contemplation
    We sweetly then pursue   10
The theme of God's salvation,
    And find it ever new;
Set free from present sorrow,
    We cheerfully can say,
E'en let the unknown to-morrow   15
    Bring with it what it may!

It can bring with it nothing,
    But He will bear us through;
Who gives the lilies clothing,
    Will clothe his people too;   20
Beneath the spreading heavens
    No creature but is fed;
And He who feeds the ravens
    Will give his children bread.

Though vine nor fig tree neither   25
    Their wonted fruit shall bear,
Though all the field should wither,
    Nor flocks nor herds be there:
Yet God the same abiding,
    His praise shall tune my voice;   30
For, while in him confiding,
    I cannot but rejoice.

85. from *The Task*

from *Book III, The Garden*

As one whom long in thickets and in brakes
Entangled, winds now this way and now that
His devious course uncertain, seeking home;
Or, having long in miry ways been foiled
And sore discomfited, from slough to slough   5

Plunging, and half despairing of escape,
If chance at length he find a green-sward smooth
And faithful to the foot, his spirits rise,
He chirrups brisk his ear-erecting steed,
And winds his way with pleasure and with ease;   10
So I, designing other themes, and called
To adorn the Sofa with eulogium due,
To tell its slumbers and to paint its dreams,
Have rambled wide. In country, city, seat
Of academic fame, (howe'er deserved,)   15
Long held, and scarcely disengaged at last.
But now, with pleasant pace, a cleanlier road
I mean to tread. I feel myself at large,
Courageous, and refreshed for future toil,
If toil await me, or if dangers new.   20
    Since pulpits fail, and sounding-boards reflect
Most part an empty ineffectual sound,
What chance that I, to fame so little known,
Nor conversant with men or manners much,
Should speak to purpose, or with better hope   25
Crack the satiric thong? 'Twere wiser far
For me enamoured of sequestered scenes,
And charmed with rural beauty, to repose
Where chance may throw me, beneath elm or vine,
My languid limbs when summer sears the plains,   30
Or when rough winter rages, on the soft
And sheltered Sofa, while the nitrous air
Feeds a blue flame and makes a cheerful hearth;
There undisturbed by Folly, and apprized
How great the danger of disturbing her,   35
To muse in silence, or at least confine
Remarks that gall so many, to the few
My partners in retreat. Disgust concealed
Is oft-times proof of wisdom, when the fault
Is obstinate, and cure beyond our reach.   40
    Domestic happiness, thou only bliss
Of Paradise that has survived the fall!
Though few now taste thee unimpaired and pure,
Or tasting, long enjoy thee, too infirm
Or too incautious to preserve thy sweets   45
Unmixt with drops of bitter, which neglect
Or temper sheds into thy crystal cup;
Thou art the nurse of virtue. In thine arms

She smiles, appearing, as in truth she is,
Heaven-born and destined to the skies again.   50
Thou art not known where Pleasure is adored,
That reeling goddess with the zoneless waist
And wandering eyes, still leaning on the arm
Of Novelty, her fickle frail support;
For thou art meek and constant, hating change,   55
And finding in the calm of truth-tied love
Joys that her stormy raptures never yield.
Forsaking thee, what shipwreck have we made
Of honour, dignity, and fair renown,
Till prostitution elbows us aside   60
In all our crowded streets, and senates seem
Convened for purposes of empire less,
Than to release the adult'ress from her bond.
The adulteress! what a theme for angry verse,
What provocation to the indignant heart   65
That feels for injured love! but I disdain
The nauseous task to paint her as she is,
Cruel, abandoned, glorying in her shame.
No. Let her pass, and charioted along
In guilty splendour, shake the public ways!   70
The frequency of crimes has washed them white;
And verse of mine shall never brand the wretch,
Whom matrons now of character unsmirched
And chaste themselves, are not ashamed to own.
Virtue and vice had boundaries in old time   75
Not to be passed; and she that had renounced
Her sex's honour, was renounced herself
By all that prized it; not for prudery's sake,
But dignity's, resentful of the wrong.
'Twas hard perhaps on here and there a waif   80
Desirous to return and not received;
But was an wholesome rigour in the main,
And taught the unblemished to preserve with care
That purity, whose loss was loss of all.
Men too were nice in honour in those days,   85
And judged offenders well. And he that sharped,
And pocketed a prize by fraud obtained,
Was marked and shunned as odious. He that sold
His country, or was slack when she required
His every nerve in action and at stretch,   90
Paid with the blood that he had basely spared,

The price of his default. But now, yes, now
We are become so candid and so fair,
So liberal in construction, and so rich
In Christian charity, (good-natured age)   95
That they are safe, sinners of either sex,
Transgress what laws they may. Well dressed, well bred,
Well equipaged, is ticket good enough
To pass us readily through every door.
Hypocrisy, detest her as we may,   100
(And no man's hatred ever wronged her yet,)
May claim this merit still, that she admits
The worth of what she mimics with such care,
And thus gives virtue indirect applause;
But she has burnt her mask not needed here,   105
Where vice has such allowance, that her shifts
And specious semblances have lost their use.
  I was a stricken deer that left the herd
Long since; with many an arrow deep infixed
My panting side was charged, when I withdrew   110
To seek a tranquil death in distant shades.
There was I found by one who had himself
Been hurt by the archers. In his side he bore
And in his hands and feet the cruel scars.
With gentle force soliciting the darts   115
He drew them forth, and healed, and bade me live.
Since then, with few associates, in remote
And silent woods I wander, far from those
My former partners of the peopled scene,
With few associates, and not wishing more.   120
Here much I ruminate, as much I may,
With other views of men and manners now
Than once, and others of a life to come.
I see that all are wanderers, gone astray,
Each in his own delusions; they are lost   125
In chase of fancied happiness, still wooed
And never won. Dream after dream ensues,
And still they dream that they shall still succeed,
And still are disappointed; rings the world
With the vain stir. I sum up half mankind,   130
And add two-thirds of the remaining half,
And find the total of their hopes and fears
Dreams, empty dreams. The million flit as gay
As if created only, like the fly

That spreads his motley wings in the eye of noon,   135
To sport their season and be seen no more.
The rest are sober dreamers, grave and wise,
And pregnant with discoveries new and rare.
Some write a narrative of wars and feats
Of heroes little known, and call the rant   140
An history; describe the man, of whom
His own coevals took but little note,
And paint his person, character and views,
As they had known him from his mother's womb.
They disentangle from the puzzled skein   145
In which obscurity has wrapped them up,
The threads of politic and shrewd design
That ran through all his purposes, and charge
His mind with meanings that he never had,
Or having, kept concealed. Some drill and bore   150
The solid earth, and from the strata there
Extract a register, by which we learn
That He who made it and revealed its date
To Moses, was mistaken in its age.
Some more acute and more industrious still   155
Contrive creation; travel nature up
To the sharp peak of her sublimest height,
And tell us whence the stars; why some are fixt,
And planetary some; what gave them first
Rotation, from what fountain flowed their light.   160
Great contest follows, and much learnèd dust
Involves the combatants, each claiming truth,
And truth disclaiming both. And thus they spend
The little wick of life's poor shallow lamp,
In playing tricks with nature, giving laws   165
To distant worlds and trifling in their own . . . .

86. Yardley Oak

Survivor sole, and hardly such, of all
That once lived here, thy brethren, at my birth,
(Since which I number threescore winters past)
A shattered veteran, hollow-trunked perhaps,
As now, and with excoriate forks deform,   5
Relics of ages! Could a mind, imbued

With truth from Heaven, created thing adore,
I might with reverence kneel, and worship thee.
　　It seems idolatry, with some excuse,
When our forefather Druids in their oaks　　　　　　　　　　10
Imagined sanctity. The conscience, yet
Unpurified by an authentic act
Of amnesty, the meed of blood divine,
Loved not the light, but, gloomy, into gloom
Of thickest shades, like Adam after taste　　　　　　　　　15
Of fruit proscribed, as to a refuge, fled.
　　Thou wast a bauble once; a cup and ball,
Which babes might play with; and the thievish jay,
Seeking her food, with ease might have purloined
The auburn nut that held thee, swallowing down　　　　　20
Thy yet close-folded latitude of boughs
And all thine embryo vastness at a gulp.
But Fate thy growth decreed; autumnal rains
Beneath thy parent tree mellowed the soil
Designed thy cradle; and a skipping deer,　　　　　　　　25
With pointed hoof dibbling the glebe, prepared
The soft receptacle, in which, secure,
Thy rudiments should sleep the winter through.
　　So fancy dreams. Disprove it, if ye can,
Ye reasoners broad awake, whose busy search　　　　　　30
Of argument, employed too oft amiss,
Sifts half the pleasures of short life away!
　　Thou fell'st mature; and in the loamy clod
Swelling with vegetative force instinct
Didst burst thine egg, as theirs the fabled Twins,　　　. 35
Now stars; two lobes, protruding, paired exact;
A leaf succeeded, and another leaf,
And, all the elements thy puny growth
Fostering propitious, thou becamest a twig.
　　Who lived when thou wast such? Oh, couldst thou speak,　　40
As in Dodona once thy kindred trees
Oracular, I would not curious ask
The future, best unknown, but at thy mouth
Inquisitive, the less ambiguous past.
　　By thee I might correct, erroneous oft,　　　　　　　　45
The clock of history, facts and events
Timing more punctual, unrecorded facts
Recovering, and misstated setting right –
Desperate attempt, till trees shall speak again!

Time made thee what thou wast, king of the woods;　　　50
And Time hath made thee what thou art – a cave
For owls to roost in. Once thy spreading boughs
O'erhung the champaign; and the numerous flocks,
That grazed it, stood beneath that ample cope
Uncrowded, yet safe-sheltered from the storm.　　　55
No flock frequents thee now. Thou hast outlived
Thy popularity, and art become
(Unless verse rescue thee awhile) a thing
Forgotten, as the foliage of thy youth.
　　While thus through all the stages thou hast pushed　　　60
Of treeship – first a seedling, hid in grass;
Then twig; then sapling; and, as century rolled
Slow after century, a giant-bulk
Of girth enormous, with moss-cushioned root
Upheaved above the soil, and sides embossed　　　65
With prominent wens globose – till at the last
The rottenness, which time is charged to inflict
On other mighty ones, found also thee.
　　What exhibitions various hath the world
Witnessed of mutability in all　　　70
That we account most durable below!
Change is the diet, on which all subsist,
Created changeable, and change at last
Destroys them. Skies uncertain now the heat
Transmitting cloudless, and the solar beam　　　75
Now quenching in a boundless sea of clouds, –
Calm and alternate storm, moisture and drought,
Invigorate by turns the springs of life
In all that live, plant, animal, and man,
And in conclusion mar them. Nature's threads,　　　80
Fine passing thought, e'en in her coarsest works,
Delight in agitation, yet sustain
The force, that agitates, not unimpaired;
But, worn by frequent impulse, to the cause
Of their best tone their dissolution owe.　　　85
　　Thought cannot spend itself, comparing still
The great and little of thy lot, thy growth
From almost nullity into a state
Of matchless grandeur, and declension thence,
Slow, into such magnificent decay.　　　90
Time was, when, settling on thy leaf, a fly
Could shake thee to the root – and time has been

When tempests could not. At thy firmest age
Thou hadst within thy bole solid contents,
That might have ribbed the sides and planked the deck   95
Of some flagged admiral; and tortuous arms,
The shipwright's darling treasure, didst present
To the four-quartered winds, robust and bold,
Warped into tough knee-timber, many a load!
But the axe spared thee. In those thriftier days   100
Oaks fell not, hewn by thousands, to supply
The bottomless demands of contest, waged
For senatorial honours. Thus to Time
The task was left to whittle thee away
With his sly scythe, whose ever-nibbling edge,   105
Noiseless, an atom and an atom more
Disjoining from the rest, has, unobserved,
Achieved a labour, which had far and wide,
By man performed, made all the forest ring.
    Embowelled now, and of thy ancient self   110
Possessing nought but the scooped rind, that seems
A huge throat, calling to the clouds for drink,
Which it would give in rivulets to thy root,
Thou temptest none, but rather much forbidd'st
The feller's toil, which thou couldst ill requite.   115
Yet is thy root sincere, sound as the rock,
A quarry of stout spurs, and knotted fangs,
Which, crook'd into a thousand whimsies, clasp
The stubborn soil, and hold thee still erect.
    So stands a kingdom, whose foundation yet   120
Fails not, in virtue and in wisdom laid,
Though all the superstructure, by the tooth
Pulverised of venality, a shell
Stands how, and semblance only of itself!
    Thine arms have left thee. Winds have rent them off   125
Long since, and rovers of the forest wild
With bow and shaft, have burnt them. Some have left
A splintered stump, bleached to a snowy white;
And some, memorial none, where once they grew.
Yet life still lingers in thee, and puts forth   130
Proof not contemptible of what she can,
Even where death predominates. The spring
Finds thee not less alive to her sweet force,
Than yonder upstarts of the neighbouring wood,
So much thy juniors, who their birth received   135

Half a millennium since the date of thine.
  But since, although well qualified by age
To teach, no spirit dwells in thee, nor voice
May be expected from thee, seated here
On thy distorted root, with hearers none,   140
Or prompter, save the scene, I will perform
Myself the oracle, and will discourse
In my own ear such matter as I may.
  One man alone, the father of us all,
Drew not his life from woman; never gazed,   145
With mute unconsciousness of what he saw,
On all around him; learn'd not by degrees,
Nor owed articulation to his ear;
But, moulded by his Maker into man
At once, upstood intelligent, surveyed   150
All creatures, with precision understood
Their purport, uses, properties, assigned
To each his name significant, and filled
With love and wisdom, rendered back to Heaven
In praise harmonious the first air he drew.   155
He was excused the penalties of dull
Minority. No tutor charged his hand
With the thought-tracing quill, or tasked his mind
With problems. History, not wanted yet,
Leaned on her elbow, watching Time, whose course,   160
Eventful, should supply her with a theme;

James Macpherson (1736–1796)

87. from *Carrick-Thura*

87a. *'Autumn is dark on the mountains'*

Autumn is dark on the mountains; grey mist rests on the hills. The whirl-
wind is heard on the heath. Dark rolls the river through the narrow plain.
A tree stands alone on the hill, and marks the grave of Connal. The leaves
whirl round with the wind, and strew the graves of the dead. At times are
seen here the ghosts of the deceased, when the musing hunter alone stalks
slowly over the heath. *Appear in thy armour of light, thou ghost of the mighty*

Connal! Shine, near thy tomb, Crimora! like a moon-beam from a cloud.

Who can search the source of thy race, O Connal? and who recount thy fathers? Thy family grew like an oak on the mountain, which meeteth the wind with its lofty head. But now it is torn from the earth. Who shall supply the place of Connal?

Here was the din of arms; and here the groans of the dying. Mournful are the wars of Fingal! O Connal! it was here thou didst fall. Thine arm was like a storm; thy sword, a beam of the sky; thy height, a rock on the plain; thine eyes, a furnace of fire. Louder than a storm was thy voice, when thou confoundedst the field. Warriors fell by thy sword, as the thistle by the staff of a boy.

Dargo the mighty came on, like a cloud of thunder. His brows were contracted and dark. His eyes like two caves in a rock. Bright rose their swords on each side; dire was the clang of their steel.

The daughter of Rinval was near; Crimora, bright in the armour of man; her hair loose behind, her bow in her hand. She followed the youth to the war, Connal her much-beloved. She drew the string on Dargo; but erring pierced her Connal. He falls like an oak on the plain; like a rock from the shaggy hill. What shall she do, hapless maid! He bleeds; her Connal dies. All the night long she cries, and all the day, O Connal, my love, and my friend! With grief the sad mourner died.

Earth here incloseth the loveliest pair on the hill. The grass grows between the stones of their tomb; I sit in the mournful shade. The wind sighs through the grass; and their memory rushes on my mind. Undisturbed you now sleep together; in the tomb of the mountain you rest alone.

87b. *Fragment of a Northern Tale*

Where Harold, with golden hair, spread o'er Lochlin his high commands; where, with justice, he ruled the tribes, who sunk, subdued, beneath his sword; abrupt rises Gormal in snow! The tempests roll dark on his sides, but calm, above, his vast forehead appears. White-issuing from the skirt of his storms, the troubled torrents pour down his sides. Joining, as they roar along, they bear the Torno, in foam, to the main.

Grey on the bank and far from men, half-covered by ancient pines from the wind, a lonely pile exalts its head, long-shaken by the storms of the north. To this fled Sigurd, fierce in fight, from Harold the leader of armies, when fate had brightened his spear with renown: When he conquered in that rude field, where Lulan's warriors fell in blood, or rose, in terror, on the waves of the main. Darkly sat the grey-haired chief; yet sorrow dwelt not in his soul. But when the warrior thought on the past, his proud heart heaved against his side: Forth flew his sword from its place, he wounded Harold in all the winds.

One daughter, and only one, but bright in form and mild of soul, the last beam of the setting line, remained to Sigurd of all his race. His son, in Lulan's battle slain, beheld not his father's flight from his foes. Nor finished seemed the ancient line! The splendid beauty of bright-eyed Fithon covered still the fallen king with renown. Her arm was white like Gormal's snow; her bosom whiter than the foam of the main, when roll the waves beneath the wrath of the winds. Like two stars were her radiant eyes, like two stars that rise on the deep, when dark tumult embroils the night. Pleasant are their beams aloft, as stately they ascend the skies.

Nor Odin forgot, in aught, the maid. Her form scarce equalled her lofty mind. Awe moved around her stately steps. Heroes loved – but shrunk away in their fears. Yet midst the pride of all her charms, her heart was soft, and her soul was kind. She saw the mournful with tearful eyes. Transient darkness arose in her breast. Her joy was in the chase. Each morning, when doubtful light wandered dimly on Lulan's waves, she roused the resounding woods, to Gormal's head of snow. Nor moved the maid alone, etc.

87c. *Oina-Morul: a poem*

As flies the inconstant sun, over Larmon's grassy hill; so pass the tales of old, along my soul, by night! When bards are removed to their place; when harps are hung in Selma's hall; then comes a voice to Ossian, and awakes his soul! It is the voice of years that are gone! they roll before me, with all their deeds! I seize the tales, as they pass, and pour them forth in song. Not a troubled stream is the song of the king, it is like the rising of music from Lutha of the strings. Lutha of many strings, not silent are thy streamy rocks, when the white hands of Malvina move upon the harp! Light of the shadowy thoughts, that fly across my soul, daughter of Toscar of helmets, wilt thou not hear the song! We call back, maid of Lutha, the years that have rolled away.

It was in the days of the king, while yet my locks were young, that I marked Con-cathlin, on high, from ocean's nightly wave. My course was towards the isle of Fuärfed, woody dweller of seas! Fingal had sent me to the aid of Mal-orchol, king of Fuärfed wild: for war was around him, and our fathers had met, at the feast.

In Col-coiled, I bound my sails; I sent my sword to Mal-orchol of shells. He knew the signal of Albion, and his joy arose. He came from his own high hail, and seized my hand in grief. 'Why comes the race of heroes to a falling king? Ton-thormod of many spears is the chief of wavy Sar-dronlo. He saw and loved my daughter, white-bosomed Oina-morul. He sought; I denied the maid; for our fathers had been foes. He came, with battle, to Fuärfed; my people are rolled away. Why comes the race of heroes to a falling king?'

'I come not,' I said, 'to look, like a boy, on the strife. Fingal remembers Mal-orchol, and his hall for strangers. From his waves, the warrior descended, on thy woody isle. Thou wert no cloud before him. Thy feast was spread with songs. For this my sword shall rise; and thy foes perhaps may fail. Our friends are not forgot in their danger, though distant is our land.'

'Descendant of the daring Trenmor, thy words are like the voice of Cruthloda, when he speaks, from his parting cloud, strong dweller of the sky! Many have rejoiced at my feast; but they all have forgot Mal-orchol. I have looked towards all the winds; but no white sails were seen. But steel resounds in my hall; and not the joyful shells. Come to my dwelling, race of heroes; dark-skirted night is near. Hear the voice of songs, from the maid of Fuärfed wild.'

We went. On the harp arose the white hands of Oina-morul. She waked her own sad tale, from every trembling string. I stood in silence; for bright in her locks was the daughter of many isles! Her eyes were two stars, looking forward through a rushing shower. The mariner marks them on high, and blesses the lovely beams. With morning we rushed to battle, to Tormul's resounding stream: the foe moved to the sound of Ton-thormod's bossy shield. From wing to wing the strife was mixed. I met Ton-thormod in fight. Wide flew his broken steel. I seized the king in war. I gave his hand, bound fast with thongs, to Mal-orchol, the giver of shells. Joy rose at the feast of Fuärfed; for the foe had failed. Ton-thormod turned his face away, from Oina-morul of isles!

'Son of Fingal,' begun Mal-orchol, 'not forgot shalt thou pass from me. A light shall dwell in thy ship, Oina-morul of slow-rolling eyes. She shall kindle gladness, along thy mighty soul. Nor unheeded shall the maid move in Selma, through the dwelling of kings!'

In the hall I lay in night. Mine eyes were half-closed in sleep. Soft music came to mine ear: it was like the rising breeze, that whirls, at first, the thistle's beard; then flies, dark-shadowy, over the grass. It was the maid of Fuärfed wild! she raised the nightly song; she knew that my soul was a stream, that flowed at pleasant sounds. 'Who looks,' she said, 'from his rock, on ocean's closing mist? His long locks, like the raven's wing, are wandering on the blast. Stately are his steps in grief! The tears are in his eyes! His manly breast is heaving over his bursting soul! Retire, I am distant far; a wanderer in lands unknown. Though the race of kings are around me, yet my soul is dark. Why have our fathers been foes, Ton-thormod, love of maids!'

'Soft voice of the streamy isle,' I said, 'why dost thou mourn by night? The race of daring Trenmor are not the dark in soul. Thou shalt not wander, by streams unknown, blue-eyed Oina-morul! Within this bosom is a voice; it comes not to other ears: it bids Ossian hear the hapless, in their hour of woe. Retire, soft singer by night; Ton-thormod shall not mourn on his rock!'

With morning I loosed the king. I gave the long-haired maid. Mal-orchol heard my words, in the midst of his echoing halls. 'King of Fuärfed wild, why should Ton-thormod mourn? He is of the race of heroes, and a flame in war. Your fathers have been foes, but now their dim ghosts rejoice in death. They stretch their hands of mist to the same shell in Loda. Forget their rage, ye warriors, it was the cloud of other years.'

Such were the deeds of Ossian, while yet his locks were young: though loveliness, with a robe of beams, clothed the daughter of many isles. We call back, maid of Lutha, the years that have rolled away!

87d. *The War of Inis-Thona: a poem*

Our youth is like the dream of the hunter on the hill of heath. He sleeps in the mild beams of the sun; he awakes amidst a storm; the red lightning flies around: trees shake their heads to the wind! He looks back, with joy, on the day of the sun, and the pleasant dreams of his rest! When shall Ossian's youth return? When his ear delight in the sound of arms? When shall I, like Oscar, travel in the light of my steel! Come, with your streams, ye hills of Cona! listen to the voice of Ossian. The song rises, like the sun, in my soul. I feel the joys of other times!

I behold thy towers, O Selma! the oaks of thy shaded wall: thy streams sound in my ear; thy heroes gather around. Fingal sits in the midst. He leans on the shield of Trenmor: his spear stands against the wall; he listens to the song of his bards. The deeds of his arm are heard; the actions of the king in his youth! Oscar had returned from the chase, and heard the hero's praise. He took the shield of Branno from the wall; his eyes were filled with tears. Red was the cheek of youth. His voice was trembling, low. My spear shook its bright head in his hand: he spoke to Morven's king.

'Fingal! thou king of heroes! Ossian, next to him in war! Ye have fought in your youth; your names are renowned in song. Oscar is like the mist of Cona; I appear, and I vanish away: The bard will not know my name. The hunter will not search in the heath for my tomb. Let me fight, O heroes, in the battle of Inis-thona. Distant is the land of my war! ye shall not hear of Oscar's fall! Some bard may find me there; some bard may give my name to song. The daughter of the stranger shall see my tomb, and weep over the youth, that came from afar. The bard shall say, at the feast, "Hear the song of Oscar from the distant land!"'

'Oscar,' replied the king of Morven, 'thou shalt fight, son of my fame! Prepare my dark-bosomed ship to carry my hero to Inis-thona. Son of my son, regard our fame; thou art of the race of renown! Let not the children of strangers say, feeble are the sons of Morven! Be thou, in battle, a roaring storm; mild as the evening sun in peace! Tell, Oscar, to Inis-thona's king, that Fingal remembers his youth; when we strove in the combat together, in the days of Agandecca.'

They lifted up the sounding sail; the wind whistled through the thongs of their masts. Waves lash the oozy rocks; the strength of ocean roars. My son beheld, from the wave, the land of groves. He rushed into Runa's sounding bay, and sent his sword to Annir of spears. The grey-haired hero rose, when he saw the sword of Fingal. His eyes were full of tears; he remembered his battles in youth. Twice had they lifted the spear, before the lovely Agandecca: heroes stood far distant, as if two spirits were striving in winds.

'But now,' began the king, 'I am old; the sword lies useless in my hall. Thou, who art of Morven's race! Annir has seen the battle of spears; but now he is pale and withered, like the oak of Lano. I have no son to meet thee with joy, to bring thee to the halls of his fathers. Argon is pale in the tomb, and Ruro is no more.

'My daughter is in the hall of strangers: she longs to behold my tomb. Her spouse shakes ten thousand spears; he comes, a cloud of death from Lano. Come, to share the feast of Annir, son of echoing Morven!'

Three days they feasted together; on the fourth Annir heard the name of Oscar. They rejoiced in the shell. They pursued the boars of Runa. Beside the fount of mossy stones, the weary heroes rest. The tear steals in secret from Annir: he broke the rising sigh. 'Here darkly rest,' the hero said, 'the children of my youth. This stone is the tomb of Ruro; that tree sounds over the grave of Argon. Do ye hear my voice, O my sons, within your narrow house? Or do ye speak in these rustling leaves, when the winds of the desert rise?'

'King of Inis-thona,' said Oscar, 'how fell the children of youth? The wild boar rushes over their tombs, but he does not disturb their repose. They pursue deer formed of clouds, and bend their airy bow. They still love the sport of their youth; and mount the wind with joy.'

'Cormalo,' replied the king, 'is a chief of ten thousand spears. He dwells at the waters of Lano, which send forth the vapour of death. He came to Runa's echoing halls, and sought the honour of the spear. The youth was lovely as the first beam of the sun; few were they who could meet him in fight! My heroes yielded to Cormalo: my daughter was seized in his love. Argon and Ruro returned from the chace; the tears of their pride descend: they roll their silent eyes on Runa's heroes, who had yielded to a stranger. Three days they feasted with Cormalo: on the fourth young Argon fought. But who could fight with Argon! Cormalo is overcome. His heart swelled with the grief of pride; he resolved, in secret, to behold the death of my sons. They went to the hills of Runa: they pursued the dark-brown hinds. The arrow of Cormalo flew in secret: my children fell in blood. He came to the maid of his love; to Inis-thona's long-haired maid. They fled over the desert.

'Annir remained alone. Night came on, and day appeared; nor Argon's voice, nor Ruro's came. At length their much-loved dog was seen; the fleet and bounding Runar. He came into the hall and howled; and seemed to look toward the place of their fall. We followed him: we found them here: we laid them by this mossy stream. This is the haunt of Annir, when the chase of the hinds is past. I bend like the trunk of an aged oak; my tears for ever flow!'

'O Ronnan!' said the rising Oscar, 'Ogar, king of spears! call my heroes to my side, the sons of streamy Morven. To-day we go to Lano's water, that sends forth the vapour of death. Cormalo will not long rejoice: death is often at the point of our swords!'

They came over the desert like stormy clouds, when the winds roll them along the heath: their edges are tinged with lightning; the echoing groves foresee the storm! The horn of Oscar's battle is heard; Lano shook over all its waves. The children of the lake convened around the sounding shield of Cormalo. Oscar fought, as he was wont in war. Cormalo fell beneath his sword: the sons of dismal Lano fled to their secret vales! Oscar brought the daughter of Inis-thona to Annir's echoing halls. The face of age is bright with joy; he blest the king of swords!

How great was the joy of Ossian, when he beheld the distant sail of his son! it was like a cloud of light that rises in the east, when the traveller is sad in a land unknown; and dismal night, with her ghosts, is sitting around in shades! We brought him, with songs, to Selma's halls. Fingal spread the feast of shells. A thousand bards raised the name of Oscar: Morven answered to the sound. The daughter of Toscar was there; her voice was like the harp; when the distant sound comes, in the evening, on the soft-rustling breeze of the vale!

O lay me, ye that see the light, near some rock of my hills! let the thick hazels be around, let the rustling oak be near. Green be the place of my rest; let the sound of the distant torrent be heard. Daughter of Toscar, take the harp, and raise the lovely song of Selma; that sleep may overtake my soul in the midst of joy; that the dreams of my youth may return, and the days of the mighty Fingal. Selma! I behold thy towers, thy trees, thy shaded wall! I see the heroes of Morven; I hear the song of bards! Oscar lifts the sword of Cormalo; a thousand youths admire its studded thongs. They look with wonder on my son: They admire the strength of his arm. They mark the joy of his father's eyes; they long for an equal fame. And ye shall have your fame, O sons of streamy Morven! My soul is often brightened with song; I remember the friends of my youth. But sleep descends, in the sound of the harp! pleasant dreams begin to rise! Ye sons of the chace, stand far distant, nor disturb my rest. The bard of other times holds discourse with his fathers, the chiefs of the days of old! Sons of the chace, stand far distant! disturb not the dreams of Ossian!

Anna Letitia Barbauld (1743–1825)

88. The Rights of Woman

Yes, injured Woman! rise, assert thy right!
Woman! too long degraded, scorned, oppressed;
O born to rule in partial Law's despite,
Resume thy native empire o'er the breast!

Go forth arrayed in panoply divine;   5
That angel pureness which admits no stain;
Go, bid proud Man his boasted rule resign,
And kiss the golden sceptre of thy reign.

Go, gird thyself with grace; collect thy store
Of bright artillery glancing from afar;   10
Soft melting tones thy thundering cannon's roar,
Blushes and fears thy magazine of war.

Thy rights are empire: urge no meaner claim, –
Felt, not defined, and if debated, lost;
Like sacred myst'ries, which, withheld from fame,   15
Shunning discussion, are reverèd the most.

Try all that wit and art suggest to bend
Of thy imperial foe the stubborn knee;
Make treacherous man thy subject, not thy friend;
Thou may'st command, but never can'st be free.   20

Awe the licentious, and restrain the rude;
Soften the sullen, clear the cloudy brow:
Be, more than princes' gifts, thy favours sued; –
She hazards all, who will the least allow.

But hope not, courted idol of mankind,   25
On this proud eminence secure to stay;
Subduing and subdued, thou soon shalt find
Thy coldness soften, and thy pride give way.

Then, then, abandon each ambitious thought,
Conquest or rule thy heart shall feebly move,   30
In Nature's school, by her soft maxims taught,
That separate rights are lost in mutual love.

89. Washing-Day

– and their voice,
Turning again towards childish treble, pipes
And whistles in its sound –

The Muses are turned gossips; they have lost
The buskined step, and clear high-sounding phrase,
Language of gods. Come then, domestic Muse,
In slipshod measure loosely prattling on
Of farm or orchard, pleasant curds and cream,   5
Or drowning flies, or shoe lost in the mire
By little whimpering boy, with rueful face;
Come, Muse, and sing the dreaded Washing-Day.
Ye who beneath the yoke of wedlock bend,
With bowèd soul, full well ye ken the day   10
Which week, smooth sliding after week, brings on
Too soon; – for to that day nor peace belongs
Nor comfort; – ere the first gray streak of dawn,
The red-armed washers come and chase repose.
Nor pleasant smile, nor quaint device of mirth,   15
E'er visited that day: the very cat,
From the wet kitchen scared and reeking hearth,
Visits the parlour, – an unwonted guest.
The silent breakfast-meal is soon dispatched;
Uninterrupted, save by anxious looks   20
Cast at the lowering sky, if sky should lower.
From that last evil, O preserve us, heavens!
For should the skies pour down, adieu to all
Remains of quiet: then expect to hear
Of sad disasters, – dirt and gravel stains   25
Hard to efface, and loaded lines at once
Snapped short, – and linen-horse by dog thrown down,
And all the petty miseries of life.
Saints have been calm while stretched upon the rack,
And Guatimozin smiled on burning coals;   30

But never yet did housewife notable
Greet with a smile a rainy washing-day.
– But grant the welkin fair, require not thou
Who call'st thyself perchance the master there,
Or study swept, or nicely dusted coat, 35
Or usual 'tendance; – ask not, indiscreet,
Thy stockings mended, though the yawning rents
Gape wide as Erebus; nor hope to find
Some snug recess impervious: shouldst thou try
The 'customed garden walks, thine eye shall rue 40
The budding fragrance of thy tender shrubs,
Myrtle or rose, all crushed beneath the weight
Of coarse checked apron, – with impatient hand
Twitched off when showers impend: or crossing lines
Shall mar thy musings, as the wet cold sheet 45
Flaps in thy face abrupt. Woe to the friend
Whose evil stars have urged him forth to claim
On such a day the hospitable rites!
Looks, blank at best, and stinted courtesy,
Shall he receive. Vainly he feeds his hopes 50
With dinner of roast chicken, savoury pie,
Or tart or pudding: - pudding he nor tart
That day shall eat; nor, though the husband try,
Mending what can't be helped, to kindle mirth
From cheer deficient, shall his consort's brow 55
Clear up propitious: – the unlucky guest
In silence dines, and early slinks away.
I well remember, when a child, the awe
This day struck into me; for then the maids,
I scarce knew why, looked cross, and drove me from them: 60
Nor soft caress could I obtain, nor hope
Usual indulgencies; jelly or creams,
Relic of costly suppers, and set by
For me their petted one; or buttered toast,
When butter was forbid; or thrilling tale 65
Of ghost or witch, or murder – so I went
And sheltered me beside the parlour fire:
There my dear grandmother, eldest of forms,
Tended the little ones, and watched from harm,
Anxiously fond, though oft her spectacles 70
With elfin cunning hid, and oft the pins
Drawn from her ravelled stocking, might have soured
One less indulgent. –

At intervals my mother's voice was heard,
Urging dispatch: briskly the work went on,   75
All hands employed to wash, to rinse, to wring,
To fold, and starch, and clap, and iron, and plait.
Then would I sit me down, and ponder much
Why washings were. Sometimes through hollow bowl
Of pipe amused we blew, and sent aloft   80
The floating bubbles; little dreaming then
To see, Montgolfier, thy silken ball
Ride buoyant through the clouds – so near approach
The sports of children and the toils of men.
Earth, air, and sky, and ocean, hath its bubbles,   85
And verse is one of them – this most of all.

90. An Inventory of the Furniture in Dr Priestley's Study

A map of every country known,
With not a foot of land his own.
A list of folks that kicked a dust
On this poor globe, from Ptol. the First;
He hopes, – indeed it is but fair, –   5
Some day to get a corner there.
A group of all the British kings,
Fair emblem! on a packthread swings.
The Fathers, ranged in goodly row,
A decent, venerable show,   10
Writ a great while ago, they tell us,
And many an inch o'ertop their fellows.
A Juvenal to hunt for mottos;
And Ovid's tales of nymphs and grottos.
The meek-robed lawyers, all in white;   15
Pure as the lamb, – at least, to sight.
A shelf of bottles, jar and phial,
By which the rogues he can defy all, –
All filled with lightning keen and genuine,
And many a little imp he'll pen you in;   20
Which, like Le Sage's sprite, let out,
Among the neighbours makes a rout;
Brings down the lightning on their houses,
And kills their geese, and frights their spouses.
A rare thermometer, by which   25

He settles, to the nicest pitch,
The just degrees of heat, to raise
Sermons, or politics, or plays.
Papers and books, a strange mixed olio,
From shilling touch to pompous folio;   30
Answer, remark, reply, rejoinder,
Fresh from the mint, all stamped and coined here;
Like new-made glass, set by to cool,
Before it bears the workman's tool.
A blotted proof-sheet, wet from Bowling.   35
– 'How can a man his anger hold in?' –
Forgotten rimes, and college themes,
Worm-eaten plans, and embryo schemes; –
A mass of heterogeneous matter,
A chaos dark, nor land nor water; –   40
New books, like new-born infants, stand,
Waiting the printer's clothing hand; –
Others, a motley ragged brood,
Their limbs unfashioned all, and rude,
Like Cadmus' half-formed men appear;   45
One rears a helm, one lifts a spear,
And feet were lopped and fingers torn
Before their fellow limbs were born;
A leg began to kick and sprawl
Before the head was seen at all,   50
Which quiet as a mushroom lay
Till crumbling hillocks gave it way;
And all, like controversial writing,
Were born with teeth, and sprung up fighting.
    'But what is this,' I hear you cry,   55
'Which saucily provokes my eye?' –
A thing unknown, without a name,
Born of the air and doomed to flame.

Charlotte Smith (1749–1806)

91. Beachy Head

On thy stupendous summit, rock sublime!
That o'er the channel reared, halfway at sea
The mariner at early morning hails,
I would recline; while Fancy should go forth,
And represent the strange and awful hour   5
Of vast concussion; when the Omnipotent
Stretched forth his arm, and rent the solid hills,
Bidding the impetuous main flood rush between
The rifted shores, and from the continent
Eternally divided this green isle.   10
Imperial lord of the high southern coast!
From thy projecting headland I would mark
Far in the east the shades of night disperse,
Melting and thinned, as from the dark blue wave
Emerging, brilliant rays of arrowy light   15
Dart from the horizon; when the glorious sun
Just lifts above it his resplendent orb.
Advances now, with feathery silver touched,
The rippling tide of flood; glisten the sands,
While, inmates of the chalky clefts that scar   20
Thy sides precipitous, with shrill harsh cry,
Their white wings glancing in the level beam,
The terns, and gulls, and tarrocks, seek their food,
And thy rough hollows echo to the voice
Of the gray choughs, and ever restless daws,   25
With clamour, not unlike the chiding hounds,
While the lone shepherd, and his baying dog,
Drive to thy turfy crest his bleating flock.
The high meridian of the day is past,
And ocean now, reflecting the calm heaven,   30
Is of cerulean hue; and murmurs low
The tide of ebb, upon the level sands.
The sloop, her angular canvas shifting still,
Catches the light and variable airs
That but a little crisp the summer sea,   35

Dimpling its tranquil surface.
                  Afar off,
And just emerging from the arch immense
Where seem to part the elements, a fleet
Of fishing vessels stretch their lesser sails;   40
While more remote, and like a dubious spot
Just hanging in th' horizon, laden deep,
The ship of commerce richly freighted, makes
Her slower progress, on her distant voyage,
Bound to the orient climates, where the sun   45
Matures the spice within its odorous shell,
And, rivalling the gray worm's filmy toil,
Bursts from its pod the vegetable down;
Which in long turbaned wreaths, from torrid heat
Defends the brows of Asia's countless casts.   50
There the earth hides within her glowing breast
The beamy adamant, and the round pearl
Enchased in rugged covering; which the slave,
With perilous and breathless toil, tears off
From the rough sea-rock, deep beneath the waves.   55
These are the toys of nature; and her sport
Of little estimate in reason's eye:
And they who reason, with abhorrence see
Man, for such gauds and baubles, violate
The sacred freedom of his fellow man –   60
Erroneous estimate! As heaven's pure air,
Fresh as it blows on this aerial height,
Or sound of seas upon the stony strand,
Or inland, the gay harmony of birds,
And winds that wander in the leafy woods;   65
Are to the unadulterate taste more worth
Than the elaborate harmony, brought out
From fretted stop, or modulated airs
Of vocal science. – So the brightest gems,
Glancing resplendent on the regal crown,   70
Or trembling in the high born beauty's ear,
Are poor and paltry, to the lovely light
Of the fair star, that as the day declines,
Attendant on her queen, the crescent moon,
Bathes her bright tresses in the eastern wave.   75
For now the sun is verging to the sea,
And as he westward sinks, the floating clouds
Suspended, move upon the evening gale,

And gathering round his orb, as if to shade
The insufferable brightness, they resign   80
Their gauzy whiteness; and more warmed, assume
All hues of purple. There, transparent gold
Mingles with ruby tints, and sapphire gleams,
And colours, such as nature through her works
Shows only in the ethereal canopy.   85
Thither aspiring fancy fondly soars,
Wandering sublime through visionary vales,
Where bright pavilions rise, and trophies, fanned
By airs celestial; and adorned with wreaths
Of flowers that bloom amid Elysian bowers.   90
Now bright, and brighter still the colours glow,
Till half the lustrous orb within the flood
Seems to retire: the flood reflecting still
Its splendour, and in mimic glory dressed;
Till the last ray shot upward, fires the clouds   95
With blazing crimson; then in paler light,
Long lines of tenderer radiance, lingering yield
To partial darkness; and on the opposing side
The early moon distinctly rising, throws
Her pearly brilliance on the trembling tide.   100
The fishermen, who at set seasons pass
Many a league off at sea their toiling night,
Now hail their comrades, from their daily task
Returning; and make ready for their own,
With the night tide commencing. The night tide   105
Bears a dark vessel on, whose hull and sails
Mark her a coaster from the north. Her keel
Now ploughs the sand; and sidelong now she leans,
While with loud clamours her athletic crew
Unload her; and resounds the busy hum   110
Along the wave-worn rocks. Yet more remote,
Where the rough cliff hangs beetling o'er its base,
All breathes repose; the water's rippling sound
Scarce heard; but now and then the sea-snipe's cry
Just tells that something living is abroad;   115
And sometimes crossing on the moonbright line,
Glimmers the skiff, faintly discerned awhile,
Then lost in shadow.
                            Contemplation here,
High on her throne of rock, aloof may sit,   120
And bid recording memory unfold

Her scroll voluminous – bid her retrace
The period, when from Neustria's hostile shore
The Norman launched his galleys, and the bay
O'er which that mass of ruin frowns even now   125
In vain and sullen menace, then received
The new invaders; a proud martial race,
Of Scandinavia the undaunted sons,
Whom Dogon, Fier-a-bras, and Humfroi led
To conquest: while Trinacria to their power   130
Yielded her wheaten garland; and when thou,
Parthenope! within thy fertile bay
Received the victors.
                    In the mailèd ranks
Of Normans landing on the British coast   135
Rode Taillefer; and with astounding voice
Thundered the war song daring Roland sang
First in the fierce contention: vainly brave,
One not inglorious struggle England made –
But failing, saw the Saxon heptarchy   140
Finish for ever. Then the holy pile,
Yet seen upon the field of conquest, rose,
Where to appease heaven's wrath for so much blood,
The conqueror bade unceasing prayers ascend,
And requiems for the slayers and the slain.   145
But let not modern Gallia form from hence
Presumptuous hopes, that ever thou again,
Queen of the isles! shalt crouch to foreign arms.
The enervate sons of Italy may yield;
And the Iberian, all his trophies torn   150
And wrapped in superstition's monkish weed,
May shelter his abasement, and put on
Degrading fetters. Never, never thou!
Imperial mistress of the obedient sea;
But thou, in thy integrity secure,   155
Shalt now undaunted meet a world in arms.
    England! 'twas where this promontory rears
Its rugged brow above the channel wave,
Parting the hostile nations, that thy fame,
Thy naval fame was tarnished, at what time   160
Thou, leagued with the Batavian, gavest to France
One day of triumph – triumph the more loud,
Because even then so rare. Oh! well redeemed,
Since, by a series of illustrious men,

Such as no other country ever reared,   165
To vindicate her cause. It is a list
Which, as fame echoes it, blanches the cheek
Of bold Ambition; while the despot feels
The extorted sceptre tremble in his grasp.
From even the proudest roll by glory filled,   170
How gladly the reflecting mind returns
To simple scenes of peace and industry,
Where, bosomed in some valley of the hills
Stands the lone farm; its gate with tawny ricks
Surrounded, and with granaries and sheds,   175
Roofed with green mosses, and by elms and ash
Partially shaded; and not far removed
The hut of sea-flints built; the humble home
Of one, who sometimes watches on the heights,
When hid in the cold mist of passing clouds,   180
The flock, with dripping fleeces, are dispersed
O'er the wide down; then from some ridged point
That overlooks the sea, his eager eye
Watches the bark that for his signal waits
To land its merchandise: – quitting for this   185
Clandestine traffic his more honest toil,
The crook abandoning, he braves himself
The heaviest snow-storm of December's night,
When with conflicting winds the ocean raves,
And on the tossing boat, unfearing mounts   190
To meet the partners of the perilous trade,
And share their hazard. Well it were for him,
If no such commerce of destruction known,
He were content with what the earth affords
To human labour; even where she seems   195
Reluctant most. More happy is the hind,
Who, with his own hands rears on some black moor,
Or turbary, his independent hut
Covered with heather, whence the slow white smoke
Of smouldering peat arises. A few sheep,   200
His best possession, with his children share
The rugged shed when wintry tempests blow;
But, when with spring's return the green blades rise
Amid the russet heath, the household live
Joint tenants of the waste throughout the day,   205
And often, from her nest, among the swamps,
Where the gemmed sun-dew grows, or fringed buck bean

They scare the plover, that with plaintive cries
Flutters, as sorely wounded, down the wind.
Rude, and but just removed from savage life   210
Is the rough dweller among scenes like these,
(Scenes all unlike the poet's fabling dreams
Describing Arcady). But he is free,
The dread that follows on illegal acts
He never feels; and his industrious mate   215
Shares in his labour. Where the brook is traced
By crowding osiers, and the black coot hides
Among the plashy reeds, her diving brood,
The matron wades; gathering the long green rush
That well prepared hereafter lends its light   220
To her poor cottage, dark and cheerless else
Through the drear hours of winter. Otherwhile
She leads her infant group where charlock grows
'Unprofitably gay',° or to the fields,   [Goldsmith]
Where congregate the linnet and the finch,   225
That on the thistles, so profusely spread,
Feast in the desert; the poor family
Early resort, extirpating with care
These, and the gaudier mischief of the ground;
Then flames the high raised heap; seen afar off   230
Like hostile war-fires flashing to the sky.
Another task is theirs: on fields that show
As angry heaven had rained sterility,
Stony and cold, and hostile to the plough,
Where clamouring loud, the evening curlew runs   235
And drops her spotted eggs among the flints;
The mother and the children pile the stones
In rugged pyramids; and all this toil
They patiently encounter; well content
On their flock bed to slumber undisturbed   240
Beneath the smoky roof they call their own.
Oh! little knows the sturdy hind, who stands
Gazing, with looks where envy and contempt
Are often strangely mingled, on the car
Where prosperous fortune sits; what secret care   245
Or sick satiety is often hid,
Beneath the splendid outside. *He* knows not
How frequently the child of luxury
Enjoying nothing, flies from place to place
In chase of pleasure that eludes his grasp;   250

And that content is e'en less found by him,
Than by the labourer, whose pick-axe smooths
The road before his chariot; and who doffs
What *was* an hat; and as the train pass on,
Thinks how one day's expenditure, like this,   255
Would cheer him for long months, when to his toil
The frozen earth closes her marble breast.
    Ah! who *is* happy? Happiness! a word
That like false fire, from marsh effluvia born,
Misleads the wand'rer, destined to contend   260
In the world's wilderness, with want or woe –
Yet *they* are happy, who have never asked
What good or evil means. The boy
That on the river's margin gaily plays,
Has heard that death is there – he knows not death,   265
And therefore fears it not; and venturing in
He gains a bullrush, or a minnow – then,
At certain peril, for a worthless prize,
A crow's, or raven's nest, he climbs the boll
Of some tall pine; and of his prowess proud,   270
Is for a moment happy. Are *your* cares,
Ye who despise him, never worse applied?
The village girl is happy, who sets forth
To distant fair, gay in her Sunday suit,
With cherry coloured knots, and flourished shawl,   275
And bonnet newly purchased. So is he
Her little brother, who his mimic drum
Beats, till he drowns her rural lovers' oaths
Of constant faith, and still increasing love;
Ah! yet a while, and half those oaths believed,   280
Her happiness is vanished; and the boy
While yet a stripling, finds the sound he loved
Has led him on, till he has given up
His freedom, and his happiness together.
I once was happy, when while yet a child,   285
I learned to love these upland solitudes,
And, when elastic as the mountain air,
To my light spirit, care was yet unknown
And evil unforeseen. Early it came,
And childhood scarcely passed, I was condemned,   290
A guiltless exile, silently to sigh,
While memory, with faithful pencil, drew
The contrast; and regretting, I compared

With the polluted smoky atmosphere
And dark and stifling streets, the southern hills   295
That to the setting sun, their graceful heads
Rearing, o'erlook the frith, where Vecta breaks
With her white rocks, the strong impetuous tide,
When western winds the vast Atlantic urge
To thunder on the coast. Haunts of my youth!   300
Scenes of fond day-dreams, I behold ye yet!
Where 'twas so pleasant by thy northern slopes
To climb the winding sheep-path, aided oft
By scattered thorns: whose spiny branches bore
Small woolly tufts, spoils of the vagrant lamb   305
There seeking shelter from the noon-day sun;
And pleasant, seated on the short soft turf,
To look beneath upon the hollow way
While heavily upward moved the labouring wain,
And stalking slowly by, the sturdy hind   310
To ease his panting team, stopped with a stone
The grating wheel.
            Advancing higher still
The prospect widens, and the village church
But little, o'er the lowly roofs around   315
Rears its gray belfry, and its simple vane;
Those lowly roofs of thatch are half concealed
By the rude arms of trees, lovely in spring,
When on each bough, the rosy-tinctured bloom
Sits thick, and promises autumnal plenty.   320
For even those orchards round the Norman farms,
Which, as their owners mark the promised fruit,
Console them for the vineyards of the south,
Surpass not these.
           Where woods of ash, and beech,   325
And partial copses, fringe the green hill foot,
The upland shepherd rears his modest home,
There wanders by, a little nameless stream
That from the hill wells forth, bright now and clear,
Or after rain with chalky mixture gray,   330
But still refreshing in its shallow course,
The cottage garden; most for use designed,
Yet not of beauty destitute. The vine
Mantles the little casement; yet the briar
Drops fragrant dew among the July flowers;   335
And pansies rayed, and freaked and mottled pinks

Grow among balm, and rosemary and rue:
There honeysuckles flaunt, and roses blow
Almost uncultured: some with dark green leaves
Contrast their flowers of pure unsullied white;   340
Others, like velvet robes of regal state
Of richest crimson, while in thorny moss
Enshrined and cradled, the most lovely, wear
The hues of youthful beauty's glowing cheek –
With fond regret I recollect e'en now   345
In spring and summer, what delight I felt
Among these cottage gardens, and how much
Such artless nosegays, knotted with a rush
By village housewife or her ruddy maid,
Were welcome to me; soon and simply pleased.   350
   An early worshipper at nature's shrine,
I loved her rudest scenes – warrens, and heaths,
And yellow commons, and birch-shaded hollows,
And hedge rows, bordering unfrequented lanes
Bowered with wild roses, and the clasping woodbine   355
Where purple tassels of the tangling vetch
With bittersweet, and bryony inweave,
And the dew fills the silver bindweed's cups –
I loved to trace the brooks whose humid banks
Nourish the harebell, and the freckled pagil;   360
And stroll among o'ershadowing woods of beech,
Lending in Summer, from the heats of noon
A whispering shade; while haply there reclines
Some pensive lover of uncultured flowers,
Who, from the tumps with bright green mosses clad,   365
Plucks the wood sorrel, with its light thin leaves,
Heart-shaped, and triply folded; and its root
Creeping like beaded coral; or who there
Gathers, the copse's pride, anémones,
With rays like golden studs on ivory laid   370
Most delicate: but touched with purple clouds,
Fit crown for April's fair but changeful brow.
   Ah! hills so early loved! in fancy still
I breathe your pure keen air; and still behold
Those widely spreading views, mocking alike   375
The poet and the painter's utmost art.
And still, observing objects more minute,
Wondering remark the strange and foreign forms
Of sea-shells; with the pale calcareous soil

Mingled, and seeming of resembling substance.   380
Though surely the blue ocean (from the heights
Where the Downs westward trend, but dimly seen)
Here never rolled its surge. Does nature then
Mimic, in wanton mood, fantastic shapes
Of bivalves, and inwreathed volutes, that cling   385
To the dark sea-rock of the wat'ry world?
Or did this range of chalky mountains, once
Form a vast basin, where the ocean waves
Swelled fathomless? What time these fossil shells,
Buoyed on their native element, were thrown   390
Among the imbedding calx: when the huge hill
Its giant bulk heaved, and in strange ferment
Grew up a guardian barrier, 'twixt the sea
And the green level of the sylvan weald.
    Ah! very vain is science's proudest boast,   395
And but a little light its flame yet lends
To its most ardent votaries; since from whence
These fossil forms are seen, is but conjecture,
Food for vague theories, or vain dispute,
While to his daily task the peasant goes,   400
Unheeding such inquiry; with no care
But that the kindly change of sun and shower,
Fit for his toil the earth he cultivates.
As little recks the herdsman of the hill,
Who on some turfy knoll, idly reclined,   405
Watches his wether flock; that deep beneath
Rest the remains of men, of whom is left
No traces in the records of mankind,
Save what these half obliterated mounds
And half filled trenches doubtfully impart   410
To some lone antiquary; who on times remote,
Since which two thousand years have rolled away,
Loves to contemplate. He perhaps may trace,
Or fancy he can trace, the oblong square
Where the mailed legions, under Claudius, reared   415
The rampire, or excavated fossé delved;
What time the huge unwieldy elephant,
Auxiliary reluctant, hither led,
From Afric's forest glooms and tawny sands,
First felt the northern blast, and his vast frame   420
Sunk useless; whence in after ages found,
The wondering hinds, on those enormous bones

Gazed; and in giants dwelling on the hills
Believed and marvelled.
                  Hither, ambition, come!   425
Come and behold the nothingness of all
For which you carry through the oppressed earth,
War, and its train of horrors – see where tread
The innumerous hoofs of flocks above the works
By which the warrior sought to register   430
His glory, and immortalise his name –
The pirate Dane, who from his circular camp
Bore in destructive robbery, fire and sword
Down through the vale, sleeps unremembered here;
And here, beneath the green sward, rests alike   435
The savage native, who his acorn meal
Shared with the herds, that ranged the pathless woods;
And the centurion, who on these wide hills
Encamping, planted the imperial eagle.
All, with the lapse of time, have passed away,   440
Even as the clouds, with dark and dragon shapes,
Or like vast promontories crowned with towers,
Cast their broad shadows on the downs: then sail
Far to the northward, and their transient gloom
Is soon forgotten.   445
              But from thoughts like these,
By human crimes suggested, let us turn
To where a more attractive study courts
The wanderer of the hills; while shepherd girls
Will from among the fescue bring him flowers,   450
Of wonderous mockery; some resembling bees
In velvet vest, intent on their sweet toil,
While others mimic flies, that lightly sport
In the green shade, or float along the pool,
But here seem perched upon the slender stalk,   455
And gathering honey dew. While in the breeze
That wafts the thistle's plumèd seed along,
Blue bells wave tremulous. The mountain thyme
Purples the hassock of the heaving mole,
And the short turf is gay with tormentil,   460
And bird's foot trefoil, and the lesser tribes
Of hawkweed; spangling it with fringèd stars.
Near where a richer tract of cultured land
Slopes to the south; and burnished by the sun,
Bend in the gale of August, floods of corn;   465

The guardian of the flock, with watchful care,
Repels by voice and dog the encroaching sheep –
While his boy visits every wirèd trap
That scars the turf; and from the pit-falls takes
The timid migrants, who from distant wilds,   470
Warrens, and stone quarries, are destined thus
To lose their short existence. But unsought
By luxury yet, the shepherd still protects
The social bird, who from his native haunts
Of willowy current, or the rushy pool,   475
Follows the fleecy crowd, and flirts and skims,
In fellowship among them.
                                            Where the knoll
More elevated takes the changeful winds,
The windmill rears its vanes; and thitherward   480
With his white load, the master travelling,
Scares the rooks rising slow on whispering wings,
While o'er his head, before the summer sun
Lights up the blue expanse, heard more than seen,
The lark sings matins; and above the clouds   485
Floating, embathes his spotted breast in dew.
Beneath the shadow of a gnarlèd thorn,
Bent by the sea blast, from a seat of turf
With fairy nosegays strewn, how wide the view!
Till in the distant north it melts away,   490
And mingles indiscriminate with clouds:
But if the eye could reach so far, the mart
Of England's capital, its domes and spires
Might be perceived. Yet hence the distant range
Of Kentish hills, appear in purple haze;   495
And nearer, undulate the wooded heights,
And airy summits, that above the mole
Rise in green beauty; and the beaconed ridge
Of Blackdown shagged with heath, and swelling rude
Like a dark island from the vale; its brow   500
Catching the last rays of the evening sun
That gleam between the nearer park's old oaks,
Then lighten up the river, and make prominent
The portal, and the ruined battlements
Of that dismantled fortress; raised what time   505
The Conqueror's successors fiercely fought,
Tearing with civil feuds the desolate land.
But now a tiller of the soil dwells there,

And of the turret's looped and raftered halls
Has made an humbler homestead – where he sees,   510
Instead of armèd foemen, herds that graze
Along his yellow meadows; or his flocks
At evening from the upland driv'n to fold.
   In such a castellated mansion once
A stranger chose his home; and where hard by   515
In rude disorder fallen, and hid with brushwood
Lay fragments gray of towers and buttresses,
Among the ruins, often he would muse –
His rustic meal soon ended, he was wont
To wander forth, listening the evening sounds   520
Of rushing milldam, or the distant team,
Or night-jar, chasing fern-flies: the tired hind
Passed him at nightfall, wondering he should sit
On the hill top so late: they from the coast
Who sought bye paths with their clandestine load,   525
Saw with suspicious doubt, the lonely man
Cross on their way: but village maidens thought
His senses injured; and with pity say
That he, poor youth! must have been crossed in love –
For often, stretched upon the mountain turf   530
With folded arms, and eyes intently fixed
Where ancient elms and firs obscured a grange,
Some little space within the vale below,
They heard him, as complaining of his fate,
And to the murmuring wind, of cold neglect   535
And baffled hope he told. The peasant girls
These plaintive sounds remember, and even now
Among them may be heard the stranger's songs.

Were I a shepherd on the hill
   And ever as the mists withdrew   540
Could see the willows of the rill
Shading the footway to the mill
   Where once I walked with you –

And as away night's shadows sail,
   And sounds of birds and brooks arise,   545
Believe, that from the woody vale
I hear your voice upon the gale
   In soothing melodies;

And viewing from the Alpine height,
 The prospect dressed in hues of air,   550
Could say, while transient colours bright
Touched the fair scene with dewy light,
 'Tis, that *her* eyes are there!

I think, I could endure my lot
 And linger on a few short years,   555
And then, by all but you forgot,
Sleep, where the turf that clothes the spot
 May claim some pitying tears.

For 'tis not easy to forget
 One, who through life has loved you still,   560
And you, however late, might yet
With sighs to memory giv'n, regret
 The shepherd of the hill.

Yet otherwhile it seemed as if young hope
Her flattering pencil gave to fancy's hand,   565
And in his wanderings, reared to sooth his soul
Ideal bowers of pleasure. Then, of solitude
And of his hermit life, still more enamoured,
His home was in the forest; and wild fruits
And bread sustained him. There in early spring 570
The barkmen found him, e'er the sun arose,
There at their daily toil, the wedgecutters
Beheld him through the distant thicket move.
The shaggy dog following the truffle hunter,
Barked at the loiterer; and perchance at night 575
Belated villagers from fair or wake,
While the fresh night-wind let the moonbeams in
Between the swaying boughs, just saw him pass,
And then in silence, gliding like a ghost
He vanished! Lost among the deepening gloom. 580
But near one ancient tree, whose wreathèd roots
Formed a rude couch, love-songs and scattered rhymes,
Unfinished sentences, or half erased,
And rhapsodies like this, were sometimes found –

Let us to woodland wilds repair   585
 While yet the glittering night-dews seem
To wait the freshly-breathing air,

Precursive of the morning beam,
That rising with advancing day,
Scatters the silver drops away.   590

An elm, uprooted by the storm,
    The trunk with mosses gray and green,
Shall make for us a rustic form,
    Where lighter grows the forest scene;
And far among the bowery shades,   595
Are ferny lawns and grassy glades.

Retiring May to lovely June
    Her latest garland now resigns;
The banks with cuckoo-flowers are strewn,
    The woodwalks blue with columbines,   600
And with its reeds, the wandering stream
Reflects the flag-flower's golden gleam.

There, feathering down the turf to meet,
    Their shadowy arms the beeches spread,
While high above our sylvan seat,   605
    Lifts the light ash its airy head;
And later leaved, the oaks between
Extend their bows of vernal green.

The slender birch its paper rind
    Seems offering to divided love,   610
And shuddering even without a wind
    Aspens, their paler foliage move,
As if some spirit of the air
Breathed a low sigh in passing there.

The squirrel in his frolic mood,   615
    Will fearless bound among the boughs;
Yaffils° laugh loudly through the wood,   *woodpeckers*
    And murmuring ring-doves tell their vows;
While we, as sweetest woodscents rise,
Listen to woodland melodies.   620

And I'll contrive a sylvan room
    Against the time of summer heat,
Where leaves, inwoven in nature's loom,
    Shall canopy our green retreat;

And gales that 'close the eye of day'   625
Shall linger, e'er they die away.

And when a sear and sallow hue
 From early frost the bower receives,
I'll dress the sand rock cave for you,
 And strew the floor with heath and leaves,   630
That you, against the autumnal air
May find securer shelter there.

The nightingale will then have ceased
 To sing her moonlight serenade;
But the gay bird with blushing breast,   635
 And woodlarks still will haunt the shade,
And by the borders of the spring
Reed-wrens will yet be carolling.

The forest hermit's lonely cave
 None but such soothing sounds shall reach,   640
Or hardly heard, the distant wave
 Slow breaking on the stony beach;
Or winds, that now sigh soft and low,
Now make wild music as they blow.

And then, before the chilling north   645
 The tawny foliage falling light,
Seems, as it flits along the earth,
 The footfall of the busy sprite,
Who wrapt in pale autumnal gloom,
Calls up the mist-born mushroom.   650

Oh! could I hear your soft voice there,
 And see you in the forest green
All beauteous as you are, more fair
 You'd look, amid the sylvan scene,
And in a wood-girl's simple guise,   655
Be still more lovely in mine eyes.

Ye phantoms of unreal delight,
 Visions of fond delirium born!
Rise not on my deluded sight,
 Then leave me drooping and forlorn   660
To know, such bliss can never be,
Unless – loved like me.

The visionary, nursing dreams like these,
Is not indeed unhappy. Summer woods
Wave over him, and whisper as they wave,   665
Some future blessings he may yet enjoy.
And as above him sail the silver clouds,
He follows them in thought to distant climes,
Where, far from the cold policy of this,
Dividing him from her he fondly loves,   670
He, in some island of the southern sea,
May haply build his cane-constructed bower
Beneath the bread-fruit, or aspiring palm,
With long green foliage rippling in the gale.
Oh! let him cherish his ideal bliss –   675
For what is life, when hope has ceased to strew
Her fragile flowers along its thorny way?
And sad and gloomy are his days, who lives
Of hope abandoned!
                    Just beneath the rock   680
Where Beachy overpeers the channel wave,
Within a cavern mined by wintry tides
Dwelt one, who long disgusted with the world
And all its ways, appeared to suffer life
Rather than live; the soul-reviving gale,   685
Fanning the bean-field, or the thymy heath,
Had not for many summers breathed on him;
And nothing marked to him the season's change,
Save that more gently rose the placid sea,
And that the birds which winter on the coast   690
Gave place to other migrants; save that the fog,
Hovering no more above the beetling cliffs
Betrayed not then the little careless sheep
On the brink grazing, while their headlong fall
Near the lone Hermit's flint-surrounded home,   695
Claimed unavailing pity; for his heart
Was feelingly alive to all that breathed;
And outraged as he was, in sanguine youth,
By human crimes, he still acutely felt
For human misery.   700
                  Wandering on the beach,
He learned to augur from the clouds of heaven,
And from the changing colours of the sea,
And sullen murmurs of the hollow cliffs,
Or the dark porpoises, that near the shore   705

Gamboled and sported on the level brine
When tempests were approaching: then at night
He listened to the wind; and as it drove
The billows with o'erwhelming vehemence
He, starting from his rugged couch, went forth 710
And hazarding a life, too valueless,
He waded through the waves, with plank or pole
Towards where the mariner in conflict dread
Was buffeting for life the roaring surge;
And now just seen, now lost in foaming gulfs, 715
The dismal gleaming of the clouded moon
Showed the dire peril. Often he had snatched
From the wild billows, some unhappy man
Who lived to bless the hermit of the rocks.
But if his generous cares were all in vain, 720
And with slow swell the tide of morning bore
Some blue swol'n cor'se to land; the pale recluse
Dug in the chalk a sepulchre – above
Where the dank sea-wrack marked the utmost tide,
And with his prayers performed the obsequies 725
For the poor helpless stranger.
                              One dark night
The equinoctial wind blew south by west,
Fierce on the shore; the bellowing cliffs were shook
Even to their stony base, and fragments fell 730
Flashing and thundering on the angry flood.
At day-break, anxious for the lonely man,
His cave the mountain shepherds visited,
Though sand and banks of weeds had choked their way –
He was not in it; but his drownèd cor'se 735
By the waves wafted, near his former home
Received the rites of burial. Those who read
Chiselled within the rock, these mournful lines,
Memorials of his sufferings, did not grieve,
That dying in the cause of charity 740
His spirit, from its earthly bondage freed,
Had to some better region fled for ever.

92. The Spider

Arachne! poor degraded maid!
Doomed to obscurity's cold shade,

The price your vanity has paid
    Excites my pity.
No wonder you should take alarm,
Lest vengeance in a housewife's form,
Your fortress should attack by storm,   5
    And raze your city.

In truth you are not much befriended,
For since with wisdom you contended,   10
And the stern Goddess so offended,
    Each earthly Pallas
Views you with horror and affright,
Shrinks with abhorence from your sight,
Signing your death-warrant in spite,   15
    To pity callous.

You were not cast in Beauty's mould,
You have no shard of burnished gold,
No painted wing can you unfold
    With gems bespotted.   20
Your form disgusting to all eyes,
The Toad in ugliness outvies,
And nature has her homeliest guise
    To you allotted.

Yet, if with philosophic eye,   25
The young would but observe you ply
Your patient toil, and fortify
    Your habitation;
Spreading your net of slenderest twine,
Each artful mesh contrived to join,   30
Strengthening with doubled thread the line
    Of circumvallation.

Methinks your curious progress would
Give them a lecture full as good
As some; so little understood,   35
    So much affected.
And as you dart upon your prey,
Might they not moralise and say,
Spiders and men alike betray
    The unprotected?   40

Might you not tell the light coquette,
Who spreads for some poor youth her net,
Entangling thus without regret
   Her simple lover;
That such ensnarers of the heart,   45
Might in contemplating your art,
Her own unworthy counterpart
   In you discover?

Your sober habits then compare,
With those bright insects who repair   50
To sport and frolic through the air,
   All gay and winning;
While you your household cares attend,
Your toils no vain pursuits suspend,
But carefully your nets you mend,   55
   And mind your spinning.

The Butterfly, while life is new,
As he has nothing else to do,
May like a Bond Street beau pursue
   His vagrant courses;   60
But nature to her creatures kind,
You to an humbler fate consigned,
Yet taught you in yourself to find
   Your own resources.

93. The Nautilus

Where southern suns and winds prevail,
And undulate the summer seas;
The Nautilus expands his sail,
And scuds before the fresh'ning breeze.

Oft is a little squadron seen   5
Of mimic ships all rigged complete;
Fancy might think the fairy queen
Was sailing with her elfin fleet.

With how much beauty is designed
Each channelled barque of purest white!   10

With orient pearl each cabin lined,
Varying with every change of light,

While with his little slender oars,
His silken sail, and tapering mast,
The dauntless mariner explores   15
The dangers of the watery waste.

Prepared, should tempests rend the sky,
From harm his fragile bark to keep,
He furls his sail, his oar lays by,
And seeks his safety in the deep,   20

Then safe on ocean's shelly bed,
He hears the storm above him roar;
Mid groves of coral glowing red,
Or rocks o'erhung with madrepore.

So let us catch life's favouring gale,   25
But if fate's adverse winds be rude,
Take calmly in th' adventurous sail,
And find repose in Solitude.

94. The Heath

Even the wide heath, where the unequal ground
Has never on its rugged surface felt
The hand of industry, though wild and rough,
Is not without its beauty; here the furze,
Enriched among its spines, with golden flowers   5
Scents the keen air; while all its thorny groups
Wide scattered o'er the waste are full of life;
For 'midst its yellow bloom, the assembled chats
Wave high the tremulous wing, and with shrill notes,
But clear and pleasant, cheer the extensive heath. 10
Linnets in numerous flocks frequent it too,
And bashful, hiding in these scenes remote
From his congeners (they who make the woods
And the thick copses echo to their song),
The heath-thrush makes his domicile; and while   15
His patient mate with downy bosom warms

Their future nestlings, he his love lay sings
Loud to the shaggy wild. The Erica here,
That o'er the Caledonian hills sublime
Spreads its dark mantle (where the bees delight   20
To seek their purest honey), flourishes,
Sometimes with bells like amethysts, and then
Paler, and shaded like the maiden's cheek
With gradual blushes. Other while, as white,
As rime that hangs upon the frozen spray.   25
Of this, old Scotia's hardy mountaineers
Their rustic couches form; and there enjoy
Sleep, which beneath his velvet canopy
Luxurious idleness implores in vain!
Between the matted heath and ragged gorse   30
Wind natural walks of turf, as short and fine
As clothe the chalky downs; and there the sheep
Under some thorny bush, or where the fern
Lends a light shadow from the sun, resort,
And ruminate or feed; and frequent there   35
Nourished by evening mists, the mushroom spreads
From a small ivory bulb, his circular roof,
The fairies fabled board. Poor is the soil,
And of the plants that clothe it few possess
Succulent moisture; yet a parasite   40
Clings even to them; for its entangling stalk
The wire like dodder winds; and nourishes,
Rootless itself, its small white flowers on them.
So to the most unhappy of our race
Those, on whom never prosperous hour has smiled,   45
Towards whom nature as a step-dame stern
Has cruelly dealt, and whom the world rejects,
To these forlorn ones, ever there adheres
Some self-consoling passion; round their hearts
Some vanity entwines itself; and hides,   50
And is perhaps in mercy given to hide,
The mortifying sad realities
Of their hard lot.

95. Verses Written in Early Spring

As in the woods, where leathery lichen weaves
Its wintry web among the sallow leaves,

Which (through cold months in whirling eddies blown)
Decay beneath the branches once their own.
From the brown shelter of their foliage sear,   5
Spring the young blooms that lead the floral year,
When waked by vernal suns, the pilewort dares,
Expand her clouded leaves and shining stars;
And, veins empurpling all her tassels pale,
Bends the soft wind-flower in the vernal gale.   10
Uncultured bells of azure jacinths blow,
And the breeze scenting violet lurks below.
So views the wanderer, with delighted eyes,
Reviving hopes from black despondence rise;
When blighted by adversity's chill breath,   15
Those hopes had felt a temporary death;
Then with gay heart he looks to future hours,
When love and friendship dress the summer bowers;
And, as delicious dreams enchant his mind,
Forgets his sorrows past, and gives them to the wind.   20

96. Thirty-Eight

addressed to Mrs H— Y

In early youth's unclouded scene,
The brilliant morning of eighteen,
With health and sprightly joy elate
   We gazed on life's enchanting spring,
   Nor thought how quickly time would bring   5
The mournful period – Thirty-eight.

Then the starch maid, or matron sage,
Already of that sober age,
We viewed with mingled scorn and hate;
   In whose sharp words, or sharper face,   10
   With thoughtless mirth we loved to trace
The sad effects of – Thirty-eight.

Till saddening, sickening at the view,
We learned to dread what time might do;
And then preferred a prayer to fate   15

To end our days ere that arrived;
    When (power and pleasure long survived)
We met neglect and – Thirty-eight.

But time, in spite of wishes flies,
And fate our simple prayer denies,   20
And bids us death's own hour await:
    The auburn locks are mixed with grey,
    The transient roses fade away,
But reason comes at – Thirty-eight.

Her voice the anguish contradicts   25
That dying vanity inflicts;
Her hand new pleasures can create,
    For us she opens to the view
    Prospects less bright – but far more true,
And bids us smile at – Thirty-eight.   30

No more shall scandal's breath destroy
The social converse we enjoy
With bard or critic tête-à-tête; –
    O'er youth's bright blooms her blights shall pour,
    But spare the improving friendly hour   35
That science gives to – Thirty-eight.

Stripped of their gaudy hues by truth,
We view the glitt'ring toys of youth,
And blush to think how poor the bait
    For which to public scenes we ran   40
    And scorned of sober sense the plan
Which gives content at – Thirty-eight.

Though time's inexorable sway
Has torn the myrtle bands away,
For other wreaths 'tis not too late,   45
    The amaranth's purple glow survives,
    And still Minerva's olive lives
On the calm brow of – Thirty-eight.

With eye more steady we engage
To contemplate approaching age,   50
And life more justly estimate;
    With firmer souls, and stronger powers,

With reason, faith, and friendship ours,
   We'll not regret the stealing hours
That lead from Thirty – even to Forty-eight.   55

97. Sonnet Written in the Churchyard at Middleton in Sussex

Pressed by the moon, mute arbitress of tides,
   While the loud equinox its power combines,
   The sea no more its swelling surge confines,
But o'er the shrinking land sublimely rides.
The wild blast, rising from the western cave,   5
   Drives the huge billows from their heaving bed;
   Tears from their grassy tombs the village dead,
And breaks the silent sabbath of the grave!
With shells and sea-weed mingled, on the shore
   Lo! their bones whiten in the frequent wave;   10
   But vain to them the winds and waters rave;
They hear the warring elements no more:
   While I am doomed – by life's long storm oppressed,
   To gaze with envy on their gloomy rest.

Robert Fergusson (1750–1774)

98. Auld Reikie°   *Old Smoky*

   Auld Reikie, wale° o' ilka* town   *best, every*
That Scotland kens beneath the moon;
Where couthy° chiels* at ev'ning meet   *cosy, friends*
Their bizzing° craigs* and mouths to weet+; *parched, gullets, wet*
And blithely gar° auld care gae* bye   *make, go* 5
Wi° blinkit and wi bleering eye: *With*
O'er lang frae thee the Muse has been
Sae frisky on the simmer's Green,
Whan flowers and gowans° wont to glent* *daisies, glint*
In bonny blinks upo' the bent°;   *grass* 10
But now the leaves a' yellow die,
Peeled frae the branches, quickly fly;

And now frae nouther° bush nor brier   *neither*
The spreckled mavis° greets your ear;   *song-thrush*
Nor bonny blackbird skims and roves   15
To seek his Love in yonder groves.
    Then, Reikie, welcome! Thou can'st charm
Unfleggit° by the year's alarm;   *unruffled*
Not Boreas that sae snelly° blows,   *swiftly*
Dare here pap° in his angry nose: *pop* 20
Thanks to our dads, whase° biggin* stands   *whose, building*
A shelter to surrounding lands.
    Now morn, with bonny purpie-smiles°,   *blushes*
Kisses the air-cock° o' St. Giles;   *weather-cock*
Rakin° their een*, the servant lasses   *rubbing, eyes* 25
Early begin their lies and clashes;
Ilk° tells her friend o' saddest distress,   *each*
That still she brooks frae scowling mistress;
And wi her Joe in turnpike stair
She'd rather snuff the stinking air,   30
As be subjected to her tongue,
When justly censured in the wrong.
    On stair wi tub, or pat° in hand,   *pot*
The barefoot housemaids loo° to stand,   *love*
That antrin° fock* may ken how snell§   *other, folk, keen* 35
Auld Reikie will at morning smell:
Then, with an inundation big as
The burn that 'neath the Nore Loch brig° is,   *North Loch bridge*
They kindly shower Edina's° roses*   *Edinburgh's, [chamber pot contents]*
To quicken and regale our noses.   40
Now some for this, wi satire's leesh°,   *lash*
Hae gi'en auld Edinburgh a creesh°:   *thrashing*
But without souring nocht° is sweet;   *nothing*
The morning smells that hail our street,
Prepare, and gently lead the way   45
To simmer canty,° braw* and gay: *cheery, fine*
Edina's sons mair° eithly* share,   *more, easily*
Her spices and her dainties rare,
Then he that's never yet been called
Aff frae his plaidie° or his fauld*.   *field, sheepfold* 50
    Now stairhead critics, senseless fools,
Censure their aim, and pride their rules,
In Luckenbooths°, wi glow'ring eye,   *closed shops along the High Street*
Their neighbours sma'est° faults descry: *smallest*
If ony loun° should dander* there,   *chap, wander* 55

Of awkward gait, and foreign air,
They trace his steps, till they can tell
His pedigree as weel's himsel.
    Whan Phoebus blinks wi warmer ray
And schools at noonday get the play, 60
Then bus'ness, weighty bus'ness comes;
The trader glow'rs; he doubts, he hums:
The lawyers eke to Cross repair,
Their wigs to shaw°, and toss an air; *show*
While busy agent closely plies, 65
And a' his kittle° cases tries. *risky*
    Now night, that's cunzied° chief for fun, *created*
Is wi her usual rites begun;
Through ilka gate the torches blaze,
And globes send out their blinking rays. 70
The usefu' Cadie° plies in street, *messenger*
To bide the profits o' his feet;
For by thir lads Auld Reikie's fock
Ken but a sample o' the stock
O' thieves, that nightly wad oppress, 75
And make baith goods and gear the less.
Near him the lazy chairman stands
And wats° na how to turn his hands, *knows*
Till some daft birky°, ranting fu'*, *chap, drunk*
Has matters somewhere else to do; 80
The chairman willing, gies° his light *gives*
To deeds o' darkness and o' night:
Its never sax° pence for a lift *six*
That gars° thir lads wi fu'ness rift*; *makes, belch*
For they wi better gear are paid, 85
And whores and culls° support their trade. *fools or gulls*
    Near some lamp-post, wi dowy° face, *melancholy*
Wi' heavy een, and sour grimace,
Stands she that beauty lang had kend°, *known*
Whoredom her trade, and vice her end. 90
But see whare now she wuns° her breid *earns*
By that which nature ne'er decreed,
And sings sad music to the lugs°, *ears*
'Mang° burachs* o' damned whores and rogues. *Among, crowds*
Whane'er we reputation loss 95
Fair chastity's transparent gloss,
Redemption seenil° kens the name, *seldom*
But a's black misery and shame.

Frae joyous tavern, reeling drunk,
Wi' fiery phizz, and een half sunk,
Behad° the bruiser, fae* to a'   *Behold, foe*
That in the reek° o' gardies* fa':   *area, raised fists*
Close by his side, a feckless race
O' macaronies° show their face,   *fops*
And think they're free frae skaith° or harm,   *peril* 105
While pith befriends their leaders arm:
Yet fearfu' aften o' their maught°,   *might*
They quat° the glory o' the faught*   *leave, fight*
To this same warrior wha led
Thae heroes to bright honour's bed;   110
And aft the hack o' honour shines
In bruiser's face wi broken lines:
Of them sad tales he tells anon,
Whan ramble and whan fighting's done;
And, like Hectorian, ne'er impairs   115
The brag and glory o' his sairs°.   *wounds*
    Whan feet in dirty gutters plash,
And fock to wale their fitstaps° fash*;   *pick their way, strive*
At night the macaroni drunk,
In pools or gutters aftimes sunk: 120
Hegh! what a fright he now appears,
Whan he his corpse dejected rears!
Look at that head, and think if there
The pomet° slaistered* up his hair!   *pomade, greased*
The cheeks observe, where now could shine   125
The scancing° glories o' carmine?   *shining*
Ah, legs! in vain the silk-worm there
Displayed to view her eidant° care;   *busy*
For stink, instead of perfumes, grow,
And clarty° odours fragrant flow.   *filthy* 130
    Now some to porter, some to punch,
Some to their wife, and some their wench,
Retire, while noisy ten-hours° drum   *closing time for the sober*
Gars a' your trades gae dandring° Home.   *sauntering*
Now mony a club, jocose and free,   135
Gie a' to merriment and glee,
Wi' sang and glass, they fley° the pow'r   *scare off*
O' care that wad harrass the hour:
For wine and Bacchus still bear down
Our thrawart° fortunes' wildest frown: *contrary* 140
It maks you stark°, and bauld* and brave,   *strong, bold*

Ev'n whan descending to the grave.
   Now some, in Pandemonium's[35] shade
Resume the gormandizing trade;
Whare eager looks, and glancing een,   145
Forespeak a heart and stamack keen.
Gang on, my lads; it's lang sin syne
We kent auld Epicurus' line;
Save you, the board wad cease to rise,
Bedight wi daintiths to the skies;   150
And Salamanders cease to swill
The comforts of a burning gill.
   But chief, O Cape°, we crave thy aid,   *club*
To get our cares and poortith° laid: *cravings*
Sincerity, and genius true,   155
Of Knights have ever been the due:
Mirth, music, porter deepest dyed,
Are never here to worth denied;
And health, o' happiness the queen,
Blinks° bonny, wi her smile serene.   *looks* 160
   Though joy maist part Auld Reikie owns,
Eftsoons° she kens sad sorrow's frowns;   *soon enough*
What group is yon sae dismal grim,
Wi' horrid aspect, cleeding° dim?   *clothing*
Says Death, *They'r mine, a dowy° crew,*   *miserable* 165
To me they'll quickly pay their last adieu.
   How come mankind, whan lacking woe,
In saulie's° face their heart to show,   *paid mourner*
As if they were a clock, to tell
That grief in them had rung her bell?   170
Then, what is man? why a' this phraze°?   *empty talk*
Life's spunk° decayed, nae mair can blaze.   *spark*
Let sober grief alone declare
Our fond anxiety and care:
Nor let the undertakers be   175
The only waefu'° friends we see.   *woeful*
   Come on, my Muse, and then rehearse
The gloomiest theme in a' your verse:
In morning, whan ane keeks° about,   *peeps*
Fu' blyth and free frae ail°, nae doubt   *ill* 180
He lippens° not to be misled   *expects*

---

[35] Pandemonium, Salamander, Cape and other terms were the names of Edinburgh Clubs dedicated to camaraderie and debauchery. Fergusson was a 'Knight Companion' of the Cape Club.

Amang the regions of the dead:
But straight a painted corp° he sees, *corpse*
Lang streekit 'neath its canopies.
Soon, soon will this his mirth controul, 185
And send damnation to his soul:
Or when the dead-deal° (awful shape!) *board for laying out a corpse*
Makes frighted mankind girn° and gape, *wince*
Reflection then his reason sours,
For the neist° dead-deal may be ours. *next* 190
Whan Sibyl led the Trojan° down *Aeneas*
To haggard Pluto's dreary town,
Shapes waur nor thae°, I freely ween *worse than those*
Could never meet the soldier's een.
    If kail° sae green, or herbs delight, *cabbage* 195
Edina's street attracts the sight;
Not Covent Garden, clad sae braw,
Mair fouth° o' herbs can eithly shaw: *abundance*
For mony a yeard is here sair sought,
That kail and cabbage may be bought; 200
And healthfu' sallad to regale,
Whan pampered wi a heavy meal.
Glowr° up the street in simmer morn, *look*
The birks° sae green, and sweet brier thorn, *birches*
Wi' spraingit° flow'rs that scent the gale, *parti-coloured* 205
Ca' far awa' the morning smell,
Wi' which our ladies flow'r-pats° filled, *flower-pots*
And every noxious vapour killed.
O Nature! canty, blyth and free,
Whare is there keeking glass° like thee? *looking-glass* 210
Is there on earth that can compare
Wi' Mary's shape, and Mary's air,
Save the empurpled speck, that grows
In the saft faulds of yonder rose?
How bonny seems the virgin breast, 215
Whan by the lillies here carest,
And leaves the mind in doubt to tell
Whichmaist in sweets and hue excel?
    Gillespie's snuff should prime the nose
Of her that to the market goes, 220
If they wad like to shun the smells
That buoy up frae mirkest cells;
Whare wames° o' paunches sav'ry scent *bellies*
To nostrils gi'e great discontent.

Now wha in Albion could expect 225
O' cleanliness sic great neglect?
Nae Hottentot that daily lairs° *lies*
'Mang tripe, or ither clarty wares,
Hath ever yet conceived, or seen
Beyond the Line°, sic* scenes unclean. *Equator, such* 230
   On Sunday here, an altered scene
O' men and manners meets our een:
Ane wad maist° trow* some people chose *almost, believe*
To change their faces wi their clo'es°, *clothes*
And fain wad gar ilk neighbour think 235
They thirst for goodness, as for drink:
But there's an unco dearth o' grace,
That has nae mansion but the face,
And never can obtain a part
In benmost° corner of the heart. *innermost* 240
Why should religion make us sad,
If good frae virtue's to be had?
Na, rather gleefu' turn your face;
Forsake hypocrisy, grimace;
And never have it understood 245
You fleg° mankind frae being good. *frighten*
   In afternoon, a' brawly° buskit*, *lavishly, clad*
The joes and lasses loo° to frisk it: *love*
Some tak a great delight to place
The modest *bongrace*° o'er the face; *straw bonnet* 250
Though you may see, if so inclined,
The turning o' the leg behind.
Now Comely-Garden, and the Park,
Refresh them, after forenoon's wark°; *work*
Newhaven, Leith or Canon-mills, 255
Supply them in their Sunday's gills;
Whare writers aften spend their pence,
To stock their heads wi drink and sense.
   While dand'ring° cits delight to stray *promenading*
To Castlehill, or public way, 260
Whare they nae other purpose mean,
Than that fool cause o' being seen;
Let me to Arthur's Seat pursue,
Whare bonny pastures meet the view;
And mony a wild-lorn scene accrues, 265
Befitting Willie Shakespeare's muse:
If Fancy there would join the thrang°, *throng*

The desert rocks and hills amang,
To echoes we should lilt and play,
And gie to mirth the lee-lang day.   270
    Or should some cankered biting shour°   *shower*
The day and a' her sweets deflour,
To Holy-rood-house let me stray,
And gie to musing a' the day;
Lamenting what auld Scotland knew   275
Bien° days for ever frae her view: *comfortable*
O Hamilton, for shame! the Muse
Would pay to thee her couthy vows,
Gin ye wad tent° the humble strain   *attend to*
And gie's our dignity again: 280
For o, waes° me! the Thistle springs   *woe's*
In domicile of ancient kings,
Without a patriot to regret
Our palace, and our ancient State.
    Blest place! whare debtors daily run,   285
To rid themselves frae jail and dun°;   *writs*
Here, though sequestered frae the din
That rings Auld Reikie's waas° within,   *walls*
Yet they may tread the sunny braes,
And brook Apollo's cheery rays;   290
Glowr frae St Anthon's grassy height,
O'er vales in simmer claise° bedight,   *clothes*
Nor ever hing their head, I ween,
Wi' jealous fear o' being seen.
May I, whenever duns come nigh,   295
And shake my garret wi their cry,
Scour° here wi haste, protection get,   *scuttle*
To screen mysell frae them and debt;
To breathe the bliss of open sky,
And Simon Fraser's° bolts defy.   *keeper of Tolbooth Prison* 300
    Now gin a lown° should hae his clase   *chap*
In threadbare autumn o' their days,
St Mary, brokers' guardian saint,
Will satisfy ilk ail and want;
For mony a hungry writer there   305
Dives down at night, wi cleading bare,
And quickly rises to the view
A gentleman, perfyte and new.
Ye rich fock, look no wi disdain
Upo' this ancient Brokage Lane!   310

For naked poets are supplied,
With what you to their wants denied.
    Peace to thy shade, thou wale° o' men,   *chief*
Drummond! relief to poortith's° pain: *poverty's*
To thee the greatest bliss we owe;   315
And tribute's tear shall grateful flow:
The sick are cured, the hungry fed,
And dreams of comfort tend their bed:
As lang as Forth weets° Lothian's shore,   *wets*
As lang's on Fife her billows roar,   320
Sae lang shall ilk whase country's dear,
To thy remembrance gie a Tear.
By thee Auld Reikie thrave°, and grew   *prospered*
Delightfu' to her childers' view:
Nae mair shall Glasgow striplings threap°   *brag about* 325
Their city's beauty and its shape,
While our new city spreads around
Her bonny wings on fairy ground.
    But provosts now that ne'er afford
The smaest dignity to *lord*°,   *the title 'Lord Provost'* 330
Ne'er care though every scheme gae wild
That Drummond's sacred hand has culled:
The spacious *Brig*° neglected lies,   *bridge*
Though plagued wi pamphlets, dunned wi cries;
They heed not though destruction come   335
To gulp us in her gaunting° womb.   *yawning*
O shame! that safety canna claim
Protection from a provost's name,
But hidden danger lies behind
To torture and to fleg° the mind;   *afright* 340
I may as weel bid Arthur's Seat
To Berwick-Law make gleg° retreat,   *hasty*
As think that either will or art
Shall get the gate to win their heart;
For *politics* are a' their mark,   345
Bribes latent, and corruption dark:
If they can eithly turn the pence,
Wi' city's good they will dispense;
Nor care though a' her sons were lair'd°   *buried*
Ten fathom i' the auld kirk-yard.   350
    To sing yet meikle does remain,
Undecent for a modest strain;
And since the poet's daily bread is

The favour of the Muse or ladies,
He downa like to gie offence   355
To delicacy's bonny sense;
Therefore the stews remain unsung,
And bawds in silence drop their tongue.
    Reikie, farewel! I ne'er could part
Wi' thee but wi a dowy heart;   360
Aft frae the Fifan coast I've seen,
Thee tow'ring on thy summit green;
So glowr the saints when first is given
A fav'rite keek° o' glore and heaven;   *glimpse*
On earth nae mair they bend their een,   365
But quick assume angelic mein;
So I on Fife wad glowr no more,
But galloped to Edina's shore.

99. Food for a new Edition of his Dictionary

To Doctor Samuel Johnson

    Let Wilkes and Churchill rage no more,
        Though scarce provision, learning's good;
    What can these hungry's next implore,
        Even Samuel Johnson loves our food.
                    Rodondo:

    Great Pedagogue, whose literanian lore,
With syllable and syllable conjoined
To transmutate and varyfy, has learned
The whole revolving scientific names
That in the alphabetic columns lie,   5
Far from the knowledge of mortalic shapes,
As we, who never can peroculate
The miracles by thee miraculised,
The Muse silential long, with mouth apert
Would give vibration to stagnatic tongue,   10
And loud encomiate thy puissant name,
Eulogiated from the green decline
Of Thames's banks to Scoticanian shores,
Where Lochiomondian liquids undulise.
    To meminate thy name in after times,   15

The mighty Mayor of each regalian town
Shall consignate thy work to parchment fair
In roll burgharian, and their tables all
Shall fumigate with fumigation strong:
Scotland, from perpendicularian hills,   20
Shall emigrate her fair muttonian store,
Which late had there in pedestration walked,
And o'er her airy heights perambulised.
    Oh, blackest execrations on thy head,
Edina shameless! though he came within   25
The bounds of your notation; though you knew
His honorific name, you noted not,
But basely suffered him to chariotise
Far from your tow'rs, with smoke that nubilate,
Nor drank one amicitial swelling cup   30
To welcome him convivial. Bailies all,
With rage inflated, Catenations tear,
Nor ever after be you vinculised,
Since you that sociability denied
To him whose potent Lexiphanian style   35
Words can prolongate, and inswell his page
With what in others to a line's confined.
    Welcome, thou verbal potentate and prince!
To hills and vallies, where emerging oats
From earth assurge our pauperty to bay,   40
And bless thy name, thy dictionarian skill,
Which there definitive will still remain,
And oft be speculised by taper blue,
While youth studentious turn thy folio page.
    Have you as yet, in per'patetic mood,   45
Regarded with the texture of the eye
The cave caverick, where fraternal bard,
Churchill, depicted pauperated swains
With thraldom and black want, reduced sore,
Where Nature, colourised, so coarsely fades,   50
And puts her russet par'phernalia on?
Have you as yet the way explorified,
To let lignarian chalice, swelled with oats,
Thy orofice approach? Have you as yet,
With skin fresh rubified by scarlet spheres,   55
Applied brimstonic unction to your hide,
To terrify the salamandrian fire
That from involuntary digits asks

The strong allaceration? – Or can you swill
The usquebalian flames of *whisky* blue   60
In fermentation strong? Have you applied
The kelt aerian to your Anglian thighs,
And with renunciation assignised
Your breeches in Londona to be worn?
Can you, in frigor of Highlandian sky,   65
On heathy summits take nocturnal rest?
It cannot be – You may as well desire
An alderman leave *plumb-puddenian* store,
And scratch the tegument from pottage-dish,
As bid thy countrymen, and thee conjoined,   70
Forsake stomachic joys. Then hie you home,
And be a malcontent, that naked hinds,
On lentiles fed, can make your kingdom quake,
And tremulate Old England libertised.

100. Robert Fergusson's Last Will

   While sober folks, in humble prose,
Estate, and goods, and gear dispose,
A poet surely may disperse
His *moveables* in doggrel verse;
And fearing death my blood will fast chill,   5
I hereby constitute my last will.
   Then *wit ye me* to have made o'er
To Nature my *poetic* lore;
To her I give and grant the freedom
Of paying to the bards who need 'em   10
As many talents as she gave,
When I became the Muses slave.
   Thanks to the gods, who made me poor!
No *lukewarm* friends molest my door,
Who always show a busy care   15
For being legatee or heir:
Of this stamp none will ever follow
The youth that's favoured by Apollo.
   But to those few who know my case,
Nor thought a *poet's friend* disgrace,   20
The following trifles I bequeath,
And leave them with my kindest breath;

Nor will I burden them with payment
Of debts incurred, or coffin raiment,
As yet 'twas never my intent   25
To pass an Irish compliment.
    To Jamie Rae, who oft *jocosus*,
With me partook of cheering doses,
I leave my snuff-box, to regale
His senses after drowsy meal,   30
And wake remembrance of a friend
Who loved him to his latter end:
But if this pledge should make him sorry,
And argue like *memento mori*,
He may bequeath't 'mong stubborn fellows,   35
To all the finer feelings callous,
Who think that parting breath's a sneeze
To set sensations all at ease.
    To Oliphant, my friend, I legate
Those scrolls poetic which he may get,   40
With ample freedom to correct
Those writs I ne'er could retrospect,
With power to him and his succession
To print and sell a new impression:
And here I fix on Ossian's Head,   45
A domicile for Doric reed,
With as much power *ad Musæ bona*,
As I *in propria persona*.
    To Hamilton I give the task
Outstanding debts to crave and ask;   50
And that my Muse he may not dub ill,
For loading him with so much trouble,
My debts I leave him *singulatim*,
As they are mostly *desperatim*.
    To Woods, whose genius can provoke   55
His passions to the bowl or sock,
For love to thee, and to the nine,
Be my immortal Shakespeare thine:
Here may you through the alleys turn,
Where Falstaff laughs, where heroes mourn,   60
And boldly catch the glowing fire
That dwells in raptures on his lyre.
    Now at my dirge (if dirge there be!),
Due to the Muse and poetry,
Let Hutcheson attend, for none is   65

More fit to guide the ceremonies;
As I in health with him would often
This clay-built mansion wash and soften,
So let my friends with him partake
The gen'rous wine at dirge or wake –   70
   And I consent to registration
Of this my will for preservation,
That patent it may be, and seen
In Walter's Weekly Magazine.
Witness whereof, these presents wrote are   75
By William Blair, the public notar,
And, for the tremor of my hand,
Are signed by him at my command.
   R.F. † his Mark

Sir Walter Scott (1771–1832)

101. The Rover

A weary lot is thine, fair maid,
   A weary lot is thine!
To pull the thorn thy brow to braid,
   And press the rue for wine.
A lightsome eye, a soldier's mien,   5
   A feather of the blue,
A doublet of the Lincoln green –
   No more of me you knew
      My Love!
   No more of me you knew.   10

'This morn is merry June, I trow,
   The rose is budding fain;
But she shall bloom in winter snow
   Ere we two meet again.'
He turned his charger as he spake   15
   Upon the river shore,
He gave the bridle-reins a shake,
   Said, 'Adieu for evermore
      My Love!
   And adieu for evermore.'   20

102. My Native Land

Breathes there the man, with soul so dead,
Who never to himself hath said,
This is my own, my native land!
Whose heart hath ne'er within him burned,
As home his footsteps he hath turned   5
From wandering on a foreign strand!
If such there breathe, go, mark him well;
For him no Minstrel raptures swell;
High though his titles, proud his name,
Boundless his wealth as wish can claim;   10
Despite those titles, power, and pelf,
The wretch, concentred all in self,
Living, shall forfeit fair renown,
And, doubly dying, shall go down
To the vile dust, from whence he sprung,   15
Unwept, unhonoured, and unsung.

103. The Dance of Death

I
Night and morning were at meeting
    Over Waterloo;
Cocks had sung their earliest greeting;
    Faint and low they crew,
For no paly beam yet shone   5
On the heights of Mount Saint John;
Tempest-clouds prolonged the sway
Of timeless darkness over day;
Whirlwind, thunder-clap, and shower
Marked it a predestined hour.   10
Broad and frequent through the night
Flashed the sheets of levin-light:
Muskets, glancing lightnings back,
Showed the dreary bivouac
    Where the soldier lay,   15
Chill and stiff, and drenched with rain,
Wishing dawn of morn again,
    Though death should come with day.

II

'Tis at such a tide and hour
Wizard, witch, and fiend have power,   20
And ghastly forms through mist and shower
   Gleam on the gifted ken;
And then the affrighted prophet's ear
Drinks whispers strange of fate and fear
Presaging death and ruin near   25
   Among the sons of men;
Apart from Albyn's war-array,
'Twas then grey Allan sleepless lay;
Grey Allan, who, for many a day,
   Had followed stout and stern,   30
Where, through battle's rout and reel,
Storm of shot and edge of steel,
Led the grandson of Lochiel,
   Valiant Fassiefern.
Through steel and shot he leads no more,   35
Low laid 'mid friends' and foemen's gore
But long his native lake's wild shore,
And Sunart rough, and high Ardgower,
   And Morven long shall tell,
And proud Bennevis hear with awe   40
How, upon bloody Quatre-Bras,
Brave Cameron heard the wild hurrah
   Of conquest as he fell.

III

Lone on the outskirts of the host,
The weary sentinel held post,   45
And heard, through darkness far aloof,
The frequent clang of courser's hoof,
Where held the cloaked patrol their course,
And spurred 'gainst storm the swerving horse;
But there are sounds in Allan's ear,   50
Patrol nor sentinel may hear,
And sights before his eye aghast
Invisible to them have passed,
   When down the destined plain,
'Twixt Britain and the bands of France,   55
Wild as marsh-borne meteor's glance,
Strange phantoms wheeled a revel dance,
   And doomed the future slain.

Such forms were seen, such sounds were heard,
When Scotland's James his march prepared   60
    For Flodden's fatal plain;
Such, when he drew his ruthless sword,
As Choosers of the Slain, adored
    The yet unchristened Dane.
An indistinct and phantom band,   65
They wheeled their ring-dance hand in hand,
    With gestures wild and dread;
The Seer, who watched them ride the storm,
Saw through their faint and shadowy form
    The lightning's flash more red;   70
And still their ghastly roundelay
Was of the coming battle-fray,
    And of the destined dead.

IV. SONG
Wheel the wild dance
While lightnings glance,   75
    And thunders rattle loud,
And call the brave
To bloody grave,
    To sleep without a shroud.
Our airy feet,   80
So light and fleet,
    They do not bend the rye
That sinks its head when whirlwinds rave,
And swells again in eddying wave,
    As each wild gust blows by;   85
But still the corn,
At dawn of morn,
    Our fatal steps that bore,
At eve lies waste,
A trampled paste   90
    Of blackening mud and gore.
Wheel the wild dance
While lightnings glance,
    And thunders rattle loud,
And call the brave   95
To bloody grave,
    To sleep without a shroud.

V

Wheel the wild dance!
Brave sons of France,
  For you our ring makes room;   100
Make space full wide
For martial pride,
  For banner, spear, and plume.
Approach, draw near,
Proud cuirassier!   105
  Room for the men of steel!
Through crest and plate
The broadsword's weight
  Both head and heart shall feel.

VI

Wheel the wild dance   110
While lightnings glance,
  And thunders rattle loud,
And call the brave
To bloody grave,
  To sleep without a shroud.   115
Sons of the spear!
You feel us near
  In many a ghastly dream;
With fancy's eye
Our forms you spy,   120
  And hear our fatal scream.
With clearer sight
Ere falls the night,
  Just when to weal or woe
Your disembodied souls take flight   125
On trembling wing each startled sprite
  Our choir of death shall know.

VII

Wheel the wild dance
While lightnings glance,
  And thunders rattle loud,   130
And call the brave
To bloody grave,
  To sleep without a shroud.
Burst, ye clouds, in tempest showers,
Redder rain shall soon be ours –   135

See the east grows wan –
Yield we place to sterner game,
Ere deadlier bolts and direr flame
Shall the welkin's thunders shame,
Elemental rage is tame   140
   To the wrath of man.

VIII
At morn, grey Allan's mates with awe
Heard of the visioned sights he saw,
   The legend heard him say;
But the Seer's gifted eye was dim,   145
Deafened his ear, and stark his limb,
   Ere closed that bloody day.
He sleeps far from his Highland heath,
But often of the Dance of Death
   His comrades tell the tale   150
On picquet-post, when ebbs the night,
And waning watch-fires glow less bright,
   And dawn is glimmering pale.

104. Pibroch[36] of Donuil Dhu

Pibroch of Donuil Dhu,
   Pibroch of Donuil,
Wake thy wild voice anew,
   Summon Clan Conuil.
Come away, come away,   5
   Hark to the summons!
Come in your war array,
   Gentles and commons.
Come from deep glen, and
   From mountain so rocky,   10
The war-pipe and pennon
   Are at Inverlochy.
Come every hill-plaid, and
   True heart that wears one,
Come every steel blade, and   15
   Strong hand that bears one.

[36] Musical variations for the bagpipe, dirges or battle-tunes

Leave untended the herd,
   The flock without shelter;
Leave the corpse uninterred,
   The bride at the altar;   20
Leave the deer, leave the steer,
   Leave nets and barges:
Come with your fighting gear,
   Broadswords and targes.
Come as the winds come, when   25
   Forests are rended;
Come as the waves come, when
   Navies are stranded:
Faster come, faster come,
   Faster and faster,   30
Chief, vassal, page and groom,
   Tenant and master.
Fast they come, fast they come;
   See how they gather!
Wide waves the eagle plume,   35
   Blended with heather.
Cast your plaids, draw your blades,
   Forward each man set!
Pibroch of Donuil Dhu,
   Knell for the onset!   40

Thomas Chatterton (1752–1770)

105. from *Aella*: The Minstrels' Song

Man	Tourne thee to thie shepsterr° swayne;
	Bryghte sonne has ne droncke the dewe
	From the floures of yelowe hue;
	Tourne thee, Alyce, back again.
Wom	No, bestoikerre°, I wylie goe,
	Softlie tryppynge o'ere the mees,
	Lyche the sylver-footed doe,
	Seekeynge shelterr yn grene trees.
Man	See the moss growne daisey'd banke,
	Pereynge ynne the streme belowe;

Man Tourne thee to thie shepsterr° swayne;   *shepherd*
     Bryghte sonne has ne droncke the dewe
     From the floures of yelowe hue;
     Tourne thee, Alyce, back again.   90
Wom No, bestoikerre°, I wylie goe,   *deceiver*
     Softlie tryppynge o'ere the mees,
     Lyche the sylver-footed doe,
     Seekeynge shelterr yn grene trees.
Man See the moss growne daisey'd banke,   95
     Pereynge ynne the streme belowe;

Here we'lle sytte, yn dewie danke,
Tourne thee, Alyce, do notte goe.

Wom I've hearde erste mie grandame saie,
Yonge damoyselles schulde ne bee,   100
Inne the swotie monthe of Maie,
Wythe yonge menne bie the grene wode tree.

Man Sytte thee, Alice, sytte, and harke,
Howe the ouzle° chauntes hys noate,   blackbird
The chelandree°, greie-morn larke,   goldfinch 105
Chauntynge from theyre lyttel throate;

Wom I heare them from eche grene wode tree,
Chauntynge owte so blatauntlie,
Tellynge lecturnyes° to mee,   warning tales
Myscheefe ys whanne you are nygh.   110

Man See alonge the mees° so grene   meeds
Pièd daisies, kynge-coppes swote;
Alle we see, bie non bee seene,
Nete° botte shepe settes here a fote.   none

Wom Shepster swayne, you tare mie gratche°,   shawl 115
Oute uponne ye! lette me goe.
Leave me swythe°, or I'lle alatche*   swiftly, call for help
Robynne, thys youre dame shall knowe.

Man See! the crokynge brionie
Rounde the poplar twyste hys spraie;   120
Rounde the oake the greene ivie
Florryshcethe and lyveth aie.

Lette us seate us bie thys tree,
Laughe, and synge to lovynge ayres;
Comme, and doe notte coyen bee;   125
Nature made all thynges bie payres.

Drooried° cattes wille after kynde;   dainty
Gentle doves wylle kyss and coe:

Wom Botte manne, hee moste be ywrynde°,   declined
Tylle syr preeste make on of two.   130

Tempte me ne to the foule thynge;
I wylle no mannes lemanne be;
Till syr preeste hys songe doethe synge,
Thou shalt neere fynde aught of mee.

Man Bie our ladie her yborne,   135
To-morrowe, soone as ytte ys daie,

I'lle make thee wyfe, ne bee forsworne,
So tyde me lyfe or dethe for aie.
Wom Whatt dothe lette°, botte thatte nowe   *hinder*
Wee attenes, thos honde yn honde,   140
Unto divinstre° goe,   *holy clerk*
And bee lyncked yn wedlocke bonde?
Man I agree, and thus I plyghte
Honde, and harte, and all that's myne;
Goode syr Rogerr, do us ryghte,   145
Make us one, at Cothbertes shryne.
Both We wylle ynn a bordelle° lyve,   *cottage*
Hailie, thoughe of no estate;
Everyche clocke moe love shall gyve;
Wee ynn godenesse wylle be greate.   150

106. from *Aella:* Song

O! synge untoe mie roundelaie,
O! droppe the brynie teare wythe mee,
Daunce ne moe atte hallie daie,   845
Lycke a reynynge ryver bee;
   Mie love ys dedde,
   Gon to hys death-bedde,
   Al under the wyllowe tree.

Black hys cryne° as the wyntere nyghte,   *hair* 850
Whyte hys rode° as the sommer snowe,   *skin*
Rodde hys face as the mornynge lyghte,
Cale° he lyes ynne the grave belowe;   *cold*
   Mie love ys dedde,
   Gon to hys death-bedde,   855
   Al under the wyllowe tree.

Swote hys tynge as the throstles note,
Quycke ynn daunce as thoughte canne bee,
Defte hys taboure, codgelle stote,
O! hee lyes bie the wyllowe tree: 860
   Mie love ys dedde,
   Gone to hys death-bedde,
   Alle underre the wyllowe tree.

Harke! the ravenne flappes hys wynge,
In the briered delle belowe;   865
Harke! the dethe-owle loude dothe synge,
To the nyghte-mares as heie goe;
 Mie love ys dedde,
 Gon to hys death-bedde,
 Al under the wyllowe tree.   870

See! the whyte moone sheenes onne hie;
Whyterre ys mie true loves shroude;
Whyterre thanne the mornynge skie,
Whyterre thanne the evenynge cloude;
 Mie love ys dedde,   875
 Gon to hys death-bedde,
 Al under the wyllowe tree.

Heere, uponne mie true loves grave,
Schalle the baren fleurs be layde,
Nee one hallie Seyncte to save   880
Al the celness° of a mayde.   *coldness*
 Mie love ys dedde,
 Gonne to hys death-bedde,
 Alle under the wyllowe tree.

Wythe mie hondes I'lle dente the brieres   885
Rounde his hallie corse to gre,
Ouphante° fairie, lyghte youre fyres,   *elfin*
Heere mie boddie stylle schall bee.
 Mie love ys dedde,
 Gon to hys death-bedde,   890
 Al under the wyllowe tree.

Comme, wythe acorne-coppe and thorne,
Drayne mie hartys blodde awaie;
Lyfe and all yttes goode I scorne,
Daunce bie nete, or feaste by daie.   895
 Mie love ys dedde,
 Gon to hys death-bedde,
 Al under the wyllowe tree.

Waterre wytches, crownede wythe reytes°,   *reeds*
Bere mee to yer leathalle tyde.   900
I die; I comme; mie true love waytes.
Thos the damselle spake, and dyed.

107. An Excelente Balade of Charitie

As written by the good priest Thomas Rowley, 1464

In Virgynë the sweltrie sun gan sheene,
And hotte upon the mees° did caste his raie;   *meeds*
The apple rodded° from its palie greene,   *reddened*
And the mole° peare did bende the leafy spraie;   *soft*
The peede chelandri° sunge the livelong daie;   *pied goldfinch* 5
'Twas nowe the pride, the manhode of the yeare,
And eke the grounde was dighte in its moste defte aumere°.   *neatest mantle*

The sun was glemeing in the midde of daie,
Deadde still the aire, and eke the welken blue,
When from the sea arist in drear arraie   10
A hepe of cloudes of sable sullen hue,
The which full fast unto the woodlande drewe,
Hiltring° attenes the sunnis fetive* face,   *shrouding, lovely*
And the blacke tempeste swolne and gatherd up apace.

Beneathe an holme, faste by a pathwaie side,   15
Which dide unto Seyncte Godwine's covent lede,
A hapless pilgrim moneynge° did abide.   *moaning*
Pore in his viewe, ungentle in his weede,
Longe bretful° of the miseries of neede,   *full*
Where from the hail-stone coulde the almer flie?   20
He had no housen theere, ne anie covent nie.

Look in his glommed face, his sprighte there scanne;
Howe woe-be-gone, how withered, forwynd°, deade!   *sapless*
Haste to thie church-glebe-house°, asshrewed manne!   *the grave*
Haste to thie kiste°, thie onlie dortoure* bedde.   *coffin, sleeping room* 25
Cale, as the claie whiche will gre on thie hedde,
Is Charitie and Love aminge highe elves;
Knightis and Barons live for pleasure and themselves.

The gatherd storme is rype; the bigge drops falle;
The forswat° meadowes smethe*, and drenche§ the raine;
        sun-burnt, steam, drink 30
The comyng ghastness do the cattle pall,
And the full flockes are drivynge ore the plaine;
Dashde from the cloudes the waters flott againe;
The welkin opes; the yellow levynne° flies;   *lightning*

And the hot fierie smothe° in the wide lowings* dies.   *steam, flames* 35

Liste! now the thunder's rattling clymmynge sound
Cheves slowlie on, and then embollen° clangs,   *swelled*
Shakes the hie spyre, and losst, dispended, drown'd,
Still on the gallard° eare of terroure hanges;   *frightened*
The windes are up; the lofty elmen swanges°;   *swings* 40
Again the levynne and the thunder poures,
And the full cloudes are braste attenes in stonen showers.

Spurreynge his palfrie oere the watrie plaine,
The Abbote of Seyncte Godwynes convente came;
His chapournette° was drented with the reine,   *small round hat* 45
And his pencte gyrdle met with mickle shame;
He ayneward tolde his bederoll° at the same;   *told his beads backwards*
The storme encreasen, and he drew aside,
With the mist° almes craver neere to the holme to bide.   *poor*

His cope was all of Lyncolne clothe so fyne,   50
With a gold button fasten'd neere his chynne;
His autremete° was edged with golden twynne,   *priest's robe*
And his shoone pyke° a loverds* mighte have binne;   *pointed, lord's*
Full well it shewn he thoughten coste no sinne:
The trammels of the palfrye pleasde his sighte,   55
For the horse-millanare° his head with roses dighte.   *horse-milliner*

'An almes, sir prieste!' the droppynge pilgrim saide,
'O! let me waite within your covente dore,
Till the sunne sheneth hie above our heade,
And the loude tempeste of the aire is oer;   60
Helpless and ould am I alas! and poor;
No house, ne friend, ne moneie in my pouche;
All thatte I call my owne is this my silver crouche°.'   *crucifix*

'Varlet,' replyd the Abbatte, 'cease your dinne;
This is no season almes and prayers to give;   65
Mie porter never lets a faitour° in;   *tramp*
None touch mie rynge who not in honour live.'
And now the sonne with the blacke cloudes did stryve,
And shettynge° on the grounde his glairie raie,   *shooting*
The Abbatte spurrde his steede, and eftsoones roadde awaie.   70

Once moe the skie was blacke, the thunder rolde;
Faste reyneynge o'er the plaine a prieste was seen;

Ne dighte full proude, ne buttoned up in golde;
His cope and jape° were graie, and eke were clene;   *short surplice*
A Limitoure° he was of order seene;   *a friar licensed to beg* 75
And from the pathwaie side then turnèd hee,
Where the pore almer laie binethe the holmen tree.

'An almes, sir priest!' the droppynge pilgrim sayde,
'For sweete Seyncte Marie and your order sake.'
The Limitoure then loosen'd his pouche threade,   80
And did thereoute a groate of silver take;
The mister° pilgrim dyd for halline* shake.   *poor, joy*
'Here take this silver, it maie eathe° thie care;   *ease*
We are Goddes stewards all, nete° of oure owne we bare.   *nothing*

'But ah! unhailie pilgrim, lerne of me,   85
Scathe° anie give a rentrolle to their Lorde.   *scarcely*
Here take my semecope, thou arte bare I see;
Tis thyne; the Seynctes will give me mie rewarde.'
He left the pilgrim, and his waie aborde°.   *went on*
Virgynne and hallie Seyncte, who sitte yn gloure,   90
Or give the mittee° will, or give the gode man power.   *mighty*

108. The Art of Puffing

By a Bookseller's Journeyman

Versed by experience in the subtle art,
The myst'ries of a title I impart:
Teach the young author how to please the town,
And make the heavy drug of rhyme go down.
Since Curl, immortal never-dying name!   5
A double pica in the book of fame,
By various arts did various dunces prop,
And tickled every fancy to his shop,
Who can, like Pottinger, ensure a book?
Who judges with the solid taste of Cooke?   10
Villains, exalted in the midway sky,
Shall live again to drain your purses dry:
Nor yet unrivalled they; see Baldwin comes,
Rich in inventions, patents, cuts, and hums:
The honourable Boswell writes, 'tis true, –   15

What else can Paoli's supporter do?
The trading wits endeavour to attain,
Like booksellers, the world's first idol – gain.
For this they puff the heavy Goldsmith's line,
And hail his sentiment, though trite, divine;   20
For this the patriotic bard complains,
And Bingley binds poor liberty in chains:
For this was every reader's faith deceived,
And Edmunds swore what nobody believed:
For this the wits in close disguises fight;   25
For this the varying politicians write;
For this each month new magazines are sold,
With dullness filled and transcripts of the old.
The 'Town and Country' struck a lucky hit,
Was novel, sentimental, full of wit: 30
Aping her walk the same success to find,
The 'Court and City' hobbles far behind.
Sons of Apollo, learn: merit's no more
Than a good frontispiece to grace the door;
The author who invents a title well   35
Will always find his covered dullness sell:
Flexney and every bookseller will buy –
Bound in neat calf, the work will never die.

Phillis Wheatley (1753–1784)

109. On Being Brought from Africa to America

'Twas mercy brought me from my pagan land,
Taught my benighted soul to understand
That there's a God, that there's a Saviour too:
Once I redemption neither sought nor knew.
Some view that sable race with scornful eye,   5
'Their colour is a diabolic dye.'
Remember, Christians, Negroes, black as Cain,
May be refined, and join th' angelic train.

110. To a Lady on the Death of Three Relations

We trace the pow'r of death from tomb to tomb,
And his are all the ages yet to come.
'Tis his to call the planets from on high,
To blacken Phoebus, and dissolve the sky;
His too, when all in his dark realms are hurled, 5
From its firm base to shake the solid world;
His fatal sceptre rules the spacious whole,
And trembling nature rocks from pole to pole.
   Awful he moves, and wide his wings are spread:
Behold thy brother numbered with the dead! 10
From bondage freed, the exulting spirit flies
Beyond Olympus, and these starry skies.
Lost in our woe for thee, blest shade, we mourn
In vain; to earth thou never must return.
Thy sisters too, fair mourner, feel the dart 15
Of death, and with fresh torture rend thine heart.
Weep not for them, who wish thine happy mind
To rise with them, and leave the world behind.
   As a young plant by hurricanes up torn,
So near its parent lies the newly born – 20
But 'midst the bright ethereal train behold
It shines superior on a throne of gold:
Then, mourner, cease; let hope thy tears restrain,
Smile on the tomb, and sooth the raging pain.
On yon blest regions fix thy longing view, 25
Mindless of sublunary scenes below;
Ascend the sacred mount, in thought arise,
And seek substantial and immortal joys;
Where hope receives, where faith to vision springs,
And raptured seraphs tune th' immortal strings 30
To strains ecstatic. Thou the chorus join,
And to thy father tune the praise divine.

111. To S.M.A., a Young African Painter, on Seeing his Works

To show the lab'ring bosom's deep intent,
And thought in living characters to paint,
When first thy pencil did those beauties give,
And breathing figures learnt from thee to live,

How did those prospects give my soul delight, 5
A new creation rushing on my sight?
Still, wond'rous youth! each noble path pursue,
On deathless glories fix thine ardent view:
Still may the painter's and the poet's fire
To aid thy pencil, and thy verse conspire! 10
And may the charms of each seraphic theme
Conduct thy footsteps to immortal fame!
High to the blissful wonders of the skies
Elate thy soul, and raise thy wishful eyes.
Thrice happy, when exalted to survey 15
That splendid city, crowned with endless day,
Whose twice six gates on radiant hinges ring:
Celestial Salem blooms in endless spring.
    Calm and serene thy moments glide along,
And may the muse inspire each future song! 20
Still, with the sweets of contemplation blessed,
May peace with balmy wings your soul invest!
But when these shades of time are chased away,
And darkness ends in everlasting day,
On what seraphic pinions shall we move, 25
And view the landscapes in the realms above?
There shall thy tongue in heav'nly murmurs flow,
And there my muse with heav'nly transport glow:
No more to tell of Damon's tender sighs,
Or rising radiance of Aurora's eyes, 30
For nobler themes demand a nobler strain,
And purer language on th' ethereal plain.
Cease, gentle muse! the solemn gloom of night
Now seals the fair creation from my sight.

George Crabbe (1754–1832)

112. from *The Village,* Book I

The village life, and every care that reigns
O'er youthful peasants and declining swains;
What labour yields, and what, that labour past,
Age, in its hour of languor, finds at last;

What form the real picture of the poor,   5
Demand a song – the Muse can give no more.
  Fled are those times, when, in harmonious strains,
The rustic poet praised his native plains:
No shepherds now, in smooth alternate verse,
Their country's beauty or their nymphs' rehearse;   10
Yet still for these we frame the tender strain,
Still in our lays fond Corydons complain,
And shepherds' boys their amorous pains reveal,
The only pains, alas! they never feel.
  On Mincio's banks, in Caesar's bounteous reign,   15
If Tityrus found the Golden Age again,
Must sleepy bards the flattering dream prolong,
Mechanic echoes of the Mantuan song?
From truth and nature shall we widely stray,
Where Virgil, not where fancy, leads the way?   20
  Yes, thus the Muses sing of happy swains,
Because the Muses never knew their pains:
They boast their peasants' pipes; but peasants now
Resign their pipes and plod behind the plough;
And few, amid the rural-tribe, have time   25
To number syllables, and play with rhyme;
Save honest Duck[37], what son of verse could share
The poet's rapture, and the peasant's care?
Or the great labours of the field degrade,
With the new peril of a poorer trade?   30
  From this chief cause these idle praises spring,
That themes so easy few forbear to sing;
For no deep thought the trifling subjects ask;
To sing of shepherds is an easy task:
The happy youth assumes the common strain,   35
A nymph his mistress, and himself a swain;
With no sad scenes he clouds his tuneful prayer
But all, to look like her, is painted fair.
  I grant indeed that fields and flocks have charms
For him that grazes or for him that farms;   40
But when amid such pleasing scenes I trace
The poor laborious natives of the place,
And see the mid-day sun, with fervid ray,
On their bare heads and dewy temples play;
While some with feebler heads and fainter hearts,   45

---

[37] see note, p. 138

Deplore their fortune, yet sustain their parts:
Then shall I dare these real ills to hide
In tinsel trappings of poetic pride?
   No; cast by fortune on a frowning coast,
Which neither groves nor happy valleys boast;   50
Where other cares than those the Muse relates,
And other shepherds dwell with other mates;
By such examples taught, I paint the cot°,   *cottage*
As truth will paint it, and as bards will not:
Nor you, ye poor, of lettered scorn complain,   55
To you the smoothest song is smooth in vain;
O'ercome by labour, and bowed down by time,
Feel you the barren flattery of a rhyme?
Can poets soothe you, when you pine for bread,
By winding myrtles round your ruined shed?   60
Can their light tales your weighty griefs o'erpower
Or glad with airy mirth the toilsome hour?
   Lo! where the heath, with withering brake grown o'er,
Lends the light turf that warms the neighbouring poor;
From thence a length of burning sand appears,   65
Where the thin harvest waves its withered ears;
Rank weeds, that every art and care defy,
Reign o'er the land, and rob the blighted rye:
There thistles stretch their prickly arms afar,
And to the ragged infant threaten war;   70
There poppies nodding, mock the hope of toil;
There the blue bugloss paints the sterile soil;
Hardy and high, above the slender sheaf,
The slimy mallow waves her silky leaf;
O'er the young shoot the charlock throws a shade,   75
And clasping tares cling round the sickly blade;
With mingled tints the rocky coasts abound,
And a sad splendour vainly shines around.
   So looks the nymph whom wretched arts adorn,
Betrayed by man, then left for man to scorn;   80
Whose cheek in vain assumes the mimic rose,
While her sad eyes the troubled breast disclose;
Whose outward splendour is but folly's dress,
Exposing most, when most it gilds distress.
   Here joyous roam a wild amphibious race,   85
With sullen woe displayed in every face;
Who, far from civil arts and social fly,
And scowl at strangers with suspicious eye.

Here too the lawless merchant of the main
Draws from his plough th' intoxicated swain;   90
Want only claimed the labour of the day,
But vice now steals his nightly rest away.
    Where are the swains, who, daily labour done,
With rural games played down the setting sun;
Who struck with matchless force the bounding ball,   95
Or made the pond'rous quoit obliquely fall;
While some huge Ajax, terrible and strong,
Engaged some artful stripling of the throng,
And fell beneath him, foiled, while far around
Hoarse triumph rose, and rocks returned the sound?   100
Where now are these? – Beneath yon cliff they stand,
To show the freighted pinnace where to land;
To load the ready steed with guilty haste,
To fly in terror o'er the pathless waste,
Or, when detected, in their straggling course,   105
To foil their foes by cunning or by force;
Or, yielding part (which equal knaves demand),
To gain a lawless passport through the land.
    Here, wand'ring long amid these frowning fields,
I sought the simple life that nature yields;   110
Rapine and wrong and fear usurped her place,
And a bold, artful, surly, savage race;
Who, only skilled to take the finny tribe,
The yearly dinner, or septennial bribe,
Wait on the shore, and, as the waves run high,   115
On the tossed vessel bend their eager eye,
Which to their coast directs its vent'rous way;
Theirs, or the ocean's, miserable prey.
    As on their neighb'ring beach yon swallows stand,
And wait for fav'ring winds to leave the land;   120
While still for flight the ready wing is spread:
So waited I the fav'ring hour, and fled;
Fled from those shores where guilt and famine reign,
And cried, Ah! hapless they who still remain;
Who still remain to hear the ocean roar,   125
Whose greedy waves devour the lessening shore;
Till some fierce tide, with more imperious sway,
Sweeps the low hut and all it holds away;
When the sad tenant weeps from door to door,
And begs a poor protection from the poor!   130
    But these are scenes where nature's niggard hand

Gave a spare portion to the famished land;
Hers is the fault, if here mankind complain
Of fruitless toil and labour spent in vain;
But yet in other scenes more fair in view,   135
Where plenty smiles – alas! she smiles for few –
And those who taste not, yet behold her store,
Are as the slaves that dig the golden ore,
The wealth around them makes them doubly poor.
   Or will you deem them amply paid in health,   140
Labour's fair child, that languishes with wealth?
Go then! and see them rising with the sun,
Through a long course of daily toil to run;
See them beneath the dog-star's raging heat,
When the knees tremble and the temples beat;   145
Behold them, leaning on their scythes, look o'er
The labour past, and toils to come explore;
See them alternate suns and showers engage,
And hoard up aches and anguish for their age;
Through fens and marshy moors their steps pursue,   150
When their warm pores imbibe the evening dew;
Then own that labour may as fatal be
To these thy slaves, as thine excess to thee.
   Amid this tribe too oft a manly pride
Strives in strong toil the fainting heart to hide;   155
There may you see the youth of slender frame
Contend with weakness, weariness, and shame:
Yet, urged along, and proudly loth to yield,
He strives to join his fellows of the field.
Till long-contending nature droops at last,   160
Declining health rejects his poor repast,
His cheerless spouse the coming danger sees,
And mutual murmurs urge the slow disease.
   Yet grant them health, 'tis not for us to tell,
Though the head droops not, that the heart is well;   165
Or will you praise that homely, healthy fare,
Plenteous and plain, that happy peasants share!
Oh! trifle not with wants you cannot feel,
Nor mock the misery of a stinted meal;
Homely, not wholesome, plain, not plenteous, such   170
As you who praise would never deign to touch.
   Ye gentle souls, who dream of rural ease,
Whom the smooth stream and smoother sonnet please;
Go! if the peaceful cot your praises share,

Go look within, and ask if peace be there; 175
If peace be his – that drooping weary sire,
Or theirs, that offspring round their feeble fire;
Or hers, that matron pale, whose trembling hand
Turns on the wretched hearth th' expiring brand!
 Nor yet can time itself obtain for these 180
Life's latest comforts, due respect and ease;
For yonder see that hoary swain, whose age
Can with no cares except his own engage;
Who, propped on that rude staff, looks up to see
The bare arms broken from the withering tree, 185
On which, a boy, he climbed the loftiest bough,
Then his first joy, but his sad emblem now.
 He once was chief in all the rustic trade;
His steady hand the straightest furrow made;
Full many a prize he won, and still is proud 190
To find the triumphs of his youth allowed;
A transient pleasure sparkles in his eyes,
He hears and smiles, then thinks again and sighs:
For now he journeys to his grave in pain;
The rich disdain him; nay, the poor disdain; 195
Alternate masters now their slave command,
Urge the weak efforts of his feeble hand,
And, when his age attempts its task in vain,
With ruthless taunts, of lazy poor complain.
 Oft may you see him, when he tends the sheep, 200
His winter-charge, beneath the hillock weep;
Oft hear him murmur to the winds that blow
O'er his white locks and bury them in snow,
When, roused by rage and muttering in the morn,
He mends the broken hedge with icy thorn: – 205
 'Why do I live, when I desire to be
At once from life and life's long labour free?
Like leaves in spring, the young are blown away,
Without the sorrows of a slow decay;
I, like yon withered leaf, remain behind, 210
Nipped by the frost, and shivering in the wind;
There it abides till younger buds come on,
As I, now all my fellow-swains are gone;
Then, from the rising generation thrust,
It falls, like me, unnoticed to the dust. 215
 'These fruitful fields, these numerous flocks I see,
Are others' gain, but killing cares to me;

To me the children of my youth are lords,
Cool in their looks, but hasty in their words:
Wants of their own demand their care; and who   220
Feels his own want and succours others too?
A lonely, wretched man, in pain I go,
None need my help, and none relieve my woe;
Then let my bones beneath the turf be laid,
And men forget the wretch they would not aid.'   225
    Thus groan the old, till, by disease oppressed,
They taste a final woe, and then they rest.
    Theirs is yon house that holds the parish-poor,
Whose walls of mud scarce bear the broken door;
There, where the putrid vapours, flagging, play,   230
And the dull wheel hums doleful through the day; –
There children dwell who know no parents' care;
Parents, who know no children's love, dwell there;
Heart-broken matrons on their joyless bed,
Forsaken wives, and mothers never wed;   235
Dejected widows with unheeded tears,
And crippled age with more than childhood fears;
The lame, the blind, and, far the happiest they!
The moping idiot and the madman gay.
    Here too the sick their final doom receive,   240
Here brought, amid the scenes of grief, to grieve,
Where the loud groans from some sad chamber flow,
Mixed with the clamours of the crowd below;
Here, sorrowing, they each kindred sorrow scan,
And the cold charities of man to man: 245
Whose laws indeed for ruined age provide,
And strong compulsion plucks the scrap from pride;
But still that scrap is bought with many a sigh,
And pride embitters what it can't deny.
    Say ye, oppressed by some fantastic woes,   250
Some jarring nerve that baffles your repose;
Who press the downy couch, while slaves advance
With timid eye, to read the distant glance;
Who with sad prayers the weary doctor tease,
To name the nameless ever-new disease;   255
Who with mock patience dire complaints endure,
Which real pain and that alone can cure;
How would ye bear in real pain to lie,
Despised, neglected, left alone to die?
How would ye bear to draw your latest breath,   260

Where all that's wretched paves the way for death?
  Such is that room which one rude beam divides,
And naked rafters form the sloping sides;
Where the vile bands that bind the thatch are seen,
And lath and mud are all that lie between;   265
Save one dull pane, that, coarsely patched, gives way
To the rude tempest, yet excludes the day:
Here, on a matted flock, with dust o'erspread,
The drooping wretch reclines his languid head;
For him no hand the cordial cup applies,   270
Or wipes the tear that stagnates in his eyes;
No friends with soft discourse his pain beguile,
Or promise hope till sickness wears a smile.
  But soon a loud and hasty summons calls,
Shakes the thin roof, and echoes round the walls;   275
Anon, a figure enters, quaintly neat,
All pride and business, bustle and conceit;
With looks unaltered by these scenes of woe,
With speed that, entering, speaks his haste to go,
He bids the gazing throng around him fly,   280
And carries fate and physic in his eye:
A potent quack, long versed in human ills,
Who first insults the victim whom he kills;
Whose murd'rous hand a drowsy bench protect,
And whose most tender mercy is neglect.   285
  Paid by the parish for attendance here,
He wears contempt upon his sapient sneer;
In haste he seeks the bed where misery lies,
Impatience marked in his averted eyes;
And, some habitual queries hurried o'er,   290
Without reply, he rushes on the door:
His drooping patient, long inured to pain,
And long unheeded, knows remonstrance vain;
He ceases now the feeble help to crave
Of man; and silent sinks into the grave.   295
  But ere his death some pious doubts arise,
Some simple fears, which 'bold bad' men despise;
Fain would he ask the parish-priest to prove
His title certain to the joys above:
For this he sends the murmuring nurse, who calls   300
The holy stranger to these dismal walls:
And doth not he, the pious man, appear,
He, 'passing rich with forty pounds a year'?

Ah! no; a shepherd of a different stock,
And far unlike him, feeds this little flock: 305
A jovial youth, who thinks his Sunday's task
As much as God or man can fairly ask;
The rest he gives to loves and labours light,
To fields the morning, and to feasts the night;
None better skilled the noisy pack to guide,   310
To urge their chase, to cheer them or to chide;
A sportsman keen, he shoots through half the day,
And, skilled at whist, devotes the night to play:
Then, while such honours bloom around his head,
Shall he sit sadly by the sick man's bed,   315
To raise the hope he feels not, or with zeal
To combat fears that e'en the pious feel?
    Now once again the gloomy scene explore,
Less gloomy now; the bitter hour is o'er,
The man of many sorrows sighs no more. –   320
Up yonder hill, behold how sadly slow
The bier moves winding from the vale below;
There lie the happy dead, from trouble free,
And the glad parish pays the frugal fee:
No more, O death! thy victim starts to hear   325
Churchwarden stern, or kingly overseer;
No more the farmer claims his humble bow,
Thou art his lord, the best of tyrants thou!
    Now to the church behold the mourners come,
Sedately torpid and devoutly dumb;   330
The village children now their games suspend,
To see the bier that bears their ancient friend;
For he was one in all their idle sport,
And like a monarch ruled their little court.
The pliant bow he formed, the flying ball,   335
The bat, the wicket, were his labours all;
Him now they follow to his grave, and stand
Silent and sad, and gazing, hand in hand;
While bending low, their eager eyes explore
The mingled relics of the parish poor;   340
The bell tolls late, the moping owl flies round,
Fear marks the flight and magnifies the sound;
The busy priest, detained by weightier care,
Defers his duty till the day of prayer;
And, waiting long, the crowd retire distressed,   345
To think a poor man's bones should lie unblessed.

113. Procrastination

Love will expire – the gay, the happy dream
Will turn to scorn, indiff'rence, or esteem:
Some favoured pairs, in this exchange, are blest,
Nor sigh for raptures in a state of rest;
Others, ill matched, with minds unpaired, repent   5
At once the deed, and know no more content;
From joy to anguish they, in haste, decline,
And, with their fondness, their esteem resign;
More luckless still their fate, who are the prey
Of long-protracted hope and dull delay: 10
'Mid plans of bliss the heavy hours pass on,
Till love is withered, and till joy is gone.
    This gentle flame two youthful hearts possessed,
The sweet disturber of unenvied rest:
The prudent Dinah was the maid beloved,   15
And the kind Rupert was the swain approved:
A wealthy Aunt her gentle niece sustained,
He, with a father, at his desk remained,
The youthful couple, to their vows sincere,
Thus loved expectant; year succeeding year,   20
With pleasant views and hopes, but not a prospect near.
Rupert some comfort in his station saw,
But the poor virgin lived in dread and awe;
Upon her anxious looks the widow smiled,
And bade her wait, 'for she was yet a child'.   25
She for her neighbour had a due respect,
Nor would his son encourage or reject;
And thus the pair, with expectations vain,
Beheld the seasons change and change again:
Meantime the nymph her tender tales perused,   30
Where cruel aunts impatient girls refused:
While hers, though teasing, boasted to be kind,
And she, resenting, to be all resigned.
    The dame was sick, and when the youth applied
For her consent, she groaned, and coughed and cried,   35
Talked of departing, and again her breath
Drew hard, and coughed, and talked again of death:
'Here you may live, my Dinah! here the boy
And you together my estate enjoy:'
Thus to the lovers was her mind expressed,   40
Till they forbore to urge the fond request.

Servant, and nurse, and comforter, and friend,
Dinah had still some duty to attend;
But yet their walk, when Rupert's evening call
Obtained an hour, made sweet amends for all;   45
So long they now each other's thoughts had known,
That nothing seemed exclusively their own:
But with the common wish, the mutual fear,
They now had travelled to their thirtieth year.

At length a prospect opened – but alas!   50
Long time must yet, before the union, pass:
Rupert was called, in other clime, t' increase
Another's wealth, and toil for future peace.
Loth were the lovers; but the aunt declared
'Twas fortune's call, and they must be prepared: 55
'You now are young, and for this brief delay,
And Dinah's care, what I bequeath will pay;
All will be yours, nay, love, suppress that sigh,
The kind must suffer, and the best must die.'
Then came the cough, and strong the signs it gave   60
Of holding long contention with the grave.

The lovers parted with a gloomy view,
And little comfort, but that both were true;
He for uncertain duties doomed to steer,
While hers remained too certain and severe.   65
Letters arrived, and Rupert fairly told
'His cares were many, and his hopes were cold:
The view more clouded, that was never fair,
And love alone preserved him from despair':
In other letters brighter hopes he drew,   70
'His friends were kind, and he believed them true.'

When the sage widow Dinah's grief descried,
She wondered much why one so happy sighed:
Then bade her see how her poor aunt sustained
The ills of life, nor murmured nor complained.   75
To vary pleasures, from the lady's chest
Were drawn the pearly string and tabby vest,
Beads, jewels, laces, all their value shown,
With the kind notice – 'They will be your own.'

This hope, these comforts, cherished day by day,   80
To Dinah's bosom made a gradual way;
Till love of treasure had as large a part,
As love of Rupert, in the virgin's heart.
Whether it be that tender passions fail,

From their own nature, while the strong prevail: 85
Or whether av'rice, like the poison-tree,
Kills all beside it, and alone will be;
Whatever cause prevailed, the pleasure grew
In Dinah's soul, – she loved the hoards to view;
With lively joy those comforts she surveyed,   90
And love grew languid in the careful maid.
   Now the grave niece partook the widow's cares,
Looked to the great, and ruled the small affairs:
Saw cleaned the plate, arranged the china-show,
And felt her passion for a shilling grow: 95
Th' indulgent aunt increased the maid's delight,
By placing tokens of her wealth in sight;
She loved the value of her bonds to tell,
And spake of stocks, and how they rose and fell.
   This passion grew, and gained at length such sway,   100
That other passions shrank to make it way;
Romantic notions now the heart forsook,
She read but seldom, and she changed her book;
And for the verses she was wont to send,
Short was her prose, and she was Rupert's friend.   105
Seldom she wrote, and then the widow's cough,
And constant call, excused her breaking off;
Who, now oppressed, no longer took the air,
But sate and dozed upon an easy chair.
The cautious doctor saw the case was clear,   110
But judged it best to have companions near;
They came, they reasoned, they prescribed – at last,
Like honest men, they said their hopes were past;
Then came a priest – 'tis comfort to reflect,
When all is over, there was no neglect: 115
And all was over – by her husband's bones,
The widow rests beneath the sculptured stones,
That yet record their fondness and their fame,
While all they left, the virgin's care became:
Stock, bonds, and buildings; – it disturbed her rest,   120
To think what load of troubles she possessed:
Yet, if a trouble, she resolved to take
Th' important duty for the donor's sake;
She too was heiress to the widow's taste,
Her love of hoarding, and her dread of waste.   125
   Sometimes the past would on her mind intrude,
And then a conflict full of care ensued;

The thoughts of Rupert on her mind would press,
His worth she knew, but doubted his success:
Of old she saw him heedless; what the boy   130
Forbore to save, the man would not enjoy;
Oft had he lost the chance that care would seize,
Willing to live, but more to live at ease:
Yet could she not a broken vow defend,
And Heav'n, perhaps, might yet enrich her friend.   135
    Month after month was passed, and all were spent
In quiet comfort and in rich content:
Miseries there were, and woes the world around,
But these had not her pleasant dwelling found;
She knew that mothers grieved, and widows wept,   140
And she was sorry, said her prayers, and slept:
Thus passed the seasons, and to Dinah's board
Gave what the seasons to the rich afford;
For she indulged, nor was her heart so small,
That one strong passion should engross it all.   145
    A love of splendour now with av'rice strove,
And oft appeared to be the stronger love:
A secret pleasure filled the widow's breast,
When she reflected on the hoards possessed;
But livelier joy inspired th' ambitious maid,   150
When she the purchase of those hoards displayed:
In small but splendid room she loved to see
That all was placed in view and harmony;
There, as with eager glance she looked around,
She much delight in every object found;   155
While books devout were near her – to destroy,
Should it arise, an overflow of joy.
    Within that fair apartment guests might see
The comforts culled for wealth by vanity:
Around the room an Indian paper blazed,   160
With lively tint and figures boldly raised;
Silky and soft upon the floor below,
Th' elastic carpet rose with crimson glow;
All things around implied both cost and care,
What met the eye was elegant or rare: 165
Some curious trifles round the room were laid,
By hope presented to the wealthy maid;
Within a costly case of varnished wood,
In level rows, her polished volumes stood;
Shown as a favour to a chosen few,   170

To prove what beauty for a book could do:
A silver urn with curious work was fraught;
A silver lamp from Grecian pattern wrought:
Above her head, all gorgeous to behold,
A time-piece stood on feet of burnished gold;   175
A stag's-head crest adorned the pictured case,
Through the pure crystal shone the enamelled face;
And while on brilliants moved the hands of steel,
It clicked from pray'r to pray'r, from meal to meal.
    Here as the lady sate, a friendly pair   180
Stepped in t' admire the view, and took their chair:
They then related how the young and gay
Were thoughtless wandering in the broad highway:
How tender damsels sailed in tilted boats,
And laughed with wicked men in scarlet coats;   185
And how we live in such degen'rate times,
That men conceal their wants, and show their crimes;
While vicious deeds are screened by fashion's name,
And what was once our pride is now our shame.
    Dinah was musing, as her friends discoursed,   190
When these last words a sudden entrance forced
Upon her mind, and what was once her pride
And now her shame, some painful views supplied;
Thoughts of the past within her bosom pressed,
And there a change was felt, and was confessed: 195
While thus the virgin strove with secret pain,
Her mind was wandering o'er the troubled main;
Still she was silent, nothing seemed to see,
But sate and sighed in pensive reverie.
    The friends prepared new subjects to begin,   200
When tall Susannah, maiden starch, stalked in;
Not in her ancient mode, sedate and slow,
As when she came, the mind she knew, to know;
Nor as, when list'ning half an hour before,
She twice or thrice tapped gently at the door;   205
But, all decorum cast in wrath aside,
'I think the devil's in the man!' she cried;
'A huge tall sailor, with his tawny cheek,
And pitted face, will with my lady speak;
He grinned an ugly smile, and said he knew,   210
Please you, my lady, 't would be joy to you:
What must I answer?' – Trembling and distressed
Sank the pale Dinah by her fears oppressed;

When thus alarmed, and brooking no delay,
Swift to her room the stranger made his way.   215
   'Revive, my love!' said he, 'I've done thee harm,
Give me thy pardon,' and he looked alarm:
Meantime the prudent Dinah had contrived
Her soul to question, and she then revived.
   'See! my good friend,' and then she raised her head,   220
'The bloom of life, the strength of youth is fled;
Living we die; to us the world is dead;
We parted blessed with health, and I am now
Age-struck and feeble – so I find art thou;
Thine eye is sunken, furrowed is thy face,   225
And downward look'st thou – so we run our race;
And happier they whose race is nearly run,
Their troubles over, and their duties done.'
   'True, lady, true – we are not girl and boy,
But time has left us something to enjoy.'   230
   'What! thou hast learned my fortune? – yes, I live
To feel how poor the comforts wealth can give:
Thou too perhaps art wealthy; but our fate
Still mocks our wishes, wealth is come too late.'
   'To me nor late nor early; I am come   235
Poor as I left thee to my native home:
Nor yet,' said Rupert, 'will I grieve; 'tis mine
To share thy comforts, and the glory thine:
For thou wilt gladly take that generous part
That both exalts and gratifies the heart;   240
While mine rejoices' – 'Heavens!' returned the maid,
'This talk to one so withered and decayed?
No! all my care is now to fit my mind
For other spousal, and to die resigned:
As friend and neighbour, I shall hope to see   245
These noble views, this pious love in thee;
That we together may the change await,
Guides and spectators in each other's fate;
When, fellow-pilgrims, we shall daily crave
The mutual prayer that arms us for the grave.'   250
   Half angry, half in doubt, the lover gazed
On the meek maiden, by her speech amazed;
'Dinah,' said he, 'dost thou respect thy vows?
What spousal mean'st thou? – thou art Rupert's spouse;
The chance is mine to take, and thine to give;   255
But, trifling this, if we together live:

Can I believe, that, after all the past,
Our vows, our loves, thou wilt be false at last?
Something thou hast – I know not what – in view;
I find thee pious – let me find thee true.'   260
  'Ah! cruel this; but do, my friend, depart;
And to its feelings leave my wounded heart.'
  'Nay, speak at once; and Dinah, let me know,
Mean'st thou to take me, now I'm wrecked, in tow?
Be fair; nor longer keep me in the dark;   265
Am I forsaken for a trimmer spark?
Heaven's spouse thou art not; nor can I believe
That God accepts her who will man deceive:
True I am shattered, I have service seen,
And service done, and have in trouble been;   270
My cheek (it shames me not) has lost its red,
And the brown buff is o'er my features spread;
Perchance my speech is rude; for I among
Th' untamed have been, in temper and in tongue;
Have been trepanned, have lived in toil and care,   275
And wrought for wealth I was not doomed to share;
It touched me deeply, for I felt a pride
In gaining riches for my destined bride:
Speak then my fate; for these my sorrows past,
Time lost, youth fled, hope wearied, and at last   280
This doubt of thee – a childish thing to tell,
But certain truth – my very throat they swell;
They stop the breath, and but for shame could I
Give way to weakness, and with passion cry;
These are unmanly struggles, but I feel   285
This hour must end them, and perhaps will heal.' –
  Here Dinah sighed, as if afraid to speak –
And then repeated – 'They were frail and weak
His soul she loved, and hoped he had the grace
To fix his thoughts upon a better place.'   290
  She ceased; – with steady glance, as if to see
The very root of this hypocrisy, –
He her small fingers moulded in his hard
And bronzed broad hand; then told her his regard,
His best respect were gone, but love had still   295
Hold in his heart, and governed yet the will –
Or he would curse her: – saying this, he threw
The hand in scorn away, and bade adieu
To every lingering hope, with every care in view.

Proud and indignant, suffering, sick, and poor,   300
He grieved unseen; and spoke of love no more –
Till all he felt in indignation died,
As hers had sunk in avarice and pride.
    In health declining, as in mind distressed,
To some in power his troubles he confessed,   305
And shares a parish-gift; – at prayers he sees
The pious Dinah dropped upon her knees;
Thence as she walks the street with stately air
As chance directs, oft meet the parted pair;
When he, with thickset coat of badge-man's blue,   310
Moves near her shaded silk of changeful hue;
When his thin locks of grey approach her braid,
A costly purchase made in beauty's aid;
When his frank air, and his unstudied pace,
Are seen with her soft manner, air, and grace,   315
And his plain artless look with her sharp meaning face;
It might some wonder in a stranger move,
How these together could have talked of love.
    Behold them now! – see there a tradesman stands,
And humbly hearkens to some fresh commands;   320
He moves to speak, she interrupts him – 'Stay,'
Her air expresses – 'Hark! to what I say':
Ten paces off, poor Rupert on a seat
Has taken refuge from the noon-day heat,
His eyes on her intent, as if to find   325
What were the movements of that subtle mind:
How still! – how earnest is he! – it appears
His thoughts are wand'ring through his earlier years;
Through years of fruitless labour, to the day
When all his earthly prospects died away: 330
'Had I,' he thinks, 'been wealthier of the two,
Would she have found me so unkind, untrue?
Or knows not man when poor, what man when rich will do?
Yes, yes! I feel that I had faithful proved,
And should have soothed and raised her, blessed and loved.'   335
    But Dinah moves – she had observed before,
The pensive Rupert at an humble door.
Some thoughts of pity raised by his distress,
Some feeling touch of ancient tenderness;
Religion, duty urged the maid to speak,   340
In terms of kindness to a man so weak:
But pride forbad, and to return would prove

She felt the shame of his neglected love;
Nor wrapped in silence could she pass, afraid
Each eye should see her, and each heart upbraid;   345
One way remained – the way the Levite took,
Who without mercy could on misery look;
(A way perceived by craft, approved by pride),
She crossed and passed him on the other side.

114. Peter Grimes

Old Peter Grimes made fishing his employ,
His wife he cabined with him and his boy,
And seemed that life laborious to enjoy:
To town came quiet Peter with his fish,
And had of all a civil word and wish.   5
He left his trade upon the sabbath-day,
And took young Peter in his hand to pray:
But soon the stubborn boy from care broke loose,
At first refused, then added his abuse:
His father's love he scorned, his power defied,   10
But being drunk, wept sorely when he died.
   Yes! then he wept, and to his mind there came
Much of his conduct, and he felt the shame, –
How he had oft the good old man reviled,
And never paid the duty of a child;   15
How, when the father in his Bible read,
He in contempt and anger left the shed:
'It is the word of life,' the parent cried;
– 'This is the life itself,' the boy replied;
And while old Peter in amazement stood,   20
Gave the hot spirit to his boiling blood: –
How he, with oath and furious speech, began
To prove his freedom and assert the man;
And when the parent checked his impious rage,
How he had cursed the tyranny of age, –   25
Nay, once had dealt the sacrilegious blow
On his bare head, and laid his parent low;
The father groaned – 'If thou art old,' said he,
'And hast a son – thou wilt remember me:
Thy mother left me in a happy time,   30
Thou kill'dst not her – Heav'n spares the double-crime.'

On an inn-settle, in his maudlin grief,
This he revolved, and drank for his relief.
　　Now lived the youth in freedom, but debarred
From constant pleasure, and he thought it hard;　　　　35
Hard that he could not every wish obey,
But must awhile relinquish ale and play;
Hard! that he could not to his cards attend,
But must acquire the money he would spend.
　　With greedy eye he looked on all he saw,　　　　40
He knew not justice, and he laughed at law;
On all he marked he stretched his ready hand;
He fished by water, and he filched by land:
Oft in the night has Peter dropped his oar,
Fled from his boat and sought for prey on shore;　　　　45
Oft up the hedge-row glided, on his back
Bearing the orchard's produce in a sack,
Or farm-yard load, tugged fiercely from the stack;
And as these wrongs to greater numbers rose,
The more he looked on all men as his foes.　　　　50
　　He built a mud-walled hovel, where he kept
His various wealth, and there he oft-times slept;
But no success could please his cruel soul,
He wished for one to trouble and control;
He wanted some obedient boy to stand　　　　55
And bear the blow of his outrageous hand;
And hoped to find in some propitious hour
A feeling creature subject to his power.
　　Peter had heard there were in London then, –
Still have they being! – workhouse clearing men,　　　　60
Who, undisturbed by feelings just or kind,
Would parish-boys to needy tradesmen bind:
They in their want a trifling sum would take,
And toiling slaves of piteous orphans make.
　　Such Peter sought, and when a lad was found,　　　　65
The sum was dealt him, and the slave was bound.
Some few in town observed in Peter's trap
A boy, with jacket blue and woollen cap;
But none inquired how Peter used the rope,
Or what the bruise, that made the stripling stoop;　　　　70
None could the ridges on his back behold,
None sought his shiv'ring in the winter's cold;
None put the question, – 'Peter, dost thou give
The boy his food? – What, man! the lad must live:

Consider, Peter, let the child have bread,   75
He'll serve thee better if he's stroked and fed.'
None reasoned thus – and some, on hearing cries,
Said calmly, 'Grimes is at his exercise.'
　　Pinned, beaten, cold, pinched, threatened, and abused –
His efforts punished and his food refused, –   80
Awake tormented, – soon aroused from sleep, –
Struck if he wept, and yet compelled to weep,
The trembling boy dropped down and strove to pray,
Received a blow, and trembling turned away,
Or sobbed and hid his piteous face; – while he,   85
The savage master, grinned in horrid glee:
He'd now the power he ever loved to show,
A feeling being subject to his blow.
　　Thus lived the lad, in hunger, peril, pain,
His tears despised, his supplications vain: 90
Compelled by fear to lie, by need to steal,
His bed uneasy and unblessed his meal,
For three sad years the boy his tortures bore,
And then his pains and trials were no more.
　　'How died he, Peter?' when the people said,   95
He growled – 'I found him lifeless in his bed';
Then tried for softer tone, and sighed, 'Poor Sam is dead.'
Yet murmurs were there, and some questions asked, –
How he was fed, how punished, and how tasked?
Much they suspected, but they little proved,   100
And Peter passed untroubled and unmoved.
　　Another boy with equal ease was found,
The money granted, and the victim bound;
And what his fate? – One night it chanced he fell
From the boat's mast and perished in her well.   105
Where fish were living kept, and where the boy
(So reasoned men) could not himself destroy: –
　　'Yes! so it was,' said Peter, 'in his play,
(For he was idle both by night and day),
He climbed the main-mast and then fell below'; –   110
Then showed his corpse and pointed to the blow:
'What said the jury?' – they were long in doubt,
But sturdy Peter faced the matter out:
So they dismissed him, saying at the time,
'Keep fast your hatchway when you've boys who climb.'   115
This hit the conscience, and he coloured more
Than for the closest questions put before.

Thus all his fears the verdict set aside,
And at the slave-shop Peter still applied.
  Then came a boy, of manners soft and mild, –   120
Our seamen's wives with grief beheld the child;
All thought (the poor themselves) that he was one
Of gentle blood, some noble sinner's son,
Who had, belike, deceived some humble maid,
Whom he had first seduced and then betrayed: 125
However this, he seemed a gracious lad,
In grief submissive and with patience sad.
  Passive he laboured, till his slender frame
Bent with his loads, and he at length was lame:
Strange that a frame so weak could bear so long   130
The grossest insult and the foulest wrong;
But there were causes – in the town they gave
Fire, food, and comfort, to the gentle slave;
And though stern Peter, with a cruel hand,
And knotted rope, enforced the rude command,   135
Yet he considered what he'd lately felt,
And his vile blows with selfish pity dealt.
  One day such draughts the cruel fisher made,
He could not vend them in his borough-trade,
But sailed for London-mart. The boy was ill,   140
But ever humbled to his master's will;
And on the river, where they smoothly sailed,
He strove with terror and awhile prevailed;
But new to danger on the angry sea,
He clung affrighten'd to his master's knee: 145
The boat grew leaky and the wind was strong,
Rough was the passage and the time was long;
His liquor failed, and Peter's wrath arose, –
No more is known – the rest we must suppose,
Or learn of Peter; – Peter says, he 'spied   150
The stripling's danger and for harbour tried;
Meantime the fish, and then th' apprentice died.'
  The pitying women raised a clamour round,
And weeping said, 'Thou hast thy 'prentice drowned.'
  Now the stern man was summoned to the hall,   155
To tell his tale before the burghers all:
He gave th' account; professed the lad he loved,
And kept his brazen features all unmoved.
  The mayor himself with tone severe replied,
'Henceforth with thee shall never boy abide;   160

Hire thee a freeman, whom thou durst not beat,
But who, in thy despite, will sleep and eat:
Free thou art now! – again shouldst thou appear,
Thou'lt find thy sentence, like thy soul, severe.'
 Alas! for Peter not a helping hand,   165
So was he hated, could he now command;
Alone he rowed his boat, alone he cast
His nets beside, or made his anchor fast;
To hold a rope or hear a curse was none, –
He toiled and railed; he groaned and swore alone. 170
 Thus by himself compelled to live each day,
To wait for certain hours the tide's delay;
At the same times the same dull views to see,
The bounding marsh-bank and the blighted tree;
The water only, when the tides were high,   175
When low, the mud half-covered and half-dry;
The sun-burnt tar that blisters on the planks,
And bank-side stakes in their uneven ranks;
Heaps of entangled weeds that slowly float,
As the tide rolls by the impeded boat.   180
 When tides were neap, and, in the sultry day,
Through the tall bounding mud-banks made their way,
Which on each side rose swelling, and below
The dark warm flood ran silently and slow;
There anchoring, Peter chose from man to hide, 185
There hang his head, and view the lazy tide
In its hot slimy channel slowly glide;
Where the small eels that left the deeper way
For the warm shore, within the shallows play;
Where gaping mussels, left upon the mud,   190
Slope their slow passage to the fallen flood; –
Here dull and hopeless he'd lie down and trace
How sidelong crabs had scrawled their crooked race;
Or sadly listen to the tuneless cry
Of fishing gull or clanging golden-eye;   195
What time the sea-birds to the marsh would come,
And the loud bittern, from the bulrush home,
Gave from the salt-ditch side the bellowing boom:
He nursed the feelings these dull scenes produce,
And loved to stop beside the opening sluice;   200
Where the small stream, confined in narrow bound,
Ran with a dull, unvaried, sadd'ning sound;
Where all, presented to the eye or ear,

Oppressed the soul with misery, grief, and fear.
　　Besides these objects, there were places three,   205
Which Peter seemed with certain dread to see;
When he drew near them he would turn from each,
And loudly whistle till he passed the reach.
　　A change of scene to him brought no relief;
In town, 'twas plain, men took him for a thief: 210
The sailors' wives would stop him in the street,
And say, 'Now, Peter, thou'st no boy to beat':
Infants at play, when they perceived him, ran,
Warning each other – 'That's the wicked man':
He growled an oath, and in an angry tone   215
Cursed the whole place and wished to be alone.
　　Alone he was, the same dull scenes in view,
And still more gloomy in his sight they grew:
Though man he hated, yet employèd alone
At bootless labour, he would swear and groan,   220
Cursing the shoals that glided by the spot,
And gulls that caught them when his arts could not.
　　Cold nervous tremblings shook his sturdy frame,
And strange disease – he couldn't say the name;
Wild were his dreams, and oft he rose in fright,   225
Waked by his view of horrors in the night, –
Horrors that would the sternest minds amaze,
Horrors that demons might be proud to raise:
And though he felt forsaken, grieved at heart,
To think he lived from all mankind apart;   230
Yet, if a man approached, in terrors he would start.
　　A winter passed since Peter saw the town,
And summer-lodgers were again come down;
These, idly curious, with their glasses spied
The ships in bay as anchored for the tide, –   235
The river's craft, – the bustle of the quay, –
And sea-port views, which landmen love to see.
　　One, up the river, had a man and boat
Seen day by day, now anchored, now afloat;
Fisher he seemed, yet used no net nor hook;   240
Of sea-fowl swimming by no heed he took,
But on the gliding waves still fixed his lazy look:
At certain stations he would view the stream,
As if he stood bewildered in a dream,
Or that some power had chained him for a time,   245
To feel a curse or meditate on crime.

This known, some curious, some in pity went,
And others questioned – 'Wretch, dost thou repent?'
He heard, he trembled, and in fear resigned
His boat: new terror filled his restless mind;   250
Furious he grew, and up the country ran,
And there they seized him – a distempered man: –
Him we received, and to a parish-bed,
Followed and cursed, the groaning man was led.
  Here when they saw him, whom they used to shun,   255
A lost, lone man, so harassed and undone;
Our gentle females, ever prompt to feel,
Perceived compassion on their anger steal;
His crimes they could not from their memories blot,
But they were grieved, and trembled at his lot.   260
  A priest too came, to whom his words are told
And all the signs they shuddered to behold.
  'Look! look!' they cried; 'his limbs with horror shake.
And as he grinds his teeth, what noise they make!
How glare his angry eyes, and yet he's not awake: 265
See! what cold drops upon his forehead stand,
And how he clenches that broad bony hand.'
  The priest attending, found he spoke at times
As one alluding to his fears and crimes:
'It was the fall,' he muttered, 'I can show   270
The manner how – I never struck a blow': –
And then aloud – 'Unhand me, free my chain;
An oath, he fell – it struck him to the brain: –
Why ask my father? – that old man will swear
Against my life; besides, he wasn't there: –   275
What, all agreed? – Am I to die to-day? –
My Lord, in mercy, give me time to pray.'
  Then, as they watched him, calmer he became,
And grew so weak he couldn't move his frame,
But murmuring spake, – while they could see and hear   280
The start of terror and the groan of fear;
See the large dew-beads on his forehead rise,
And the cold death-drop glaze his sunken eyes;
Nor yet he died, but with unwonted force
Seemed with some fancied being to discourse: 285
He knew not us, or with accustomed art
He hid the knowledge, yet exposed his heart;
'Twas part confession, and the rest defence,
A madman's tale, with gleams of waking sense.

'I'll tell you all,' he said, 'the very day   290
When the old man first placed them in my way:
My father's spirit – he who always tried
To give me trouble, when he lived and died -
When he was gone, he could not be content
To see my days in painful labour spent,   295
But would appoint his meetings, and he made
Me watch at these, and so neglect my trade.
　　'Twas one hot noon, all silent, still, serene,
No living being had I lately seen;
I paddled up and down and dipped my net,   300
But (such his pleasure) I could nothing get, –
A father's pleasure, when his toil was done,
To plague and torture thus an only son!
And so I sat and looked upon the stream,
How it ran on, and felt as in a dream: 305
But dream it was not: no! – I fixed my eyes
On the mid stream and saw the spirits rise,
I saw my father on the water stand,
And hold a thin pale boy in either hand;
And there they glided ghastly on the top   310
Of the salt flood, and never touched a drop:
I would have struck them, but they knew th' intent,
And smiled upon the oar, and down they went.
　　'Now, from that day, whenever I began
To dip my net, there stood the hard old man –   315
He and those boys: I humbled me and prayed
They would be gone; – they heeded not, but stayed;
Nor could I turn, nor would the boat go by,
But gazing on the spirits, there was I:
They bade me leap to death, but I was loth to die: 320
And every day, as sure as day arose,
Would these three spirits meet me ere the close;
To hear and mark them daily was my doom,
And "Come" they said, with weak, sad voices, "come".
To row away with all my strength I tried,   325
But there were they, hard by me in the tide,
The three unbodied forms – and "Come", still "come", they cried.
　　'Fathers should pity – but this old man shook
His hoary locks, and froze me by a look:
Thrice, when I struck them, through the water came   330
A hollow groan, that weakened all my frame:
"Father," said I, "have mercy": – He replied,

I know not what – the angry spirit lied, –
"Didst thou not draw thy knife?" said he: – 'Twas true,
But I had pity and my arm withdrew: 335
He cried for mercy which I kindly gave,
But he has no compassion in his grave.
   'There were three places, where they ever rose, –
The whole long river has not such as those, –
Places accursed, where, if a man remain,   340
He'll see the things which strike him to the brain;
And there they made me on my paddle lean,
And look at them for hours; – accursèd scene!
When they would glide to that smooth eddy-space,
Then bid me leap and join them in the place;   345
And at my groans each little villain sprite
Enjoyed my pains and vanished in delight.
   'In one fierce summer-day, when my poor brain
Was burning hot, and cruel was my pain,
Then came this father-foe, and there he stood   350
With his two boys again upon the flood;
There was more mischief in their eyes, more glee
In their pale faces when they glared at me:
Still did they force me on the oar to rest,
And when they saw me fainting and oppressed,   355
He, with his hand, the old man, scooped the flood,
And there came flame about him mixed with blood;
He bade me stoop and look upon the place,
Then flung the hot-red liquor in my face;
Burning it blazed, and then I roared for pain,   360
I thought the demons would have turned my brain.
   'Still there they stood, and forced me to behold
A place of horrors – they cannot be told –
Where the flood opened, there I heard the shriek
Of tortured guilt – no earthly tongue can speak: 365
"All days alike! for ever!" did they say,
"And unremitted torments every day:"
Yes, so they said': – But here he ceased and gazed
On all around, affrightened and amazed;
And still he tried to speak, and looked in dread   370
Of frightened females gathering round his bed;
Then dropped exhausted, and appeared at rest,
Till the strong foe the vital powers possessed:
Then with an inward, broken voice he cried,
'Again they come,' and muttered as he died.   375

William Blake (1757–1827)

115. To Autumn

O autumn, laden with fruit, and stained
With the blood of the grape, pass not, but sit
Beneath my shady roof; there thou may'st rest,
And tune thy jolly voice to my fresh pipe;
And all the daughters of the year shall dance!   5
Sing now the lusty song of fruits and flowers.

'The narrow bud opens her beauties to
The sun, and love runs in her thrilling veins;
Blossoms hang round the brows of morning, and
Flourish down the bright cheek of modest eve,   10
Till clust'ring summer breaks forth into singing,
And feathered clouds strew flowers round her head.

'The spirits of the air live on the smells
Of fruit; and joy, with pinions light, roves round
The gardens, or sits singing in the trees.'   15
Thus sang the jolly Autumn as he sat,
Then rose, girded himself, and o'er the bleak
Hills fled from our sight; but left his golden load.

116. Auguries of Innocence

To see a world in a grain of sand
And a heaven in a wild flower:
Hold infinity in the palm of your hand
And eternity in an hour.
A robin red breast in a cage   5
Puts all heaven in a rage.
A dove house filled with doves and pigeons
Shudders hell through all its regions.
A dog starved at his master's gate
Predicts the ruin of the state.   10
A horse misused upon the road

Calls to heaven for human blood.
Each outcry of the hunted hare
A fibre from the brain does tear.
A skylark wounded in the wing,   15
A cherubim does cease to sing.
The game cock clipped and armed for fight
Does the rising sun affright.
Every wolf's and lion's howl
Raises from hell a human soul.   20
The wild deer wand'ring here and there
Keeps the human soul from care.
The lamb misused breeds public strife
And yet forgives the butcher's knife.
The bat that flits at close of eve   25
Has left the brain that wont believe.
The owl that calls upon the night
Speaks the unbeliever's fright.
He who shall hurt the little wren
Shall never be belov'd by men.   30
He who the ox to wrath has moved
Shall never be by woman loved.
The wanton boy that kills the fly
Shall feel the spider's enmity.
He who torments the chafer's sprite   35
Weaves a bower in endless night.
The caterpillar on the leaf
Repeats to thee thy mother's grief.
Kill not the moth nor butterfly
For the last judgement draweth nigh.   40
He who shall train the horse to war
Shall never pass the polar bar.
The beggar's dog and widow's cat,
Feed them and thou wilt grow fat.
The gnat that sings his summer's song   45
Poison gets from slander's tongue.
The poison of the snake and newt
Is the sweat of envy's foot.
The poison of the honey bee
Is the artist's jealousy.   50
The prince's robes and beggar's rags
Are toadstools on the miser's bags.
A truth that's told with bad intent
Beats all the lies you can invent.

It is right it should be so. 55
Man was made for joy and woe.
And when this we rightly know
Through the world we safely go.
Joy and woe are woven fine,
A clothing for the soul divine. 60
Under every grief and pine
Runs a joy with silken twine.
The babe is more than swaddling bands.
Throughout all these human lands
Tools were made and born were hands. 65
Every farmer understands.
Every tear from every eye
Becomes a babe in eternity.
This is caught by females bright
And returned to its own delight. 70
The bleat, the bark, bellow, and roar
Are waves that beat on heaven's shore.
The babe that weeps the rod beneath
Writes revenge in realms of death.
The beggar's rags fluttering in air 75
Does to rags the heavens tear.
The soldier armed with sword and gun
Palsied strikes the summer's sun.
The poor man's farthing is worth more
Than all the gold on Afric's shore. 80
One mite wrung from the lab'rer's hands
Shall buy and sell the miser's lands;
Or if protected from on high
Does that whole nation sell and buy.
He who mocks the infant's faith 85
Shall be mocked in age and death.
He who shall teach the child to doubt
The rotting grave shall ne'er get out.
He who respects the infant's faith
Triumphs over hell and death. 90
The child's toys and the old man's reasons
Are the fruits of the two seasons.
The questioner who sits so sly
Shall never know how to reply.
He who replies to words of doubt 95
Doth put the light of knowledge out.
The strongest poison ever known

Came from Caesar's laurel crown.
Nought can deform the human race
Like to the armour's iron brace. 100
When gold and gems adorn the plough
To peaceful arts shall envy bow.
A riddle or the cricket's cry
Is to doubt a fit reply.
The emmet's inch and eagle's mile 105
Make lame philosophy to smile.
He who doubts from what he sees
Will ne'er believe, do what you please.
If the sun and moon should doubt
They'd immediately go out. 110
To be in a passion you good may do
But no good if a passion is in you.
The whore and gambler by the state
Licenced build that nation's fate.
The harlot's cry from street to street 115
Shall weave old England's winding sheet.
The winner's shout the loser's curse
Dance before dead England's hearse.
Every night and every morn
Some to misery are born. 120
Every morn and every night
Some are born to sweet delight.
Some are born to sweet delight.
Some are born to endless night.
We are led to believe a lie 125
When we see not through the eye.
Which was born in a night to perish in a night,
When the soul slept in beams of light.
God appears and God is light
To those poor souls who dwell in night, 130
But does a human form display
To those who dwell in realms of day

117. Long John Brown and Little Mary Bell

Little Mary Bell had a fairy in a nut,
Long John Brown had the devil in his gut.
Long John Brown loved little Mary Bell,

And the fairy drew the devil into the nut-shell.

Her fairy skipped out and her fairy skipped in;   5
He laughed at the devil saying *love is a sin.*
The devil he raged and the devil he was wroth
And the devil entered into the young man's broth.

He was soon in the gut of the loving young swain
For John eat and drank to drive away love's pain;   10
But all he could do he grew thinner and thinner
Though he eat and drank as much as ten men for his dinner.

Some said he had a wolf in his stomach day and night,
Some said he had the devil and they guessed right:
The fairy skipped about in his glory, joy, and pride,   15
And he laughed at the devil till poor John Brown died.

Then the fairy skipped out of the old nut shell
And woe and alack for pretty Mary Bell!
For the devil crept in when the fairy skipped out
And there goes miss Bell with her fusty old nut.   20

118. from *An Island in the Moon*

118a. *Little Phoebus came strutting in*

Little Phoebus came strutting in
With his fat belly and his round chin,
What is it you would please to have?
Ho! ho!
I wont let it go at only so and so.   5

118b. *When old corruption first begun*

When old corruption first begun,
Adorned in yellow vest,
He committed on flesh a whoredom –
O what a wicked beast!

From them a callow babe did spring,   5
And old corruption smiled

To think his race should never end,
For now he had a child

He called him surgery and fed
The babe with his own milk,   10
For flesh and he could ne'er agree,
She would not let him suck.

And this he always kept in mind,
And formed a crooked knife,
And ran about with bloody hands   15
To seek his mother's life.

And as he ran to seek his mother
He met with a dead woman,
He fell in love and married her,
A deed which is not common   20

She soon grew pregnant and brought forth
Scurvy and spotted fever.
The father grind and skipped about
And said, I'm made for ever

For now I have procured these imps   25
I'll try experiments.
With that he tied poor scurvy down
And stopped up all its vents.

And when the child began to swell,
He shouted out aloud,   30
'I've found the dropsy out and soon
Shall do the world more good.

He took up fever by the neck
And cut out all its spots,
And through the holes which he had made   35
He first discovered guts.

118c. *As I walked forth one may morning*

As I walked forth one may morning
To see the fields so pleasant and so gay,
O there did I spy a young maiden sweet,

Among the violets that smell so sweet,
   Smell so sweet,   5
   Smell so sweet,
Among the violets that smell so sweet.

118d. *This frog he would a wooing ride*

This frog he would a wooing ride,
   Kitty alone – Kitty alone –
This frog he would a wooing ride:
   Kitty alone and I.
Sing cock; I cary Kitty alone: 5
   Kitty alone – Kitty alone –
Cock, I cary Kitty alone:
   Kitty alone and I.

118e. *Fa ra so bo ro*

   Fa ra so bo ro
Fa ra bo ra
Sa ba ra ra ba rare roro
Sa ra ra ra bo ro ro ro
Radara   5
Sarapodo no flo ro

119. The Book of Thel

Thel's motto,

Does the eagle know what is in the pit?
Or wilt thou go ask the mole:
Can wisdom be put in a silver rod?
Or love in a golden bowl?

The daughters of Mne Seraphim led round their sunny flocks,   5
All but the youngest: she in paleness sought the secret air
To fade away like morning beauty from her mortal day:
Down by the river of Adona her soft voice is heard:
And thus her gentle lamentation falls like morning dew.

'O life of this our spring! why fades the lotus of the water?   10

Why fade these children of the spring? born but to smile and fall.
Ah! Thel is like a wat'ry bow, and like a parting cloud,
Like a reflection in a glass, like shadows in the water
Like dreams of infants, like a smile upon an infant's face,
Like the dove's voice, like transient day, like music in the air;   15
Ah! gentle may I lay me down, and gentle rest my head.
And gentle sleep the sleep of death. and gentle hear the voice
Of him that walketh in the garden in the evening time.'

The lily of the valley breathing in the humble grass
Answered the lovely maid and said: 'I am a wat'ry weed,   20
And I am very small, and love to dwell in lowly vales;
So weak, the gilded butterfly scarce perches on my head.
Yet I am visited from heaven and he that smiles on all
Walks in the valley and each morn over me spreads his hand
Saying, Rejoice thou humble grass, thou new-born lily flower,   25
Thou gentle maid of silent valleys and of modest brooks;
For thou shalt be clothed in light, and fed with morning manna:
Till summer's heat melts thee beside the fountains and the springs
To flourish in eternal vales." Then why should Thel complain,
Why should the mistress of the vales of Har, utter a sigh.'   30

She ceased and smiled in tears, then sat down in her silver shrine.
Thel answered, 'O thou little virgin of the peaceful valley
Giving to those that cannot crave, the voiceless, the o'ertired.
Thy breath doth nourish the innocent lamb, he smells thy milky garments,
He crops thy flowers while thou sittest smiling in his face,   35
Wiping his mild and meekin mouth from all contagious taints.
Thy wine doth purify the golden honey, thy perfume,
Which thou dost scatter on every little blade of grass that springs
Revives the milked cow, and tames the fire-breathing steed.
But Thel is like a faint cloud kindled at the rising sun: 40
I vanish from my pearly throne, and who shall find my place?'

'Queen of the vales,' the lily answered, 'ask the tender cloud,
And it shall tell thee why it glitters in the morning sky,
And why it scatters its bright beauty through the humid air.
Descend O little cloud and hover before the eyes of Thel.'   45

The cloud descended, and the lily bowed her modest head:
And went to mind her numerous charge among the verdant grass.

'O little cloud,' the virgin said, 'I charge thee tell to me,

Why thou complainest not when in one hour thou fade away:
Then we shall seek thee but not find; ah, Thel is like to thee.   50
I pass away: yet I complain, and no one hears my voice.'

The cloud then showed his golden head and his bright form emerged,
Hovering and glittering on the air before the face of Thel.

'O virgin know'st thou not our steeds drink of the golden springs
Where Luvah doth renew his horses: look'st thou on my youth,   55
And fearest thou because I vanish and am seen no more.
Nothing remains? O maid I tell thee, when I pass away,
It is to tenfold life, to love, to peace, and raptures holy:
Unseen descending, weigh my light wings upon balmy flowers;
And court the fair eyed dew to take me to her shining tent;   60
The weeping virgin, trembling kneels before the risen sun,
Till we arise linked in a golden band, and never part;
But walk united, bearing food to all our tender flowers.'

'Dost thou O little cloud? I fear that I am not like thee;
For I walk through the vales of Har, and smell the sweetest flowers;   65
But I feed not the little flowers: I hear the warbling birds
But I feed not the warbling birds; they fly and seek their food,
But Thel delights in these no more because I fade away,
And all shall say, without a use this shining woman lived,
Or did she only live to be at death the food of worms?'   70

The cloud reclined upon his airy throne and answered thus.

'Then if thou art the food of worms, O virgin of the skies,
How great thy use, how great thy blessing; every thing that lives,
Lives not alone, nor for itself: fear not and I will call
The weak worm from its lowly bed, and thou shalt hear its voice.   75
Come forth worm of the silent valley, to thy pensive queen.'

The helpless worm arose, and sat upon the lily's leaf,
And the bright cloud sailed on, to find his partner in the vale.

Then Thel astonished viewed the worm upon its dewy bed.

Art thou a worm? 'Image of weakness, art thou but a worm?   80
I see thee like an infant wrapped in the lily's leaf:
Ah weep not little voice, thou can'st not speak, but thou can'st weep,
Is this a worm? I see thee lay helpless and naked: weeping,

And none to answer, none to cherish thee with mother's smiles.'

The clod of clay heard the worm's voice, and raised her pitying head;   85
She bowed over the weeping infant, and her life exhaled
In milky fondness, then on Thel she fixed her humble eyes.

'O beauty of the vales of Har, we live not for ourselves,
Thou see'st me the meanest thing, and so I am indeed;
My bosom of itself is cold, and of itself is dark,   90
But he that loves the lowly pours his oil upon my head
And kisses me, and binds his nuptial bands around my breast,
And says: "Thou mother of my children, I have loved thee
And I have given thee a crown that none can take away."
But how this is sweet maid, I know not, and I cannot know,   95
I ponder, and I cannot ponder, yet I live and love.'

The daughter of beauty wiped her pitying tears with her white veil,
And said: 'Alas! I knew not this, and therefore did I weep
That God would love a worm I knew, and punish the evil foot
That wilful bruised its helpless form: but that he cherished it   100
With milk and oil, I never knew; and therefore did I weep,
And I complained in the mild air, because I fade away,
And lay me down in thy cold bed, and leave my shining lot.'

'Queen of the vales,' the matron clay answered; 'I heard thy sighs.
And all thy moans flew o'er my roof, but I have called them down: 105
Wilt thou O queen enter my house? 'tis given thee to enter,
And to return; fear nothing, enter with thy virgin feet.'

The eternal gate's terrific porter lifted the northern bar:
Thel entered in and saw the secrets of the land unknown;
She saw the couches of the dead, and where the fibrous roots   110
Of every heart on earth infixes deep its restless twists:
A land of sorrows and of tears where never smile was seen.

She wandered in the land of clouds through valleys dark, list'ning
Dolours and lamentations: waiting oft beside a dewy grave
She stood in silence, list'ning to the voices of the ground,   115
Till to her own grave plot she came, and there she sat down,
And heard this voice of sorrow breathed from the hollow pit.

'Why cannot the ear be closed to its own destruction?
Or the glist'ning eye to the poison of a smile!

Why are eyelids stored with arrows ready drawn,   120
Where a thousand fighting men in ambush lie?
Or an eye of gifts and graces, show'ring fruits and coined gold?
Why a tongue impressed with honey from every wind?
Why an ear, a whirlpool fierce to draw creations in?
Why a nostril wide inhaling terror, trembling, and affright?   125
Why a tender curb upon the youthful burning boy?
Why a little curtain of flesh on the bed of our desire?'

The virgin started from her seat, and with a shriek
Fled back unhindered till she came into the vales of Har.

120. from *Songs of Innocence*

120a. *Introduction*

Piping down the valleys wild
Piping songs of pleasant glee
On a cloud I saw a child
And he laughing said to me:

'Pipe a song about a lamb!'   5
So I piped with merry cheer.
'Piper pipe that song again'–
So I piped, he wept to hear.

'Drop thy pipe, thy happy pipe,
Sing thy songs of happy cheer.'   10
So I sung the same again
While he wept with joy to hear.

'Piper sit thee down and write
In a book that all may read'–
So he vanished from my sight   15
And I plucked a hollow reed

And I made a rural pen,
And I stained the water clear,
And I wrote my happy songs
Every child may joy to hear.   20

120b. *The Lamb*

   Little lamb who made thee?
   Dost thou know who made thee?
Gave thee life and bid thee feed
By the stream and o'er the mead;
Gave thee clothing of delight,   5
Softest clothing woolly bright;
Gave thee such a tender voice,
Making all the vales rejoice;
   Little lamb who made thee?
   Dost thou know who made thee?   10

   Little lamb I'll tell thee,
   Little lamb I'll tell thee:
He is callèd by thy name,
For he calls himself a lamb:
He is meek and he is mild,   15
He became a little child:
I a child and thou a lamb,
We are callèd by his name.
   Little lamb God bless thee.
   Little lamb God bless thee: 20

120c. *The Chimney Sweeper*

When my mother died I was very young,
And my father sold me while yet my tongue,
Could scarcely cry 'weep weep weep weep'.
So your chimneys I sweep and in soot I sleep.

There's little Tom Dacre, who cried when his head   5
That curled like a lamb's back, was shaved, so I said,
'Hush Tom never mind it, for when your head's bare,
You know that the soot cannot spoil your white hair.'

And so he was quiet, and that very night,
As Tom was a sleeping he had such a sight,   10
That thousands of sweepers Dick, Joe, Ned and Jack
Were all of them locked up in coffins of black

And by came an angel who had a bright key,
And he opened the coffins and set them all free.

Then down a green plain leaping laughing they run 15
And wash in a river and shine in the sun.

Then naked and white, all their bags left behind,
They rise upon clouds, and sport in the wind.
And the angel told Tom if he'd be a good boy,
He'd have God for his father and never want joy. 20

And so Tom awoke and we rose in the dark
And got with our bags and our brushes to work.
Though the morning was cold, Tom was happy and warm,
So if all do their duty, they need not fear harm.

120d. *The Divine Image*

To mercy pity peace and love,
All pray in their distress:
And to these virtues of delight
Return their thankfulness.

For mercy pity peace and love, 5
Is God our father dear:
And mercy pity peace and love,
Is man his child and care.

For mercy has a human heart,
Pity, a human face: 10
And love, the human form divine,
And peace, the human dress.

Then every man of every clime,
That prays in his distress,
Prays to the human form divine 15
Love mercy pity peace.

And all must love the human form,
In heathen, Turk or Jew.
Where mercy, love and pity dwell
There God is dwelling too. 20

120e. *Holy Thursday*

'Twas on a holy Thursday, their innocent faces clean,

The children walking two and two in red and blue and green,
Grey headed beadles walked before with wands as white as snow
Till into the high dome of Paul's they like Thames waters flow.

O what a multitude they seemed, these flowers of London town; 5
Seated in companies they sit with radiance all their own.
The hum of multitudes was there but multitudes of lambs
Thousands of little boys and girls raising their innocent hands.

Now like a mighty wind they raise to heaven the voice of song
Or like harmonious thunderings the seats of heaven among. 10
Beneath them sit the aged men, wise guardians of the poor.
Then cherish pity, lest you drive an angel from your door.

120f. *Nurse's Song*

When the voices of children are heard on the green
And laughing is heard on the hill,
My heart is at rest within my breast
And every thing else is still.

'Then come home my children, the sun is gone down 5
And the dews of night arise;
Come come leave off play, and let us away
Till the morning appears in the skies.'

'No, no, let us play, for it is yet day
And we cannot go to sleep; 10
Besides in the sky, the little birds fly
And the hills are all covered with sheep.'

'Well well go and play till the light fades away
And then go home to bed.'
The little ones leaped and shouted and laughed 15
And all the hills echoèd.

121. from *Songs of Experience*

121a. *Introduction*

Hear the voice of the bard!
Who present, past, and future sees,

Whose ears have heard,
The holy word,
That walked among the ancient trees.   5

Calling the lapsed soul
And weeping in the evening dew:
That might control
The starry pole:
And fallen fallen light renew!   10

'O earth O earth return!
Arise from out the dewy grass;
Night is worn,
And the morn
Rises from the slumberous mass.   15

Turn away no more:
Why wilt thou turn away?
The starry floor,
The wat'ry shore
Is giv'n thee till the break of day.'   20

121b. *The Clod and the Pebble*

'Love seeketh not itself to please,
Nor for itself hath any care;
But for another gives its ease,
And builds a heaven in hell's despair.'

    So sang a little clod of clay,   5
    Trodden with the cattle's feet:
    But a pebble of the brook,
    Warbled out these metres meet.

'Love seeketh only self to please,
To bind another to its delight;   10
Joys in another's loss of ease,
And builds a hell in heaven's despite.'

121c. *The Chimney Sweeper*

A little black thing among the snow:
Crying 'weep, weep', in notes of woe!

'Where are thy father and mother? Say?'
'They are both gone up to the church to pray.

'Because I was happy upon the heath,   5
And smiled among the winter's snow:
They clothed me in the clothes of death,
And taught me to sing the notes of woe.

'And because I am happy, and dance and sing,
They think they have done me no injury: 10
And are gone to praise God and his priest and king
Who make up a heaven of our misery.'

121d. *The Sick Rose*

O rose thou art sick.
The invisible worm,
That flies in the night
In the howling storm:

Has found out thy bed   5
Of crimson joy:
And his dark secret love
Does thy life destroy.

121e. *The Tiger*

Tiger, tiger, burning bright,
In the forests of the night:
What immortal hand or eye,
Could frame thy fearful symmetry?

In what distant deeps or skies   5
Burnt the fire of thine eyes?
On what wings dare he aspire?
What the hand dare seize the fire?

And what shoulder, and what art,
Could twist the sinews of thy heart?   10
And when thy heart began to beat,
What dread hand? and what dread feet?

What the hammer? what the chain?
In what furnace was thy brain?
What the anvil? what dread grasp,   15
Dare its deadly terrors clasp?

When the stars threw down their spears
And watered heaven with their tears:
Did he smile his work to see?
Did he who made the lamb make thee?   20

Tiger, tiger, burning bright,
In the forests of the night:
What immortal hand or eye
Dare frame thy fearful symmetry?

121f. *Ah! Sun-Flower*

Ah! sun-flower! weary of time,
Who countest the steps of the sun:
Seeking after that sweet golden clime
Where the traveller's journey is done.

Where the youth pined away with desire,   5
And the pale virgin shrouded in snow:
Arise from their graves and aspire,
Where my sun-flower wishes to go.

121g. *The Garden of Love*

I went to the garden of love,
And saw what I never had seen:
A chapel was built in the midst,
Where I used to play on the green.

And the gates of this chapel were shut,   5
And 'Thou shalt not' writ over the door;
So I turned to the garden of love,
That so many sweet flowers bore,

And I saw it was fillèd with graves,
And tomb-stones where flowers should be: 10
And priests in black gowns, were walking their rounds,
And binding with briars, my joys and desires.

121h. *London*

I wander through each chartered street,
Near where the chartered Thames does flow.
And mark in every face I meet
Marks of weakness, marks of woe.

In every cry of every man, 5
In every infant's cry of fear,
In every voice, in every ban,
The mind-forged manacles I hear:

How the chimney-sweeper's cry
Every black'ning church appals, 10
And the hapless soldier's sigh,
Runs in blood down palace walls.

But most through midnight streets I hear
How the youthful harlot's curse
Blasts the new-born infant's tear 15
And blights with plagues the marriage hearse.

121i. *Infant Sorrow*

My mother groaned! my father wept.
Into the dangerous world I leapt:
Helpless, naked, piping loud:
Like a fiend hid in a cloud.

Struggling in my father's hands: 5
Striving against my swaddling bands:
Bound and weary I thought best
To sulk upon my mother's breast.

121j. *A Poison Tree*

I was angry with my friend:
I told my wrath, my wrath did end.
I was angry with my foe:
I told it not, my wrath did grow.

And I watered it in fears, 5
Night and morning with my tears:

And I sunnèd it with smiles,
And with soft deceitful wiles.

And it grew both day and night.
Till it bore an apple bright.   10
And my foe beheld it shine,
And he knew that it was mine.

And into my garden stole
When the night had veiled the pole;
In the morning glad I see   15
My foe outstretched beneath the tree.

123. from *The Marriage of Heaven and Hell*

Rintrah roars and shakes his fires in the burdened air;
Hungry clouds swag on the deep.

Once meek, and in a perilous path,
The just man kept his course along
The vale of death.   5
Roses are planted where thorns grow,
And on the barren heath
Sing the honey bees.

Then the perilous path was planted:
And a river, and a spring   10
On every cliff and tomb;
And on the bleached bones
Red clay brought forth.

Till the villain left the paths of ease,
To walk in perilous paths, and drive   15
The just man into barren climes.

Now the sneaking serpent walks
In mild humility.
And the just man rages in the wilds
Where lions roam.   20

Rintrah roars and shakes his fires in the burdened air:
Hungry clouds swag on the deep.

123. from *Milton: a Poem in Books*

To justify the Ways of God to Men

PREFACE: The stolen and perverted writings of Homer and Ovid, of Plato
and Cicero, which all men ought to contemn, are set up by artifice against
the sublime of the Bible. But when the new age is at leisure to pronounce,
all will be set right: and those grand works of the more ancient and con-
sciously and professedly inspired men, will hold their proper rank, and the
daughters of memory shall become the daughters of inspiration. Shake-
speare and Milton were both curbed by the general malady and infection
from the silly Greek and Latin slaves of the sword.

Rouse up O young men of the new age! Set your foreheads against the
ignorant hirelings! For we have hirelings in the camp, the court, and the
university: who would if they could, for ever depress mental and prolong
corporeal war. Painters! on you I call! Sculptors! Architects! Suffer not the
fashionable fools to depress your powers by the prices they pretend to give
for contemptible works or the expensive advertising boasts that they make
of such works; believe Christ and his apostles that there is a class of men
whose whole delight is in destroying. We do not want either Greek or
Roman models if we are just and true to our own imaginations, those
worlds of eternity in which we shall live for ever; in Jesus our Lord.

And did those feet in ancient time
Walk upon England's mountains green:
And was the holy Lamb of God
On England's pleasant pastures seen!

And did the countenance divine   5
Shine forth upon our clouded hills?
And was Jerusalem builded here,
Among these dark satanic mills?

Bring me my bow of burning gold:
Bring me my arrows of desire: 10
Bring me my spear: O clouds unfold!
Bring me my chariot of fire!

I will not cease from mental fight,
Nor shall my sword sleep in my hand:
Till we have built Jerusalem,   15
In England's green and pleasant land.

Mary Robinson (1758–1800)

124. Female Fashions for 1799

A form, as any taper, fine;
A head like half-pint bason;
Where golden cords, and bands entwine,
As rich as fleece of Jason.

A pair of shoulders strong and wide,   5
Like country clown enlisting;
Bare arms long dangling by the side,
And shoes of ragged listing!

Cravats like towels, thick and broad,
Long tippets made of bear-skin,   10
Muffs that a Russian might applaud,
And rouge to spoil a fair skin.

Long petticoats to hide the feet,
Silk hose with clocks of scarlet;
A load of perfume, sick'ning sweet,   15
Bought of Parisian varlet.

A bush of hair, the brow to shade,
Sometimes the eyes to cover;
A necklace that might be displayed
By Otaheitean lover!   20

A bowl of straw to deck the head,
Like porringer unmeaning;
A bunch of poppies flaming red,
With motly ribands streaming.

Bare ears on either side the head,   25
Like wood-wild savage satyr;
Tinted with deep vermilion red,
To shame the blush of nature.

Red elbows, gauzy gloves, that add
An icy cov'ring merely;   30
A wadded coat, the shape to pad,
Like Dutch-women – or nearly.

Such is caprice! but, lovely kind!
Oh! let each mental feature
Proclaim the labour of the mind,   35
And leave your charms to nature.

125. Male Fashions for 1799

Crops like hedgehogs, high-crowned hats,
Whiskers like Jew Moses;
Padded collars, thick cravats,
And cheeks as red as roses.

Faces painted pink and brown;   5
Waistcoats striped and gaudy,
Sleeves thrice doubled thick with down,
And straps to brace the body.

Short great-coats that reach the knees,
Boots like French postillion;   10
Worn the German race to please,
But laughed at by the million.

Square-toed shoes, with silken strings,
Pantaloons not fitting;
Finger decked with wedding rings,   15
And small-clothes made of knitting.

Curricles so low, that they
Along the ground seem dragging;
Hacks that weary half the day
In Rotten-row are fagging.   20

Bull-dogs grim, and boxers bold,
In noble trains attending;
Science which is bought with gold,
And flatt'rers vice commending.

Hair-cords, and plain rings, to show   25
Many a Lady's favour,
Bought by ev'ry vaunting beau,
With mischievous endeavour.

Such is giddy Fashion's son!
Such a Modern Lover!   30
Oh! would their reign had ne'er begun!
And may it soon be over!

126. London's Summer Morning

Who has not waked to list the busy sounds
Of summer's morning, in the sultry smoke
Of noisy London? On the pavement hot
The sooty chimney-boy, with dingy face
And tattered covering, shrilly bawls his trade,   5
Rousing the sleepy housemaid. At the door
The milk-pail rattles, and the tinkling bell
Proclaims the dustman's office; while the street
Is lost in clouds impervious. Now begins
The din of hackney-coaches, waggons, carts;   10
While tinmen's shops, and noisy trunk-makers,
Knife-grinders, coopers, squeaking cork-cutters,
Fruit-barrows, and the hunger-giving cries
Of vegetable vendors, fill the air.
Now ev'ry shop displays its varied trade,   15
And the fresh-sprinkled pavement cools the feet
Of early walkers. At the private door
The ruddy housemaid twirls the busy mop,
Annoying the smart 'prentice, or neat girl,
Tripping with band-box lightly. Now the sun   20
Darts burning splendour on the glitt'ring pane,
Save where the canvas awning throws a shade
On the gay merchandise. Now, spruce and trim,
In shops (where beauty smiles with industry,)

Sits the smart damsel; while the passenger   25
Peeps through the window, watching ev'ry charm.
Now pastry dainties catch the eye minute
Of humming insects, while the limy snare
Waits to enthral them. Now the lamp-lighter
Mounts the tall ladder, nimbly vent'rous,   30
To trim the half-filled lamp; while at his feet
The pot-boy yells discordant! All along
The sultry pavement, the old-clothes-man cries
In tone monotonous, and side-long views
The area for his traffic: now the bag   35
Is slily opened, and the half-worn suit
(Sometimes the pilfered treasure of the base
Domestic spoiler), for one half its worth,
Sinks in the green abyss. The porter now
Bears his huge load along the burning way;   40
And the poor poet wakes from busy dreams,
To paint the summer morning.

Robert Burns (1759–1796)

127. A Red, Red Rose

Tune: Major Graham

My luve is like a red, red rose,
    That's newly sprung in June.
My luve is like the melodie,
    That's sweetly played in tune.

As fair art thou, my bonie lass,   5
    So deep in luve am I,
And I will luve thee still, my dear,
    Till a' the seas gang dry.
        [repeat]

Till a' the seas gang dry, my dear,
    And the rocks melt wi the sun!   10
And I will luve thee still, my dear,
    While the sands o' life shall run,

And fare thee weel, my only luve,
  And fare thee weel a while!
And I will come again, my luve,   15
  Though it were ten thousand mile.
    [repeat]

128. The White Cockade

Chorus   *O, he's a ranting, roving lad!*
       He is a brisk an' a bonie lad!
       Betide what may, I will be wed,
       And follow the boy wi' the white cockade!

My love was born in Aberdeen,   5
The boniest lad that e'er was seen;
But now he makes our hearts fu' sad,
He takes the field wi' his white cockade.

I'll sell my rock°, my reel, my tow*,   *distaff, flax*
My guid gray mare and hawkit° cow,   *spotted* 10
To buy myself a tartan plaid,
To follow the boy wi the white cockade.

129. To a Louse on Seeing one on a Lady's Bonnet at Church

Ha! whare ye gaun, ye crowlan ferlie°?   *weirdy*
Your impudence protects you sairly°,   *quite*
I canna say but ye strunt° rarely   *stride*
  Owre gauze and lace,
Though faith! I fear ye dine but sparely   5
  On sic° a place.   *such*

Ye ugly, creepin, blastit wonner°,   *wonder*
Detested, shunned by saunt an' sinner,
How daur ye set your fit° upon her –   *feet*
  Sae fine a lady!   10
Gae somewhere else and seek your dinner
  On some poor body.

Swith°! in some beggar's hauffet* squattle§:   *Now, sideburns, burrow in*
There ye may creep, and sprawl, and sprattle,
Wi' ither kindred, jumping cattle,   15
    In shoals and nations;
Whare horn nor bane° ne'er daur unsettle   *bone comb*
    Your thick plantations.

Now haud you there! ye're out o' sight,
Below the fatt'rels°, snug an' tight;   *ribbon-ends* 20
Na, faith ye yet! ye'll no be right,
    Till ye've got on it –
The vera tapmost, tow'ring height
    O' Miss's bonnet.

My sooth! right bauld ye set your nose out,   25
As plump an' grey as onie grozet°:   *gooseberry*
O for some rank, mercurial rozet°,   *resin (used as insecticide)*
    Or fell, red smeddum°,   *disinfectant powder*
I'd gie ye sic a hearty dose o't,
    Wad dress your droddum°.   *rump* 30

I wad na been surprised to spy
You on an auld wife's flainen toy°;   *flannel cap*
Or aiblins° some bit duddie* boy,   *perhaps, little ragged*
    On's wyliecoat°;   *flannel vest*
But Miss's fine Lunardi°! fye!   *bonnet* 35
    How daur ye do't?

O Jenny, dinna toss your head,
An' set your beauties a' abroad!
Ye little ken what cursèd speed
    The blastie's makin!   40
Thae winks an' finger-ends, I dread,
    Are notice takin!

O wad some power the giftie gie us
To see oursels as ithers see us!
It wad frae monie a blunder free us,   45
    An' foolish notion:
What airs in dress an' gait wad lea'e us,
    An' ev'n devotion!

130. The Banks o' Doon

Ye banks and braes o' bonnie Doon,
   How can ye bloom sae fresh and fair?
How can ye chant, ye little birds,
   And I sae weary fu' o' care!
Thou'll break my heart, thou warbling bird,   5
   That wantons through the flowering thorn!
Thou minds me o' departed joys,
   Departed never to return.

Aft hae I roved by bonie Doon
   To see the rose and woodbine twine,   10
And ilka bird sang o' its luve,
   And fondly sae did I o' mine.
Wi' lightsome heart I pu'd a rose,
   Fu' sweet upon its thorny tree;
And my fause° luver staw* my rose –   *false, stole* 15
   But ah! he left the thorn wi me.

131. Charlie He's My Darling

Chorus   *An' Charlie he's my darling, my darling, my darling,*
        Charlie he's my darling, the young Chevalier. –

'Twas on a Monday morning   5
   Right early in the year
That Charlie came to our town –
   The young Chevalier. –

As he was walking up the street
   The city for to view,   10
O there he spied a bonie lass
   The window looking through. –

Sae light's he jimpèd up the stair,
   And tirlèd at the pin°   *rattled at the door*
And wha sae ready as hersel'   15
   To let the laddie in. –

He set his Jenny on his knee,
    All in his Highland dress;
For brawlie° weel he kend the way   *admirably*
    To please a bonie lass. –   20

It's up yon heathery mountain
    And down yon scroggy glen,
We daur na gang a-milking
    For Charlie and his men. –

132. Comin' thro the Rye

Chorus   O Jenny's a' weet°, poor body,   *wet*
          Jenny's seldom dry:
          She draigl't° a' her petticoatie,   *bedraggled*
          Comin through the rye!

Comin through the rye, poor body,   5
    Comin through the rye,
She draigl't a' her petticoatie,
    Comin through the rye!

Gin a body meet a body
    Comin through the rye,   10
Gin a body kiss a body,
    Need a body cry?

Gin a body meet a body
    Comin through the glen,
Gin a body kiss a body,   15
    Need the warld ken?

133. My Heart's in the Highlands

Chorus   *My heart's in the Highlands, my heart is not here,*
My heart's in the Highlands a-chasing the deer,
A-chasing the wild deer and following the roe –
My heart's in the Highlands, wherever I go!

Farewell to the Highlands, farewell to the North,   5
The birthplace of valour, the country of worth!
Wherever I wander, wherever I rove,
The hills of the Highlands for ever I love.

Farewell to the mountains high covered with snow,
Farewell to the straths and green valleys below,   10
Farewell to the forests and wild-hanging woods,
Farewell to the torrents and loud-pouring floods!

134. Robert Bruce's March to Bannockburn

Scots, wha hae° wi Wallace bled,   *who have*
Scots, wham Bruce has aften led,
Welcome to your gory bed,
   Or to victorie. –

Now's the day, and now's the hour: 5
See the front o' battle lour,
See approach proud Edward's power –
   Chains and slaverie. –

Wha will be a traitor knave?
Wha can fill a coward's grave?   10
Wha sae base as be a slave? –
   Let him turn, and flee: –

Wha for Scotland's king and law
Freedom's sword will strongly draw,
Freeman stand or freeman fa',   15
   Let him follow me. –

By oppression's woes and pains,
By your sons in servile chains,
We will drain our dearest veins
    But they *shall* be free!   20

Lay the proud usurpers low!
Tyrants fall in every foe!
Liberty's in every blow!
    Let us DO – or DIE!

135. Auld Lang Syne

Chorus   *For auld lang syne, my jo,*
        For auld lang syne,
        We'll tak a cup° o' kindness yet   *[or 'kiss']*
        For auld lang syne°!   *long ago*

Should auld acquaintance be forgot,   5
    And never brought to mind?
Should auld acquaintance be forgot,
    And auld lang syne!

And surely ye'll be your pint-stowp°,   *tankard*
    And surely I'll be mine,   10
And we'll tak a cup o' kindness yet
    For auld lang syne!

We twa hae run about the braes,
    And poued° the gowans* fine,   *pulled, wild-flowers*
But we've wandered monie a weary fit   15
    Sin' auld lang syne.

We twa hae paidled in the burn
    Frae morning sun till dine°,   *dinner time*
But seas between us braid hae roared
    Sin' auld lang syne.   20

And there's a hand, my trusty fiere,
    And gie's a hand o' thine,
And we'll tak a right guid-willie° waught*   *hospitable, draught*
    For auld lang syne!

136. Address to the Deil°   *devil*

> *O Prince! O Chief of many thronèd pow'rs!*
> *That led th' embattled seraphim to war . . .*
>   John Milton, *Paradise* Lost I, 1.129f

O Thou! whatever title suit thee –
Auld Hornie, Satan, Nick, or Clootie° –   *cloven-hoofed*
Wha in yon cavern grim an' sootie,
   Closed under hatches,
Spairges° about the brunstane cootie*,   *stains, little tub* 5
   To scaud° poor wretches!   *scald*

Hear me, auld Hangie°, for a wee,   *hangman*
An' let poor damned bodies be;
I'm sure sma' pleasure it can gie,
   Ev'n to a deil,   10
To skelp an' scaud poor dogs like me
   An' hear us squeel.

Great is thy pow'r an' great thy fame;
Far kenned an' noted is thy name;
An' though yon lowin heugh's° thy hame,   *crag* 15
   Thou travels far;
An' faith! thou's neither lag, nor lame,
   Nor blate°, nor scaur*.   *hold back, scare*

Whyles, ranging like a roarin lion,
For prey, a' holes an' corners trying;   20
Whyles, on the strong-winged tempest flyin,
   Tirlin° the kirks;   *uncovering*
Whyles, in the human bosom pryin',
   Unseen thou lurks.

I've heard my rev'rend graunie say,   25
In lanely glens ye like to stray;
Or, where auld ruined castles grey
   Nod to the moon,
Ye fright the nightly wand'rer's way
   Wi' eldritch° croon.   *elfin* 30

When twilight did my graunie summon,
To say her pray'rs, douce, honest woman!
Aft yont° the dyke she's heard you bummin*,   *beyond, humming*
   Wi' eerie drone;
Or, rustlin, through the boortrees° comin',   *hedge trees* 35
   Wi' heavy groan.

Ae dreary, windy, winter night,
The stars shot down wi sklentin° light,   *slanting*
Wi you mysel, I gat a fright:
   Ayont the lough°,   *loch* 40
Ye, like a rash-buss°, stood in sight,   *bush of rushes*
   Wi' waving sugh°.   *sough*

The cudgel in my nieve° did shake,   *fist*
Each bristled hair stood like a stake;
When wi an eldritch, stoor° 'quaick, quaick,'   *hoarse* 45
   Amang the springs,
Awa ye squattered° like a drake,   *flapped*
   On whistling wings.

Let warlocks grim, an' withered hags,
Tell how wi you, on ragweed nags,   50
They skim the muirs an' dizzy crags,
   Wi' wicked speed;
And in kirk-yards renew their leagues,
   Owre howkit° dead.   *exhumed*

Thence, countra° wives, wi toil an' pain,   *country* 55
May plunge an' plunge the kirn° in vain;   *churn*
For O! the yellow treasure's taen
   By witching skill;
An' dawtit°, twal-pint* Hawkie's§ gaen   *patted, twelve-pint, cow*
   As yell's the bill.   60

Thence, mystic knots mak great abuse
On young guidmen, fond, keen an' croose;
When the best wark-lume i' the house,
   By cantraip° wit,   *magic*
Is instant made no worth a louse,   65
   Just at the bit.

When thowes° dissolve the snawy hoord,   *thaws*
An' float the jinglin icy boord,
Then, water-kelpies haunt the foord,
    By your direction,   70
An' nighted trav'llers are allured
    To their destruction.

An' aft your moss-traversing spunkies°   *will-o-wisps*
Decoy the wight that late an' drunk is:
The bleezin°, cursed, mischievous monkies   *blazing* 75
    Delude his eyes,
Till in some miry slough he sunk is,
    Ne'er mair to rise.

When Masons' mystic word an' grip
In storms an' tempests raise you up,   80
Some cock or cat your rage maun stop,
    Or, strange to tell!
The youngest brother ye wad whip
    Aff straught to hell.

Lang syne in Eden's bonie yard,   85
When youthfu' lovers first were paired,
An' all the soul of love they shared,
    The raptured hour,
Sweet on the fragrant flow'ry swaird,
    In shady bow'r: 90

Then you, ye auld, snick-drawing° dog!   *scheming*
Ye cam to Paradise incog,
An' played on man a cursèd brogue
    (Black be your fa'!),
An' gied the infant warld a shog°,   *shake* 95
    'Maist ruined a'.

D'ye mind that day when in a bizz°   *buzz*
Wi' reekit duds°, an' reestit gizz*,   *smoky rags, withered wig*
Ye did present your smoutie phiz*   *smutty face*
    'Mang better folk;   100
An' sklented° on the man of Uzz   *played*
    Your spitefu' joke?

An' how ye gat him i' your thrall,
An' brak him out o' house an' hal',
While scabs an' botches did him gall,   105
    Wi' bitter claw;
An' lowsed his ill-tongued wicked scaul° –   *scolding wife*
    Was warst ava°?   *of all*

But a' your doings to rehearse,
Your wily snares an' fechtin° fierce,   *fighting* 110
Sin' that day Michael did you pierce
    Down to this time,
Wad ding° a Lallan* tongue, or Erse,   *defeat, Lowland*
    In prose or rhyme.

An' now, auld Cloots, I ken ye're thinkin,   115
A certain bardie's rantin, drinkin,
Some luckless hour will send him linkin,
    To your black pit;
But, faith! he'll turn a corner jinkin°,   *elusively*
    An' cheat you yet.   120

But fare-you-weel, auld Nickie-Ben!
O, wad ye tak a thought an' men'!
Ye aiblins° might – I dinna ken –   *maybe*
    Still hae a stake:
I'm wae to think upo' yon den,   125
    Ev'n for your sake!

137. To a Mouse, on Turning Her Up in her Nest with the Plough, November 1785

Wee, sleekit°, cowrin, tim'rous beastie,   *glossy*
O, what a panic's in thy breastie!
Thou need na start awa sae hasty
    Wi' bickering brattle!
I wad be laith° to rin an' chase thee,   *loath* 5
    Wi' murdering pattle°!   *trowel*

I'm truly sorry man's dominion
Has broken nature's social union,
An' justifies that ill opinion
    Which makes thee startle   10

At me, thy poor, earth-born companion
   An' fellow mortal!

I doubt na, whyles, but thou may thieve;
What then? poor beastie, thou maun live!
A daimen-icker° in a thrave*   *occasional ear of corn, stook* 15
   'S a sma' request;
I'll get a blessin wi the lave°,   *rest*
   An' never miss't!

Thy wee-bit housie, too, in ruin!
Its silly wa's the win's are strewin!   20
An' naething, now, to big° a new ane,   *build*
   O' foggage° green!   *pasture grass*
An' bleak December's win's ensuin,
   Baith snell° an' keen!   *fast*

Thou saw the fields laid bare an' waste,   25
An' weary winter comin fast,
An' cozie here, beneath the blast,
   Thou thought to dwell,
Till crash! the cruel coulter° past   *front plough-blade*
   Out through thy cell.   30

That wee bit heap o' leaves an' stibble,
Has cost thee monie a weary nibble!
Now thou's turned out, for a' thy trouble,
   But house or hald,
To thole° the winter's sleety dribble,   *endure* 35
   An' cranreuch° cauld!   *hoarfrost*

But Mousie, thou art no thy lane°,   *alone*
In proving foresight may be vain:
The best-laid schemes o' mice an' men
   Gang aft agley°,   *awry* 40
An' lea'e us nought but grief an' pain,
   For promised joy!

Still thou art blest, compared wi' me!
The present only toucheth thee:
But och! I backward cast my e'e,   45
   On prospects drear!
An' forward, though I canna see,
   I guess an' fear!

138. Tam o' Shanter°: a Tale   *a Carrick farm*

'Of Biownyis and of Bogillis full is this buke.'
Gavin Douglas

When chapman billies° leave the street,   *fellow-pedlars*
And drouthy° neebors neebors meet,   *thirsty*
As market-days are wearing late,
An' folk begin to tak the gate;
While we sit bousing° at the nappy*,   *boozing, ale* 5
An' getting fou and unco happy,
We think na on the lang Scots miles,
The mosses, waters, slaps, and styles,
That lie between us and our hame,   10
Whare sits our sulky, sullen dame,
Gathering her brows like gathering storm,
Nursing her wrath to keep it warm.
This truth fand honest Tam o' Shanter,
As he frae Ayr ae night did canter: 15
(Auld Ayr, wham ne'er a town surpasses,
For honest men and bonie lasses).
O Tam, had'st thou but been sae wise,
As taen thy ain wife Kate's advice!
She tauld thee weel thou was a skellum°,   *scoundrel*
A blethering, blustering, drunken blellum°;   *blusterer* 20
That frae November till October,
Ae market-day thou was nae sober;
That ilka melder° wi the miller,   *grinding-time*
Thou sat as lang as thou had siller;
That ev'ry naig was ca'd a shoe on,   25
The smith and thee gat roaring fou on;
That at the Lord's house, even on Sunday,
Thou drank wi Kirkton Jean till Monday.
She prophesied, that, late or soon,
Thou would be found deep drowned in Doon,   30
Or catched wi warlocks in the mirk
By Alloway's auld, haunted kirk.
Ah! gentle dames, it gars me greet,
To think how monie counsels sweet,
How monie lengthened, sage advices   35
The husband frae the wife despises!
But to our tale: – Ae market-night,

Tam had got planted unco right,
Fast by an ingle, bleezing finely,
Wi' reaming swats°, that drank divinely;   *frothy new beer* 40
And at his elbow, souter° Johnnie,   *cobbler*
His ancient, trusty, drouthy cronie;
Tam lo'ed him like a very brither;
They had been fou for weeks thegither.
The night drave on wi sangs and clatter;   45
And ay the ale was growing better:
The landlady and Tam grew gracious
Wi secret favours, sweet and precious:
The souter tauld his queerest stories;
The landlord's laugh was ready chorus: 50
The storm without might rair and rustle,
Tam did na mind the storm a whistle.
    Care, mad to see a man sae happy,
E'en drowned himsel amang the nappy.
As bees flee hame wi' lades o' treasure,   55
The minutes winged their way wi' pleasure:
Kings may be blest but Tam was glorious,
O'er a' the ills o' life victorious!
    But pleasures are like poppies spread:
You seize the flow'r, its bloom is shed;   60
Or like the snow falls in the river,
A moment white – then melts for ever;
Or like the borealis race,
That flit ere you can point their place;
Or like the rainbow's lovely form   65
Evanishing amid the storm.
Nae man can tether time or tide;
The hour approaches Tam maun ride:
That hour, o' night's black arch the key-stane,
That dreary hour Tam mounts his beast in;   70
And sic a night he taks the road in,
As ne'er poor sinner was abroad in.
    The wind blew as 'twad blawn its last;
The rattling showers rose on the blast;
The speedy gleams the darkness swallowed;   75
Loud, deep, and lang the thunder bellowed:
That night, a child might understand,
The Deil° had business on his hand.   *devil*
    Weel mounted on his gray mare Meg,
A better never lifted leg,   80

Tam skelpit° on through dub and mire,   *thrashed*
Despising wind, and rain, and fire;
Whiles holding fast his guid blue bonnet,
Whiles crooning o'er some auld Scots sonnet,
Whiles glow'ring round wi prudent cares,   85
Lest bogles° catch him unawares: *spectres*
Kirk-Alloway was drawing nigh,
Whare ghaists and houlets nightly cry.
    By this time he was cross the ford,
Whare in the snaw the chapman smoored°;   *smothered* 90
And past the birks° and meikle* stane,   *birches, abundant*
Whare drunken Charlie brak's neck-bane;
And through the whins, and by the cairn,
Whare hunters fand the murdered bairn;
And near the thorn, aboon the well,   95
Whare Mungo's mither hanged hersel.
Before him Doon pours all his floods;
The doubling storm roars through the woods;
The lightnings flash from pole to pole;
Near and more near the thunders roll: 100
When, glimmering through the groaning trees,
Kirk-Alloway seemed in a bleeze°,   *blaze*
Through ilka bore° the beams were glancing,   *crack*
And loud resounded mirth and dancing.
    Inspiring bold John Barleycorn,   105
What dangers thou can'st make us scorn!
Wi' tippenny, we fear nae evil;
Wi' usquabae°, we'll face the Devil!   *whisky*
The swats sae reamed in Tammie's noddle,
Fair play, he cared na deils a boddle°.   *farthing* 110
But Maggie stood, right sair astonished,
Till, by the heel and hand admonished,
She ventured forward on the light;
And, vow! Tam saw an unco sight!
    Warlocks and witches in a dance: 115
Nae cotillion, brent new frae France,
But hornpipes, jigs, strathspeys, and reels,
Put life and mettle in their heels.
A winnock-bunker° in the east,   *window-seat*
There sat auld Nick, in shape o' beast;   120
A tousie tyke°, black, grim, and large,   *shaggy cur*
To gie them music was his charge:
He screwed the pipes and gart them skirl°,   *made them screech*

Till roof and rafters a' did dirl°.   rattle
Coffins stood round, like open presses,   125
That shawed the dead in their last dresses;
And, by some devilish cantraip° sleight,   witchy
Each in its cauld hand held a light:
By which heroic Tam was able
To note upon the haly table,   130
A murderer's banes, in gibbet-airns°;   gibbet-fetters
Twa span-lang, wee, unchristened bairns;
A thief new-cutted frae a rape –
Wi his last gasp his gab did gape;
Five tomahawks wi bluid red-rusted;   135
Five scymitars wi' murder crusted;
A garter which a babe had strangled;
A knife a father's throat had mangled –
Whom his ain son o' life bereft –
The grey-hairs yet stack to the heft;   140
Wi' mair o' horrible and awefu',
Which even to name wad be unlawfu'.
    As Tammie glowered, amazed, and curious,
The mirth and fun grew fast and furious;
The piper loud and louder blew,   145
The dancers quick and quicker flew,
They reeled, they set, they crossed, they cleekit°,   linked arms
Till ilka carlin swat and reekit,
And coost° her duddies to the wark,   threw off
And linket at it in her sank°!   under-garment 150
    Now Tam, o Tam! had thae been queans,
A' plump and strapping in their teens!
Their sarks, instead o' creeshie flannen,
Been snaw-white seventeen hunder linen! –
Thir breeks o' mine, my only pair,   155
That ance were plush, o' guid blue hair,
I wad hae gi'en them off my hurdies°   buttocks
For ae blink o' the bonie burdies!
    But withered beldams, auld and droll,
Rigwoodie° hags wad spean* a foal,   withered, wean 160
Louping° and flinging on a crummock*,   leaping, crutch
I wonder didna turn thy stomach!
    But Tam kend what was what fu' brawlie:
There was ae winsome wench and wawlie°,   buxom
That night enlisted in the core,   165
Lang after kend on Carrick shore;

(For monie a beast to dead she shot,
An' perished monie a bonie boat,
And shook baith meikle corn and bear,
And kept the country-side in fear).   170
Her cutty sark°, o' Paisley harn*,   *short shift, coarse linen*
That while a lassie she had worn,
In longitude though sorely scanty,
It was her best, and she was vauntie.
Ah! little kend thy reverend grannie,   175
That sark she coft° for her wee Nannie,   *bought*
Wi twa pund Scots ('twas a' her riches),
Wad ever graced a dance of witches!
    But here my Muse her wing maun cour°,   *fold*
Sic flights are far beyond her power: 180
To sing how Nannie lap and flang
(A souple jade she was and strang),
And how Tam stood like ane bewitched,
And thought his very een enriched;
Even Satan glowred, and fidged fu' fain,   185
And hotched and blew wi might and main;
Till first ae caper, syne anither,
Tam tint° his reason a' thegither,   *lost*
And roars out: 'Weel done, Cutty-sark!'
And in an instant all was dark;   190
And scarcely had he Maggie rallied,
When out the hellish legion sallied.
    As bees bizz out wi angry fyke°,   *commotion*
When plundering herds assail their byke°   *swarm*
As open pussie's° mortal foes,   *hare* 195
When, pop! she starts before their nose;
As eager runs the market-crowd,
When 'Catch the thief!' resounds aloud:
So Maggie runs, the witches follow,
Wi monie an eldritch skriech and hollo.   200
    Ah, Tam! Ah, Tam! thou'll get thy fairin°!   *reward*
In hell they'll roast thee like a herrin!
In vain thy Kate awaits thy comin!
Kate soon will be a woefu' woman!
Now, do thy speedy utmost, Meg,   205
And win the key-stane of the brig;
There, at them thou thy tail may toss,
A running stream they dare na cross!
But ere the key-stane she could make,

The fient° a tail she had to shake;   *fiend* 210
For Nannie, far before the rest,
Hard upon noble Maggie prest,
And flew at Tam wi furious ettle°;   *aim*
But little wist she Maggie's mettle!
Ae spring brought off her master hale,   215
But left behind her ain grey tail:
The carlin claught° her by the rump,   *witch clutched*
And left poor Maggie scarce a stump.
     Now, wha this tale o' truth shall read,
Ilk man, and mother's son, take heed: 220
Whene'er to drink you are inclined,
Or cutty sarks run in your mind,
Think! ye may buy the joys o'er dear:
Remember Tam o' Shanter's mare.

139. Is There for Honest Poverty

Is there for honest poverty
    That hings his head, an' a' that?
The coward-slave, we pass him by –
    We dare be poor for a' that!
For a' that, an' a' that,   5
    Our toils obscure, an' a' that,
The rank is but the guinea's stamp,
    The man's the gowd° for a' that.   *gold*

What though on hamely° fare we dine,   *homely*
    Wear hoddin° grey, an' a' that?   *homespun wool* 10
Gie fools their silks, and knaves their wine –
    A man's a man for a' that.
For a' that, an' a' that,
    Their tinsel show, an' a' that,
The honest man, though e'er sae poor,   15
    Is king o' men for a' that.

Ye see yon birkie ca'd 'a lord,'
    Wha struts, an' stares, an' a' that?
Though hundreds worship at his word,
    He's but a cuif° for a' that.   *fool* 20
For a' that, an' a' that,

His ribband, star, an' a' that,
The man o' independent mind,
   He looks an' laughs at a' that.

A prince can mak a belted knight,   25
   A marquis, duke, an' a' that!
But an honest man's aboon° his might –   *above*
   Guid faith, he mauna fa' that!
For a' that, an' a' that,
   Their dignities, an' a' that,   30
The pith o' sense an' pride o' worth
   Are higher rank than a' that.

Then let us pray that come it may
   (As come it will for a' that)
That sense and worth o'er a' the earth   35
   Shall bear the gree° an' a' that!   *social degree*
For a' that, an' a' that,
   It's comin yet for a' that,
That man to man the world o'er
   Shall brothers be for a' that.   40

ACKNOWLEDGMENTS

I am indebted to many individuals for support and help with *The Story of Poetry*. Neil Powell assisted with preparing the text; Evelyn Schlag commented on much of what I call the informal history as it was written or adapted from *Lives of the Poets*. Colleagues at Carcanet, Pamela Heaton in particular, encouraged me. At the John Rylands University Library, Stella Halkyard provided a reassuring presence. Angel García-Gómez was as always a great support.

Some passages in this book draw upon material included in my *50 British Poets 1300–1900* (1980), in *The Story of Poetry* (1999) and on essays and reviews I have written over the last thirty-five years.

OUTLINE BIBLIOGRAPHY

A full bibliography for a book of this nature would be as long as the book itself. This is a summary list of editions of poetry and poets' prose I have consulted, or recent and modern editions available to readers (some of them now on the Web) wishing to pursue the poets further. Other editions exist. The dates I give are of editions I have consulted. I provide a merely preliminary list of anthologies and secondary works, critical and contextual. I omit most monographs. In the cases of some poets, critical volumes are in print while no edition of the work is currently available.

I have a preference for critical writing by practising poets, from Dryden through Johnson, Coleridge, Arnold, Pound, Ford, Eliot, Rickword, Graves, Sisson, Davie, down to the present day.

EDITIONS AND SELECTIONS (VERSE AND PROSE)
Addison and Steele *The Tatler,* 4 vols, ed. Donald Bond (Oxford, 1987)
— *Critical Essays from the Spectator* (Oxford, 1970)
Barbauld, Anna Letitia *The Poems* ed. William McCarthy and Elizabeth Kraft (Athens, Georgia, 1994)
Blake, William *Complete Writings, with variant readings* ed. Geoffrey Keynes (London, 1966)
— *Poetry and Designs* ed. M.L. Johnson and J.E. Grant (New York, 1979)
— *Songs of Innocence and of Experience* ed. Geoffrey Keynes (London, 1967)
Burns, Robert *Poems and Songs* ed. James Kinsley, 3 vols (Oxford, 1968)
— *Poems and Songs* ed. James Kinsley (Oxford, 1969)
— *Selected Poems* ed. Carol McGuirk (Harmondsworth, 1993)
— *Selected Poetry* ed. A. Calder and W. Donnelly (Harmondsworth, 1991)
Chatterton, Thomas *The Complete Works* ed. Donald S. Taylor, 2 vols (Oxford, 1971)
— *Selected Poems* ed. Grevel Lindop (Manchester, 2003)
Collins, William *The Works* ed. R. Wendforf and C. Ruyskamp (Oxford, 1979)
— *The Poems of Gray, Collins and Goldsmith* ed. Roger Lonsdale (London, 1969)
— *Thomas Gray and William Collins. Poetical Works* ed. Roger Lonsdale (Oxford, 1977)
— *Selected Poems of Thomas Gray and William Collins* ed. Arthur Johnston (London, 1967)
Cowper, William *The Poems* ed. J. D. Baird and C. Ruyskamp, 3 vols (Oxford, 1980–95)

— *The Task and Selected Other Poems* ed. James Sambrook (London, 1994)

— *Selected Poems* ed. Nicholas Rhodes (Manchester, 2003)

— *The Centenary Letters* ed. Simon Malpas (Manchester, 2000)

Crabbe, George *The Complete Poetical Works* ed. N. Dalrymple-Champneys and A. Pollard, 3 vols (Oxford, 1988)

— *Selected Poems* ed. Gavin Edwards (Harmondsworth, 1991)

— *Tales, 1812 and other selected poems* ed. Howard Mills (Cambridge, 1967)

Fergusson, Robert *The Poems* ed. Matthew P. McDiarmid, 2 vols (Edinburgh, 1954, 1956)

— *Selected Poems* ed. James Robertson (Edinburgh, 2000)

Gay, John *Poetry and Prose* ed. V.A. Dearing with C.E. Beckwith, 2 vols (Oxford, 1974)

— *Selected Poems* ed. Marcus Walsh (Carcanet, 2003)

Goldsmith, Oliver *Collected Works* ed. Arthur Friedman, 5 vols (Oxford, 1966)

— *The Poems of Gray, Collins and Goldsmith* ed. Roger Lonsdale (London, 1969)

— *Selected Writings* ed. John Lucas (Manchester, 2003)

Gray, Thomas *The Complete Poems* ed. H.W. Starr and J.R. Hendrickson (Oxford, 1966)

— *The Poems of Gray, Collins and Goldsmith* ed. Roger Lonsdale (London, 1969)

— *Thomas Gray and William Collins: Poetical Works* ed. Roger Lonsdale (Oxford, 1977)

— *Selected Poems of Thomas Gray and William Collins* ed. Arthur Johnston (London, 1967)

— *Selected Poems* ed. John Heath-Stubbs (Manchester, 1981)

Johnson, Samuel *The Yale Edition of the Works,* vol. 4, *Poems* ed. E. L. McAdam Jr with G. Milne (New Haven, 1964)

— *The Poems* ed. D.N. Smith and E.L. McAdam Jr, revised by J.D. Fleeman (Oxford, 1974)

— *The Complete English Poems* ed. J.D. Fleeman (New Haven, 1971)

— *The Letters* ed. Bruce Redford, 5 vols (Princeton, 1992–94)

— *Lives of the English Poets* ed. L Archer-Hind, 2 vols (New York, 1964)

Leapor, Mary *Poems upon Several Occasions*, 2 vols (1748, 1751, available online as PDF files at www.orgs.muohio.edu/womenpoets/leapor/) in *Eighteenth-Century Women Poets* ed. Roger Lonsdale (Oxford, 1989)

Macpherson, James *The Poems of Ossian and Related Works* ed. Howard Gaskill (Edinburgh, 1996)

Parnell, Thomas *Collected Poems* ed. C. Rawson and F.P. Lock (Newark, Delaware, 1989)

Pope, Alexander *The Twickenham Edition of the Poems* ed. John Butt et al., 11 vols (London, 1939–69)

— *The Prose Works: The Earlier Works, 1711–1720* ed. Norman Ault (Oxford, 1936)

— *Poetry and Prose of Alexander Pope* ed. Aubrey Williams (Boston, 1969)

— *Selected Poetry* ed. Pat Rogers (Oxford, 1998)

— *The Works* ed. Andrew Crozier (Ware, 1995)

— *Selected Prose* ed. Paul Hammond (Cambridge, 1987)

— *The Correspondence* ed. George Sherburn, 5 vols (Oxford, 1956)

— *Selected Letters* ed. Howard Erskine-Hill (Oxford, 2000)

Prior, Matthew *Literary Works* ed. H.B. Wright and M.K. Spears, 2 vols (Oxford, 1971)

— *The Poetical Works* (digital reprint) (Ann Arbor, 2005)

Robinson, Mary *Selected Poems* ed. Judith Pascoe (Calgary, 1999)

— *Memoirs of the Late Mrs Robinson, written by herself*, 4 vols (London, 1801) in *Eighteenth-Century Women Poets* ed. Roger Lonsdale (Oxford, 1989)

Scott, Sir Walter *The Poetical Works* ed. J. Logie Robertson (Oxford, 1906)

— *New Love Poems* ed. Davidson Cook (Oxford, 1932)

— *Selected Poems* ed. James Reed (Manchester, 1992)

Smart, Christopher *The Poetical Works* ed. M. Walsh and K. Williamson, 6 vols (Oxford, 1980–96)

— *The Religious Poetry* ed. Marcus Walsh (Manchester, 1988)

Smith, Charlotte *The Poems* ed. Stuart Curran (Oxford, 1993)

— *Selected Poems* ed. Judith Willson (Manchester, 2004)

— in *Eighteenth-Century Women Poets* ed. Roger Lonsdale (Oxford, 1989)

Swift, Jonathan *The Poems* ed. Harold Williams, 3 vols (Oxford, 1958)

— *Selected Prose and Poetry* ed. Edward Rosenheim (New York, 1966)

— *Complete Poems* ed. Pat Rogers (Harmondsworth, 1983)

— *Selected Poems* ed. C.H. Sisson (Manchester, 1988)

Thomson, James *Poetical Works* ed. J. L. Robertson (London, 1908)

— *The Seasons* and *The Castle of Indolence* ed. James Sambrook (Oxford, 1972)

— *The Seasons* ed. James Sambrook (Oxford, 1981)

Watts, Isaac *The Works of the Rev. Isaac Watts D.D.,* ed. G. Burder, 9 vols (Leeds, 1812–13)

— *The Works* ed. P. Jennings and J. Dodderidge (Brooklyn, 1989)

— *Selected Poems* ed. Gordon Jackson (Manchester, 1999)

Wesley, Charles *A Reader* ed. John R. Tyson (New York, 2000)

— *Selected Prayers, Hymns and Sermons* by John and Charles Wesley, foreword Peter J. Gomes (New York, 2000)

Wheatley, Phillis *Complete Writings* ed. Vincent Carretta (New York, 2001)

— *Collected Works* ed. John C. Shields (New York, 1988)

Young, Edward *Night Thoughts* ed. S.A. Cornford (Cambridge, 1989)

— *The Poetical Works,* 4 vol. facsimile (Chestnut Hill, Massachusetts, 2005)

ANTHOLOGIES

Fifteen Poets from Gower to Arnold (Oxford, 1940)

Hymns Ancient and Modern (London, 1916)

Allison, A.W. et al. *The Norton Anthology of Poetry* (New York, 1983)

Davie, Donald *Augustan Lyric* (London, 1974)

— *The New Oxford Book of Christian Verse* (Oxford, 1981)

DeMaria, Robert, Jr. (ed.) *British Literature 1640–1789: An Anthology* (Oxford, 1996)

Fairer, David *Eighteenth-Century Poetry: An Annotated Anthology* (London, 2003)

Graves, Robert *English and Scottish Ballads* (London, 1957)

Gilbert, Sandra M. and Susan Gubar *The Norton Anthology of Literature by Women: the traditions in English* (New York, 1996)

Greer, G. et al. *Kissing the Rod: an anthology of seventeenth-century women's verse* (London, 1988)

Johnson, Samuel, *The Works of the English Poets, with prefaces, biographical and critical,* 75 vols (London, 1790)

Kerr, William *Restoration Verse 1660–1715* (London, 1930)

Lonsdale, Roger (ed.) *Eighteenth-Century Women Poets* (Oxford, 1989)

Moore, Geoffrey *American Literature: a representative anthology of American writing from Colonial times to the present* (London, 1964)

Percy, Thomas *Reliques of Ancient English Poetry* (London, 1765)

Rennison, Nick and Michael Schmidt *Poets on Poets* (Manchester, 1997)

Scott, Tom *The Penguin Book of Scottish Verse* (Harmondsworth, 1970)

Smith, David Nichol *The Oxford Book of Eighteenth-Century Verse* (Oxford, 1926)

Spender, D. and J. Todd (eds) *British Women Writers: An Anthology from the Fourteenth Century to the Present* (London, 1989)

Tomlinson, Charles *Oxford Book of Verse in English Translation* (Oxford, 1980)

HISTORY AND SECONDARY

Abrams, M.H. *The Mirror and the Lamp: romantic theory and the critical tradition* (Oxford, 1953)

— *Natural Supernaturalism: tradition and revolution in romantic literature* (New York, 1971)

Addison, Joseph *Critical Essays from the Spectator* (Oxford, 1970)

Attridge, Derek *Poetic Rhythm* (Cambridge, 1995)

Barrell, John *English Literature in History, 1730–1780: An Equal, Wide Survey* (London, 1983)

Bate, Walter Jackson *The Burden of the Past and the English Poet* (London, 1971)

— *From Classic to Romantic: premises of taste in eighteenth-century England* (New York, 1961)

Baugh, A.C. (ed.) *A Literary History of England* (New York, 1967)

Bloom, Harold *The Anxiety of Influence* (Oxford, 1973)

— *Figures of Capable Imagination* (New York, 1976)

— *Ruin the Sacred Truths: poetry and belief from the Bible to the present* (Cambridge, Mass., 1989)

— *Poets of Sensibility and the Sublime* (New York, 1986)

Boswell, James *The Life of Samuel Johnson* (New York, 1965)

Bradford, Richard *A Linguistic History of English Poetry* (London, 1993)

Brewer, Derek (ed.) *Writers and Their Background* (London, 1974)

Brogan, T.V.F. (ed.) *The New Princeton Handbook of Poetic Terms* (Princeton, 1994)

Brooks, Cleanth *The Well Wrought Urn* (London, 1968)

Brooks, Cleanth and Robert Penn Warren *Understanding Poetry* (New York, 1938)

Cambridge History of English Literature ed. Sir A.W. Ward and A.R. Waller, 15, vols (Cambridge, 1907)

Craig, Cairns (ed.) *History of Scottish Literature,* 4 vols (Aberdeen, 1987–89)

Crawford, Thomas *Society and the Lyric: A Study of the Song Culture of Eighteenth-Century Scotland* (Edinburgh, 1979)

— *Devolving English Literature* (Oxford, 1992)

Croft, P. J. *Autograph Poetry in the English Language,* 2 vols (London, 1973)

Daiches, David (ed.) *A Critical History of English Literature,* 4 vols (London, 1969)

Davie, Donald *The Language of Science and the Language of Literature, 1700–1740* (London, 1963)

— *Older Masters* (Manchester, 1992)

— *Purity of Diction in English Verse* and *Articulate Energy* (Manchester, 1994)

Edwards, Michael *Towards a Christian Poetics* (London, 1984)

Eliot, Thomas Stearns *The Sacred Wood: essays on poetry and criticism* (London, 1920)

— *Notes Towards the Definition of Culture* (London, 1948)

— *To Criticize the Critic and other writings* (London, 1965)

— *The Letters of T.S. Eliot 1898–1922* (London, 1971)

— *Selected Essays* (London, 1975)

Empson, William *Some Versions of Pastoral* (Harmondsworth, 1966)

— *Seven Types of Ambiguity* (Harmondsworth, 1973)

Erskine-Hill, Howard *Poetry of Opposition and Revolution: Dryden to Wordsworth* (Oxford, 1996)

— *The Augustan Idea in English Literature* (London, 1983)

Everett, Barbara *Poets in Their Time: essays on English poetry from Donne to Larkin* (London, 1986)

Feather, John *A History of British Publishing* (London, 1988)

Ford, Boris (ed.) *The New Penguin Companion to English Literature,* vol. IV, *From Dryden to Johnson* (Harmondsworth, 1982)

Ford, Ford Madox *The March of Literature* (London, 1947)

Fowler, Alastair *A History of English Literature: forms and kinds from the Middle Ages to the present* (Oxford, 1987)

Fussell, Paul *Poetic Metre and Poetic Form* (New York, 1979)

Graves, Robert *Collected Writings on Poetry* (Manchester, 1995)

Gunn, Thom *The Occasions of Poetry, Essays in Criticism and Autobiography* (London, 1985)

— *Shelf Life: essays, memoirs and an interview* (London, 1993)

Hill, Geoffrey *The Lords of Limit* (London, 1984)

Hunt, John Dixon *The Figure in the Landscape: Poetry, Painting, and Gardening During the Eighteenth Century* (Baltimore, 1976)

Johnson, Samuel *Lives of the English Poets* ed. L. Archer-Hind, 2 vols (New York, 1964)

Kermode, Frank (ed.) *The Classic* (London, 1975)

— *Poetry, Narrative, History* (1990)

Leavis, Frank Raymond *The Common Pursuit* (London, 1952)

— *Revaluation: tradition and development in English poetry* (Harmondsworth, 1964)

Lucas, John *England and Englishness: ideas of nationhood in English poetry 1688–1900* (London, 1990)

McGann, Jerome J. *The Poetics of Sensibility: a revolution in literary style* (Oxford, 1996)

Nowottny, Winifred *The Language Poets Use* (London, 1962)

Plant, Marjorie *The English Book Trade: an economic history of the making and sale of books* (London, 1939)

Pound, Ezra *The Literary Essays of Ezra Pound* (London, 1954)

— *Selected Prose 1909–1965* (London, 1973)

— *The ABC of Reading* (London, 1991)

Preminger, Alex and T. V. F. Brogan (eds) The *New Princeton Encyclopaedia of Poetry and Poetics* (Princeton, 1993)

Richards, I.A. *Principles of Literary Criticism* (London, 1967)

Ricks, Christopher *The Force of Poetry* (Oxford, 1984)

Rickword, Edgell *Essays and Opinions 1921–1931* (Manchester, 1974)

— *Literature in Society* (Manchester, 1978)

Rogers, Pat *Grub Street: Studies in a Sub-Culture* (London, 1972)

— *Hacks and Dunces: Pope, Swift, and Grub Street* (London, 1980)

Rothstein, Eric *Restoration and Eighteenth-Century Poetry 1660–1780* (*Routledge History of English Poetry*, vol. three) (Boston, 1981)

Sambrook, James *The Eighteenth Century: The Intellectual and Cultural Context of English Literature, 1700–1789* (New York, 1986)

Sisson, Charles Hubert *The Avoidance of Literature: collected essays* (Manchester, 1979)

— *In Two Minds* (Manchester, 1990)

— *English Perspectives* (Manchester, 1992)

Sitter, John *Literary Loneliness in Mid-Eighteenth-Century England* (Ithaca, NY, 1982)

Stone, P.W.K. *The Art of Poetry 1750–1820: Theories of Composition and Style in the Late Neo-Classic and Early Romantic Periods* (London, 1967)

Sutherland, James *A Preface to Eighteenth-Century Poetry* (Oxford, 1948)

Tate, Allen *Essays of Four Decades* (London, 1970)

Tillotson, G. *Augustan Studies* (London, 1961)

Vaisey, David and David McKitterick *The Foundations of Scholarship: Libraries and Collecting, 1650–1750* (Los Angeles, 1992)

Warton, Thomas *The History of English Poetry: from the close of the eleventh to the commencement of the eighteenth century,* 4 vols (London, 1924)

Watson, J.R. (ed.) *Pre-Romanticism in English Poetry of the Eighteenth Century: The Poetic Art and Significance of Thomas Gray, Collins, Goldsmith, Cowper, Crabbe* (Basingstoke, 1989)

Weinbrot, Howard D. *Britannia's Issue: The Rise of British Literature from Dryden to Ossian* (Cambridge, 1993)

Willey, Basil *The Eighteenth Century Background* (London, 1940)

Womersley, David (ed.)*Augustan Critical Writing* (Harmondsworth, 1997)

GENERAL INDEX

INDEX OF FIRST LINES AND EXTRACTS

INDEX OF TITLES